Dr. Batch File's
Ultimate Collection

Dr. Batch File's Ultimate Collection

Ronny Richardson

Windcrest®/McGraw-Hill

FIRST EDITION
FIRST PRINTING

© 1993 by **Windcrest Books**, an imprint of TAB Books.
TAB Books is a division of McGraw-Hill, Inc.
The name "Windcrest" is a registered trademark of TAB Books.

Library of Congress Cataloging-in-Publication Data

Richardson, Ronny.
    Dr. Batch File's ultimate collection / by Ronny Richardson.
      p.   cm.
    Includes index.
    ISBN 0-8306-4112-2   ISBN 0-8306-4113-0 (pbk.)
    1. Electronic data processing—Batch processing. 2. File
organization (Computer science) I. Title.
QA76.9.B38R535 1992
005.4'46—dc20   92-9172
                                      CIP

TAB Books offers software for sale. For information and a catalog, please contact TAB Software Department, Blue Ridge Summit, PA 17294-0850.

Acquisitions Editor: Brad Schepp
Book Editor: Kellie Hagan
Series Design: Jaclyn J. Boone
Director of Production: Katherine G. Brown
Cover: Sandra Blair Design
   and Brent Blair Photography, Harrisburg, Pa.   WR1

Contents

Acknowledgments   *xiii*

Introduction   *xv*

PART ONE

BATCH FILE STRUCTURE

---

1 Anatomy of a batch file   3

There's no such thing as too much documentation   *3*
Self documentation   *4*
Batch file components   *4*
Summary   *7*

2 Hiding what a batch file does   9

Logging computer usage   *9*
Better messages   *10*
Password protection   *11*
A less powerful approach   *12*
Warning   *12*
Summary   *12*

PART TWO

WORKING WITH BATCH FILES

---

3 Batch file help   29

Customized help   *29*
Specific help   *30*
Summary   *31*

4 Batch files that use less space   41

DOS upgrade   *41*
Combining batch files   *42*
Compressing batch files   *42*
Technical notes   *43*
Summary   *44*

5 Counting in batch files   **55**

Math rules   *55*
A basic math batch file   *56*
A brute-force math approach   *58*
Stripping off the digits   *58*
Utility programs   *60*
Summary   *60*

_____ PART THREE _____

WORKING WITH DOS

6 Command-line enhancements   **93**

You might not need a batch file   *93*
Entering multiple commands on the command line   *94*
When the command line isn't enough   *94*
Reusing commands   *95*
Keyboard macros in the environment   *96*
Keyboard macros in a batch file   *97*
Storing the command line in the environment   *97*
Storing the command line in a batch file   *98*
Summary   *99*

7 Making DOS run smoothly   **127**

A more intelligent AUTOEXEC.BAT file   *127*
Unloading memory-resident programs   *127*
Shelling out to DOS   *128*
Running inflexible programs   *129*
Running commands occasionally   *129*
Running under different versions of DOS   *131*
Summary   *132*

8 Working with subdirectories   **145**

Changing subdirectories   *145*
A custom batch file for each subdirectory   *145*
Returning home   *145*
Quick changes   *146*
Finding files   *148*
Summary   *148*

9 DOS-based virus protection   **159**

Writing program protection files   *159*
Hiding COMMAND.COM   *160*

Testing your critical files   *161*
DOS 5.0   *161*
Summary   *162*

10   Miscellaneous batch files   **167**

A floppy-disk catalog   *167*
Stopping your batch files   *168*
Making CHKDSK smarter   *168*
Counting backup files   *169*
Summary   *169*

_____ PART FOUR _____

CONFIGURING DOS

11   Custom configurations   **179**

The basic approach   *179*
Putting it together   *180*
Environmental surveying   *181*
Conditionally loading memory-resident software   *182*
DR DOS is even better   *182*
As close as MS-DOS can come   *183*
Summary   *184*

12   Accessing global information   **199**

Date and time   *199*
Volume label   *200*
Serial number   *201*
Using Batcmd   *201*
Calling technical support   *202*
Summary   *202*

13   Working with your path   **217**

Adding to your path   *218*
Deleting from your path   *218*
Summary   *219*

14   Modifying DOS without version 5.0   **237**

A word of warning   *237*
Your AUTOEXEC.BAT and CONFIG.SYS files   *238*
Changing DOS   *239*
Changing commands   *240*
Summary   *240*

15 Modifying DOS 5.0 with DOSKEY   **247**

DOSKEY basics *248*
What can you do with DOSKEY? *248*
Putting it together *249*
Command-line recall *252*
Summary *252*

_____ **PART FIVE** _____

THE ENVIRONMENT

16 The DOS environment   **261**

What is the environment? *261*
The SET command *262*
Increasing the size of the environment *265*
Testing the environment *267*
Summary *267*

17 The DOS errorlevel   **273**

The brute-force approach *274*
Combining IF statements *274*
Shorter errorlevel tests *274*
Programs that use errorlevel *275*
Summary *279*

18 Working with ANSI   **287**

An ANSI tutorial *288*
The keyboard *291*
Summary *295*

_____ **PART SIX** _____

DOCUMENTATION

19 Advanced batch file techniques   **305**

List of techniques *305*
Case construction *306*
Creating a boot disk *307*
Dealing with capitalization *308*
Environmental variables *310*
FOR command tricks *310*
Label testing *312*

Nesting IF statements *313*
Quicker than GOTO END *313*
Quotation marks *314*
Replacing commands with environmental variables *315*
Subroutines in batch files *315*
Using reserve names in batch files *318*
Writing batch files with a spreadsheet program *319*
Zero-length files *320*
Summary *320*

20   Batch file documentation   343

01.BAT *343*
02.BAT *343*
1-LOG.BAT *344*
ANSIDEMO.BAT *344*
ANSIHIDE.BAT *344*
AUTOASK.BAT *344*
AUTOBOOT.BAT *345*
BIGMENU.BAT *345*
BLANK.BAT *345*
CAPITAL1.BAT *345*
CAPITAL2.BAT *346*
CAPITAL3.BAT *346*
CAPITAL4.BAT *346*
CAPITAL5.BAT *346*
CASE.BAT *347*
CATALOG.BAT *347*
CHECKERR.BAT *347*
CHECKER2.BAT *347*
CHKDSKCD *348*
CL.BAT *348*
CL2.BAT *348*
CNTBOOTS.BAT *348*
CNTFILES *349*
CONFIG.BAT *349*
CTTYKEY.BAT *349*
CURRENT.BAT *349*
CURRENT1.BAT *350*
DEL.BAT *350*
DIGIT-1.BAT *350*
DIGIT-2.BAT *350*
DIGIT-3.BAT *351*
DIRECTOR.BAT *351*
EDIT1.BAT *351*
EDIT2.BAT *351*

EDITPAT2.BAT   *351*
EDITPATH.BAT   *352*
ENV__SIZE.BAT   *352*
FASTFIND.BAT   *352*
GET-TIME.BAT   *352*
GETVOL.BAT   *353*
HELP.BAT   *353*
HELP1.BAT   *353*
HELPBAT.BAT   *353*
HELPBAT2.BAT   *353*
HELPBAT3.BAT   *354*
KEYASSGN.BAT   *354*
KEYERASE.BAT   *354*
LOCK.BAT   *355*
LOGBOOT.BAT   *355*
LOTUS.BAT   *355*
LOTUS1.BAT   *355*
MACRO.BAT   *356*
MACRO2.BAT   *356*
MATH.BAT   *356*
MATH1.BAT   *357*
MATH2.BAT   *357*
MOVEIT.BAT   *357*
MULTI.BAT   *357*
MULTI1.BAT   *358*
MULTI2.BAT   *358*
MULTI3.BAT   *358*
MULTI4.BAT   *358*
NEST1.BAT   *359*
NEST2.BAT   *359*
NEXTFILE.BAT   *359*
NICEPROM.BAT   *359*
NOT-DEL.BAT   *360*
NUMBER.BAT   *360*
NUMBER1.BAT   *360*
NUMBER2−6.BAT   *360*
NUMBER9.BAT   *360*
OCCASION.BAT   *361*
PASSWRD2.BAT   *361*
PATH1.BAT   *361*
PATH2.BAT   *361*
PATH3.BAT   *362*
PATH4.BAT   *362*
PHONE.BAT   *362*

PREPARE.BAT   *362*
QCD.BAT   *363*
RCD.BAT   *363*
RECONFIG.BAT   *363*
REMOVE.BAT   *363*
RETURN.BAT   *364*
RETURN2.BAT   *364*
RETURN3.BAT   *364*
RMD.BAT   *364*
SAVE-ERR.BAT   *365*
SAVESPAC.BAT   *365*
SENDANS2.BAT   *365*
SENDANSI.BAT   *365*
SERIAL.BAT   *365*
SETPATH.BAT   *366*
SHOWLOOP.BAT   *366*
SMALLBAT.BAT   *366*
SMARTCHK.BAT   *367*
SP.BAT   *367*
STARTAPP.BAT   *367*
STARTDAT.BAT   *367*
STARTWOR.BAT   *367*
STORE.BAT   *368*
STOREVOL.BAT   *368*
TECH-AID.BAT   *368*
TESTCOM5.BAT   *368*
TESTCOMM.BAT   *369*
TESTENVI.BAT   *369*
TESTGOTO.BAT   *369*
TEXTFND4.BAT   *369*
TEXTFND5.BAT   *370*
TP.BAT   *370*
UNBLANK.BAT   *370*
USEOVER.BAT   *370*
VERSION.BAT   *371*
VOLUME.BAT   *371*
VOLUME1.BAT   *371*

21   Batch file utilities   **373**

BatScreen   *373*
Batcmd   *373*
LHA, version 2.13   *380*
Summary   *382*

Appendix A   DOS command summary   385

Appendix B   Batch file information
              for popular programs   397

Index   401

Acknowledgments

I want to thank the folks at Hyperkinetix. Chris Bascom, the President, agreed to let one of his programmers, Doug Amaral, write Batcmd and BatScreen especially for this book. Doug did a wonderful job on those custom programs and I appreciate all his work. I think you'll find BatScreen and Batcmd to both be wonderful programs. Best of all, full-use unrestricted copies of both programs come free with this book.

Personally, I want to thank my wife Cicinda, my son Tevin, and my daughter Dawna for their support and patience. Because I have only a limited pool of time available, some of the time I spent writing this book had to come from the time I would have spent with my family. They were all very understanding and supportive.

Introduction

My first batch book was *MS-DOS Batch File Programming*, also available from Windcrest. I wrote it between 1987 and 1988, and it was published shortly thereafter. This book was a complete course in batch files. It began by assuming that you knew nothing about batch files and, therefore, covered the very basics. It continued all the way through some very advanced batch topics. If you're looking for the most detailed batch coverage available, that is the book for you.

MS-DOS Batch File Programming (now in its third edition) was one of the first books that was dedicated solely to batch files. Before that, the only place to learn about batch files was the single chapter most DOS books devoted to them. Because this book has been so popular, the market has become glutted with imitators. Some of them have the words *advanced* or *power* in their titles, but all they do is rehash the material from the first edition of my book.

In the third edition of *MS-DOS Batch File Programming*, I introduced a concept that was entirely new to computer books, a line-by-line explanation of every batch file in the book (all 200 of them). No other programming book has ever done that for more than a handful of its programs. You'll see these same line-by-line explanations in this book. As a result, you should be able to understand how even the most complex batch file works.

What's in this book?

Part 1: Batch file structure

This section shows you how to structure your batch files for maximum usefulness and easy understanding. The chapters in this section are:

Chapter 1: Anatomy of a batch file   It's much easier to write and use batch files if they follow a particular structure and always use certain commands. This chapter covers these concepts.

Chapter 2: Hiding everything a batch file does   If you structure your batch files properly, you can hide as much of what goes on as you like. You can even hide those stubborn DOS messages that turning echo off and piping to nul don't hide!

Part 2: Working with batch files

This section shows you how to make the batch files themselves work better. This, in turn, allows your batch files to be more powerful. The chapters in this section are:

Chapter 3: Batch file help Because DOS limits filenames to eight characters or less, it's often difficult to look at a program name and figure out exactly what that program does—especially if you haven't used it for a while. Using batch file help, you can quickly find out what a particular batch file does.

Chapter 4: Batch files that use less space Because DOS allocates a full cluster to each file no matter how small it is, and because most people tend to accumulate a lot of batch files, your batch files can end up taking a lot of hard disk space. This chapter shows you how to reduce the space used by your batch files.

Chapter 5: Counting in batch files Wouldn't it be nice if your batch files could count and perform simple mathematics? Well, they can and this chapter shows you how.

Part 3: Working with DOS

The primary use for batch files is to improve the way DOS operates. This section will show you ways to improve DOS with batch files that you might have never even considered. The chapters in this section are:

Chapter 6: Command line enhancements If you have DOS 5.0, then you know how nice it is to be able to enter multiple commands on one command line. You also know how nice it is to use DOSKEY to write macros and recall command lines you've already entered. If you don't have DOS 5.0 or you don't like the amount of memory DOSKEY requires, then this chapter will show you how to perform the same tasks using batch files.

Chapter 7: Making DOS run more smoothly This chapter will show you how you can use batch files to run inflexible programs, make sure a second program isn't loaded while shelled out from another program, and others to make DOS easier to use.

Chapter 8: Working with subdirectories Normally, batch files are fairly ignorant of subdirectories. Once a batch file changes to a new subdirectory, it can't even automatically return to the subdirectory it just left! This chapter will show you how to make batch files work more intelligently with subdirectories.

Chapter 9: DOS-based virus protection While users in high-risk situations will still need an antiviral package, low-risk users can usually find all the protection they need using DOS batch files.

Chapter 10: Miscellaneous batch files This chapter presents some DOS-related batch files that are useful but didn't easily fit into one of the other chapters.

Part 4: Configuring DOS

Wouldn't it be nice if you could just turn your computer on and it was ready to run? With issues like networks, expanded and extended memory, and memory-resident software, very few users can work with just one configuration. This section will show you how to work with multiple configurations and how to change many other aspects of DOS operation. The chapters in this section are:

Chapter 11: Booting with custom configurations   If you need to boot your computer with different sets of CONFIG.SYS and AUTOEXEC.BAT configuration files for different purposes, then this chapter is for you. It will show you how to automate the process and even how to have the batch file start applications. Make sure the proper environment is in place prior to starting an application.

Chapter 12: Accessing global information   This chapter will show you how to access global information such as the volume label, and the time and disk serial numbers in batch files.

Chapter 13: Working with your path   This chapter will show you how to easily modify your path, and includes batch files that allow you to quickly swap paths and remove subdirectories from an existing path.

Chapter 14: Modifying DOS without version 5.0   Even if you haven't upgraded to DOS 5.0, you can change the way internal DOS commands work—this chapter shows you how. It also shows you how to change the name DOS uses for its configuration files.

Chapter 15: Modifying DOS with version 5.0   The DOS 5.0 DOSKEY program makes it a snap to change the operation of any of the DOS internal commands. This chapter shows you how.

Part 5: The environment

This section shows you how to take advantage of the environment provided by DOS. The chapters in this section are:

Chapter 16: Expanding the environment   The default size of the environment is paltry. This chapter shows you how to expand it.

Chapter 17: The DOS errorlevel   Some programs use the errorlevel to communicate rather than the environment. This chapter shows you how to use the errorlevel.

Chapter 18: Working with ANSI   Loading ANSI.SYS in your CONFIG.SYS file gives you the power to modify the screen environment your batch files work with. This chapter shows you how.

Part 6: Documentation   This section documents the batch files and programs that comes with this book. The chapters in this section are:

Chapter 19: Advanced batch file technique   Many of the batch files in this book rely on advanced batch file techniques you might not have had a chance to master. This section summarizes those techniques in one quick reference for easy study.

Chapter 20: Batch file documentation   This chapter provides a quick-reference explanation of each of the batch files that comes with this book. It quickly tells you what the batch file expects as an input and what the batch file does.

Chapter 21: Software documentation   The disk that comes with this book includes three programs: Batcmd, LHA, and BatScreen. Some of the batch files use the Batcmd utility to perform tasks that either can't be performed with a DOS command or are easier to perform with Batcmd. One of the batch files in this book (SMALLBAT.BAT) uses LHA to compress several batch files into one file. I've also used LHA to compress the files on the enclosed disk. While none of the batch files uses BatScreen, it's a very nice program for producing batch file screens and can easily replace many of the ECHO commands in these batch files. This chapter documents these three programs.

Technical notes

Many of the batch files in this book make extensive use of the environment. In many cases, they'll fail to run if you haven't expanded the size of your environment. Chapter 16 explains how to expand the environment.

In addition, many of these batch files also use "tricks" that may be difficult to understand when you first review them. All the advanced tricks are explained in detail in part 6. Some of the batch files in this book also use a utility program called Batcmd. It's described in chapter 21.

Hardware

Writing a computer book is difficult. You never know what type of hardware and software the reader has. You don't even know what version of the operating system he's using. In writing about batch files, I'm more fortunate than many writers because most batch files will run on any hardware configuration. Most of the batch files in this book will also run on any version of DOS, 3.3 or higher. Many of them will even run under earlier versions. I've indicated where this isn't true.

For most of the examples in this book, I assume that the files supporting DOS external commands (like FORMAT.COM and BACKUP.COM) are either in the current subdirectory or in the path when an example batch file example requires one of these programs.

Book defaults

There are a few important pieces of information you need to keep in mind when reading this book:

F1 through F12   This means to press the appropriate function key. On most older keyboards, there are ten function keys on the left side or top of the keyboard, labeled from F1 to F10. Newer keyboards have twelve function keys, F1 to F12.

Enter, Tab, Shift, etc.   Keys that have a name on them are referred to by that name. Arrow keys and keys that don't have a name (like the spacebar) are called names like *right arrow*, *left arrow*, and *spacebar* (all are lowercase).

Control keys   In general, a ^ symbol followed by another character means to hold down the Ctrl key while pressing the following key. So a ^z means to hold down the Ctrl key while pressing the z key. These Ctrl-key combinations are also displayed as follows:

Ctrl–F1, Ctrl–z, and Ctrl–ST. This second kind of display applies also to the Alt and Shift keys.

[ ]   Any command inside brackets is optional. Brackets are generally used when explaining command. In DIR [/P], for example, the /P switch is optional. It causes the listing to pause each time the screen is full. Pressing any key restarts the listing.

Italics   Any lowercase, italic text in a batch file command or program stands for variable information. In CD \ *subdirectory* \ *filename*, for example, CD is the command (change directory) and *subdirectory* and *filename* are pieces of information that will change almost every time you use the command.

Uppercase/lowercase   Most of the commands in this book are shown in uppercase. For the most part, the computer doesn't care. The commands DIR, dir, DiR are all the same to the computer. About the only time it matters is when you're using the equal sign to compare two things.

About the author

Ronny Richardson was born in Oak Ridge, Tennessee and raised in Atlanta, Georgia. He has undergraduate degrees in Electronics and Mathematics, graduate degrees in Decision Sciences and Business Administration, and a Ph.D. in Business Administration.

Ronny began using computers in 1983. The next year he won an IBM clone at the Atlanta Comdex, which spurred his interest in learning about computers. Later that year he began teaching computer classes at a local computer store, and in 1986 began writing articles for *Computer Shopper*. Since then, Ronny has published over 200 articles. He currently writes for *PC/Computing*, *Atlanta Computer Currents*, and *Computer Monthly*.

Note to readers

If this book causes you to develop a nice batch file hint, write to me in care of TAB Books and let me know. While I can't respond to individual letters, your hint or question just might show up in the next edition of this book. The address is:

Ronny Richardson
c/o TAB Books
P.O. Box 40
Blue Ridge Summit, PA 17294-0214

If you're active in the on-line community, you can contact me through CompuServe. My address is 70322,3100.

About this book

You might be interested in knowing about the hardware and software I used to write this book. I used a Northgate Super Micro 386/20 and an HP Laserjet III. The word processing program I used for everything except the batch files and tables was Microsoft Word 5.5. I edited batch files and other ASCII files with the extremely nice editor built into DOS 5.0. Finally, I created all the tables using Word for Windows. While too slow for general writing, it has the best table editing engine I've ever seen.

Disclaimer

All the batch files in this book were tested on a wide variety of DOS versions. I've done everything possible to ensure that the programs and batch files included with this book and on the disk either will run under all versions of DOS or are clearly labeled as to which version(s) they require. I've also done my best to make sure that every program and batch file does exactly what I claim it will do. I make no guarantee of any type, expressed or implied, regarding the programs, batch files, and documentation included in this book and on the included disk. In addition, I'm not liable for incidental or consequential damages in connection with, or arising from, the performance of these programs and batch files.

PART ONE
Batch file structure

1
Anatomy of a batch file

In the process of writing all of my batch file books, I've written over 500 batch files and looked at countless batch files written by others. In doing so, I've developed some ideas on what constitutes a well-organized batch file. I've tried to follow these ideas in writing the batch files in this book and I've found that it made the process much easier.

There's no such thing as too much documentation

Before starting this book, I went back and reviewed my collection of batch files and it struck me just how difficult it is to figure out what a batch file does just by looking at the code itself.

The primary method you have for documenting a batch file is by burying remark lines inside the batch file. That way, anyone looking at the batch file will be able to read your comments as they try to follow along. Of course, these comments are useful only if you use a lot of them and make them truly explanatory. And, unless you have a very slow computer, even a large number of remarks won't significantly slow down your batch files.

A second form of documentation is written. You'll find this form of documentation in the tables in this book that list most of the batch files. The batch file code is on the left and a detailed explanation is on the right. Of course, you probably won't need to document your batch files in this level of detail. You might find it adequate to simply print out a listing of your batch files and write notes in the margin.

In my other batch file books, these two forms (internal remarks and tables) were the only documentation I used. In this book, I've added a third form: user documentation. In chapter 20, you'll find a brief description of what each batch file does and what it requires for input. If you use a lot of batch files on your system, you might find it useful to keep a similar listing of your own batch files. You might also want to keep this sort of documentation on the utility programs you add to your system.

Self documentation

DOS 5.0 adds a nifty new feature to most of its commands. If you're not sure what they do or how to use them, you can start them with a /? switch and get a screen of helpful information. That makes it quick and easy to find out what a program does or what inputs it needs. I expect that, over time, this will be added to most programs.

Implementing this feature in batch files is fairly easy. A section of code near the top of each batch file in this book tests to see if the first replaceable parameter is a /?. If it is, the batch file displays a help screen and exits to DOS. I used the /? switch to be consistent with DOS 5.0, but I don't really see the need to type in two characters to get help. Therefore, my batch files will also respond to just the question mark without the slash.

Batch file components

Some information is important enough to be contained in every batch file. Because it's so important, you might as well put it at the top of each batch file. The first five lines of each batch file should be as follows:

@ECHO OFF   Unless you have some very good reason for echoing the commands, the first line of every batch file you write should turn command-echoing off. If you leave echo on, the screen will quickly become cluttered and confuse the user.

REM NAME: The second line of the batch file gives the batch file's name. This isn't crucial because you should know the name from the DOS filename. However, some of the very useful batch files in chapter 3 depend on finding this line, so it's important to include it in each batch file.

REM PURPOSE: The third line of the batch file gives the purpose of the batch file. It's important that you enter the word *purpose* in all capital letters and follow it immediately with a colon. It's also a good idea to put the complete purpose on one line. (Although many of the purpose lines in this book's batch files are multiline, this was done for table formatting reasons.)

REM VERSION   The first version of a batch file is 1.00. A tiny change would make it 1.01, a larger change would make it 1.10, and a major change would make it 2.00. Batch files tend to evolve over time, so this line is a good indicator of how long a batch file has been in use. You might notice that many of the batch files in the book are version 1.0. This is because I begin numbering my batch files at zero. They reach number 1.00 only after they've finished an extensive amount of "pre-release" testing. As a result, they don't get a number higher than 1.00 unless I enhance them or fix a bug after they're finished.

REM DATE: This is the date of the last modification to the batch file. A batch file that hasn't been updated for a very long time is either very stable or not used very often.

Following this scheme, the top of a typical batch file will look something like this:

```
@ECHO OFF
REM NAME:      MULTI.BAT
REM PURPOSE:   Issue Multiple DOS Commands On A Single Line
```

```
REM VERSION:   1.10
REM DATE:      May 7, 1991
```

If you study the sample batch files that come with this book, you'll see that almost all of them follow this documentation scheme. It's also important that you decide on a capitalization scheme for the text. Some of the batch files in chapter 3 allow you to search for specific text in these batch files, so it's easier if you know how that text is capitalized.

A different kind of top

The scheme in the previous batch file requires an REM at the beginning of each line so DOS will treat the line as a remark and skip it. If you plan on entering a lot of documentation at the top of the batch file, it can be tiring to type REM at the beginning of each line. You can avoid this by adding a label below the documentation where the working commands of the batch file start and making the second line of the batch file a GOTO command to jump over the remarks. Using that scheme, the above batch file fragment would look like this:

```
@ECHO OFF
GOTO TOP
NAME:      MULTI.BAT
PURPOSE:   Issue Multiple DOS Commands On A Single Line
VERSION:   1.10
DATE:      May 7, 1991
:TOP
```

The GOTO TOP command causes DOS to skip over all the remarks. This approach can look a little confusing to users not expecting it, however, so you might want to reserve using it in batch files with a lot of comments at the top.

Capitalization

In working with batch files, I've developed the following style of capitalization:

- I use all capital letters for batch commands, DOS commands, and program names.
- I capitalize the first letter of each word in most messages and remarks.
- When a message tells you what to enter on the command line, I capitalize the command line.
- When a message is very important, I capitalize the entire message, something like WARNING: THIS TAKES AN HOUR.
- When a message is extremely important, I surround it with asterisks, like this: **WARNING: THIS TAKES ALL NIGHT**.

Spacing

In a long batch file, it can be difficult to see the different sections if you enter text on each line. To visually break the batch file up into different sections, I leave one or more blank lines between each section. These blank lines don't affect the operation of the batch file, but they do make it much easier to read.

While the batch files in this book have blank lines between the sections, I've left them out of the tables, again for legibility reasons.

Section markers

Many of my batch files have discrete sections that perform one task, like displaying help or an error message. As I mentioned above, I often separate these sections with blank lines. In addition, I also use markers to differentiate the sections.

Most sections begin with a label (like :HELP) so the batch file can jump to that section when needed. When a section begins with a label, I also end it with a label. I construct this label by adding END plus an underscore to the label at the top of the section—so the :HELP section would end with an END__HELP label, like this:

```
:HELP
ECHO  This Batch File Runs Your Backup Program
ECHO  You Must Start It With Either An F Or I
ECHO  On The Command Line
ECHO  The F Is For A Full Backup
ECHO  The I Is For An Incremental Backup
GOTO  END
:END__HELP
```

Adding four characters to the beginning of a label will often make that label exceed eight characters, and most versions of DOS limit labels to eight characters or less. When a label exceeds eight characters, most versions of DOS will consider only the first eight characters. As a result, DOS will treat END__ERROR1, END__ERROR2 and END__ERROR3 as the same label, namely END__ERROR. You therefore wouldn't be able to jump to a label marking the end of a section. This shouldn't be a problem, however, because these labels are at the end of sections and you shouldn't need to jump to them.

Additionally, some batch file compilers and a few versions of DOS will object if you use long labels. If you face that problem, you can add an REM to the front of the label so DOS or your compiler treats the offending line as a remark.

Indenting sections

I've also found that it can be useful to indent the lines of a section between the beginning and ending label of the section. If you do that, the previous batch file segment will look like this:

```
:HELP
     ECHO  This Batch File Runs Your Backup Program
     ECHO  You Must Start It With Either An F or I
     ECHO  On The Command Line
     ECHO  The F Is For A Full Backup
     ECHO  The I Is For An Incremental Backup
     GOTO  END
:END__HELP
```

As you can see, indenting makes it clear which statements belong in which sections. This is especially useful in longer batch files.

Because of the limited space in the table format, I haven't indented sections for batch files in this book. However, this is something I do use on my own personal batch files. Also note that some batch file compilers require labels to start at the left margin, so you might not be able to indent labels.

Message length

You'll notice that most of the ECHO commands in my batch files have fairly short lines. For longer messages, I use multiple ECHO commands rather than longer lines. It's been my experience that shorter lines are easier to read on the screen than longer ones.

Summary

- Internal documentation makes it easier to modify a batch file at a later date.
- Batch files that can display help when started with a /? switch make it easier for the user to find out how to use them.
- Most batch files should start with a line to turn off command-echoing and lines giving the name, purpose, revision number, and revision date of the batch file.
- You can avoid using an REM command at the start of each remark line in your batch files by using a GOTO command to jump over the remarks.
- Using consistent capitalization makes it easier to read and search through batch files.
- Blank lines between sections can make a batch file more readable.
- Using labels to mark the end of a section can make a batch file easier to follow.
- Indenting the commands within a section is a nice way to visually highlight the boundaries of a section.
- Messages using shorter lines are easier to read than messages using longer lines. Of course, using shorter lines requires additional lines to display the entire message.

2

Hiding what a batch file does

You can hide much of what goes on in your batch files with commands like @ECHO OFF and COPY *.* A: > NUL, but some DOS error messages might still get through. For example, when a batch file tries to delete a file that doesn't exist, the DOS error message will be displayed even if the batch file uses the above commands to try and suppress that message.

There are other DOS error messages, like *File not found*, that can't be turned off with the ECHO command or piped to the NUL device. However, you can still get rid of them. DOS has an internal command called CTTY. When you first start the computer, DOS recognizes your keyboard as the default input device and your screen as the standard display device. Normally, you use the CTTY command to change to an alternative input/output device—for example, a data collection device connected to COM1. However, CTTY has two features that make it useful here. First, you can use any legal device name as the alternative console, including NUL. With NUL as the alternative console, DOS has no way of receiving input or displaying output. That's where the second advantage of CTTY comes in—programs continue to run while a CTTY NUL command is in effect.

NOT-DEL.BAT in Fig. 2-1 takes advantage of CTTY. (Batch files in this book are located at the end of the chapter.) Nothing, including DOS error messages, will show on the screen between a CTTY NUL command and a CTTY CON command. In fact, the console (keyboard) is almost completely inactive. Ctrl-Break will stop the batch file but any other keystrokes will simply remain in the keyboard buffer waiting for control to return to the console. As a result, you can't regain control by issuing a CTTY CON command from the keyboard if you abort the batch file. To regain control, you must reboot.

Logging computer usage

You can create a log that records every time a computer is rebooted using the CTTY command. While this log doesn't need the CTTY command to operate, you greatly reduce the chance that the log will be spotted and neutralized by using the CTTY command to hide the logging activity. LOGBOOT.BAT in Fig. 2-2 shows the code that creates this log. The important points are:

- ECHO ¦ MORE is used to supply the necessary Return so you don't have to answer the DATE and TIME questions.
- The > piping symbol adds the new text to the bottom of the log rather than over-writing it.
- You should probably change the name of the log file to something less meaningful, like ABC.QVL. You can also specify the full path to the file, so it doesn't have to be in the root directory.

The log doesn't show how long the computer is used, so it would be difficult to use this kind of batch file to determine client billing or even the utilization of certain computers. You could, however, combine it with a batch file menu system and have the batch files that run the specific applications record additional information. 1-LOG.BAT in Fig. 2-3 is just such a batch file. Keep in mind that these batch files will run without the CTTY commands, but it's easier for the user to see what's going on.

Better messages

I routinely use programs that stubbornly refuse to allow their messages to be turned off with ECHO OFF or rerouted with >NUL. This is often acceptable for an experienced user, who understands what's going on, but will only add more confusion for a new user. I could add explanations using ECHO statements but they tend to get lost inside the multiple messages from the programs I'm using.

When you issue a CTTY NUL, all output is directed to the NUL device, including all DOS error messages and messages from programs. However, the output from the ECHO command is also routed to NUL. Luckily, DOS piping still works, so an ECHO statement can be piped to the screen using >CON, where CON is short for console.

PREPARE.BAT in Fig. 2-4 illustrates this. I perform a backup every few days using Fastback. In between, I like to make twice-daily incremental backups. An incremental backup is one where only the few files that have changed are backed up. I also rotate my backups and store the most recent one off-site. Unfortunately, Fastback makes it difficult to make an incremental backup if you don't have the original backup handy, so I use the DOS Backup program. Because it's much slower than Fastback, I want to back up only important files. This is where PREPARE.BAT comes in. It goes through my hard disk and makes sure the archive bit is set off for all the working files I don't want to back up. That makes my backup much faster. Notice that I use a CTTY NUL to stop all the program messages and I pipe the ECHO statements to the console to put messages on the screen.

While CTTY NUL is in effect, the keyboard is essentially disconnected. If you need to get input from the keyboard, you can bypass the CTTY NUL with piping. For example:

```
PAUSE < CON
```

will accept a single keystroke from the keyboard for the PAUSE command. You can use this with programs designed to take input from the keyboard for an error level test, as CTTYKEY.BAT in Fig. 2-5 shows. Notice that I redirect the prompt first. Because the console isn't active, the program can't display the prompt itself.

Password protection

One way to keep casual users from accessing your hard disk is to add password protection. Password protection ranges from simple programs that require you to enter a password, to complex systems that encrypt the file allocation table (FAT) and won't access the hard disk at all until the proper password is entered. If all you need is light protection, then you can put together a batch file password system that's very effective.

Keep in mind that this system won't keep a user from booting off a floppy disk and then accessing your hard disk. In addition, because you can't encrypt the batch file, anyone with access to the hard disk can look at the batch file and figure out your password—although not in a very straightforward way. With that caveat in mind, let's construct the password system.

The password batch file, PASSWRD2.BAT, is shown in Fig. 2-6. It uses Batcmd to get the first character of the password. If that character is correct, it uses Batcmd to get the second character. If the first character is incorrect, it increments a counter and asks again. It repeats this process for the second and third character. Anytime an incorrect character is entered, the program begins prompting for the password from the beginning. If the counter reaches three—after entering three incorrect passwords—the batch file will enter an endless loop and the keyboard will appear to lock up.

With any batch file, you have the problem of the user pressing Ctrl-Break to stop the batch file. PASSWRD2.BAT avoids this problem almost completely by using CTTY NUL at the top. This turns off the console so the computer won't accept input from the keyboard and won't write output to the screen. It's interesting to note that the batch file will still accept the Ctrl-Break; it just won't accept the Y in response to the *Terminate batch job (y/n) message*. This effectively locks the computer. Notice that after the correct response is entered, the batch file restores the screen and keyboard with the CTTY CON command.

Because the keyboard and screen don't respond to the batch file under the CTTY NUL command, the batch file forces them to work by piping output to the screen using the >CON piping command and grabbing input from the keyboard with the <CON piping command.

If you add password protection to the top of your AUTOEXEC.BAT file, anyone booting the computer from the hard disk will have to enter a password. It should be at the very top of the AUTOEXEC.BAT file so the user won't have time to enter Ctrl-Break before the password part of the AUTOEXEC.BAT file takes over.

You can also create a stand-alone batch file to lock your computer but leave it running. Figure 2-7 shows LOCK.BAT, a batch file to do just this. As written, the password for LOCK.BAT is 205. LOCK.BAT uses the GN option of Batcmd, which accepts only numbers 0 through 9. If the user enters any other character, Batcmd will beep and continue waiting.

Control doesn't pass back to the batch file, so if the user tries to enter a keystroke other than a number it's not counted as a password attempt by LOCK.BAT. As a result, using the GN option allows an intruder to make more password attempts than does the GK option shown in PASSWRD2.BAT above. It also makes the password easier to figure out when reading the batch file. Users concerned about either of these issues should modify LOCK.BAT to use the GK option of Batcmd as illustrated in PASSWRD2.BAT.

A less powerful approach

Using CTTY NUL to hide program messages is the only way to deal with programs that bypass DOS and write to the screen themselves. However, if the program whose messages you want to hide is a DOS program or uses DOS to write to the screen, and you load ANSI.SYS, there's a method that will hide the messages without using CTTY NUL.

The trick is to use ANSI command sequences to make the foreground and background colors the same when an unwanted message is due to appear, which effectively hides the message from the user. By alternating between the same colors for the programs and different colors for your messages, you can make sure the user sees only your messages. ANSIHIDE.BAT in Fig. 2-8 illustrates this.

While this approach works, it too suffers drawbacks. First, it will work only on systems that are running ANSI.SYS. Second, it will work only for programs that use DOS to write to the screen. And third, while the messages are indeed invisible, the screen will still scroll for those messages. As a result, there tends to be a lot of space between the messages you write to the screen. See chapter 18 for more information on using ANSI.SYS with your batch files.

Warning

Because of the way DOS works, you should never use the CTTY NUL command while loading memory-resident programs (also called TSRs, for terminate and stay resident). Consider the batch file with the following lines:

```
CTTY NUL
TSR
CTTY CON
```

This batch file segment turns off the console, loads a memory-resident program, and turns the console back on. When the TSR program loads, DOS will clear the file buffers and file handles used by the memory-resident program but not the file handle it used in CTTY NUL. Thus, this batch file segment needlessly uses one file handle. You have the same problem if you try to hide a TSR's messages by loading it with the command:

```
TSR > NUL
```

Because DOS has a limited number of file handles, you should avoid using either method when loading memory-resident programs. In the best case, you could end up trying to run a program and getting a *Not enough file handles* error message. In the worse case, you wouldn't get this error message until you try to save your data. In that case, you would lose all your work.

Summary

- You can avoid many DOS messages by turning command-echoing off in your batch file with the command @ECHO OFF.

- When issuing a DOS command, you can avoid many more messages by piping the results to NUL by adding >NUL to the end of the command.
- The CTTY command allows you to prevent anything from reaching the screen.
- NOT-DEL.BAT illustrates how to turn off the console with the CTTY command to keep all error messages off the screen.
- LOGBOOT.BAT will record each time the computer is turned on or rebooted.
- 1-LOG.BAT will record each time Lotus is started and when the user exits Lotus.
- When the console is turned off with a CTTY NUL, a batch file can still display information on the screen by piping it there.
- When the console is turned off with a CTTY NUL, a batch file can still get input from the keyboard by piping the information from the keyboard into the batch file.
- PASSWRD2.BAT uses the unique characteristics of CTTY NUL to force the user to enter a password before the batch file will run.

2-1 NOT-DEL.BAT will try to delete a nonexistent file to show the ability of the CTTY command to hide DOS error messages.

Batch File Line	Explanation
`@ECHO OFF`	Turn command-echoing off.

`REM NAME:     NOT-DEL.BAT`
`REM PURPOSE: Show CTTY Command`
`REM VERSION: 1.00`
`REM DATE:     January 3, 1991`
`REM FILE C:\QQQ DOES NOT EXIST`
	Documentation remarks.

`IF (%1)==(/?) GOTO HELP` `IF (%1)==(?)  GOTO HELP`	If the user starts the batch file with a request for help, jump to a section to display that help.
`DEL C:\QQQ > NUL`	Delete a nonexistent file and try to pipe messages to nul.
`GOTO END`	Exit the batch file.

`:HELP`
`ECHO A Demonstration Batch File`
`ECHO Showing How Not All Error`
`ECHO Messages Can Be Piped To NUL`
`GOTO END`
`:END_HELP`
	Section that displays help when the user starts the batch file with a /? or a ? as the first replaceable parameter.

`:END`	Label marking the end of the batch file.

2-2 LOGBOOT.BAT creates a log of every time the computer is booted, without the user knowing it.

Batch File Line	Explanation
`@ECHO OFF`	Turn command-echoing off.

`REM NAME:     LOGBOOT.BAT`
`REM PURPOSE: Show Logging Booting`
`REM VERSION: 1.00`
`REM DATE:     January 3, 1991`
`REM Normally, this would be`
`REM part of AUTOEXEC.BAT file`
	Documentation remarks.

`IF (%1)==(/?)  GOTO HELP` `IF (%1)==(?)   GOTO HELP`	If the user starts the batch file with a request for help, jump to a section to display that help.
`CTTY NUL`	Turn the console off so nothing shows up on the screen.
`ECHO	MORE	TIME >> BOOTLOG.TXT`	Pipe the time to a log file. Piping through MORE keeps you from having to press Return, and the > > causes the information to be appended to the end of the file.
`ECHO	MORE	DATE >> BOOTLOG.TXT`	Pipe the date to a log file.
`CTTY CON`	Return control to the screen/keyboard.
`GOTO END`	Exit the batch file.

`:HELP`
`ECHO This Is A Demonstration Batch`
`ECHO File That Shows How The CTTY`
`ECHO Command Can Be Used To Hide`
`ECHO Batch File Activity`
`GOTO END`
`:END_HELP`
	Section that displays help when the user starts the batch file with a /? or a ? as the first replaceable parameter.

`:END`	Label marking the end of the batch file.

2-3 1-LOG.BAT is a batch file for tracking Lotus usage.

Batch File Line	Explanation
`@ECHO OFF`	Turn command-echoing off.

`REM NAME:     1-LOG.BAT`
`REM PURPOSE: Log Lotus Usage`
`REM VERSION: 1.00`
`REM DATE:     January 3, 1991`
	Documentation remarks.

Batch File Line	Explanation
IF (%1)==(/?) GOTO HELP IF (%1)==(?) GOTO HELP	If the user starts the batch file with a request for help, jump to a section to display that help.
CTTY NUL	Turn the console off by turning on the alternative console of nul. This way, nothing except what is explicitly piped to the console is shown.
ECHO Starting Lotus >> C:\LOG\LOTUSLOG.TXT	Pipe a message to the log file indicating the batch file is starting Lotus. Because the batch file uses a > > to pipe, the message is appended to the bottom of the file.
ECHO | MORE | TIME >> C:\LOG\LOTUSLOG.TXT	Pipe the time to the log file. The piping through MORE adds the return the TIME command needs to continue after displaying the time.
ECHO | MORE | DATE >> C:\LOG\LOTUSLOG.TXT	Pipe the date to the log file.
CTTY CON	Turn the console back on.
C:	Make sure the computer is logged onto the C drive. This is a very good idea when the computer has more than one hard disk or if the user sometimes uses the floppy drives.
CD\123	Change to the Lotus subdirectory.
123	Start Lotus.
CTTY NUL	Turn the console off.
ECHO Finishing Lotus >> C:\LOG\LOTUSLOG.TXT	Pipe the closing message to the log file.
ECHO | MORE | TIME >> C:\LOG\LOTUSLOG.TXT	Pipe the finishing time to the log file.

Batch File Line	Explanation
`ECHO	MORE	DATE >> C:\LOG\LOTUSLOG.TXT`	Pipe the finishing date to the log file.
`CTTY CON`	Turn the console back on.
`MENU`	Reload the menu.
`GOTO END`	Exit the batch file.

`:HELP`
`ECHO This Is A Demonstration Batch File`
`ECHO Showing How The CTTY Command Can Be`
`ECHO Used To Hide Logging Activity By A`
`ECHO Batch File`
`GOTO END`
`:END_HELP`
	Section that displays help when the user starts the batch file with a /? or a ? as the first replaceable parameter.

`:END`	Label marking the end of the batch file.

2-4 PREPARE.BAT gets my hard disk ready for an incremental backup.

Batch File Line	Explanation
`@ECHO OFF`	Turn command-echoing off.

`REM NAME:    PREPARE.BAT`
`REM PURPOSE: Prepare For Backup`
`REM VERSION: 1.00`
`REM DATE:    January 3, 1991`
	Documentation remarks.

`IF (%1)==(/?) GOTO HELP` `IF (%1)==(?)  GOTO HELP`	If the user starts the batch file with a request for help, jump to a section to display that help.
`CD\`	Change to the root directory.
`CLS`	Clear the screen.
`CTTY NUL`	Turn the console off.

`ECHO Please Wait > Con`
`ECHO Clearing Archive Attributes>Con`
`ECHO *.BAK files > Con`
	Pipe messages to the console to inform the user what's happening.

`ATTRIB *.BAK /S -A`	Use the DOS ATTRIB program to reset the archive bit to all .BAK files on the hard disk so they won't be backed up in an incremental backup. If you're using DOS 3.3 or later, you could also use the DOS ATTRIB command for this.

Batch File Line	Explanation
ECHO *.TMP files > Con	Tell the user which files are next.
ATTRIB *.TMP /S -A	Clear the archive bit on .TMP files.
ECHO JUNK*.* files > Con	Tell the user which files are next.
ATTRIB JUNK*.* /S -A	Clear the archive bit on JUNK*.* files.
ECHO MW.INI > Con	Tell the user which files are next.
ATTRIB C:\WORD\MW.INI -A	Update the Microsoft Word initialization file. Each time you run Word, it stores the name of the last document you edited here. Word will run with an older version or no MW.INI file at all if you don't change this.
ECHO Selected Fastback Files > Con	Tell the user which files are next.
ATTRIB C:\FB-OFFIC*.* -A ATTRIB C:\FB-HOME*.* -A ATTRIB C:\FASTBACK*.* -A	Clear the archive bit on selected Fastback file. You need Fastback to restore, so backing up Fastback files is redundant.
ECHO TREEINFO.NCD > Con	Tell the user which files are next.
ATTRIB C:\TREEINFO.NCD -A	This is a Norton Utility data file that's easily regenerated.
CTTY CON	Turn the console back on.
ECHO **ALL CLEARED**	Tell the user the batch file is finished.
CD\SYSLIB	Change to the DOS library.
GOTO END	Exit the batch file.
:HELP ECHO This Batch File Clears The ECHO Archive Bit From Files That Do ECHO Not Need To Be Backed Up In An ECHO Incremental Backup GOTO END :END_HELP	Section that displays help when the user starts the batch file with a /? or a ? as the first replaceable parameter.
:END	Label marking the end of the batch file.

2-5 CTTYKEY.BAT shows how you can still use the keyboard with CTTY NUL in effect, if the batch file is structured to allow it.

Batch File Line	Explanation
`@ECHO OFF`	Turn command-echoing off.

`REM NAME:    CTTYKEY.BAT`
`REM PURPOSE: Show CTTY Command`
`REM VERSION: 2.00`
`REM DATE:    January 1, 1992`
	Documentation remarks.

`IF (%1)==(/?) GOTO HELP` `IF (%1)==(?)  GOTO HELP`	If the user starts the batch file with a request for help, jump to a section to display that help.
`CLS`	Clear the screen.
`CTTY NUL`	Use NUL as the console. This turns off the screen and the keyboard.
`ECHO Press 1 2 3 or 4 > CON`	Pipe text to the screen when the screen is otherwise turned off by the CTTY NUL command..
`BATCMD GF 1234`	Obtain a keystroke from the keyboard when the keyboard is otherwise turned off.
`CTTY CON`	Return control to the keyboard and screen.
`GOTO END`	Exit the batch file.

`:HELP`
`ECHO This Is A Demonstration`
`ECHO Batch File Illustrating`
`ECHO Getting Input In A Batch`
`ECHO File When The Console Is`
`ECHO Turned Off By A CTTY NUL`
`ECHO Command`
`GOTO END`
`:END_HELP`
	Section that displays help when the user starts the batch file with a /? or a ? as the first replaceable parameter.

`:END`	Label marking the end of the batch file.

2-6 PASSWRD2.BAT requires the user to enter the correct password (RON in this example) in three tries or less.

Batch File Line	Explanation
`@ECHO OFF`	Turn command-echoing off.

`REM NAME:    PASSWRD2.BAT`
`REM PURPOSE: Batch Password`
`REM VERSION: 1.00`
`REM DATE:    January 3, 1991`
	Documentation remarks.

`IF (%1)==(/?) GOTO HELP` `IF (%1)==(?)  GOTO HELP`	If the user starts the batch file with a request for help, jump to a section to display that help.

Batch File Line	Explanation
`CTTY NUL`	Turn the console off. This prevents the user from breaking out of the batch file using Control-Break.
`SET COUNTER=1`	Create an environmental variable that's used to count the number of attempts the user makes to enter the password.
`:TOP`	Label marking the top of the section for password handling.
`ECHO Enter Password > CON`	Tell the user to enter the password. The message is piped to the console because the console is redirected to nul.
`BATCMD GK<CON`	Use Batcmd to get a single keystroke from the user. The keystroke is piped to Batcmd because the keyboard is redirected to nul.
`IF ERRORLEVEL 82 IF NOT` ℝ `ERRORLEVEL 83 GOTO SECOND`	Test the user's keystroke. If it's the first character of the password, skip to the section that gets the second character. Note this is the section to change to in order to modify the first character of the password.

`IF %COUNTER%==1 GOTO 1`
`IF %COUNTER%==2 GOTO 2`
`IF %COUNTER%==3 GOTO 3`
`:END_TOP`
	If the batch file reaches this point, the user entered an invalid first character. Where the batch file jumps to depends on how many attempts the user has already made.

`:SECOND`	Label marking the beginning of the section to get the second character of the password.
`ECHO *>CON`	Echo a character to the screen so the user will know the first character was accepted.
`BATCMD GK<CON`	Get the second character from the user.
`IF ERRORLEVEL 79 IF NOT` **O** `ERRORLEVEL 80 GOTO THIRD`	Check the second character to see if the proper one was entered. If so, jump to the section that processes the third character.

`IF %COUNTER%==1 GOTO 1`
`IF %COUNTER%==2 GOTO 2`
`IF %COUNTER%==3 GOTO 3`
`:END_SECOND`
	If the batch file reaches this point, the user entered an invalid second character. Where the batch file jumps to depends on how many attempts the user has already made.

`:THIRD`	Label marking the beginning of the section that processes the third character.
`ECHO **>CON`	Echo two characters to the screen.
`BATCMD GK<CON`	Get a character from the user.

Batch File Line	Explanation
IF ERRORLEVEL 78 IF NOT ᴎ ERRORLEVEL 79 GOTO CORRECT	Test that character. If it's correct, jump to the section for a correct password.
IF %COUNTER%==1 GOTO 1 IF %COUNTER%==2 GOTO 2 IF %COUNTER%==3 GOTO 3 :END_THIRD	If the batch file reaches this point, the user entered an invalid third character. Where the batch file jumps to depends on how many attempts the user has already made.
:1	Label marking the section that handles the first miss.
SET COUNTER=2	Increment the counter.
GOTO TOP :END_1	Start over.
:2	Label marking the section that handles the second miss.
SET COUNTER=3	Increment the counter.
GOTO TOP :END_2	Start over.
:3	Label marking the section that handles the third miss.
REM Password Attempts Up REM Stay Here And Computer Is REM Locked Into An Endless Loop	Documentation remarks.
GOTO 3 :END_3	Go back to 3--effectively putting the batch file into an endless loop. Because the console is turned off, the only way out is to reboot.
:HELP ECHO This Is A Password ECHO Demonstration Batch File ECHO You *CANNOT* Break Out Of ECHO This Batch File With ECHO Ctrl-Break ECHO ---------- ECHO WARNING ECHO ---------- ECHO Pressing Ctrl-Break While ECHO Running This Batch File ECHO Will Cause You To Have To ECHO Reboot The Computer To ECHO Regain Control GOTO END :END_HELP	Section that displays help when the user starts the batch file with a /? or a ? as the first replaceable parameter.

2-6 Continued

Batch File Line	Explanation
`:CORRECT`	Label marking the section of the batch file that handles a correct password. If this batch file was used to start an application, those commands would be here. If this batch file were used as a portion of the AUTOEXEC.BAT file, then nothing is needed here because the AUTOEXEC.BAT controls access to the computer.
`CTTY CON`	Turn the console back on.
`:END`	Label marking the end of the batch file.

2-7 LOCK.BAT uses the same approach as PASSWRD2.BAT and allows the user to lock his computer while leaving it unattended.

Batch File Line	Explanation
`@ECHO OFF`	Turn command-echoing off.
`GOTO TOP`	Skip over the documentation remarks that follow.

`NAME:    LOCK.BAT`
`PURPOSE: Lock Keyboard While Away`
`VERSION: 1.00`
`DATE:    January 3, 1992`
	Documentation remarks.

`:TOP`	Label used to jump over the non-executing documentation remarks.
`IF (%1)==(/?) GOTO HELP` `IF (%1)==(?)  GOTO HELP`	If the user starts the batch file with a request for help, jump to a section to display that help.
`CLS`	Clear the screen.
`BATCMD PC 12 25`	Use Batcmd to position the cursor in the middle of the screen.
`ECHO User Locked: Password Required`	Display a message telling the user the computer has been locked and requires a password.
`BATCMD PC 15 01`	Reposition the cursor.
`CTTY NUL`	Turn the console off. This prevents the user from breaking out of the batch file using Ctrl-Break.

Batch File Line	Explanation
SET COUNTER=1	Create an environmental variable that's used to count the number of attempts the user makes to enter the password.
:END_TOP	Label marking the end of the TOP section.
:FIRST	Label marking the beginning of the section to get the first character of the password.
ECHO Enter Password > CON	Prompt the user for a password and pipe that message to the screen because the CTTY NUL command turned off the screen.
BATCMD GN<CON	Obtain the first character of the password from the user using Batcmd. Again, piping must be used because the CTTY NUL command turned off the keyboard as well as the screen. Note that the GN option of Batcmd accepts only numbers, making it easier for someone to guess your password. When a non-number keystroke is entered, Batcmd beeps and continues waiting for a number. Because control doesn't return to the batch file, that will not count as a password attempt. Users concerned about this should modify LOCK.BAT to use the GK option, as shown in PASSWRD2.BAT.
IF ERRORLEVEL 2 IF NOT ERRORLEVEL 3 GOTO SECOND	Test the user's keystroke. If it's the first character of the password, skip to the section that gets the second character. Note that this is the section to change to modify the first character of the password. Also note that the GN option of Batcmd assigns an errorlevel equal to the number pressed, i.e., pressing five results in an errorlevel of five.

2-7**2-7** Continued

Batch File Line	Explanation
IF %COUNTER%==1 GOTO 1 IF %COUNTER%==2 GOTO 2 IF %COUNTER%==3 GOTO 3	If the batch file reaches this point, the user entered an invalid first character. Where the batch file jumps to depends on how many attempts the user has already made.
:END_FIRST	Label marking the end of the FIRST section.
:SECOND	Label marking the beginning of the section to get the second character of the password.
ECHO *>CON	Echo a character to the screen so the user will know the first character was accepted.
BATCMD GN<CON	Get the second character from the user.
IF ERRORLEVEL 0 IF NOT ERRORLEVEL 1 GOTO THIRD	Check the second character to see if the proper one was entered. If so, jump to the section that processes the third character.
IF %COUNTER%==1 GOTO 1 IF %COUNTER%==2 GOTO 2 IF %COUNTER%==3 GOTO 3	If the batch file reaches this point, the user entered an invalid second character. Where the batch file jumps to depends on how many attempts the user has already made.
:END_SECOND	Label marking the end of the SECOND section.
:THIRD	Label marking the beginning of the section that processes the third character.
ECHO **>CON	Echo two characters to the screen.
BATCMD GN<CON	Get a character from the user.
IF ERRORLEVEL 5 IF NOT ERRORLEVEL 6 GOTO CORRECT	Test that character. If it's correct, jump to the section for a correct password.
IF %COUNTER%==1 GOTO 1 IF %COUNTER%==2 GOTO 2 IF %COUNTER%==3 GOTO 3	If the batch file reaches this point, the user entered an invalid third character. Where the batch file jumps to depends on how many attempts the user has already made.

2-7 Continued

Batch File Line	Explanation
`:END_THIRD`	Label marking the end of the THIRD section.
`:1`	Label marking the section that handles the first miss.
`SET COUNTER=2`	Increment the counter.
`GOTO FIRST`	Start over.
`:END_1`	Label marking the end of section 1
`:2`	Label marking the section that handles the second miss.
`SET COUNTER=3`	Increment the counter.
`GOTO FIRST`	Start over.
`:END_2`	Label marking the end of section 2
`:3`	Label marking the section that handles the third miss.

`REM Tries Up`
`REM Stay Here And Computer Is`
`REM Locked Into An Endless Loop`
	Documentation remark.

`GOTO 3`	Go back to 3--effectively putting the batch file into an endless loop. Because the console is turned off, the only way out is to reboot.
`:END_3`	Label marking the end of section 3.

`:HELP`
`ECHO This Is A Password`
`ECHO Batch File That Locks Your`
`ECHO Computer While You Are Away`
`ECHO You *CANNOT* Break Out Of`
`ECHO This Batch File With`
`ECHO Ctrl-Break`
`ECHO ----------`
`ECHO WARNING`
`ECHO ----------`
`ECHO Pressing Ctrl-Break While`
`ECHO Running This Batch File`
`ECHO Will Cause You To Have To`
`ECHO Reboot The Computer To`
`ECHO Regain Control`
`GOTO END`
`:END_HELP`
	Section that displays help when the user starts the batch file with a /? or a ? as the first replaceable parameter.

`:CORRECT`	Label marking the section of the batch file that handles a correct password.
`CTTY CON`	Turn the console back on.

2-8 ANSIHIDE.BAT hides certain messages by making the foreground and background colors the same when those messages are being printed.

Batch File Line	Explanation
`@ECHO OFF`	Turn command-echoing off.

`REM NAME:      ANSIHIDE.BAT`
`REM PURPOSE: Use ANSI.SYS To Hide`
`            Messages`
`REM VERSION: 1.00`
`REM DATE:      December 19, 1991`
	Documentation remarks.

`IF (%1)==(/?) GOTO HELP` `IF (%1)==(?)  GOTO HELP`	If the user starts the batch file with a request for help, jump to a section to display that help.
`ECHO ON`	Turn command-echoing back on. Because the ANSI escape sequences are being sent via the prompt, the prompt must be displayed for DOS to receive the escape sequences. For the prompt to be displayed, echo must be on.
`PROMPT=$e[0;40;37m`	Send the ANSI escape sequences to change the screen color to white-on-black.
`ECHO`	Display a blank line by echoing Alt-255. The real purpose is to display the prompt so DOS will receive the ANSI escape sequence.
`@ECHO OFF`	Turn command-echoing back off.
`CLS`	Clear the screen.
`ECHO Message 1 (Visible)` `ECHO Message 2 (Visible)`	Display two messages using DOS, the same method with which the programs that come with DOS display their messages.
`ECHO ON`	Turn command-echoing on in order to send another ANSI escape sequence to DOS.
`PROMPT $e[0;30;40m`	Send the ANSI escape sequence to change the screen color to black-on-black.
`ECHO`	Echo Alt-255 to force DOS to display the prompt so it can receive the ANSI escape sequences.

Batch File Line	Explanation
`@ECHO OFF`	Turn command-echoing back off.
`ECHO Message 3 (Invisible)` `ECHO Message 4 (Invisible)`	Send two more messages using DOS. Because these are displayed as black text on a black background, they are invisible.

`ECHO ON`
`PROMPT=$e[0;40;37m`
`ECHO`
`@ECHO OFF`
	Reset the screen colors to white-on-black.

`ECHO Message 5 (Visible)` `ECHO Message 6 (Visible)`	Display two more messages.
`PROMPT $p$g`	Reset the prompt.
`GOTO END`	Exit the batch file.

`:HELP`
`ECHO This Is A Demonstration`
`ECHO Batch File That Uses ANSI`
`ECHO To Hide Messages`
`GOTO END`
`:END_HELP`
	Section that displays help when the user starts the batch file with a /? or a ? as the first replaceable parameter.

`:END`	Label marking the end of the batch file.

PART TWO
Working with batch files

3
Batch file help

One problem with having a lot of batch files is that it's difficult to remember which batch file does what. One way around this is with a menu. However, if you write a menu system with an entry for every one of your batch files, you're going to have to work through an awfully long menu to run your batch files.

Another approach is to write your own help file. The batch file HELP.BAT in Fig. 3-1 (located at the end of the chapter) will display a friendly reminder of the purpose of your batch files. As HELP1.BAT in Fig. 3-2 shows, you can use IF statements to make this help batch file somewhat context-sensitive.

Customized help

While writing custom help batch files works, it's a difficult system to maintain. Each time you write a batch file or discard an existing batch file, you must update your help screens to reflect that change. Otherwise, your help system will get out of sync with your batch files and give incorrect information.

There's an approach that allows you to add and delete batch files at will and it never gets out of sync; however, it requires some special consideration. This approach has two requirements: a common batch file subdirectory and consistent internal documentation in the batch files.

While keeping all your batch files in one subdirectory isn't absolutely necessary, it makes the help system work much better. If you have your batch file arsenal scattered across multiple subdirectories, the help system can give you information on only one sub-directory at a time. Also, for these batch files to work across different subdirectories, you'll need to modify them to either take the subdirectory as an input or always use the current subdirectory. I store all my batch files in C: \ BAT, but the name doesn't matter. (If you use a different subdirectory name, you'll need to modify these batch files to work with that name.)

In addition to keeping your batch files in a separate subdirectory, you need to create the batch files with proper internal documentation and consistent capitalization. This requirement affects only the first five lines of the batch file and every batch file should begin with the same first five lines. They are:

1. @ECHO OFF
2. REM NAME:
3. REM PURPOSE:
4. REM VERSION:
5. REM DATE:

Chapter 1 discusses this in more detail. If you haven't done so, please read this chapter before you continue.

HELPBAT.BAT in Fig. 3-3 uses the above documentation to display custom help about each batch file. It begins with a FOR loop that loops through each batch file in the C: \ BAT subdirectory. For each batch file, it calls itself with a special flag that causes HELPBAT.BAT to jump to a special routine the second time through.

This special routine first displays the name of the batch file and underlines it. It has access to the name because, when it's called the second time, the name is passed to it as a replaceable parameter. After displaying the name, the routine types the batch file using the DOS TYPE command. It pipes this information to the FIND filter, which then displays only the line containing PURPOSE:.

Note: This is the reason for the recommendation in chapter 1 to put your entire purpose statement all on one line. That way, the display completely explains the purpose of the batch file. If you must use multiple lines for your purpose statement, you could start each one with a PURPOSE: to make sure the help batch file displays the entire purpose. This does, however, tend to make the help screens look fairly cluttered.

After the PURPOSE: information is piped to the FIND filter, control is returned to HELPBAT.BAT, which will then loop through to the next batch file, if any remain.

On my 16 MHz IBM Model 80, this system runs slow enough that I can read all the lines as they scroll up the screen. However, on my Northgate 386/20, the lines scroll too fast to read. If that happens to you, you can replace the ECHO %1 line with a TYPE %1 ¦ FIND "NAME:" line. That will cut the speed of the display in half because the help batch file now has to type the batch file twice and use the find filter twice to locate specific text. If it still runs too fast, you can add lines to display the version and last modified date. If you display all four pieces of information, that version of HELPBAT.BAT will run at one fourth the speed of the original version.

When you delete a batch file, it doesn't exist to type so it's automatically removed from this system. When you add a batch file, it contains all the information required by HELPBAT.BAT, so the FOR loop automatically includes it in the system. As a result, your help system is always current with your batch files.

Specific help

While HELPBAT.BAT is a very effective method of displaying general batch file help, it can be overpowering when you have a lot of batch files. For example, I have over 500 batch files, so finding a specific batch file using HELPBAT.BAT would take a long time and a lot of reading.

Fortunately, narrowing the search is fairly easy. All that's required is adding a filter onto the line that types the batch files, as shown by HELPBAT2.BAT in Fig. 3-4. When you don't enter any text, you get all the purpose lines as you do with HELPBAT.BAT. However, when you enter a phrase, HELPBAT2.BAT displays the purpose line for only those batch files that contain that phrase.

Because you're using the DOS FIND filter, the search is case-sensitive. That's the reason for recommending that you standardize your capitalization. DOS 5.0 users can add the /I switch to ignore case.

While HELPBAT2.BAT displays only the purpose line for those batch files that contain text that the user specifies on the command line, it displays the underlined filenames of every batch file in the subdirectory. That too is avoidable, but avoiding it requires using a DOS trick.

The process begins by modifying the line that types the batch file and types the specified text to pipe the results into a temporary file called JUNK. When the text is found, JUNK contains the purpose line from the batch file. When the text isn't found, the file still exists but contains nothing.

The problem is telling if JUNK contains any text or not. You want to skip displaying the name and typing JUNK if JUNK is empty, and you want to display the batch file name and type JUNK if JUNK contains text. The FIND filter doesn't set the DOS errorlevel, so you can't test the errorlevel. And a zero-length file passes the DOS IF EXIST test, so you can't test using the IF EXIST test. However, DOS won't copy a zero-length file.

The solution, then, is to create the temporary file in one subdirectory and copy it to a second subdirectory. If it exists in the second subdirectory, it contains text and you can display the batch filename and the text. If it doesn't exist, then it contains no text and the batch file currently being processed doesn't contain text matching the search criteria. HELPBAT3.BAT in Fig. 3-5 does just that.

To avoid problems, HELPBAT3.BAT creates two temporary subdirectories at its start and removes them when finished. It also deletes the temporary file after each batch file is processed, so one test doesn't interfere with the next test.

Summary

- One way to keep track of all your batch files is to access them through a menu system.
- If you track your batch files with a menu system, you must update the menu system every time you add or delete a batch file.
- Another approach to tracking your batch files is to write a help batch file that lists and describes all your other batch files. This batch file can be noncontext-sensitive like HELP.BAT, or context-sensitive like HELP1.BAT.
- Before you can write a more advanced help system, you need to store your batch files in a common subdirectory and construct them with proper and consistent internal documentation.
- HELPBAT.BAT automatically displays the purpose line for each batch file. It doesn't require any modifications when you add or delete batch files.

- HELPBAT2.BAT uses a FIND filter to display only the purpose line for batch files that contain a specified piece of text. However, HELPBAT2.BAT still displays the name of all the batch files.
- HELPBAT3.BAT pipes the results of the FIND filter to a file and then copies that file to make sure it contains text. That allows HELPBAT3.BAT to display the name and purpose information for only those files that contain a specified piece of text.

3-1 HELP.BAT displays a help menu of other batch files.

Batch File Line	Explanation
`@ECHO OFF`	Turn command-echoing off.

`REM NAME:     HELP.BAT`
`REM PURPOSE: Display Batch Help`
`REM VERSION: 1.00`
`REM DATE:     January 3, 1991`
	Documentation remarks.

`IF (%1)==(/?) GOTO HELP` `IF (%1)==(?)  GOTO HELP`	If the user starts the batch file with a request for help, jump to a section to display that help.
`CLS`	Clear the screen.

`ECHO DISCARD.BAT`
`ECHO -----------`
`ECHO Will Move All Unwanted Files`
`ECHO To A Directory For Holding`
`ECHO SYNTAX: DISCARD FILE1 FILE2`
`BATCMD SL`
`ECHO MAINTAIN.BAT`
`ECHO ------------`
`ECHO Will Erase Temporary Files,`
`ECHO Sort Files, And Run Your`
`ECHO File Defragmentation Program`
`ECHO SYNTAX: MAINTAIN`
`ECHO WARNING: Takes Two Hours To Run`
`BATCMD SL`
`ECHO PRINT.BAT`
`ECHO ---------`
`ECHO Print ASCII Files Automatically`
`ECHO SYNTAX: PRINT FILE1 FILE2 FILE3`
`ECHO WARNING: Make Sure Printer Is On`
`ECHO Or Computer Will Lock Up`
	Print help information on the screen.

`GOTO END`	Exit the batch file.

`:HELP`
`ECHO This Is A Demonstration Batch`
`ECHO File That Displays Help`
`ECHO Information On A Few Batch Files`
`GOTO END`
`:END_HELP`
	Section that displays help when the user starts the batch file with a /? or a ? as the first replaceable parameter.

`:END`	Label marking the end of the batch file.

3-2 HELP1.BAT adds limited context sensitivity to a batch-based help facility.

Batch File Line	Explanation
`@ECHO OFF`	Turn command-echoing off.

`REM NAME:    HELP1.BAT`
`REM PURPOSE: Display Batch Help`
`REM VERSION: 1.00`
`REM DATE:    January 3, 1991`
	Documentation remarks.

`IF (%1)==(/?) GOTO HELP` `IF (%1)==(?)  GOTO HELP`	If the user starts the batch file with a request for help, jump to a section to display that help.
`IF (%1)==() GOTO NOTHING`	Jump to Nothing section if no replaceable parameter was entered.
`IF NOT %1==UTILITY GOTO NOUTIL`	If %1 is not a utility, skip to the NoUtil section.

`ECHO DISCARD.BAT`
`ECHO -----------`
`ECHO Will Move All Unwanted Files`
`ECHO To A Directory For Holding`
`ECHO SYNTAX: DISCARD FILE1 FILE2...`
`BATCMD SL`
`ECHO MAINTAIN.BAT`
`ECHO ------------`
`ECHO Will Erase Temporary Files,`
`ECHO Sort Files, And Run Your`
`ECHO File Defragmentation Program`
`ECHO SYNTAX: MAINTAIN`
`ECHO WARNING: Takes 2 Hours To Run`
`GOTO END`
	Display the help messages and exit the batch file.

`:NOUTIL`	Label marking the beginning of the NoUtil section.
`IF NOT %1==PRINTING GOTO NOPRINT`	Skip to the next section if printing help was not selected.

`ECHO PRINT.BAT`
`ECHO ---------`
`ECHO Will Print ASCII`
`ECHO Files Automatically`
`ECHO SYNTAX: PRINT FILE1 FILE2 FILE3`
`ECHO WARNING: Make Sure Printer Is`
`ECHO On Or Computer Will Lock Up`
`GOTO END`
`:END_NOUTIL`
	Display the printing help messages and exit the batch file.

`:NOPRINT`	Label marking the beginning of the NoPrint section.
`IF NOT %1==BACKUP GOTO NOBACK`	If backup was not selected, skip to the next section.

Batch File Line	Explanation

`ECHO BACKUP.BAT`
`ECHO ----------`
`ECHO Will Backup All (Or Some)`
`ECHO Subdirectories On Your Hard Disk`
`ECHO SYNTAX: BACKUP`
`ECHO To Backup Entire Hard Disk`
`ECHO SYNTAX: BACKUP directory`
`ECHO To Backup One Subdirectory`
`GOTO END`
`:END_NOPRINT`
	Display the backup help messages and exit the batch file.

`:NOBACK`	Label for NoBack section.
`IF NOT %1==MISC GOTO WRONG`	If Misc was not selected, skip to next section.

`ECHO GAME.BAT`
`ECHO --------`
`ECHO Will bring up the game menu`
`ECHO SYNTAX: GAME`
`GOTO END`
`:END_NOBACK`
	Display help message and exit batch file.

`:WRONG`
`ECHO INVALID SYNTAX`
`GOTO NOTHING`
`:END_WRONG`
	Section for invalid replaceable parameter.

`:NOTHING`
`ECHO SYNTAX IS HELP1 CATEGORY`
`ECHO ENTER CATEGORY IN ALL UPPERCASE`
`ECHO Valid categories are:`
`ECHO Utilities, Backup, Printing, Misc`
`:END_NOTHING`
	Display general help information.

`:HELP`
`ECHO HELP1.BAT Display Help On`
`ECHO Specific Batch Files`
`GOTO NOTHING`
`:END_HELP`
	Section that displays help when the user starts the batch file with a /? or a ? as the first replaceable parameter.

`:END`	Label marking end.

3-3 HELPBAT.BAT displays the name of each batch file and its purpose line.

Batch File Line	Explanation
`@ECHO OFF`	Turn command-echoing off.

`REM NAME:    HELPBAT.BAT`
`REM PURPOSE: Display .BAT Purpose`
`REM VERSION: 1.00`
`REM DATE:    November 6, 1991`
	Documentation remarks.

Batch File Line	Explanation
IF (%1)==(/?) GOTO HELP IF (%1)==(?) GOTO HELP	If the user starts the batch file with a request for help, jump to a section to display that help.
IF (%2)==(DISPLAY) GOTO DISPLAY	Normally, you would run HELPBAT.-BAT without any replaceable parameters. However, it calls itself for each batch file with the first replaceable parameter being the name of the batch file and the second being the flag DISPLAY, so the batch file knows to run the subroutine.
FOR %%J IN (C:\BAT*.BAT) DO CALL HELPBAT %%J DISPLAY	When run from the command line, this batch file loops through all the batch files. For each one, it calls this batch file again and supplies it with the name of the batch file and a flag to tell the batch file to run the subroutine. I've "hardwired" it to process the batch files in my C:\BAT subdirectories. You'll want to change this to the subdirectory you use, or remove the hardwiring altogether if you keep your batch files in a different location.
GOTO END	After looping through all the batch files, it exits this batch file.
:DISPLAY	Label marking the beginning of the subroutine that's run when the batch file calls itself.
ECHO %1 ECHO --------------------	Echo the name of the batch file and underline it.
TYPE %1 | FIND "PURPOSE:"	Type the batch file and use the DOS FIND filter to display only the line containing PURPOSE:.
BATCMD SL	Display a blank line.
GOTO END :END_DISPLAY	Jump to the end of the batch file.
:HELP ECHO Reads Batch Files & Displays ECHO The Name And Purpose Line GOTO END :END_HELP	Section that displays help when the user starts the batch file with a /? or a ? as the first replaceable parameter.
:END	Label marking the end of the batch file.

3-4 HELPBAT2.BAT allows you to get help about your batch files for a specific topic; however, it still displays the names of all the batch files.

Batch File Line	Explanation
`@ECHO OFF`	Turn command-echoing off.

`REM NAME:     HELPBAT2.BAT`
`REM PURPOSE: Display .BAT Purpose`
`REM          For Matching Text`
`REM VERSION: 1.00`
`REM DATE:    November 9, 1991`
	Documentation remarks.

`IF (%1)==(/?) GOTO HELP` `IF (%1)==(?)  GOTO HELP`	If the user starts the batch file with a request for help, jump to a section to display that help.
`IF (%2)==(DISPLAY) GOTO DISPLAY`	When HELPBAT2.BAT calls itself for each batch file, it finds the first replaceable parameter to be the name of the batch file, and the second to be the flag DISPLAY, so the batch file knows to run the subroutine.
`SET FIND=`	Store a space in the variable FIND. If the user doesn't enter anything, the batch file will carry this value forward as the value to search for, and most lines have a space.
`IF (%1)==() GOTO RUN`	If no replaceable parameter was entered, skip the find variable construction section.
`SET SPACE=`	Set the environmental variable SPACE equal to one space.
`:TOP`	Label marking the top of the section to deal with the environmental variable(s) to search for.
`SET FIND=%1`	Add the current replaceable parameter to the find variable.
`SHIFT`	Move the replaceable parameters down one level.
`IF (%1)==() GOTO RUN`	If there are no more replaceable parameters, jump to the next section.
`SET FIND=%FIND%%SPACE%`	Add a space to the FIND variable to separate the next word.
`GOTO TOP` `:END_TOP`	Go through the loop again.
`:RUN`	Label marking the beginning of the section to find the help text.

Batch File Line	Explanation
`FOR %%J IN (C:\BAT\*.BAT)` `    DO CALL HELPBAT2 %%J DISPLAY`	When run from the command line, the batch file loops through all the batch files. For each one, it calls this batch file again and supplies it with the name of the batch file and a flag to tell the batch file to run the subroutine.
`GOTO END` `:END_RUN`	After looping through all the batch files, it exits this batch file.
`:DISPLAY`	Label marking the beginning of the subroutine that's run when the batch file calls itself.
`ECHO %1` `ECHO --------------------`	Echo the name of the batch file and underline it.
`TYPE %1	FIND "%FIND%" |` ` FIND "PURPOSE:"`	Find the specified text on the purpose line. If the FIND variable is blank, that portion of the FIND filter passes all the text along to the next filter.
`BATCMD SL`	Display a blank line.
`GOTO END` `:END_DISPLAY`	Jump to the end of the batch file.

`:HELP`
`ECHO Reads Batch Files & Displays`
`ECHO The Name And Purpose Line`
`ECHO And Will Search The Purpose For`
`ECHO Text Entered On The Command`
`ECHO Line`
`GOTO END`
`:END_HELP`
	Section that displays help when the user starts the batch file with a /? or a ? as the first replaceable parameter.

`:END`	Label marking the end of the batch file.

3-5 HELPBAT3.BAT allows you to get help about your batch files for a specific topic and display only the names of the batch files that match your search criteria.

Batch File Line	Explanation
`@ECHO OFF`	Turn command-echoing off.

`REM NAME:     HELPBAT3.BAT`
`REM PURPOSE: Display .BAT Purpose`
`REM          For Matching Text`
`REM VERSION: 1.00`
`REM DATE:    November 9, 1991`
	Documentation remarks.

Batch File Line	Explanation
IF (%1)==(/?) GOTO HELP IF (%1)==(?) GOTO HELP	If the user starts the batch file with a request for help, jump to a section to display that help.
IF (%2)==(DISPLAY) GOTO DISPLAY	When HELPBAT3.BAT calls itself for each batch file, it finds the first replaceable parameter to be the name of the batch file, and the second being the flag DISPLAY so the batch file knows to run the subroutine.
MD C:\TEMP1 MD C:\TEMP2	Create two temporary subdirectories. These are removed when the batch file finishes.
SET FIND=	Store a space in the variable FIND. If the user doesn't enter anything, the batch file will carry this value forward as the value to search for, and most lines have a space.
IF (%1)==() GOTO RUN	If no replaceable parameter was entered, skip the find variable construction section.
SET SPACE=	Set the environmental variable SPACE equal to one space.
:TOP	Label marking the top of the section to deal with the environmental variable(s) to search for.
SET FIND=%1	Add the current replaceable parameter to the find variable.
SHIFT	Move the replaceable parameters down one level.
IF (%1)==() GOTO RUN	If there are no more replaceable parameters, jump to the next section.
SET FIND=%FIND%%SPACE%	Add a space to the find variable to separate the next word.
GOTO TOP :END_TOP	Go through the loop again.
:RUN	Label marking the beginning of the section to find the help text.

Batch File Line	Explanation
FOR %%J IN (C:\BAT*.BAT) DO CALL HELPBAT3 %%J DISPLAY	When run from the command line, the batch file loops through all the batch files. For each one, it calls this batch file again and supplies it with the name of the batch file and a flag to tell the batch file to run the subroutine.
RD C:\TEMP1 RD C:\TEMP2	Remove the temporary subdirectories.
SET FIND= SET SPACE=	Delete the temporary environmental variables.
GOTO END :END_RUN	After looping through all the batch files, it exits this batch file.
:DISPLAY	Label marking the beginning of the subroutine that's run when the batch file calls itself.
TYPE %1 | FIND "%FIND%" | FIND "PURPOSE:" > C:\TEMP1\JUNK	Find the specified text on the purpose line. If the FIND variable is blank, that portion of the FIND filter passes all the text along to the next filter. Pipe the results of the FIND to a file.
COPY C:\TEMP1\JUNK C:\TEMP2\JUNK > NUL	If the FIND in the above step was successful, this file exists and contains text. If the FIND was unsuccessful, a zero-length file exists. Because zero-length files won't copy, C:\TEMP2\JUNK will exist only if the FIND is successful.
DEL C:\TEMP1\JUNK	Delete the first temporary file.
IF NOT EXIST C:\TEMP2\JUNK GOTO END	If C:\TEMP2\JUNK doesn't exist, this file didn't contain the requested text, so exit the batch file.
ECHO %1 ECHO --------------------	Echo the name of the batch file and underline it.
TYPE C:\TEMP2\JUNK	Display the purpose line by typing the file containing the text.
C:\TEMP2\JUNK	After typing this file, it's no longer needed, so delete it.

Batch File Line	Explanation
BATCMD SL	Display a blank line.
GOTO END :END_DISPLAY	Jump to the end of the batch file.
:HELP ECHO Reads Batch Files & Displays ECHO The Name And Purpose Line ECHO And Will Search The Purpose For ECHO Text Entered On The Command ECHO Line GOTO END :END_HELP	Section that displays help when the user starts the batch file with a /? or a ? as the first replaceable parameter.
:END	Label marking the end of the batch file.

4

Batch files that use less space

MS-DOS allocates disk space to files in blocks called *clusters*. Clusters range in size from 1K to 8K. The DOS directory entry that's maintained for every file contains the actual size of the file. This is the size you see when you issue a DIR command, but it isn't the actual amount of disk space required for the file.

On my hard disk, every file gets allocated space in 4,096-byte clusters. If a file has one character in it, it's allocated 4,096 bytes. If it has 4,097 bytes, it's allocated two clusters, or 8,192 bytes. Some versions of DOS allocate space in clusters up to 8,192 bytes. This large space requirement for small files is especially hard on batch files because they're typically very small.

I keep most of my working batch files in a subdirectory called C:\BAT. The batch files have only 5,203 bytes of information in them, yet they require 43,000 bytes of disk space. That means that 88% of the space allocated to these files is wasted. The directory with all the batch files I'm writing for this book is even worse. With only 19,172 bytes of information, the files require 182,272 bytes of space!

There are no complete solutions to this dilemma, but there are three partial solutions: Upgrade to a new version of DOS, combine smaller batch files into larger ones, and compress the batch files files.

DOS upgrade

Upgrading to a new version of DOS can often decrease the size of the files on your hard disk. Typically, newer releases have reduced the cluster size. This isn't always true, however, and often the cluster size is a function of the hard disk size. So check first.

Upgrading DOS versions has a temporary drawback. You must back up your hard disk, reformat it, and restore the data before the change is effective—and all of this takes time. You have the additional advantage, however, in that the space reduction applies to all files, not just batch files. Because file size behaves much like a random variable, files waste an average of half a cluster. If cluster size is reduced from 8K to 4K, then the space wasted by an average file will be reduced from 4K to 2K, a savings of 2K per file. Some time ago, when I upgraded a full 20Mg hard disk from DOS 2.1 to DOS 3.2, I freed up almost 4 Megs of space as a result of reducing the cluster size from 8K to 4K.

Combining batch files

The second solution to reducing batch file disk space is to combine multiple small batch files into one larger batch file. For example, if you have a menu with six options and each option requires a batch file, you could combine all the options into one batch file called MENU.BAT. Simply pass the the option you want as the first replaceable parameter. Figure 4-1 shows BIGMENU.BAT, which runs all six of the menu options.

This solution has two primary drawbacks. The resulting batch file runs slower than six individual batch files, and this long batch file is more difficult to write, debug, and maintain than six shorter batch files.

Compressing batch files

The third solution for reducing the space required for batch files is to compress them with a file compression program like LHA by Haruyasu Yoshizaki. LHA is a copyrighted but free program that compresses files and stores them in a common file, which usually has an .LZH extension. With batch files, you get two types of space savings. First, the act of compressing batch files reduces their size a great deal. In addition, by storing all the batch files in one common file, you save because partial clusters aren't wasted on each small batch file.

The problem is that batch files can't run when they're compressed. The solution is to write one overall controlling batch file that uncompresses the batch files you want to run, runs them, and then deletes them after they run. Because the act of uncompressing them doesn't delete them from the single .LZH storage file, deleting the .BAT files after execution doesn't eliminate them. The next time you want to run the same batch file, the controlling batch file simply uncompresses it again.

As an experiment, I picked twelve batch files from other chapters in this book to experiment with: CHECKERR.BAT, CL.BAT, CL2.BAT, HELPBAT.BAT, MACRO. BAT, MACRO2.BAT, MULTI.BAT, MULTI2.BAT, NUMBER1.BAT, NUMBER9.BAT, PASSWRD2.BAT and SAVE-ERR.BAT. In addition, NUMBER1.BAT calls five more files (NUMBER2.BAT through NUMBER6.BAT) while running, so these were part of the experiment as well. These seventeen contained 30,702 bytes of data when I performed my experiment, but because each file is allocated space in full-cluster increments regardless of its size, the actual disk space used was 53,248 bytes.

I used LHA, version 2.13, to compress all seventeen files into one large file called SMALLBAT.LZH. I then wrote SMALLBAT.BAT in Fig. 4-2 to handle the individual batch files. To run a batch file, in SMALLBAT.LZH, enter the command SMALLBAT followed by the name of the batch file to run and then any parameters to pass to that batch file. SMALLBAT.BAT will uncompress the batch file you want to run, along with any other batch files it calls, run them, and then delete them. The combination of

SMALLBAT.BAT and SMALLBAT.LZH contains 11,728 bytes of data and uses 14,336 bytes of disk space, which is only 27% of the disk space required by the original files.

SMALLBAT.BAT intentionally points out a few of the problems with this approach. While CHECKERR.BAT and SAVE-ERR.BAT appear to function when running under this system, they really don't work properly. Both are batch files for reporting the errorlevel. However, SMALLBAT.BAT runs LHA before calling the batch files and running a program resets the errorlevel to zero—so these batch files will always report zero unless there's a problem running LHA. Any batch file that depends on the errorlevel being set when it begins, therefore, can't be incorporated into this system. Of course, batch files that change the errorlevel after they start will continue to work correctly under this system.

Another problem is that MULTI.BAT expects to receive a number of commands on the command line, and sometimes this will exceed the number that can be handled by the ten available replaceable parameters. SMALLBAT.BAT handles this properly, but it requires several lines of code and the construction of a large environmental variable. Of course, having to enter SMALLBAT and a space before the MULTI command reduces the number of commands that can be passed to MULTI.BAT. (Because you would have entered MULTI anyway, having to enter it after SMALLBAT doesn't reduce the space available for replaceable parameters.)

Of course, you have to do a lot of extra typing because each batch file now requires the phrase SMALLBAT and a space in front of it. You can reduce this, however, by renaming SMALLBAT.BAT to RUN.BAT or even R.BAT.

Another aspect of using the LHA-driven SMALLBAT.BAT to compress your batch files, and it can be either an advantage or a disadvantage depending on how you use your system, is that it makes it harder for others to operate your system. It takes two commands—SMALLBAT and the name of the batch file—to run each batch file instead of one. If you're trying to make your system easier for other people to use, it's a disadvantage. If you're concerned about security, making your system more complex for an uninformed user is an advantage.

SMALLBAT.BAT can run into problems when the system is rebooted or turned off while an application that's being controlled by one of its batch files is running. When that happens, SMALLBAT.BAT loses control without deleting that batch file. The system will continue to run normally, but the batch files that were uncompressed prior to rebooting won't be deleted by the system until the next time that particular option of SMALLBAT .BAT is run.

If your disk space is very tight, you can use the same approach to run programs as well as batch files. LHA tends to slow down significantly when uncompressing large files, however, so you're probably better off storing each major application in a separate subdirectory and a separate .LZH file.

Technical notes

The disk enclosed with this book contains a complete and read-to-run copy of LHA, as well as documentation prepared by the program's author. In addition, chapter 21 briefly documents LHA. If you like this approach, you'll want to modify SMALLBAT.BAT to run the batch files you use on your system. With the included version of LHA, you have all the tools you need.

Readers familiar with PkZip might want to substitute that program for LHA. If you do that, the lines that perform the decompression must include the /O switch. This allows PkZip to overwrite existing files, something the system will need to do if you reboot before SMALLBAT.BAT can delete all its files.

Summary

- DOS allocates space in full-cluster increments that can be as large as 8K, and are generally at least 2K for hard disks. As a result, even small files can take up a lot of hard disk space.
- Upgrading to a newer version of DOS can sometimes reduce the cluster size; however, it's a lot of hard work.
- You can reduce the amount of space used by small batch files by combining them into a large batch file and jumping to the right spot in this massive batch file by way of a menu or replaceable parameter.
- You can dramatically reduce the space needed to store your batch files by compressing all of them and having a controlling batch file, like SMALLBAT.BAT, uncompress the ones you need to run an application.
- Some programs, like those that expect the errorlevel to be set when they begin, aren't appropriate for a compressed system.
- Compressing all your batch files makes the system more difficult to use.
- Compressing all your batch files can cause administrative difficulties when the computer is turned off or rebooted, which doesn't allow the controlling batch file to delete all the batch files it has uncompressed.

4-1 BIGMENU.BAT consolidates six different batch files into one file to conserve disk space.

Batch File Line	Explanation
`@ECHO OFF`	Turn command-echoing off.

`REM NAME:     BIGMENU.BAT`
`REM PURPOSE: Consolidate Batch Files`
`REM VERSION: 1.00`
`REM DATE:     March 1, 1991`
`REM This Batch File Replaces 1.BAT,`
`REM 2.BAT, 3.BAT, 4.BAT, 5.BAT,`
`REM AND 6.BAT`
	Documentation remarks.

`IF (%1)==(/?) GOTO HELP` `IF (%1)==(?)  GOTO HELP`	If the user starts the batch file with a request for help, jump to a section to display that help.
`IF (%1)==() GOTO NOCODE`	If the user fails to enter a replaceable parameter, jump to an error-handling section.

Batch File Line	Explanation
IF %1==1 GOTO ONE IF %1==2 GOTO TWO IF %1==3 GOTO THREE IF %1==4 GOTO FOUR IF %1==5 GOTO FIVE IF %1==6 GOTO SIX	If the user enters one of these values, he has made a proper selection and the batch file will jump to the appropriate section to handle it.
GOTO NOTRIGHT	The user entered an invalid replaceable parameter so the batch file jumps to an error-handling section.
:ONE	Label marking the top of the section of the batch file that handles the first option.
C:	Make sure the computer is logged onto the C drive.
CD\WORD	Change to the Microsoft Word subdirectory.
WORD %2	Run Word using a replaceable parameter if the user specified one.
GOTO MENU :END_ONE	Jump to the section of the batch file that redisplays the menu.
:TWO C: CD\123 123 GOTO MENU :END_TWO	The section of the batch file that handles the second option.
:THREE C: CD\DBASE DBASE %2 %3 GOTO MENU :END_THREE	The section of the batch file that handles the third option.
:FOUR C: CD\GAME XMAN GOTO MENU :END_FOUR	The section of the batch file that handles the fourth option.
:FIVE FORMAT A:/V GOTO MENU :END_FIVE	The section of the batch file that handles the fifth option.
:SIX BACKUP C:\ A: /S GOTO MENU :END_SIX	The section of the batch file that handles the sixth option.

Batch File Line	Explanation
`:NOCODE`	Label marking the section that handles the error when the user fails to enter a menu selection code.
`CLS`	Clear the screen.

`ECHO Enter Bigmenu Followed By`
`ECHO A Menu Code To Run A Program`
`ECHO For Example BIGMENU 1`
`ECHO To Run Word Processor`
	Tell the user what happened.

`PAUSE`	Wait for the user to read the message.
`GOTO MENU` `:END_NOCODE`	Redisplay the menu.
`:NOTRIGHT`	Label marking the section of the batch file that handles the user entering an invalid code.

`ECHO You Entered An Incorrect Code`
`ECHO Only The Codes 1-6 Are Allowed`
`ECHO Enter Bigmenu Followed By`
`ECHO A Menu Code To Run A Program`
`ECHO For Example BIGMENU 1`
`ECHO To Run Word Processor`
`PAUSE`
`GOTO MENU`
`:END_NOTRIGHT`
	Tell the user what happened and how to correct the problem.

`:MENU`	Label marking the section of the batch file that displays the menu.

`REM Enter Commands Here To`
`REM Display Menu`
`REM Following Command Assumes A`
`REM Program Called MENU.COM Or`
`REM MENU.EXE Exists`
	Documentation remarks.

`MENU`	Display the menu.
`GOTO END` `:END_MENU`	Exit the batch file.

`:HELP`
`ECHO BIGMENU.BAT Is A Demonstration`
`ECHO Batch File That Shows How`
`ECHO Multiple Batch Files Can Be`
`ECHO Combined Into A Single Batch`
`ECHO File To Save Space`
`GOTO END`
`:END_HELP`
	Section that displays help when the user starts the batch file with a /? or a ? as the first replaceable parameter.

`:END`	Label marking the end of the batch file.

4-2 SMALLBAT.BAT uncompresses the batch files you tell it to run, runs them, and then deletes the batch files—leaving the compressed versions intact.

Batch File Line	Explanation
`@ECHO OFF`	Turn command-echoing off.

`REM NAME:      SMALLBAT.BAT`
`REM PURPOSE: Run Compressed Batch File`
`REM VERSION: 2.00`
`REM DATE:      January 10, 1992`
	Documentation remarks.

`IF (%1)==(/?)  GOTO HELP` `IF (%1)==(?)   GOTO HELP`	If the user starts the batch file with a request for help, jump to a section to display that help.

`SET CHECKERR=`
`SET CL=`
`SET CL2=`
`SET HELPBAT=`
`SET MACRO=`
`SET MACRO2=`
`SET MULTI=`
`SET MULTI2=`
`SET NUMBER1=`
`SET NUMBER9=`
`SET PASSWRD2=`
`SET SAVE-ERR=`
	Reset the environmental variables used by the batch file.

`IF (%1)==() GOTO MISSING`	If the user did not enter a replaceable parameter to tell SMALLBAT.BAT which batch file to run, jump to an error-handling routine.
`SET %1=YES`	Create an environmental variable with the same name as the first replaceable parameter the user entered and set its value to yes.

`IF (%CHECKERR%)==(YES)  GOTO CHECKERR`
`IF (%CL%)==(YES)        GOTO CL`
`IF (%CL2%)==(YES)       GOTO CL2`
`IF (%HELPBAT%)==(YES)   GOTO HELPBAT`
`IF (%MACRO%)==(YES)     GOTO MACRO`
`IF (%MACRO2%)==(YES)    GOTO MACRO2`
`IF (%MULTI%)==(YES)     GOTO MULTI`
`IF (%MULTI2%)==(YES)    GOTO MULTI2`
`IF (%NUMBER1%)==(YES)   GOTO NUMBER1`
`IF (%NUMBER9%)==(YES)   GOTO NUMBER9`
`IF (%PASSWRD2%)==(YES)  GOTO PASSWRD2`
`IF (%SAVE-ERR%)==(YES)  GOTO SAVE-ERR`
	First the batch file sets all the environmental variables to nul, then it sets the single variable represented by the first replaceable parameter to yes. Therefore, if any of these variables contains a value of yes, it's the replaceable parameter selected by the user.

4-2 Continued

Batch File Line	Explanation
| ```
:INVALID
ECHO You Have Entered An Invalid
ECHO Batch File To Run
BATCMD SL
GOTO LIST
:END_INVALID
``` | If the batch file reaches this point then the user made an invalid selection for the first replaceable parameter, so display an error message and jump to another section to display the valid commands. Note: BATCMD SL.COM is a small program to display a blank line of the screen. |
| ```
:MISSING
ECHO You Did Not Tell SMALLBAT.BAT
ECHO Which Batch File To Run
BATCMD SL
GOTO LIST
:END_MISSING
``` | The user didn't enter a command, so display an error message and then jump to a section to display the available commands. |
| ```
:LIST
ECHO The Valid Commands Are:
ECHO CHECKERR      CL
ECHO CL2           HELPBAT
ECHO MACRO         MACRO2
ECHO MULTI         MULTI2
ECHO NUMBER1       NUMBER9
ECHO PASSWRD2      SAVE-ERR
GOTO END
:END_LIST
``` | Display the available commands and then exit the batch file. |
| ```
:CHECKERR
``` | Label marking the beginning of the section to run CHECKERR.BAT. |
| ```
D:
CD\SMALLBAT
``` | Change to the appropriate drive and subdirectory. |
| ```
LHA E SMALLBAT CHECKERR.BAT
``` | Uncompress the batch file. |
| ```
CLS
``` | Clear the screen to remove the messages. |
| ```
CALL CHECKERR
``` | Call the batch file. |
| ```
D:
CD\SMALLBAT
``` | Change back to the appropriate drive and subdirectory in case CHECKERR.BAT changed them while running. |
| ```
DEL CHECKERR.BAT
``` | Delete the batch file called by SMALLBAT.BAT. |
| ```
GOTO END
:END_CHECKERR
``` | Exit the batch file. |
```

Batch File Line	Explanation
| ```
:CL
D:
CD\SMALLBAT
LHA E SMALLBAT CL.BAT
CLS
SHIFT
SHIFT
CALL CL %0 %1 %2 %3 %4 %5 %6 %7 %8 %9
D:
CD\SMALLBAT
DEL CL.BAT
GOTO END
:END_CL
``` | Section to handle CL.BAT. Note the use of two shifts and the replaceable parameters when CL.BAT is called. The two shifts discard SMALLBAT and CL as replaceable parameters, so CL.BAT gets all ten (%0-%9) of the replaceable parameters it expects to get when run from the command line. That way, CL.BAT requires no modifications to run under SMALLBAT.BAT. |
| ```
:CL2
D:
CD\SMALLBAT
LHA E SMALLBAT CL2.BAT
CLS
SHIFT
SHIFT
CALL CL2 %0 %1 %2 %3 %4 %5 %6 %7 %8 %9
D:
CD\SMALLBAT
DEL CL2.BAT
GOTO END
:END_CL2
``` | Section to handle CL2.BAT. |
| ```
:HELPBAT
D:
CD\SMALLBAT
LHA E SMALLBAT HELPBAT.BAT
CLS
CALL HELPBAT
D:
CD\SMALLBAT
DEL HELPBAT.BAT
GOTO END
:END_HELPBAT
``` | Section to handle HELPBAT.BAT. |
| ```
:MACRO
D:
CD\SMALLBAT
LHA E SMALLBAT MACRO.BAT
CLS
SHIFT
SHIFT
CALL MACRO %0 %1 %2 %3 %4 %5 %6
    %7 %8 %9
D:
CD\SMALLBAT
DEL MACRO.BAT
GOTO END
:END_MACRO
``` | Section to handle MACRO.BAT. |

Batch File Line	Explanation

`:MACRO2`
`D:`
`CD\SMALLBAT`
`LHA E SMALLBAT MACRO2.BAT`
`CLS`
`SHIFT`
`SHIFT`
`CALL MACRO2 %0 %1 %2 %3 %4 %5 %6`
`    %7 %8 %9`
`D:`
`CD\SMALLBAT`
`DEL MACRO2.BAT`
`GOTO END`
`:END_MACRO2`
	Section to handle MACRO2.BAT.

`:MULTI`	Label marking the beginning of the section to handle MULTI.BAT. This batch file can process more than ten replaceable parameters, so its replaceable parameters have to be passed in a special manner.

`D:`
`CD\SMALLBAT`
`LHA E SMALLBAT MULTI.BAT`
`CLS`
	Change to the appropriate subdirectory and uncompress MULTI.BAT.

`SHIFT` `SHIFT`	Discard the SMALLBAT and MULTI replaceable parameters.
`SET PASS=`	Reset the variable that will store the parameters for MULTI.BAT to nul.
`SET SPACE=`	Store a space under this environmental variable.
`:TOPMULTI`	Label marking the top of the loop to build the environmental variable for MULTI.BAT. Note that the batch file currently lacks error checking to make sure there are parameters for MULTI.BAT to act on. It's assumed that each batch file called by SMALLBAT.BAT will handle its own error checking.
`SET PASS=%PASS%%0%SPACE%`	Take the environmental variable PASS, and add a space (%SPACE%) and the next replaceable parameter.

Batch File Line	Explanation
`SHIFT`	Move the replaceable parameters down one level.
`IF NOT (%0)==() GOTO TOPMULTI`	If more replaceable parameters exist, continue looping.
`CALL MULTI %PASS%`	Call MULTI.BAT and pass it all the replaceable parameters on the command line.
`SET PASS=` `SET SPACE=`	Reset the variables used by SMALLBAT.BAT especially to call MULTI.BAT.

`D:`
`CD\SMALLBAT`
`DEL MULTI.BAT`
`GOTO END_MULTI`
	Delete the batch file and exit.

`:MULTI2`
`D:`
`CD\SMALLBAT`
`LHA E SMALLBAT MULTI2.BAT`
`CLS`
`CALL MULTI2`
`D:`
`CD\SMALLBAT`
`DEL MULTI2.BAT`
`GOTO END`
`:END_MULTI2`
	Section to handle MULTI2.BAT. Because MULTI2.BAT prompts the user for commands, it needs no replaceable parameters--unlike MULTI.BAT.

`:NUMBER1`
`D:`
`CD\SMALLBAT`
`LHA E SMALLBAT NUMBER1.BAT NUMBER2.BAT`
`LHA E SMALLBAT NUMBER3.BAT NUMBER4.BAT`
`LHA E SMALLBAT NUMBER5.BAT NUMBER6.BAT`
`CLS`
`CALL NUMBER1`
`D:`
`CD\SMALLBAT`
`DEL NUMBER1.BAT`
`DEL NUMBER2.BAT`
`DEL NUMBER3.BAT`
`DEL NUMBER4.BAT`
`DEL NUMBER5.BAT`
`DEL NUMBER6.BAT`
`GOTO END`
`:END_NUMBER1`
	Section to handle NUMBER1.BAT. Because this batch file calls several others, all of the batch files it calls must be uncompressed before running NUMBER1.BAT and deleted afterwards.

Batch File Line	Explanation

```:NUMBER9```
```D:```
```CD\SMALLBAT```
```LHA E SMALLBAT NUMBER9.BAT```
```CLS```
```CALL NUMBER9```
```D:```
```CD\SMALLBAT```
```DEL NUMBER9.BAT```
```GOTO END```
```:END_NUMBER9```
	Section to handle NUMBER9.BAT.

```:PASSWRD2```
```D:```
```CD\SMALLBAT```
```LHA E SMALLBAT PASSWRD2.BAT```
```CLS```
```CALL PASSWRD2```
```D:```
```CD\SMALLBAT```
```DEL PASSWRD2.BAT```
```GOTO END```
```:END_PASSWRD2```
	Section to handle PASSWRD2.BAT.

```:SAVE-ERR```
```D:```
```CD\SMALLBAT```
```LHA E SMALLBAT SAVE-ERR.BAT```
```CLS```
```CALL SAVE-ERR```
```D:```
```CD\SMALLBAT```
```DEL SAVE-ERR.BAT```
```GOTO END```
```:END_SAVE-ERR```
	Section to handle SAVE-ERR.BAT.

```:HELP```
```ECHO SMALLBAT.BAT Is A Demonstration```
```ECHO Batch File That Keeps Several```
```ECHO Batch Files In One Compressed```
```ECHO File And Decompresses Them```
```ECHO "On Demand"```
```BATCMD SL```
```GOTO LIST```
```:END_HELP```
	Section that displays help when the user starts the batch file with a /? or a ? as the first replaceable parameter.

```:END```	Label marking the end of the batch file.

Batch File Line	Explanation
SET CHECKERR= SET CL= SET CL2= SET HELPBAT= SET MACRO= SET MACRO2= SET MULTI= SET MULTI2= SET NUMBER1= SET NUMBER9= SET PASSWRD2= SET SAVE-ERR=	Reset the environmental variables used by the batch file before exiting.

5

Counting in batch files

Most programming languages, like BASIC or C, offer several ways to perform simple mathematics from within a program. The ability to perform math allows you to count simply by adding one to the last value of a variable.

Being able to count and perform simple mathematics would be useful in batch files. You might, for example, want to count the number of times a user selects a particular option, or you might want to do something after a specific number of operations has passed.

Unfortunately, the DOS batch file language doesn't offer any straightforward way of counting or performing simple math. Nevertheless, it's possible to write a batch file to do just this.

Math rules

When you first think about writing a batch file to add one to a number, it sounds impossible. However, if you break the math down to a simple set of rules, you'll see how to write the batch file. To keep the size of the file manageable, limit the addition to whole numbers with three digits or less and ignore negative numbers. Now, let's look at a set of rules for adding one to a three-digit number.

Addition

1. If the ones, tens, and hundreds digits all equal nine, stop because this method won't work. (When the number is 999, adding one will exceed the three-digit rule.)
2. If the ones digit is less than nine, increase its value by one and quit.
3. If the ones digit equals nine, set it equal to zero and increase the value of the tens digit by one.
4. If the tens digit needs to be increased by one and is less than nine, increase it by one and quit.

5. If the tens digit needs to be increased by one and equals nine, set it equal to zero and increase the value of the hundreds digit by one.
6. If the hundreds digit needs to be increased by one, do so. The hundreds digit will never need to be increased by one and be equal to nine because rule #1 prevents this.

Looking at these six rules, do you see the general approach to the addition problem? If not, here's a hint: assume that the three digits are stored under three different environmental variables: ONE, TEN, and HUNDRED.

Subtraction

Occasionally, you might need to perform subtraction as well as addition. The approach is almost identical. The rules for subtraction are:

1. If the ones, tens, and hundreds digits all equal zero, stop because this method won't work. (When the number is 0, subtracting one will cause the number to become negative, which isn't allowed.)
2. If the ones digit is greater than zero, decrease its value by one and quit.
3. If the ones digit equals zero, set it equal to nine and decrease the value of the tens digit by one.
4. If the tens digit needs to be decreased by one and is greater than zero, decrease it by one and quit.
5. If the tens digit needs to be decreased by one and equals zero, set it equal to nine and decrease the value of the hundreds digit by one.
6. If the hundreds digit needs to be decreased by one, do so. The hundreds digit will never need to be decreased by one and be equal to zero because rule #1 prevents this.

A basic math batch file

MATH.BAT in Fig. 5-1 shows how to use these addition and subtraction rules to write a batch file that will add one to or subtract one from a value stored in the environment. Notice that this batch file uses nothing but DOS commands. MATH.BAT is a very long batch file, but the logic behind it is fairly simple and follows directly from the addition and subtraction rules I've listed.

As you can see in looking at MATH.BAT, it never actually performs any math. Rather, it simply works through a series of IF statements and executes the true statements. These IF statements are the implementation of the math rules.

To use MATH.BAT, you must first store the individual digits of the number as separate environmental variables. Let's say you want to start the counter off at 148. You must first issue the commands:

```
SET HUNDRED = 1
SET TEN = 4
SET ONE = 8
```

Once you have the digits stored in the environment, you can run MATH.BAT by issuing the command MATH A to add one to 148, or MATH S to subtract one from 148.

If you issue the command MATH A, the batch file will add one to 148 to arrive at 149. It will then store 149 under the environmental variable ANSWER. It will also update the values of the environmental variables HUNDRED, TEN, and ONE so, after running MATH A once, their values are 1, 4, and 9, respectively.

Finding a unique filename

Before you move on, take a look at two practical applications of MATH.BAT. Sometimes your batch file needs a temporary work file that it will delete after it finishes. The difficulty is figuring out a name that doesn't already exist. Normally, I use the name JUNK. Everyone who uses my computer understands that files with the name JUNK*.* are subject to being deleted anytime.

If you want to use another method, you can loop through a series of extensions, 000-999, using MATH.BAT to find the first one that isn't in use. NEXTFILE.BAT in Fig. 5-2 shows a segment of a batch file to do exactly that. In a complete batch file, once this segment had found a free filename, the batch file would use it for some process. Because NEXTFILE.BAT tests 1,000 file extensions, it's unlikely that it would miss an unused name.

For some applications, you might be working your way through a sequence of filenames where it would be useful to store values between sessions. That way, you could pick up at the point you left off in the next session. For example, several months ago my wife was writing a book on her family history. She was making a lot of changes and occasionally wanted to revert to an earlier version when the changes didn't work out. I configured a batch file that started her word processor to automatically archive all her files using LHA each time she exited the word processor. So she could recover data from any session, I had the batch file use a new archive file each time. The first file was BOOK001.LZH, the second BOOK002.LZH, and so on.

You've already seen how to increment the counter, but there's another problem. The counter is stored as three environmental variables (ONE, TEN, and HUNDRED) and their contents are lost when the computer is switched off or rebooted. STORE.BAT in Fig. 5-3 solves this problem.

When STORE.BAT is run with the S option, it writes out a batch file called STORE-IT.BAT, containing the current values of the variables, in the root directory of the C drive. When STORE.BAT is run with the R option, it calls STORE-IT.BAT and STORE-IT.BAT resets the values of the three environment variables.

One approach would be to run STORE S just before shutting down the system to save the current values, and STORE R from the AUTOEXEC.BAT file to recall them. Another approach would be to run STORE S every time the value changed, so STORE-IT.BAT would always contain the current value. As before, the AUTOEXEC.BAT file would need to run STORE R to place the value into the environment at the beginning of a session.

Looping

In addition to finding a unique filename, another practical use for MATH.BAT is looping. Occasionally, a batch file needs to loop through a series of code more than once—for example, if you want to give a user three chances to enter a password or if you want to run your disk testing program three times to triple check your hard disk. SHOWLOOP.BAT in Fig. 5-4 is a batch file segment to do just that. SHOWLOOP.BAT loops through a set of commands thirty times. While SHOWLOOP.BAT does nothing useful, you can easily change the maximum loop value and add useful code to the batch file.

A brute-force math approach

As useful as MATH.BAT is, it has a drawback. MATH.BAT requires you to enter the ones, tens, and hundreds digits into the environment separately. (Of course, that isn't much of a limitation if you're calling MATH.BAT from another batch file or saving values between sessions with STORE.BAT.) It would be nice to be able to enter a single number in the environment and have MATH.BAT work with it. MATH1.BAT in Fig. 5-5 shows how to do so, using a brute-force approach.

Attacking the problem in this fashion has its own drawback. On my 386/20 computer, MATH.BAT completes its task in well under a second. With all its IF statements, MATH1.BAT takes over twenty seconds! That's clearly unacceptable if you're using MATH1.BAT to find a unique filename, control looping, or perform some other task where it's accessed several times.

Stripping off the digits

You've seen how to use MATH.BAT to perform addition and subtraction, but MATH.BAT works only if the three digits are stored in the environment under separate names. MATH1.BAT cures this problem with a brute-force method of looking at every single possible number, but takes much longer to run.

Another approach is to enter the number to add/subtract to/from as a single number, but have the batch file strip off the three individual digits. NUMBER.BAT in Fig. 5-6 does just that. NUMBER.BAT uses a brute-force approach of testing for every possible three-digit value. Because NUMBER.BAT contains even more IF statements than MATH1.BAT, however, it takes even longer to run. On my 386/20, NUMBER.BAT takes 56 seconds. Clearly, the brute-force approach is slow. Of course, you need to run NUMBER.BAT only once per session because it stores numbers in the environment where MATH.BAT can access them, and MATH.BAT updates those numbers when it runs.

Not only is NUMBER.BAT slow, but it's also a very long batch file. If you had to manually key in NUMBER.BAT, it would take you a long time and the probability is high that you would make several errors. (I created the batch file using Lotus 1-2-3, as explained in chapter 19.) It would be nice to be able to use a couple of loops to work through all the possible values. For example, the following Qbasic program will display all the numbers 000−999 with only seven lines:

```
FOR I = 0 TO 9
    FOR J = 0 TO 9
        FOR K = 0 TO 9
            PRINT LTRIM$(STR$(I)) + LTRIM$(STR$(J)) + LTRIM$(STR$(K))
```

```
        NEXT
      NEXT
    NEXT
```

It would be nice if you could write a similar batch file using nested FOR loops to work through all the digits. That hypothetical batch file would look like this:

```
FOR %%I IN (0 1 2 3 4 5 6 7 8 9) DO
   FOR %%J IN (0 1 2 3 4 5 6 7 8 9) DO
      FOR %%K IN (0 1 2 3 4 5 6 7 8 9) DO
         IF %%I%%J%%K = = %ANSWER% SET HUNDRED = %%I
         IF %%I%%J%%K = = %ANSWER% SET TEN = %%J
         IF %%I%%J%%K = = %ANSWER% SET ONE = %%K
      ENDDO
   ENDDO
ENDDO
```

If you enter the command:

```
FOR %I IN (0 1 2) DO FOR %J IN (0 1 2) DO ECHO %I%J
```

on the command line, you'll see that the error message FOR can't be nested. So FOR loops can't be nested—or can they?

Chapter 19 provides all the details, but the approach to nesting FOR loops is fairly simple. Each version of COMMAND.COM can run only one FOR loop at a time, but you can nest the FOR loops by having each loop load a new copy of COMMAND.COM.

NUMBER1.BAT in Fig. 5-7 starts the process. For each of the ten possible values for the hundreds digit, it loads a secondary copy of COMMAND.COM and calls NUMBER-2.BAT in Fig. 5-8 to loop through the tens digits. NUMBER2.BAT loops through the tens digits and, for each one, it loads another secondary copy of COMMAND.COM and calls NUMBER3.BAT in Fig. 5-9 to loop through the ones digits. NUMBER3.BAT loops through the ones digits and calls NUMBER4.BAT in Fig. 5-10 only if it finds a match.

NUMBER4.BAT constructs a batch file to store the ones, tens, and hundreds digits in the environment. NUMBER4.BAT can't write the information directly into the environment because it's running under a secondary copy of COMMAND.COM. Any changes NUMBER4.BAT makes to the environment, therefore, are lost when that secondary copy of COMMAND.COM unloads.

Once the looping is finished, control returns to NUMBER1.BAT, which is running under the primary copy of COMMAND.COM. If NUMBER1.BAT finds TEMP.BAT, it runs it to write the changes to the environment. If it doesn't find TEMP.BAT, then ANSWER is a single- or two-digit number without a leading zero. If that happens, NUM-BER1.BAT begins looping through the possible tens digits values. For each digit, it loads a secondary copy of COMMAND.COM and runs NUMBER5.BAT in Fig. 5-11 to loop through the ones digits. If NUMBER5.BAT finds a match, it calls NUMBER6.BAT in Fig. 5-12 to construct TEMP.BAT.

When control returns to NUMBER1.BAT, it once again checks for TEMP.BAT and runs it if it finds it. If it still doesn't find TEMP.BAT, then ANSWER is a single-digit number without leading zeros and NUMBER1.BAT sets the environmental variable ONE equal to ANSWER. It might be a good idea to go ahead and check ANSWER against the ten possible digits to make sure the user didn't enter something other than a number into ANSWER.

While the batch files NUMBER1.BAT through NUMBER6.BAT are certainly shorter and smaller than NUMBER.BAT, the requirement to repeatedly load and unload COMMAND.COM makes them run slower still. If ANSWER is a three-digit number, they take 42 seconds on my 386/20.

While running, NUMBER1.BAT calls five regular batch files and one temporary file (TEMP.BAT). Tracking six permanent files to perform one task is more cumbersome than necessary. By using a trick explained in chapter 19 to have a batch file call itself to perform different tasks, I combined NUMBER1.BAT through NUMBER6.BAT into a single batch file—NUMBER9.BAT in Fig. 5-13. While NUMBER9.BAT still calls the temporary batch file (TEMP.BAT), it calls no other files while running.

The first time you run NUMBER9.BAT, there's no replaceable parameter. Each time NUMBER1.BAT would have called another file, NUMBER9.BAT calls itself with a replaceable parameter to indicate what portion of the batch files needs to be executed. That way, all the code can be stored inside NUMBER9.BAT and executed by using a replaceable parameter to jump to that section. Because there's extra testing and jumping, however, NUMBER9.BAT takes even longer than NUMBER1.BAT to run. On my 386/20, NUMBER9.BAT took 47 seconds to process a three-digit number.

Utility programs

As already mentioned, most of these batch files run very slow. Their lack of speed is a perfect illustration of the fact that just because a batch file is capable of doing something doesn't mean that it's the perfect vehicle for performing that task.

MATH2.BAT in Fig. 5-14 illustrates this point. MATH2.BAT uses Batcmd (covered in chapter 21) to perform the same simple mathematics these batch files perform on the environmental variable MATH. While the batch files are painstakingly slow, Batcmd performs the math too fast to time.

The ease with which Batcmd performs the math that these batch files struggle with illustrates why utilities to help batch files are so popular. Often a task that's very difficult to perform with a batch file can be performed handily with a simple utility.

Summary

- MATH.BAT can add or subtract one to or from a three-digit number, as long as the three digits are stored in the environment under different variables.
- NEXTFILE.BAT uses MATH.BAT to find a unique filename a batch file can use without being concerned with overwriting an existing file.
- SHOWLOOP.BAT uses MATH.BAT to loop through a series of instructions a predetermined number of times.
- MATH1.BAT uses a brute-force approach to add or subtract to or from a three-digit number without having to store the individual digits under separate variables.
- NUMBER.BAT uses a brute-force approach to strip off the individual digits from a three-digit number.

- NUMBER1.BAT through NUMBER6.BAT use nested FOR loops to strip off the individual digits from a three-digit number.
- NUMBER9.BAT combines NUMBER1.BAT through NUMBER6.BAT into a single, massive batch file.
- MATH2.BAT uses Batcmd to easily perform addition and subtraction without all the limitations imposed when using batch files.

5-1 MATH.BAT, which has significant limitations, can increase or decrease a number by one.

Batch File Line	Explanation
`@ECHO OFF`	Turn command-echoing off.

`REM NAME:     MATH.BAT`
`REM PURPOSE: Perform Simple Adding`
`REM          And Subtracting Using`
`REM          Environmental Variables`
`REM VERSION: 1.08`
`REM DATE:    November 1, 1991`
	Documentation remarks.

`IF (%1)==(/?) GOTO HELP` `IF (%1)==(?)  GOTO HELP`	If the user starts the batch file with a request for help, jump to a section to display that help.
`REM Make Sure Everything Is` `REM Stored In Memory Correctly`	Documentation remarks.

`IF (%ONE%)==() GOTO ERROR1`
`IF (%TEN%)==() GOTO ERROR1`
`IF (%HUNDRED%)==() GOTO ERROR1`
	MATH.BAT depends on these three environmental variables being in place. If they're missing it can't run, so jump to an error-handling routine.

`IF (%1)==()   GOTO ERROR1`	If the user didn't enter a replaceable parameter it doesn't know if it is to add or subtract, so jump to an error-handling routine.
`REM Create QUESTION Variable For Use` `REM In Displaying Problem`	Documentation remarks.
`SET QUESTION=%HUNDRED%%TEN%%ONE%`	Put the three digits into a single number for neat display.
`IF %HUNDRED%==0 SET` `      QUESTION=%TEN%%ONE%`	If the hundreds digit is a zero it looks strange to have a number like 099, so redo it without the zero.
`IF %HUNDRED%==0 IF %TEN%==0` `      SET QUESTION=%ONE%`	If both the hundreds and tens digits are zero it looks strange to have a number like 008, so redo it without the zeros.
`REM Now Make Sure The First` `REM Replaceable Parameter Is OK`	Documentation remarks.

`IF %1==A GOTO ADD`
`IF %1==a GOTO ADD`
`IF %1==S GOTO SUBTRACT`
`IF %1==s GOTO SUBTRACT`
	If the first replaceable parameter was an A or S, jump to the appropriate section of the batch file.

Batch File Line	Explanation
GOTO ERROR2	If it reaches here the user entered an invalid replaceable parameter, so jump to an error-handling routine.
:ADD	Beginning of the addition section.
ECHO Number To Add One To Is %QUESTION%	Display the question.
SET QUESTION=	Reset this environmental variable.
IF %ONE%==9 IF %TEN%==9 IF %HUNDRED%==9 GOTO ERROR3	If the number is 999 then MATH.-BAT can't perform any additional addition because it's limited to three-digit numbers, so jump to an error-handling routine.
IF %ONE%==9 GOTO ADD1	If the ones digit is a nine then the tens digit must be incremented, so jump to a section to handle that.
IF %ONE%==8 SET ONE=9	If the ones digit is an eight, increase it to a nine.
IF %ONE%==9 GOTO ANSWER	If the ones digit is a nine then it was an eight at the step above, so the addition is done. Therefore, jump to the answer routine. Note that the tens digit needs to be increased only if the ones digit is a nine.
IF %ONE%==7 SET ONE=8 IF %ONE%==8 GOTO ANSWER	If the ones digit is a seven, increment it and jump to the answer routine. Note that the addition tests must be in decreasing order. Otherwise, if ONE was one, it would be set to two and would pass the IF ONE==2 test.
IF %ONE%==6 SET ONE=7 IF %ONE%==7 GOTO ANSWER	If the ones digit is a six, increment it and jump to the answer routine.
IF %ONE%==5 SET ONE=6 IF %ONE%==6 GOTO ANSWER	If the ones digit is a five, increment it and jump to the answer routine.
IF %ONE%==4 SET ONE=5 IF %ONE%==5 GOTO ANSWER	If the ones digit is a four, increment it and jump to the answer routine.
IF %ONE%==3 SET ONE=4 IF %ONE%==4 GOTO ANSWER	If the ones digit is a three, increment it and jump to the answer routine.
IF %ONE%==2 SET ONE=3 IF %ONE%==3 GOTO ANSWER	If the ones digit is a two, increment it and jump to the answer routine.

Batch File Line	Explanation
`IF %ONE%==1 SET ONE=2` `IF %ONE%==2 GOTO ANSWER`	If the ones digit is a one, increment it and jump to the answer routine.
`IF %ONE%==0 SET ONE=1` `IF %ONE%==1 GOTO ANSWER`	If the ones digit is a zero, increment it and jump to the answer routine.
`GOTO ERROR99` `:END_ADD`	MATH.BAT will never reach this point unless the variable ONE exists but is not equal to a single-digit number. This jumps to a generic error-handling section.
`:ADD1`	This label marks the beginning of the section to handle the addition of the tens digit.
`SET ONE=0`	MATH.BAT will reach this point only when ONE=9, so ONE must be reset to zero. This could not be handled in the prior section because ONE must be nine to flag the jump to this section.
`IF %TEN%==9 GOTO ADD2`	If the tens digit is nine then the hundreds digit must be incremented, so jump to a section to handle that.
`IF %TEN%==8 SET TEN=9` `IF %ONE%==9 GOTO ANSWER`	If the tens digit is eight, increment it and jump to the answer section.
`IF %TEN%==7 SET TEN=8` `IF %TEN%==8 GOTO ANSWER`	If the tens digit is seven, increment it and jump to the answer section.
`IF %TEN%==6 SET TEN=7` `IF %TEN%==7 GOTO ANSWER`	If the tens digit is six, increment it and jump to the answer section.
`IF %TEN%==5 SET TEN=6` `IF %TEN%==6 GOTO ANSWER`	If the tens digit is five, increment it and jump to the answer section.
`IF %TEN%==4 SET TEN=5` `IF %TEN%==5 GOTO ANSWER`	If the tens digit is four, increment it and jump to the answer section.
`IF %TEN%==3 SET TEN=4` `IF %TEN%==4 GOTO ANSWER`	If the tens digit is three, increment it and jump to the answer section.
`IF %TEN%==2 SET TEN=3` `IF %TEN%==3 GOTO ANSWER`	If the tens digit is two, increment it and jump to the answer section.
`IF %TEN%==1 SET TEN=2` `IF %TEN%==2 GOTO ANSWER`	If the tens digit is one, increment it and jump to the answer section.

Batch File Line	Explanation
`IF %TEN%==0 SET TEN=1` `IF %TEN%==1 GOTO ANSWER`	If the tens digit is zero, increment it and jump to the answer section.
`GOTO ERROR99` `:END_ADD1`	MATH.BAT will never reach this point unless the variable TEN exists, but is not equal to a single-digit number. This jumps to a generic error-handling section.
`:ADD2`	This label marks the beginning of the section to handle the addition of the hundreds digit.
`SET TEN=0`	MATH.BAT will reach this point only when TEN=9, so TEN must be reset to zero.
`IF %HUNDRED%==8 SET HUNDRED=9` `IF %HUNDRED%==9 GOTO ANSWER`	If the hundreds digit is eight, increment it and jump to the answer section. MATH.BAT doesn't need to test for a value of nine because the tens and ones digits must be nine to reach this point and 999 is screened out above.
`IF %HUNDRED%==7 SET HUNDRED=8` `IF %HUNDRED%==8 GOTO ANSWER`	If the hundreds digit is seven, increment it and jump to the answer section.
`IF %HUNDRED%==6 SET HUNDRED=7` `IF %HUNDRED%==7 GOTO ANSWER`	If the hundreds digit is six, increment it and jump to the answer section.
`IF %HUNDRED%==5 SET HUNDRED=6` `IF %HUNDRED%==6 GOTO ANSWER`	If the hundreds digit is five, increment it and jump to the answer section.
`IF %HUNDRED%==4 SET HUNDRED=5` `IF %HUNDRED%==5 GOTO ANSWER`	If the hundreds digit is four, increment it and jump to the answer section.
`IF %HUNDRED%==3 SET HUNDRED=4` `IF %HUNDRED%==4 GOTO ANSWER`	If the hundreds digit is three, increment it and jump to the answer section.
`IF %HUNDRED%==2 SET HUNDRED=3` `IF %HUNDRED%==3 GOTO ANSWER`	If the hundreds digit is two, increment it and jump to the answer section.
`IF %HUNDRED%==1 SET HUNDRED=2` `IF %HUNDRED%==2 GOTO ANSWER`	If the hundreds digit is one, increment it and jump to the answer section.

Batch File Line	Explanation
IF %HUNDRED%==0 SET HUNDRED=1 IF %HUNDRED%==1 GOTO ANSWER	If the hundreds digit is zero, increment it and jump to the answer section.
GOTO ERROR99 :END_ADD2	MATH.BAT will never reach this point unless the variable HUNDRED exists but is not equal to a single-digit number. This jumps to a generic error-handling section.
:SUBTRACT	Label marking the beginning of the subtraction section.
ECHO Number To Subtract One From Is %QUESTION%	Display the question.
SET QUESTION=	Reset this environmental variable.
IF %ONE%==0 IF %TEN%==0 IF %HUNDRED%==0 GOTO ERROR4	If the number is 000 then no further subtraction is possible, so jump to an error-handling section.
IF %ONE%==0 GOTO SUB1	If the ones digit is zero then the tens digit must be decreased, so jump to a section to handle that.
IF %ONE%==1 SET ONE=0 IF %ONE%==0 GOTO ANSWER	If the ones digit is one, decrease it by one and jump to the answer section. Subtraction tests must be performed in increasing order to keep the value changes from affecting the next test.
IF %ONE%==2 SET ONE=1 IF %ONE%==1 GOTO ANSWER	If the ones digit is two, decrease it by one and jump to the answer section.
IF %ONE%==3 SET ONE=2 IF %ONE%==2 GOTO ANSWER	If the ones digit is three, decrease it by one and jump to the answer section.
IF %ONE%==4 SET ONE=3 IF %ONE%==3 GOTO ANSWER	If the ones digit is four, decrease it by one and jump to the answer section.
IF %ONE%==5 SET ONE=4 IF %ONE%==4 GOTO ANSWER	If the ones digit is five, decrease it by one and jump to the answer section.
IF %ONE%==6 SET ONE=5 IF %ONE%==5 GOTO ANSWER	If the ones digit is six, decrease it by one and jump to the answer section.
IF %ONE%==7 SET ONE=6 IF %ONE%==6 GOTO ANSWER	If the ones digit is seven, decrease it by one and jump to the answer section.

Batch File Line	Explanation
`IF %ONE%==8 SET ONE=7` `IF %ONE%==7 GOTO ANSWER`	If the ones digit is eight, decrease it by one and jump to the answer section.
`IF %ONE%==9 SET ONE=8` `IF %ONE%==8 GOTO ANSWER`	If the ones digit is nine, decrease it by one and jump to the answer section.
`GOTO ERROR99` `:END_SUBTRACT`	MATH.BAT will never reach this point unless the variable ONE exists but is not equal to a single-digit number. This jumps to a generic error-handling section.
`:SUB1`	Label marking the section that handles decreasing the tens digit.
`SET ONE=9`	The ones digit must be set here for the above IF test to work properly.
`IF %TEN%==0 GOTO SUB2`	If the tens digit is a zero then the hundreds digit will have to be decreased, so jump to a section to handle that.
`IF %TEN%==1 SET TEN=0` `IF %TEN%==0 GOTO ANSWER`	If the tens digit is one, decrease it by one and jump to the answer section.
`IF %TEN%==2 SET TEN=1` `IF %TEN%==1 GOTO ANSWER`	If the tens digit is two, decrease it by one and jump to the answer section.
`IF %TEN%==3 SET TEN=2` `IF %TEN%==2 GOTO ANSWER`	If the tens digit is three, decrease it by one and jump to the answer section.
`IF %TEN%==4 SET TEN=3` `IF %TEN%==3 GOTO ANSWER`	If the tens digit is four, decrease it by one and jump to the answer section.
`IF %TEN%==5 SET TEN=4` `IF %TEN%==4 GOTO ANSWER`	If the tens digit is five, decrease it by one and jump to the answer section.
`IF %TEN%==6 SET TEN=5` `IF %TEN%==5 GOTO ANSWER`	If the tens digit is six, decrease it by one and jump to the answer section.
`IF %TEN%==7 SET TEN=6` `IF %TEN%==6 GOTO ANSWER`	If the tens digit is seven, decrease it by one and jump to the answer section.
`IF %TEN%==8 SET TEN=7` `IF %TEN%==7 GOTO ADD2`	If the tens digit is eight, decrease it by one and jump to the answer section.

Batch File Line	Explanation
IF %TEN%==9 SET TEN=8 IF %TEN%==8 GOTO ADD2	If the tens digit is nine, decrease it by one and jump to the answer section.
GOTO ERROR99 :END_SUB1	MATH.BAT will never reach this point unless the variable TEN exists but is not equal to a single-digit number. This jumps to a generic error-handling section.
:SUB2	Label marking the beginning of the section to decrease the hundreds digit by one.
SET TEN=9	Set the tens digit to nine.
IF %HUNDRED%==1 SET HUNDRED=0 IF %HUNDRED%==0 GOTO ANSWER	If the hundreds digit is one, decrease it by one and jump to the answer section. A test for a hundreds value of zero isn't required because the tens and ones digit would have to be zero to reach this point and 000 has already been screened out.
IF %HUNDRED%==2 SET HUNDRED=1 IF %HUNDRED%==1 GOTO ANSWER	If the hundreds digit is two, decrease it by one and jump to the answer section.
IF %HUNDRED%==3 SET HUNDRED=2 IF %HUNDRED%==2 GOTO ANSWER	If the hundreds digit is three, decrease it by one and jump to the answer section.
IF %HUNDRED%==4 SET HUNDRED=3 IF %HUNDRED%==3 GOTO ANSWER	If the hundreds digit is four, decrease it by one and jump to the answer section.
IF %HUNDRED%==5 SET HUNDRED=4 IF %HUNDRED%==4 GOTO ANSWER	If the hundreds digit is five, decrease it by one and jump to the answer section.
IF %HUNDRED%==6 SET HUNDRED=5 IF %HUNDRED%==5 GOTO ANSWER	If the hundreds digit is six, decrease it by one and jump to the answer section.
IF %HUNDRED%==7 SET HUNDRED=6 IF %HUNDRED%==6 GOTO ANSWER	If the hundreds digit is seven, decrease it by one and jump to the answer section.
IF %HUNDRED%==8 SET HUNDRED=7 IF %HUNDRED%==7 GOTO ANSWER	If the hundreds digit is eight, decrease it by one and jump to the answer section.

Batch File Line	Explanation
`IF %HUNDRED%==9 SET HUNDRED=8` `IF %HUNDRED%==8 GOTO ANSWER`	If the hundreds digit is nine, decrease it by one and jump to the answer section.
`GOTO ERROR99` `:END_SUB2`	MATH.BAT will never reach this point unless the variable HUNDREDS exists but is not equal to a single digit number. This jumps to a generic error-handling section.

`:ERROR1`
`ECHO One Of The Required Memory`
`ECHO Variables Does Not Exist Or`
`ECHO The Required Replaceable`
`ECHO Parameters Was Not Entered.`
`SKIPLINE`
`ECHO The Required Memory Variables`
`ECHO Are As Follows:`
`SKIPLINE`
`ECHO ONE      This Is The One's Digit`
`ECHO TEN      This Is The Ten's Digit`
`ECHO HUNDRED This Is The Hundred's`
`            Digit`
`GOTO END`
`:END_ERROR1`
	This section displays the error message explaining that one of the required environmental variables is missing. Note that SKIPLINE runs a small program that displays a blank line of the screen.

`:ERROR2`
`ECHO The First Replaceable Parameter`
`ECHO Must Be An A For Addition Or An`
`ECHO S For Subtraction. The Batch`
`ECHO File Automatically Adds Or`
`ECHO Subtracts One.`
`GOTO END`
`:END_ERROR2`
	This routine displays the error message if the user doesn't enter a replaceable parameter or enters one other than an A or S.

`:ERROR3`
`ECHO The Current Number Is 999 So No`
`ECHO Further Addition Is Possible`
`GOTO END`
`:END_ERROR3`
	This section displays an error message when the user tries to add to 999.

`:ERROR4`
`ECHO The Current Number Is 0 So No`
`ECHO Further Subtraction Is Possible`
`GOTO END`
`:END_ERROR4`
	This section displays an error message when the user tries to subtract from 0.

`:ERROR99`
`ECHO Unknown Error Occurred`
`ECHO Check MATH.BAT For Modification`
`GOTO END`
`:END_ERROR99`
	This section displays a generic error message when a nonspecific error is encountered.

`:ANSWER`	Label marking the section that constructs the answer.

Batch File Line	Explanation
`IF %HUNDRED%==0 GOTO ANSWER2`	If the hundreds digit is zero, jump to another section.
`SET ANSWER=%HUNDRED%%TEN%%ONE%`	Combine the three digits to form the answer.
`ECHO The answer is %ANSWER%`	Display the answer.
`GOTO END` `:END_ANSWER`	Exit the batch file.
`:ANSWER2`	Label marking the beginning of the section that constructs the answer when the hundreds digit is a zero.
`IF %TEN%==0 GOTO ANSWER3`	If the tens digit is a zero, jump to another section.

`SET ANSWER=%TEN%%ONE%`
`ECHO The answer is %ANSWER%`
`GOTO END`
`:END_ANSWER2`
	Construct and display the answer, and then exit.

`:ANSWER3`
`SET ANSWER=%ONE%`
`ECHO The answer is %ANSWER%`
`GOTO END`
`:END_ANSWER3`
	This section constructs and displays the answer when the tens and hundreds digits are zero.

`:HELP`
`ECHO Adds One To And Subtracts One`
`ECHO From A Number Using DOS`
`ECHO The Number Must Be 3 Digits Or`
`ECHO Smaller And The Math Must`
`ECHO Result In An Answer Of 0-999`
`ECHO The Digits Of The Number Must`
`ECHO Be Stored Under The`
`ECHO Environmental Variables ONE,`
`ECHO TEN, And HUNDRED`
`GOTO END`
`:END_HELP`
	Section that displays help when the user starts the batch file with a /? or a ? as the first replaceable parameter.

`:END`	Label marking the end of the batch file.

`:HELP`
`ECHO This Demonstration Batch File`
`ECHO Illustrates Dealing With Case`
`ECHO Problems In A Batch File`
`GOTO END`
`:END_HELP`
	Section that displays help when the user starts the batch file with a /? or a ? as the first replaceable parameter.

`:END`	Label marking the end of the batch file.

5-2 NEXTFILE.BAT illustrates using MATH.BAT to find an unused filename.

Batch File Line	Explanation
`@ECHO OFF`	Turn command-echoing off.

`REM NAME:     NEXTFILE.BAT`
`REM PURPOSE: Use MATH.BAT To Find`
`REM          Next Free Filename`
`REM VERSION: 1.00`
`REM DATE:     November 2, 1991`
	Documentation remarks.

`IF (%1)==(/?)  GOTO HELP` `IF (%1)==(?)   GOTO HELP`	If the user starts the batch file with a request for help, jump to a section to display that help.

`SET ONE=0`
`SET TEN=0`
`SET HUNDRED=0`
`SET ANSWER=000`
	Preset the environmental variables.

`:TOP`	Label marking the top of the loop.
`IF NOT EXIST JUNK.%ANSWER% GOTO SHOW`	If the file JUNK.000, where 000 is the current number, doesn't exist, it will work as a temporary file, so exit the loop.
`CALL MATH A`	Call MATH.BAT to increment the number by one.
`GOTO TOP`	Go back through the loop again.

`:SHOW`
`ECHO Next Filename is JUNK.%ANSWER%`
`GOTO END`
`:END_SHOW`
	Display the name of the next free file the batch file finds and exit the batch file.

`:HELP`
`ECHO Demonstration Batch File That`
`ECHO Shows Finding An Available`
`ECHO Filename Using Math In A Batch`
`ECHO File`
`GOTO END`
`:END_HELP`
	Section that displays help when the user starts the batch file with a /? or a ? as the first replaceable parameter.

`:END`	Label marking the end of the batch file.

5-3 STORE.BAT will store the values of the ONE, TEN, and HUNDRED environmental variables to a file for use in another session and recall their values from that file.

Batch File Line	Explanation
`@ECHO OFF`	Turn command-echoing off.

`REM NAME:     STORE.BAT`
`REM PURPOSE: Store/Recall Counter`
`REM VERSION: 1.00`
`REM DATE:     December 20, 1991`
	Documentation remarks.

Batch File Line	Explanation
| ```
IF (%1)==(S)   GOTO STORE
IF (%1)==(s)   GOTO STORE
IF (%1)==(R)   GOTO RECALL
IF (%1)==(r)   GOTO RECALL
IF (%1)==(/?)  GOTO HELP
IF (%1)==(?)   GOTO HELP
GOTO ERROR
``` | If the user entered a valid switch, jump to the appropriate section; otherwise, jump to an error-handling section. |
| ```
:STORE
``` | Label marking the beginning of the section to store the values to disk. |
| ```
IF (%ONE%)==() GOTO NOVALUE
IF (%TEN%)==() GOTO NOVALUE
IF (%HUNDRED%)==() GOTO NOVALUE
``` | If any of the values are missing, jump to an error-handling section. |
| ```
IF EXIST C:\STORE-IT.BAT
    DEL C:\STORE-IT.BAT
``` | If the storage file already exists, delete it. |
| ```
ECHO @ECHO OFF > C:\STORE-IT.BAT
``` | Pipe an ECHO OFF command to the batch file. |
| ```
ECHO SET ONE=%ONE% >> C:\STORE-IT.BAT
ECHO SET TEN=%TEN% >> C:\STORE-IT.BAT
ECHO SET HUNDRED=%HUNDRED% >>
    C:\STORE-IT.BAT
``` | Pipe the current values of the variables, along with the set commands necessary to write them to the environment, to the batch file. |
| ```
GOTO END
:END_STORE
``` | Exit the batch file. |
| ```
:RECALL
``` | Label marking the beginning of the section to restore the values from the file. |
| ```
IF EXIST C:\STORE-IT.BAT
    C:\STORE-IT.BAT
``` | If the file that stores the values exists, run it in such a way that control never returns to this batch file and it terminates at this point. |
| ```
GOTO MISSING
:END_RECALL
``` | If the batch file reaches this point then the user selected recall, but no file exists to recall from so jump to an error-handling section. |
| ```
:ERROR
ECHO You Must Start STORE.BAT With A
ECHO Parameter To Tell It What To Do
BATCMD SL
ECHO S=Store Current Values Of
ECHO ONE, TEN, And HUNDRED To A File
BATCMD SL
ECHO R=Recall These Values From A File
GOTO END
:END_ERROR
``` | Section that displays an error to enter a replaceable parameter. Notice the use of BATCMD SL to skip a line. This requires the Batcmd utility program. After displaying the message, it exits the batch file. |
```

Batch File Line	Explanation
:MISSING ECHO You Requested This Batch File To ECHO Recall The Values of ONE, TEN, ECHO And HUNDRED From A File, But That ECHO File (STORE-IT.BAT) Is Missing! GOTO END :END_MISSING	Section that displays an error message when the user asks the batch file to recall values from disk but the necessary file does not exist. After displaying the message, it exits the batch file.
:NOVALUE ECHO You Requested This Batch File To ECHO Store The Values of ONE, TEN, And ECHO HUNDRED To A File, But One Or ECHO More Of These Values Is Missing! BATCMD SL ECHO ONE=%ONE% ECHO TEN=%TEN% ECHO HUNDRED=%HUNDRED% GOTO END :END_NOVALUE	Section that displays an error message when the user asks the batch file to save values but those values do not exist. After displaying the message, it exits the batch file.
:HELP ECHO STORE S Stores The Current Values ECHO For The ONE, TEN, And ECHO HUNDRED Environmental ECHO Variables To The File ECHO C:\STORE-IT.BAT ECHO STORE R Recalls The Values Stored ECHO In This File GOTO END :END_HELP	Section that displays help when the user starts the batch file with a /? or a ? as the first replaceable parameter.
:END	Label marking the end of the batch file.

5-4 SHOWLOOP.BAT shows using MATH.BAT to go through a loop thirty times.

Batch File Line	Explanation
@ECHO OFF	Turn command-echoing off.
REM NAME: SHOWLOOP.BAT REM PURPOSE: Illustrate Looping REM With MATH.BAT REM VERSION: 1.00 REM DATE: November 2, 1991	Documentation remarks.
IF (%1)==(/?) GOTO HELP IF (%1)==(?) GOTO HELP	If the user starts the batch file with a request for help, jump to a section to display that help.
SET ONE=0 SET TEN=0 SET HUNDRED=0 SET ANSWER=0	Preset the environmental variables.
:TOP	Label marking the top of the loop.

Batch File Line	Explanation
`CALL MATH A`	Increment the loop counter by one.
`ECHO Loop Number %ANSWER%`	Echo the loop number for the user.
`IF NOT %ANSWER%==30 GOTO TOP`	If the loop counter hasn't yet reached 30, continue looping. Note that MATH.BAT stores the number as 30 and not 030.
`ECHO Done!`	The batch file will fail the above IF statement when the counter equals 30. That's when the batch file will reach this point. This line tells the user what has happened.
`GOTO END`	Exit the batch file.

`:HELP`
`ECHO This Is A Demonstration Batch`
`ECHO File To Illustrate Looping In A`
`ECHO Batch File Using Math`
`GOTO END`
`:END_HELP`
	Section that displays help when the user starts the batch file with a /? or a ? as the first replaceable parameter.

`:END`	Label marking the end of the batch file.

5-5 MATH1.BAT is a brute-force approach to batch file math.

Batch File Line	Explanation
`@ECHO OFF`	Turn command-echoing off.

`REM NAME:     MATH1.BAT`
`REM PURPOSE: "Brute Force" Math`
`REM VERSION: 1.00`
`REM DATE:     November 2, 1991`
	Documentation remarks.

`IF (%1)==(/?) GOTO HELP` `IF (%1)==(?)  GOTO HELP`	If the user starts the batch file with a request for help, jump to a section to display that help.
`IF (%QUESTION%)==() GOTO ERROR1`	If the environmental variable QUESTION doesn't exist there's no number to add/subtract to/from, so jump to an error-handling routine.
`IF (%1)==() GOTO ERROR2`	If the user didn't specify an A/S on the command line the batch file doesn't know if it's to add or subtract, so jump to an error-handling routine.

Batch File Line	Explanation
SET A=IF %QUESTION% SET B=SET ANSWER	Set some environmental variables to shorten the IF statements used by this batch file.
IF %1==A GOTO ADD IF %1==a GOTO ADD IF %1==S GOTO SUBTRACT IF %1==s GOTO SUBTRACT	Jump to the appropriate section of the batch file.
GOTO ERROR3	If the batch file reaches this point then the user entered something other than A/S on the command-line, so jump to an error-handling routine.
:ADD	Label marking the top of the addition section.
%A%==999 GOTO ERROR4	If the value of the number to add to is 999 then the batch file can't perform the addition because it's limited to three-digit numbers, so jump to an error-handling routine.
ECHO The Number To Add One To Is %QUESTION%	Tell the user what the number to add one to is. This step is optional.
%A%==998 %B%=999	If the number to add one to is 998, then store 999 in the ANSWER variable.
%A%==997 %B%=998	If the number to add one to is 997, then store 998 in the ANSWER variable.
The batch file continues in a similar fashion for 2-996	
%A%==001 %B%=2	If the number to add one to is 1, then store 2 in the ANSWER variable.
%A%==000 %B%=1	If the number to add one to is 0, then store 1 in the ANSWER variable.
GOTO ANSWER :END_ANSWER	Jump to the section of the batch file that displays the answer.
:SUBTRACT	Label marking the top of the subtraction section.
%A%==000 GOTO ERROR5	If the value of the number to subtract from is 0 then the batch file can't perform the subtraction because it's limited to numbers of zero or larger, so jump to an error-handling routine.

Batch File Line	Explanation
ECHO The Number To Subtract One From Is %QUESTION%	Tell the user what the number to subtract one from is. This step is optional.
%A%==001 %B%=0	If the number to subtract one from is 1, then store 0 in the ANSWER variable.
%A%==002 %B%=1	If the number to subtract one from is 2, then store 1 in the ANSWER variable.
The batch file continues in a similar fashion for 3-997	
%A%==998 %B%=997	If the number to subtract one from is 998, then store 997 in the ANSWER variable.
%A%==999 %B%=998	If the number to subtract one from is 999, then store 998 in the ANSWER variable.
GOTO ANSWER :END_ANSWER	Jump to the section of the batch file that displays the answer.
:ERROR1 ECHO You Must Specify The Value ECHO To Add/Subtract To/From As ECHO The Environmental Variable ECHO QUESTION GOTO END :END_ERROR1	Display an error message and exit when the user doesn't specify the number to add/subtract to/from under the environmental variable QUESTION.
:ERROR2 ECHO MATH1.BAT Needs To Know If ECHO You Want To Add Or Subtract ECHO You Tell It By Entering An ECHO A Or S On The Command Line ECHO After The MATH1 Command GOTO END :END_ERROR2	Display an error message and exit when the user doesn't specify a replaceable parameter on the command line to tell MATH1.BAT if it should add or subtract.
:ERROR3 ECHO You Specified An Input ECHO Other Than A For Add ECHO Or S For Subtract ECHO Please Try Again GOTO END :END_ERROR3	Display an error message and exit when the user doesn't specify an A or S on the command line to tell MATH1.BAT if it should add or subtract.
:ERROR4 ECHO You Cannot Add To 999 ECHO Because MATH1.BAT Is ECHO Limited To Three-Digit Numbers GOTO END :END_ERROR4	Display an error message and exit when the user tries to add to 999.

Batch File Line	Explanation

`:ERROR5`
`ECHO You Cannot Subtract From 0`
`ECHO Because MATH1.BAT Is`
`ECHO Limited To Non-Negative Numbers`
`GOTO END`
`:END_ERROR5`
	Display an error message and exit when the user tries to subtract from zero.

`:ANSWER`
`ECHO The Answer Is %ANSWER%`
`:END_ANSWER`
	Section to display the answer.

`:HELP`
`ECHO Adds One To And Subtracts One`
`ECHO From A Number Using DOS`
`ECHO The Number Must Be 3 Digits Or`
`ECHO Smaller And The Math Must`
`ECHO Result In An Answer Of 0-999`
`ECHO Number Must Be Stored In The`
`ECHO Environment Under The Name`
`ECHO QUESTION`
`GOTO END`
`:END_HELP`
	Section that displays help when the user starts the batch file with a /? or a ? as the first replaceable parameter.

`:END`	Label marking the end of the batch file.
`SET A=` `SET B=`	Reset the temporary environmental variables for exiting.

5-6 NUMBER.BAT takes a three-digit number stored under the environmental variable ANSWER, strips off the three digits, and stores them under the names ONE, TEN, and HUNDRED.

Batch File Line	Explanation
`@ECHO OFF`	Turn command-echoing off.

`REM NAME:      NUMBER.BAT`
`REM PURPOSE: Brute-Force Method`
`REM          Of Stripping Off`
`REM          Digits Individually`
`REM VERSION  1.01`
`REM DATE:    October 18, 1991`
	Documentation remarks.

`IF (%1)==(/?) GOTO HELP` `IF (%1)==(?)  GOTO HELP`	If the user starts the batch file with a request for help, jump to a section to display that help.

`IF (%ANSWER%)==() ECHO Must`
`       Set Answer`
`IF (%ANSWER%)==() GOTO END`
	If the number to break down to components doesn't exist, then display an error message and exit.

`SET A=IF %ANSWER%`
`SET B= SET ONE`
`SET C= SET TEN`
`SET D= SET HUNDRED`
	To reduce the size of the batch file, the portions of the IF statements that don't change are stored as environmental variables.

Batch File Line	Explanation
`%A%==999%B%=9`	If ANSWER=999, then set ONE=9.
`%A%==998%B%=8`	If ANSWER=998, then set ONE=8.
`%A%==997%B%=7`	If ANSWER=997, then set ONE=7.
The batch file continues in a similar fashion for 3-996	
`%A%==002%B%=2`	If ANSWER=2, then set ONE=2.
`%A%==001%B%=1`	If ANSWER=1, then set ONE=1.
`%A%==000%D%=0`	If ANSWER=0, then set ONE=0.
`%A%==999%C%=9`	If ANSWER=999, then set TEN=9.
`%A%==998%C%=9`	If ANSWER=998, then set TEN=9.
`%A%==997%C%=9`	If ANSWER=997, then set TEN=9.
The batch file continues in a similar fashion for 3-996	
`%A%==002%B%=2`	If ANSWER=2 then set TEN=0.
`%A%==001%B%=1`	If ANSWER=1, then set TEN=0.
`%A%==000%D%=0`	If ANSWER=0, then set TEN=0.
`%A%==999%B%=9`	If ANSWER=999, then set HUNDRED=9.
`%A%==998%B%=8`	If ANSWER=999, then set HUNDRED=9.
`%A%==997%B%=7`	If ANSWER=999, then set HUNDRED=9.
The batch file continues in a similar fashion for 3-996	
`%A%==002%B%=2`	If ANSWER=2, then set HUNDRED=0.
`%A%==001%B%=1`	If ANSWER=1, then set HUNDRED=0.
`%A%==000%D%=0`	If ANSWER=0, then set HUNDRED=0.
`GOTO END`	Exit the batch file.

`:HELP`
`ECHO Takes A 3-Digit Number`
`ECHO Stored In The Environment`
`ECHO Under The Name ANSWER And`
`ECHO Stores The Three Individual`
`ECHO Digits To The Environment`
`ECHO Under The Names ONE, TEN`
`ECHO And HUNDRED`
`GOTO END`
`:END_HELP`
	Section that displays help when the user starts the batch file with a /? or a ? as the first replaceable parameter.

Batch File Line	Explanation
`:END`	Label marking the end of the batch file.

`SET A=`
`SET B=`
`SET C=`
`SET D=`
	Reset the environmental variables before exiting.

5-7 NUMBER1.BAT is the first in a chain of batch files that takes a three-digit number stored under the environmental variable ANSWER, strips off the three digits, and stores them under the names ONE, TEN, and HUNDRED. This is accomplished by using three imbedded FOR loops.

Batch File Line	Explanation
`@ECHO OFF`	Turn command-echoing off.

`REM NAME:    NUMBER1.BAT`
`REM PURPOSE: Loop Through Possible`
`            Values Of Hundreds`
`REM VERSION: 1.15`
`REM DATE:    October 16, 1991`
	Documentation remarks.

`IF (%1)==(/?) GOTO HELP` `IF (%1)==(?)  GOTO HELP`	If the user starts the batch file with a request for help, jump to a section to display that help.

`IF (%ANSWER%)==() ECHO Input Value`
`                  Not Specified`
`IF (%ANSWER%)==() ECHO Set ANSWER=`
`                  Input Value`
`IF (%ANSWER%)==() GOTO END`
	If the input value doesn't exist, display an error message and exit.

`SET ONE=`
`SET TEN=`
`SET HUNDRED=`
	Reset the environmental variables.

`IF EXIST TEMP.BAT DEL TEMP.BAT`	If the temporary file exists, delete it.
`FOR %%J IN (0 1 2 3 4 5 6 7 8 9)` `    DO COMMAND/C NUMBER2 %%J`	Loop through the possible values for the hundreds digit and call another batch file for each value by loading another copy of COMMAND.COM. Notice how the current value for the hundreds digit is passed as a replaceable parameter to the next batch file.
`IF EXIST TEMP.BAT CALL TEMP.BAT`	If the batch file exists then NUMBER4.BAT found the values, so run this temporary batch file to set them into the environment.

Batch File Line	Explanation
IF (%ONE%)==() FOR %%J IN (0 1 2 3 4 5 6 7 8 9) DO COMMAND/C NUMBER5 %%J	If the IF (%ONE%)==( ) is true then the steps above didn't decode the number, so it must not have a hundreds digit. This step cycles through the tens digits. For each digit, it calls another batch file to handle the ones digits. Notice how the tens digit is passed to that batch file as a replaceable parameter.
IF EXIST TEMP.BAT CALL TEMP.BAT	If the batch file exists then NUMBER6.BAT found the values, so run this temporary batch file to set them into the environment.
IF (%TEN%)==() SET ONE=%ANSWER%	If the IF (%TEN%)==( ) is true then the steps above didn't decode the number, so it must not have a hundreds or tens digit. That means that ANSWER must contain a single ones digit, so the batch file uses that as the value of ONE.
GOTO END	Exit the batch file.
:HELP ECHO Takes A Three-Digit Number ECHO Stored In The Environment ECHO Under The Name ANSWER And ECHO Stores The Three Individual ECHO Digits To The Environment ECHO Under The Names ONE, TEN, ECHO And HUNDRED ECHO In The Process, It Calls ECHO NUMBER2.BAT - NUMBER6.BAT GOTO END :END_HELP	Section that displays help when the user starts the batch file with a /? or a ? as the first replaceable parameter.
:END	Label marking the end of the batch file.

5-8 NUMBER2.BAT is called by NUMBER1.BAT to loop through all the TENS digits.

Batch File Line	Explanation
@ECHO OFF	Turn command-echoing off.
REM NAME: NUMBER2.BAT REM PURPOSE: Loop Through Possible Values Of Tens REM VERSION: 1.08 REM DATE: October 16, 1991	Documentation remarks.

Batch File Line	Explanation
IF (%1)==(/?) GOTO HELP IF (%1)==(?) GOTO HELP	If the user starts the batch file with a request for help, jump to a section to display that help.
FOR %%J IN (0 1 2 3 4 5 6 7 8 9) DO COMMAND/C NUMBER3 %1 %%J	This is the second of a series of nested FOR loops. This line cycles through all the possible tens values. For each one, it calls another batch file and passes that batch file the value of the hundreds digit (%1) along with the value of the tens digit (%%J).
EXIT	The end of the batch file. Because this batch file was called with COMMAND/C, the exit is required to return control to the calling batch file.
:HELP ECHO This Batch File Was Intended ECHO To Be Called By NUMBER1.BAT ECHO *DO NOT RUN FROM COMMAND LINE* :END_HELP EXIT	Section that displays help when the user starts the batch file with a /? or a ? as the first replaceable parameter.

5-9 NUMBER3.BAT is called by NUMBER2.BAT to loop through all the ONES digits.

Batch File Line	Explanation
@ECHO OFF	Turn command-echoing off.
REM NAME: NUMBER3.BAT REM PURPOSE: Loop Through Possible Values Of Ones REM VERSION: 1.08 REM DATE: October 16, 1991	Documentation remarks.
IF (%1)==(/?) GOTO HELP IF (%1)==(?) GOTO HELP	If the user starts the batch file with a request for help, jump to a section to display that help.

FOR %%J IN (0 1 2 3 4 5 6 7 8 9) DO
    IF %ANSWER%==%1%2%%J COMMAND/C
    NUMBER4 %1 %2 %%J
	This line cycles through all the ones digits and calls another batch file if the environmental variable matches the number constructed from the hundreds, tens, and ones digit.

Batch File Line	Explanation
EXIT	The end of the batch file. Because this batch file was called with COMMAND/C, the exit is required to return control to the calling batch file.
:HELP ECHO This Batch File Was Intended ECHO To Be Called By NUMBER1.BAT ECHO *DO NOT RUN FROM COMMAND LINE* :END_HELP EXIT	Section that displays help when the user starts the batch file with a /? or a ? as the first replaceable parameter.

5-10 NUMBER4.BAT is called by NUMBER3.BAT when it finds a match for the environmental variable ANSWER. Then NUMBER4.BAT creates a batch file called TEMP.BAT to place that information into the environment.

Batch File Line	Explanation
@ECHO OFF	Turn command-echoing off.
REM NAME: NUMBER4.BAT REM PURPOSE: Place Correct Value Into Environment REM VERSION: 1.08 REM DATE: October 16, 1991	Documentation remarks.
IF (%1)==(/?) GOTO HELP IF (%1)==(?) GOTO HELP	If the user starts the batch file with a request for help, jump to a section to display that help.
ECHO SET ONE=%3 > TEMP.BAT	This line echoes the command to create ONE into a batch file. Using the > to pipe the information overwrites the file if it already exists.
ECHO SET TEN=%2 >> TEMP.BAT	This line echoes the command to create TEN into a batch file. Using the > > to pipe the information adds the command to the bottom of the existing batch file.
ECHO SET HUNDRED=%1 >> TEMP.BAT	This line echoes the command to create HUNDRED into a batch file.
EXIT	The end of the batch file. Because it was called with COMMAND/C, the exit is required to return control to the calling batch file.

Batch File Line	Explanation

`:HELP`
`ECHO This Batch File Was Intended`
`ECHO To Be Called By NUMBER1.BAT`
`ECHO *DO NOT RUN FROM COMMAND LINE*`
`:END_HELP`
`EXIT`
	Section that displays help when the user starts the batch file with a /? or a ? as the first replaceable parameter.

5-11 NUMBER5.BAT is called by NUMBER1.BAT to loop through the ONES digits when there's no HUNDREDS digit.

Batch File Line	Explanation
`@ECHO OFF`	Turn command-echoing off.

`REM NAME:      NUMBER5.BAT`
`REM PURPOSE: Loop Through Possible`
`             Values Of Tens`
`REM VERSION: 1.05`
`REM DATE:     October 16, 1991`
	Documentation remarks.

`IF (%1)==(/?) GOTO HELP` `IF (%1)==(?)  GOTO HELP`	If the user starts the batch file with a request for help, jump to a section to display that help.

`FOR %%J IN (0 1 2 3 4 5 6 7 8 9)`
`    DO IF %ANSWER%==%1%%J COMMAND/C`
`NUMBER6 %1 %%J`
	This line loops through all the ones digits. It is called only if there's no hundreds digit, so it ignores those. It passes the tens digit (%1) from NUMBER1.BAT and the ones digit (%%J) to another batch file if they match the environmental variable ANSWER.

`EXIT`	The end of the batch file. Because this batch file was called with COMMAND/C, the exit is required to return control to the calling batch file.

`:HELP`
`ECHO This Batch File Was Intended`
`ECHO To Be Called By NUMBER1.BAT`
`ECHO *DO NOT RUN FROM COMMAND LINE*`
`:END_HELP`
`EXIT`
	Section that displays help when the user starts the batch file with a /? or a ? as the first replaceable parameter.

5-12 When NUMBER5.BAT finds a match of the environmental variable ANSWER, it calls NUMBER6.BAT to create a batch file called TEMP.BAT to place that information into the environment.

Batch File Line	Explanation
`@ECHO OFF`	Turn command-echoing off.

`REM NAME:    NUMBER6.BAT`
`REM PURPOSE: Place Correct Value`
`            Into Environment`
`REM VERSION: 1.05`
`REM DATE:    October 16, 1991`
	Documentation remarks.

`IF (%1)==(/?) GOTO HELP` `IF (%1)==(?)  GOTO HELP`	If the user starts the batch file with a request for help, jump to a section to display that help.
`ECHO SET ONE=%2 > TEMP.BAT`	This line echoes the command to create ONE into a batch file. Using the > to pipe the information overwrites the file if it already exists.
`ECHO SET TEN=%1 >> TEMP.BAT`	This line echoes the command to create TEN into a batch file. Using the > > to pipe the information adds the command to the bottom of the existing batch file.
`EXIT`	The end of the batch file. Because it was called with COMMAND/C, the exit is required to return control to the calling batch file.

`:HELP`
`ECHO This Batch File Was Intended`
`ECHO To Be Called By NUMBER1.BAT`
`ECHO *DO NOT RUN FROM COMMAND LINE*`
`:END_HELP`
`EXIT`
	Section that displays help when the user starts the batch file with a /? or a ? as the first replaceable parameter.

5-13 NUMBER9.BAT replaces NUMBER1.BAT through NUMBER6.BAT by repeatedly calling itself.

Batch File Line	Explanation
`@ECHO OFF`	Turn command-echoing off.

`REM NAME:    NUMBER9.BAT`
`REM PURPOSE: Perform NUMBER1.BAT-`
`            NUMBER6.BAT`
`REM         Using A Single Batch`
`            File`
`REM VERSION: 1.15`
`REM DATE:    October 16, 1991`
	Documentation remarks.

Batch File Line	Explanation
| ```
IF (%1)==(/?) GOTO HELP
IF (%1)==(?)  GOTO HELP
``` | If the user starts the batch file with a request for help, jump to a section to display that help. |
| ```
IF (%1)==() GOTO NUMBER1
``` | If the first replaceable parameter is blank then the batch file was run from the command line, so jump to the equivalent of NUMBER1.BAT. |
| ```
IF (%2)==(NUMBER2) GOTO NUMBER2
IF (%2)==(NUMBER5) GOTO NUMBER5
IF (%3)==(NUMBER3) GOTO NUMBER3
IF (%4)==(NUMBER4) GOTO NUMBER4
IF (%3)==(NUMBER6) GOTO NUMBER6
``` | The batch file figures out which section to go to based on the first replaceable parameter. |
| ```
GOTO END
``` | If it reaches this point then an invalid replaceable parameter was entered, so exit the batch file. |
| ```
:NUMBER1
``` | Label marking the section of the batch file that functions as NUMBER1.BAT. |
| ```
IF (%ANSWER%)==() ECHO Input Value
                  Not Specified
IF (%ANSWER%)==() ECHO Set ANSWER=
                  Input Value
IF (%ANSWER%)==() GOTO END
``` | If the input value doesn't exist, display an error message and exit. |
| ```
SET ONE=
SET TEN=
SET HUNDRED=
``` | Reset the environmental variables. |
| ```
IF EXIST TEMP.BAT DEL TEMP.BAT
``` | If the temporary file exists, delete it. |
| ```
FOR %%J IN (0 1 2 3 4 5 6 7 8 9)
    DO COMMAND/C NUMBER9 %%J NUMBER2
``` | Loop through the possible values for the hundreds digit and call another batch file for each value by loading another copy of COMMAND.COM. Notice how the current value for the hundreds digit is passed as a replaceable parameter to the next batch file. Notice how each time this batch file calls itself, it inserts a %1 with a label name so the next version of itself will know which section to jump to. |
| ```
IF EXIST TEMP.BAT CALL TEMP.BAT
``` | If the batch file exists then NUMBER4.BAT found the values, so run this temporary batch file to set them into the environment. |

Batch File Line	Explanation
IF (%ONE%)==() FOR %%J IN (0 1 2 3 4 5 6 7 8 9) DO COMMAND/C NUMBER9 %%J NUMBER5	If the IF (%ONE%)==() is true then the steps above didn't decode the number, so it must not have a hundreds digit. This steps cycles through the tens digits. For each digit, it calls another batch file to handle the ones digits. Notice how the tens digit is passed to that batch file as a replaceable parameter.
IF EXIST TEMP.BAT CALL TEMP.BAT	If the batch file exists then NUMBER6.BAT found the values, so run this temporary batch file to set them into the environment.
IF (%TEN%)==() SET ONE=%ANSWER%	If the IF (%TEN%)==() is true then the steps above didn't decode the number, so it must not have a hundreds or tens digit. That means that ANSWER must contain a single ones digit, so the batch file uses that as the value of ONE.
GOTO END : END_NUMBER1	Once it reaches this point the batch file is finished, so it jumps to the end.
:NUMBER2	Label marking the section of the batch file that functions as NUMBER2.BAT.
FOR %%J IN (0 1 2 3 4 5 6 7 8 9) DO COMMAND/C NUMBER9 %1 %%J NUMBER3	This is the second of a series of nested FOR loops. This line cycles through all the possible tens values. For each one, it calls another batch file and passes that batch file the value of the hundreds digit (%1) along with the value of the tens digit (%%J).
EXIT : END_NUMBER2	The end of the batch file. Because this batch file was called with COMMAND/C, the exit is required to return control to the calling batch file--which in this case is another version of NUMBER9.BAT
:NUMBER3	Label marking the section of the batch file that functions as NUMBER3.BAT.

Batch File Line	Explanation

`FOR %%J IN (0 1 2 3 4 5 6 7 8 9) DO`
`    IF %ANSWER%==%1%2%%J COMMAND/C`
`    NUMBER9 %1 %2 %%J NUMBER4`
	This line cycles through all the ones digits and calls itself again if the environmental variable matches the number constructed from the hundreds, tens, and ones digit.

`EXIT` `END_NUMBER3`	The end of the batch file. Because this batch file was called with COMMAND/C, the exit is required to return control to the calling batch file--which in this case is another version of NUMBER9.BAT
`:NUMBER4`	Label marking the section of the batch file that functions as NUMBER4.BAT.
`ECHO SET ONE=%3 > TEMP.BAT`	This line echoes the command to create ONE into a batch file. Using the > to pipe the information overwrites the file if it already exists.
`ECHO SET TEN=%2 >> TEMP.BAT`	This line echoes the command to create TEN into a batch file. Using the > > to pipe the information adds the command to the bottom of the existing batch file.
`ECHO SET HUNDRED=%1 >> TEMP.BAT`	This line echoes the command to create HUNDRED into a batch file.
`EXIT` `:END_NUMBER4`	The end of the batch file. Because this batch file was called with COMMAND/C, the exit is required to return control to the calling batch file--which in this case is another version of NUMBER9.BAT
`:NUMBER5`	Label marking the section of the batch file that functions as NUMBER5.BAT.

`FOR %%J IN (0 1 2 3 4 5 6 7 8 9) DO`
`    IF %ANSWER%==%1%%J COMMAND/C`
`    NUMBER9 %1 %%J NUMBER6`
	This line loops through all the ones digits. It's called if only there's no hundreds digit, so it ignores those. It passes the tens digit (%1) from NUMBER1.BAT and the ones digit (%%J) to another batch file if they match the environmental variable ANSWER.

Batch File Line	Explanation
EXIT :END_NUMBER5	The end of the batch file. Because this batch file was called with COMMAND/C, the exit is required to return control to the calling batch file--which in this case is another version of NUMBER9.BAT
:NUMBER6	Label marking the section of the batch file that functions as NUMBER6.BAT.
ECHO SET ONE=%2 > TEMP.BAT	This line echoes the command to create ONE into a batch file. Using the > to pipe the information overwrites the file if it already exists.
ECHO SET TEN=%1 >> TEMP.BAT	This line echoes the command to create TEN into a batch file. Using the > > to pipe the information adds the command to the bottom of the existing batch file.
EXIT :END_NUMBER6	The end of the batch file. Because this batch file was called with COMMAND/C, the exit is required to return control to the calling batch file--which in this case is another version of NUMBER9.BAT
:HELP ECHO Takes A Three-Digit Number ECHO Stored In The Environment ECHO Under The Name ANSWER And ECHO Stores The Three Individual ECHO Digits To The Environment ECHO Under The Names ONE, TEN, ECHO And HUNDRED ECHO This Is A Demonstration Batch ECHO File That Replaces ECHO NUMBER1.BAT - NUMBER6.BAT GOTO END :END_HELP	Section that displays help when the user starts the batch file with a /? or a ? as the first replaceable parameter.
:END	Label marking the end of the batch file.
DEL TEMP.BAT	Delete the temporary batch file that places the information into the environment.

5-14 MATH2.BAT uses Batcmd to quickly and efficiently perform addition and subtraction in a batch file.

Batch File Line	Explanation
`@ECHO OFF`	Turn command-echoing off.

`REM NAME:     MATH2.BAT`
`REM PURPOSE: Show Math With Batcmd`
`REM VERSION: 1.00`
`REM DATE:    December 17, 1991`
	Documentation remarks.

`IF (%1)==(/?) GOTO HELP` `IF (%1)==(?)  GOTO HELP`	If the user starts the batch file with a request for help, jump to a section to display that help.
`CLS`	Clear the screen.
`SET MATH=456`	Store a value to the environmental variable MATH for this example.
`ECHO Math Variable Is %MATH%`	Display that value for the user.
`BATCMD SL`	Use the Batcmd utility to skip a line.
`ECHO Will Add One Five Times` `ECHO And Display Results`	Tell the user what will happen next.
`BATCMD AD` `ECHO Math Now %MATH%`	Add one to the contents of the MATH environmental variable using the Batcmd utility, and then display the results for the user.
The above two steps are repeated four more times.	
`SET MATH=3`	Store a new value to the MATH environmental variable.

`ECHO Resetting Math Variable To %MATH%`
`ECHO Will Subtract Five Times`
`ECHO And Display Results`
	Tell the user and explain what will happen next.

`BATCMD SU` `ECHO Math Now %MATH%`	Subtract one from the contents of the MATH environmental variable using the Batcmd utility, and then display the results for the user.
The above two steps are repeated four more times.	
`SET MATH=`	Reset the environmental variable before the batch file terminates.
`GOTO END`	Exit the batch file.

Batch File Line	Explanation

`:HELP`
`ECHO This Is A Demonstration Batch`
`ECHO File That Uses The Utility`
`ECHO Program Batcmd To Perform Math`
`ECHO Easily In A Batch File`
`GOTO END`
`:END_HELP`
	Section that displays help when the user starts the batch file with a /? or a ? as the first replaceable parameter.

`:END`	Label marking the end of the batch file.

PART THREE
Working with DOS

6

Command-line enhancements

Issuing multiple commands to DOS (pre-5.0) can be a real pain. You want to be able to give the computer several commands at the same time so you can move on to something else, but DOS makes that difficult. Sure, you can write a batch file, but writing and debugging a batch file for every set of commands is time-consuming and burns up disk space—especially if you forget to go back later and delete the extra batch files. You can try starting the first command and entering the next command blindly, but DOS's limited type-ahead buffer and your inability to see that next command while typing makes that difficult.

If all the commands can be specified without spaces, you can specify several commands simultaneously by entering something like:

    FOR %J IN (CHKDSK/F OPTIMIZE TAPEBACK) DO %J

on the command line. However, this method breaks down the first time you need to issue a command that has spaces in it, like:

    XCOPY *.* B:

This method also won't work if any of the commands run a batch file containing a FOR loop or if you need piping in one of the commands.

You might not need a batch file

If you're running DOS 5.0, then you don't need a batch file to run multiple commands from the command line. Just enter your first command and press Ctrl−T. You'll see a paragraph symbol on the screen (it looks like a P with the loop on the wrong side). Now type in the second command. If you want to enter more commands, just separate each command with the Ctrl−T.

Of course, entering all the commands on a single line limits you to the standard 127-character command line. As it turns out, this method is superior to MULTI.BAT, the first batch file you'll look at. MULTI.BAT is also limited to 127 characters, but its divider requires three characters rather than DOS 5.0's one, and DOS 5.0 supports piping while MULTI.BAT doesn't.

93

Entering multiple
commands on the command line

MULTI.BAT, in Fig. 6-1, emulates DOS 5.0's Ctrl−T function by allowing you to enter as many commands as you like on a command line, up to DOS's limit of 127 characters. The advantage of MULTI.BAT is that it will work with any version of DOS down to DOS 3.3. By replacing the CALL statement with COMMAND/C, MULTI.BAT can be modified to work with even earlier versions of DOS.

MULTI.BAT constructs an environmental variable containing the command. It does this by looping through the replaceable parameters and adding each one to the environmental variable until it reaches a replaceable parameter that's a caret (^). That tells MULTI.BAT that the command is complete. At that point, it executes the command, resets the environmental variable, and starts over. Because the replaceable parameters have to be separated by spaces, the caret must have a space on each side.

I used the caret in this batch file because it's not a character likely to be used on the command line, and because there's no lowercase version of it. Readers needing to use the caret, surrounded by spaces in commands can substitute another rarely used symbol.

MULTI.BAT uses one nifty trick and has one limitation that you need to be aware of. The trick is that it executes all of its commands using the command:

    CALL %COMMAND%

It has to do this so it can regain control if the command you enter executes a batch file. Interestingly, CALL has no impact if the command isn't a batch file, so CALL DIR and DIR would perform exactly the same function. The batch file's one limitation is piping. DOS processes pipes before handing processing over to MULTI.BAT, so the pipes will never even get to MULTI.BAT. As a result, none of the commands you execute using MULTI.BAT can use pipes. Otherwise, commands execute the same under MULTI.BAT as they do when run from the command line.

When the command line isn't enough

If you have too many commands to enter on the command line or if you find typing all those commands on one line confusing, then you need something more advanced. The batch files discussed in this section overcome both of these problems.

If you're using DOS 5.0, then you have an alternative if the commands you need to enter exceed 127 characters. Before entering the commands on the command line, you can define a DOSKEY macro to shorten the longer commands. However, if you're going to go to this much trouble you might as well go ahead and write a custom macro. See chapter 15 for details on DOSKEY macros.

MULTI1.BAT

MULTI1.BAT in Fig. 6-2 is a simple batch file that aids the user in writing a temporary batch file. First, it displays detailed instructions on the screen. Then it issues the command COPY CON TEMP.BAT to place all the user's keystrokes into a batch file called

TEMP.BAT. When the user presses the F6 key to signal to DOS that he's finished creating the batch file, MULTI1.BAT runs TEMP.BAT and then deletes it.

As written, MULTI1.BAT expects to stay in the current subdirectory. If one of the commands causes it to change subdirectories, then the DEL TEMP.BAT it uses to delete the temporary batch file won't work. Users who anticipate having MULTI1.BAT change subdirectories should specify the full path, including drive, to TEMP.BAT both for the COPY CON and DEL commands.

MULTI2.BAT

The problem with MULTI1.BAT is that once you press a Return there's no way to edit or modify that line. Of course, everyone familiar with Murphy's law knows that just as soon as you press a Return you're going to see a serious problem. If this happens to you, your only choice is to press Ctrl-Break and rerun MULTI1.BAT.

MULTI2.BAT in Fig. 6-3 overcomes all of the problems associated with MULTI-1.BAT by storing each command in memory as an environmental variable. While it doesn't allow you to edit commands, it does allow you to reenter them. MULTI2.BAT allows you to enter up to five commands, but will run with as few as one command. Once you're satisfied with the commands, MULTI2.BAT executes them sequentially.

MULTI2.BAT makes extensive use of Batcmd, a batch file utility written by Doug Amaral of Hyperkinetix. For more information on Batcmd, see chapter 21. In addition, MULTI2.BAT requires a great deal of environmental space and won't run unless you've expanded your space well beyond the default. See Part Five for details on expanding your environment.

MULTI3.BAT

Most of MULTI2.BAT is taken up with routines to enter and edit the environmental variables using Batcmd. Of course, you don't need Batcmd to enter environmental variables—you can do that directly from the command line using the SET command. Once you've entered up to five environmental variables, named CMD1 – CMD5, MULTI3.BAT in Fig. 6-4 will execute them sequentially for you without all the overhead of MULTI2.BAT.

MULTI4.BAT

One significant problem with MULTI2.BAT is its use of the environment to store the commands. When all five commands are long, storing them in the environment can be quite taxing on available space. MULTI4.BAT in Fig. 6-5 overcomes this problem by storing the five commands in five different batch files called JUNK1.BAT through JUNK5.BAT. These five files are stored in the root directory of the C drive. If either of these files exists when MULTI4.BAT starts, it deletes them. Once it finishes, MULTI4.BAT deletes all of the files it creates.

Reusing commands

I sometimes find myself reissuing the same DOS commands over and over. For example, when I'm trying to correct bugs in a program I continually compile it. There are actually a couple of solutions to this problem. You can write a batch file. That is, however, a lot of work for a command you'll use for only one session. If you're running DOS 5.0 and loading DOSKEY, you can define a macro to issue or just recall the command. For those of you without DOS 5.0, I wrote USEOVER.BAT, shown in Fig. 6-6.

If you run USEOVER.BAT with a command after the name, it first stores the command in the environment and then runs the command. Commands can contain as many parts as necessary. When you later run USEOVER.BAT without any command, it will repeat the last command it stored in memory. If you enter a new command on the command line and a different command already exists in memory, USEOVER.BAT will replace the one in memory with the one you enter on the command line, and then execute the new command.

Keyboard macros in the environment

Under DOS 5.0, you can define a macro with a command like:

    DOSKEY A = DIR *.* /P

and, from then on, every time you enter an A on the command line by itself, DOSKEY will replace it with the DIR *.* /P command. DOSKEY calls this a *macro*; some other sources call it *command aliasing*.

MACRO.BAT in Fig. 6-7 provides most of the functions of DOS 5 macros with very little memory use. MACRO.BAT uses only standard DOS batch commands, and will work with all versions of DOS after 2.0.

As written, MACRO.BAT handles only four macros. The first macro is stored in the environment under the name A, the second under B, and so on. This is necessary because MACRO.BAT runs the first macro by issuing the command %A%. If you were to store the macros with the numbers 1–4, DOS would read the %1 part of the first macro command, %1%, as the batch file's first replaceable parameter. Numbers are used to indicate macros on the command line to avoid the problem of dealing with the case of letters in the batch file—which would double the number of IF tests required. If you have adequate environmental space, MACRO.BAT can easily be expanded to handle additional macros.

If you enter the macro command followed by one of the four numbers, MACRO.BAT will execute the command defined by that macro. If you enter a macro number followed by a series of commands, MACRO.BAT will assign those commands to that macro and exit. It won't execute the macro at this point. In order to keep the batch file code fairly simple, macro commands are limited to nine commands, corresponding to the nine replaceable parameters after a Shift command is executed. (The tenth replaceable parameter—%0 in this scheme—stores the name of the macro.)

As mentioned above, MACRO.BAT stores its macros in the environment under the names A–D. There's no requirement that these variables be defined by MACRO.BAT because all it does is check to see that they exist. If you plan on using the same macros each time you use the computer, you can save yourself time by defining them in your AUTOEXEC.BAT file.

MACRO.BAT has one limitation not found in similar macro programs that comes into play when you shell out of a program (accessing the DOS command line without actually exiting the program). When you do this, you load a secondary copy of COMMAND .COM, and this copy has its own environment. Any changes you make to the environment, including storing macros, is lost when you exit this version of COMMAND.COM to return to your application.

In addition, you generally have very little free environmental space when you shell out of a program—no matter how large you've made the primary copy of the environment in your CONFIG.SYS file. That is because most programs release any free environmental space when they load so they'll have the maximum amount of memory to operate in. As a result, you might not even be able to define macros using MACRO.BAT if you shell out of a program to use it. Of course, any macros you defined before entering you application will still exist and run fine.

Keyboard macros in a batch file

MACRO.BAT stores its macros in the environment, so you need a lot of environmental space to use it. MACRO2.BAT, in Fig. 6-8, overcomes this limitation by storing its macros as batch files.

As written, MACRO2.BAT has the capacity of storing ten macros as separate batch files (0.BAT−9.BAT) in the C:\MACRO2 subdirectory. I wrote the batch file with a ten-macro limit to keep its size reasonable, but you can expand MACRO2.BAT to handle as many macros as you like. The macros aren't stored in memory, so expanding the number of macros MACRO2.BAT can handle won't reduce available memory. Also, because MACRO2.BAT doesn't use the environment to store its macros, it will run fine while you're shelled out of a program.

MACRO2.BAT uses a separate subdirectory so its batch files won't be confused with other batch files. Normally, you wouldn't include this subdirectory in your path because MACRO2.BAT can locate its batch files without having them in the path. If you want to use them without accessing them through MACRO2.BAT, however, you could include the C:\MACRO2 subdirectory in your path. If you want to create a macro longer than one line for MACRO2.BAT to access, you could create or edit the batch file outside of MACRO2.BAT and it would still run just fine.

Storing the command line in the environment

In addition to creating macros, the DOSKEY program that comes with DOS 5.0 saves all the commands you enter on the command line and allows you to replay them. I've never liked the way DOSKEY and similar programs store commands from the command line. I end up entering a lot of short commands like DIR, but there's no point storing short commands like this because they're usually more difficult to find and replay than reenter.

Most command-line recall programs store all your commands so you end having to scroll through a lot of short commands to find the one long and complex command you want to replay. In a lot of cases, all that work is just more trouble than it's worth.

CL.BAT (short for command line) in Fig. 6-9 overcomes this problem. To run a command without saving it, you enter it on the command line as you normally would. When entering a long command you want to save, you type in CL followed by the command.

CL.BAT functions like MACRO.BAT back in Fig. 6-7, but with three important exceptions. First, you don't select a name for the command line as you do for the macro. Second, when you're out of space for commands, the oldest one is discarded to make room for the next command you want to store. Finally, MACRO.BAT doesn't run a macro after you create it; CL.BAT executes the command after storing it to the environment.

CL.BAT uses the letters $W-Z$ to store its command lines so the variables it selects won't conflict with the variables used by MACRO.BAT. However, both CL.BAT and MACRO.BAT use the environmental space to store their information, so the space demands of using both batch files can be very large.

After storing one or more command lines by entering CL followed by the command, you can display the available command lines with the command CL D. Once CL.BAT has stored a command line, you can reuse that command line by entering the CL # command, where # is the number of the command line to reuse.

Like MACRO.BAT, the environmental variables used by CL.BAT to store command lines don't have to be created by CL.BAT. If you often reuse a specific command line, you can create that command line by placing the appropriate environmental variable in your AUTOEXEC.BAT file. Additionally, like MACRO.BAT, CL.BAT might not be able to store command lines if you shell out of another program to DOS. In any case, any command lines you store while shelled out are lost when you return to your application.

Storing the command line in a batch file

CL.BAT stores its command lines in the environment, so you need a lot of environmental space to use CL.BAT, especially if you plan on using it in conjunction with MACRO.BAT. CL2.BAT in Fig. 6-10 overcomes this limitation by storing its command lines as batch files.

As written, CL2.BAT has the capacity of storing nine command lines stored as separate batch files (1.BAT$-$9.BAT) in the C:\CL2 subdirectory. This is an artificial limit to keep the size of the batch file reasonable; you can expand CL2.BAT to handle as many command lines as you like. Because they're not stored in memory, expanding the number of command lines CL2.BAT can handle won't reduce available memory.

CL2.BAT uses a separate subdirectory so its batch files won't be confused with other batch files. Normally, you wouldn't include this subdirectory in your path because CL2.BAT can locate its batch files without having them in the path. If you want to use them without accessing them through CL2.BAT, you could include the C:\CL2 subdirectory in your path.

Note that both CL2.BAT and MACRO2.BAT use the names 1.BAT through 9.BAT for their respective names, although in separate subdirectories. As a result, if you included both \CL2 and \MACRO2 in your path, you would be able to run only the batch files stored in the subdirectory that came first in your path. Additionally, many menu systems use batch files with names like 1.BAT. If your menu system does and comes first in your path, you might not be able to run either set of batch files from the command line. Of course, CL2.BAT and MACRO2.BAT are able to run the batch files without problem in either case.

If you want to create a series of command lines for CL2.BAT to access, you could create or edit the batch file outside of CL2.BAT and it would still run it just fine.

In addition to not using any memory to store your command lines, CL2.BAT is the only program for reusing command-line commands that saves your commands from one computing session to the next.

Summary

- MULTI.BAT allows you to enter multiple commands, separated by a caret, on a single command line, and it executes each command sequentially.
- MULTI1.BAT has the user enter commands into a scratch batch file, runs the batch file, and then deletes the scratch batch file.
- MULTI2.BAT stores up to five commands in the environment, allows the user to change the commands, and, when the user is satisfied with the commands, executes them.
- MULTI3.BAT executes up to five commands already stored in the environment.
- MULTI4.BAT stores up to five commands in batch files, allows the user to change the commands, and, when the user is satisfied with the commands, executes them.
- USEOVER.BAT issues the command entered on the command line as well as storing it in the environment for easy reuse.
- MACRO.BAT allows you to define four macros containing up to nine command components, and easily execute those macros as many times as you like. Macro definitions can be stored in the AUTOEXEC.BAT file as well as MACRO.BAT.
- MACRO2.BAT allows you to define ten macros containing up to ten command components, and easily execute those macros as many times as you like. Unlike MACRO.BAT, the macros are stored in batch files rather than in memory, so MACRO.BAT uses no extra memory.
- CL.BAT allows you to store up to four command lines in memory for later reuse. Each command line can contain up to nine command components.
- CL2.BAT allows you to store up to nine command lines containing up to ten command components, and easily reuse those command lines as many times as you like. Unlike CL.BAT, the command lines are stored in batch files rather than in memory, so CL2.BAT uses no extra memory.

6-1 MULTI.BAT lets you enter several commands on the command line. Each command must be separated by a caret.

Batch File Line	Explanation
`@ECHO OFF`	Turn command-echoing off.

`REM NAME:     MULTI.BAT`
`REM PURPOSE: Issue Multiple DOS`
`              Commands`
`REM          On a Single Line`
`REM VERSION: 1.10`
`REM DATE:    May 7, 1991`
	Documentation remarks.

Batch File Line	Explanation
`IF (%1)==(/?) GOTO HELP` `IF (%1)==(?)  GOTO HELP`	If the user starts the batch file with a request for help, jump to a section to display that help.
`SET COMMAND=`	Make sure the environmental variable used by this batch file starts off empty.
`IF (%1)==() GOTO ERROR`	If the user entered no replaceable parameters MULTI.BAT has nothing to do, so jump to an error-handling routine.
`IF (%1)==(^) GOTO ERROR`	If the user entered the first command as the command divider symbol he really doesn't understand how to run MULTI.BAT, so jump to an error-handling routine.
`:TOP`	Label marking the top of a loop.
`SET COMMAND=%COMMAND% %1`	Add a space and the next replaceable parameter to the existing environmental variable. MULTI.BAT builds the command in this fashion, one element at a time.
`SHIFT`	Discard the %0 parameter and move all the remaining parameters down one level.
`IF (%1)==() GOTO RUNLAST`	If there are no more parameters MULTI.-BAT has reached the end of the last command, so jump to a special section to run that command and exit.
`IF (%1)==(^) GOTO RUN`	If the next replaceable parameter is a caret, then MULTI.BAT has reached the end of a command. Jump to a section to run that command.
`GOTO TOP` `END_TOP`	If MULTI.BAT reaches this point, the next replaceable parameter is neither blank or a caret. It's part of the command MULTI.BAT is currently constructing, so it continues looping.
`:RUN`	Label marking the section to run all the commands except the last one.
`SHIFT`	Discard the caret divider.
`CALL %COMMAND%`	Run the command. The CALL is required in case the command is a batch file. Without it, control wouldn't return to MULTI.BAT. The CALL command has no impact when the command isn't a batch file.
`SET COMMAND=`	Reset the environmental variable.

Batch File Line	Explanation
GOTO TOP :END_RUN	Return to the loop that builds the commands.
:RUNLAST	Label marking the section that handles the last command.
CALL %COMMAND%	Run the command, as above.
GOTO END :END_RUNLAST	Exit the batch file.
:ERROR ECHO Invalid Command Specified ECHO The Command Is Multi ECHO Followed By Command Lines ECHO Each Line Must Be ECHO Separated By A ^ PAUSE GOTO END :END_ERROR	Section to explain the problem to the user.
:HELP ECHO MULTI.BAT Runs Multiple ECHO Commands Entered On The ECHO Command Line ECHO --------------------- ECHO To Run, Enter: ECHO MULTI Command ^ Command ECHO Where The Commands Are ECHO Separated By A ^ With ECHO Spaces Around It GOTO END :END_HELP	Section that displays help when the user starts the batch file with a /? or a ? as the first replaceable parameter.
:END	Label marking the exit point of the batch file.
SET COMMAND=	Reset the environmental variable before exiting.

6-2 MULTI1.BAT aids you in creating a temporary batch file, runs that batch file, and then deletes the batch file.

Batch File Line	Explanation
@ECHO OFF	Turn command-echoing off.
REM NAME: MULTI1.BAT REM PURPOSE: On-The-Fly Batch File REM VERSION: 1.00 REM DATE: November 4, 1991	Documentation remarks.
IF (%1)==(/?) GOTO HELP IF (%1)==(?) GOTO HELP	If the user starts the batch file with a request for help, jump to a section to display that help.
IF EXIST TEMP.BAT GOTO ERROR	If the temporary batch file used by this batch file exists, jump to an error-handling routine.

Batch File Line	Explanation
CLS ECHO Enter Your Commands One ECHO Per Line, Pressing Enter ECHO Between Commands. Once You ECHO Press Enter, You Cannot ECHO Go Back And Edit That Command. ECHO When You Finish, Press The ECHO F6 Key To Quit Editing ECHO And Continue. ECHO ***** REMEMBER ***** ECHO Press F6 When Done ECHO ***** REMEMBER *****	Display detailed instructions on the screen.
COPY CON TEMP.BAT	Create a batch file from keystrokes the user enters.
CALL TEMP	Run the batch file.
DEL TEMP.BAT	Delete the batch file.
GOTO END	Exit the batch file.
:ERROR ECHO Working File TEMP.BAT Exists! ECHO You Must Delete This File If ECHO You Want To Use MULTI1.BAT GOTO END :END_ERROR	Section to display an error message when the temporary batch file already exists.
:HELP ECHO MULTI1.BAT Prompts The User To ECHO Enter Commands That Are Stored ECHO In A Batch File ECHO It Then Runs And Deletes That ECHO Temporary Batch File GOTO END :END_HELP	Section that displays help when the user starts the batch file with a /? or a ? as the first replaceable parameter.
:END	Label marking the end of the batch file.

6-3 MULTI2.BAT stores five commands in memory as environmental variables and executes them one at a time.

Batch File Line	Explanation
@ECHO OFF	Turn command-echoing off.
REM NAME: MULTI2.BAT REM PURPOSE: Enter Up To Five Commands REM One At A Time. Store Them REM In The Environment And Then REM Run Them All At Once REM VERSION: 1.10 REM DATE: September 9, 1991	Documentation remarks.

Batch File Line	Explanation
`IF (%1)==(/?) GOTO HELP` `IF (%1)==(?)  GOTO HELP`	If the user starts the batch file with a request for help, jump to a section to display that help.

`SET CMD1=`
`SET CMD2=`
`SET CMD3=`
`SET CMD4=`
`SET CMD5=`
`SET BATCMD=`
`SET TOEDIT=`
`SET EDIT=NO`
	Clear out the variables used later in the batch file.

`:1`	Label marking the beginning of the section that handles the first command. This is required so the editing phase can jump directly to the correct section and edit a specific command.
`BATCMD GE Enter First Command:`	This line gets input from the user with a utility program to store it in the environment under the name BATCMD.

`IF (%BATCMD%)==() ECHO No Command Entered`
`IF (%BATCMD%)==() ECHO Exiting Program`
`IF (%BATCMD%)==() GOTO END`
	If the user doesn't enter a first command, then explain the problem to the user and exit.

`SET CMD1=%BATCMD%`	Because the utility program Batcmd always uses BATCMD as the environmental name it stores information under, the batch file transfers the contents of BATCMD to another environmental variable before reusing the utility.
`SET BATCMD=`	This resets the environmental variable.

Batch File Line	Explanation
`IF %EDIT%==YES GOTO DONENTER`	When editing a specific variable--instead of entering a variable--the batch file sets the environmental variable EDIT to YES. This line prevents the batch file from progressing to the next variable during the editing phase.
`:END_1`	Label marking the end of section 1.
`:2`	Label marking the beginning of the section to handle the second variable.
`BATCMD GE Enter Second Command:`	Use the Batcmd utility program to have the user input the second command.
`IF (%BATCMD%)==() GOTO DONENTER`	If the user presses return, assume command entry is over and jump to the next phase.
`SET CMD2=%BATCMD%`	Store the contents of the BATCMD environmental variable in another name so the variable can be used again.
`SET BATCMD=`	Reset the environmental variable to null.
`IF %EDIT%==YES GOTO DONENTER`	If this section was used for editing rather than command entry, then return to the editing control section of the batch file.
`:END_2`	Label marking the end of section 2 .

Batch File Line	Explanation

`:3`
`BATCMD GE Enter Third Command:`
`IF (%BATCMD%)==() GOTO DONENTER`
`SET CMD3=%BATCMD%`
`SET BATCMD=`
`IF %EDIT%==YES GOTO DONENTER`
`:END_3`
	Input or edit the third command.

`:4`
`BATCMD GE Enter Fourth Command:`
`IF (%BATCMD%)==() GOTO DONENTER`
`SET CMD4=%BATCMD%`
`SET BATCMD=`
`IF %EDIT%==YES GOTO DONENTER`
`:END_4`
	Input or edit the fourth command.

`:5`
`BATCMD GE Enter Fifth Command:`
`IF (%BATCMD%)==() GOTO DONENTER`
`SET CMD5=%BATCMD%`
`SET BATCMD=`
`IF %EDIT%==YES GOTO DONENTER`
`:END_5`
	Input or edit the fifth command.

`:DONENTER`	Once data entry is complete, this section allows the user to change commands, abort the execution of any of the commands, or run the commands.
`CLS`	Clear the screen.

`ECHO You Have Entered The Following`
`IF NOT (%CMD1%)==() ECHO Command #1: %CMD1%`
`IF NOT (%CMD2%)==() ECHO Command #2: %CMD2%`
`IF NOT (%CMD3%)==() ECHO Command #3: %CMD3%`
`IF NOT (%CMD4%)==() ECHO Command #4: %CMD4%`
`IF NOT (%CMD5%)==() ECHO Command #5: %CMD5%`
	Display the commands the user has entered.

`ECHO`	Display a blank line by echoing an Alt-255.

`ECHO Enter Command Number To Reenter`
`ECHO Enter 0 To Run These Commands`
`ECHO Enter 9 To Exit Batch File`
	Tell the user what to do next.

`:END_DONENTER`	Label marking the end of the Donenter section.
`:GETNO`	Label marking the beginning of the section to get input from the user.

Batch File Line	Explanation
`BATCMD GN Enter Selection No. (0-5,9)`	Tell the user what to do and get a numeric input from the user. The GN option of Batcmd only accepts the numbers 0-9 and sets the errorlevel equal to the number.
`IF ERRORLEVEL 0 IF NOT ERRORLEVEL 1 GOTO` `    RUNTHEM`	If the user enters a zero, jump to the section to handle running the commands.
`IF ERRORLEVEL 9 GOTO EXIT`	If the user enters a nine, exit without running the commands.
`IF ERRORLEVEL 6 GOTO GETNO`	If the user entered a nine, the line above would prevent it from reaching this line. If the user entered a six or higher, then loop back through this routine to get another number from the user because that's an invalid selection.
`FOR %%J IN (1 2 3 4 5) DO IF` `    ERRORLEVEL %%J SET TOEDIT=%%J`	If the batch file reaches this point, then the user entered a number to edit. Store that number in an environmental variable.
`SET EDIT=YES`	Set the edit flag variable so the routines will know the user is editing variables rather than entering them.
`GOTO %TOEDIT%` `:END_GETNO`	Jump to the appropriate section of the batch file to edit the command.

`:RUNTHEM`
`%CMD1%`
`%CMD2%`
`%CMD3%`
`%CMD4%`
`%CMD5%`
`GOTO END`
`:END_RUNTHEM`
	Section to run each command and then exit the batch file.

Batch File Line	Explanation
`:EXIT`	Label marking the section of the batch file that handles the user selecting the exit option.

`CLS`
`ECHO You Selected Exit`
`ECHO Is This What You Want (Y/N)?`
	Tell the user what's going on.

`BATCMD GF yYnN`	Ask the user if he really wants to exit. The GF option of Batcmd accepts only characters listed on the command line. It sets the errorlevel to one for the first, two for the second, and so on. GF is case-sensitive, so both cases must be listed.
`IF NOT ERRORLEVEL 3 GOTO END`	If the user pressed either upper- or lowercase n, then exit the batch file.
`GOTO DONENTER` `:END_EXIT`	Otherwise, jump back to the editing section.

`:HELP`
`ECHO MULTI2 Prompts The User For Up To Five`
`ECHO Commands, Stores Those Commands In The`
`ECHO Environment, Allows The User To Change`
`ECHO The Commands Once They Are Entered,`
`ECHO Runs The Commands, And Deletes The`
`ECHO Associated Environmental Variables`
`GOTO END`
`:END_HELP`
	Section that displays help when the user starts the batch file with a /? or a ? as the first replaceable parameter.

`:END`	Label marking the end of the batch file.

`SET CMD1=`
`SET CMD2=`
`SET CMD3=`
`SET CMD4=`
`SET CMD5=`
`SET BATCMD=`
`SET TOEDIT=`
`SET EDIT=`
	Before exiting, reset the environmental variables.

6-4 MULTI3.BAT is a stripped-down version of MULTI2.BAT that doesn't use any utility program.

Batch File Line	Explanation
`@ECHO OFF`	Turn command-echoing off.

`REM NAME:    MULTI3.BAT`
`REM PURPOSE: Run Multiple Commands`
`REM VERSION: 1.00`
`REM DATE:    November 4, 1991`
	Documentation remarks.

`IF (%1)==(/?) GOTO HELP` `IF (%1)==(?)  GOTO HELP`	If the user starts the batch file with a request for help, jump to a section to display that help.
`IF NOT (%CMD1)==() CALL %CMD1%`	Run the first command. The CALL command is required in case the command runs a batch file. Otherwise, this batch file could not regain control
`IF NOT (%CMD2)==() CALL %CMD2%`	Run the second command.
`IF NOT (%CMD3)==() CALL %CMD3%`	Run the third command.
`IF NOT (%CMD4)==() CALL %CMD4%`	Run the fourth command.
`IF NOT (%CMD5)==() CALL %CMD5%`	Run the last command.
`GOTO END`	Exit the batch file.

`:HELP`
`ECHO This Batch File Runs Up To Five`
`ECHO Commands You've Stored In The`
`ECHO Environment Prior To Running`
`ECHO This Batch File`
`ECHO The Commands Should Be Stored`
`ECHO Under The Environmental`
`ECHO Variables CMD1 - CMD5`
`GOTO END`
`:END_HELP`
	Section that displays help when the user starts the batch file with a /? or a ? as the first replaceable parameter.

`:END`	Label marking the end of the batch file.

6-5 MULTI4.BAT is a version of MULTI2.BAT that stores the commands in batch files rather than in the environment.

Batch File Line	Explanation
`@ECHO OFF`	Turn command-echoing off.
`GOTO TOP`	Skip over the documentation remarks that follow.

`NAME:    MULTI4.BAT`
`PURPOSE: Enter Up To 5 Commands To Run`
`         Enter Them One At A Time`
`         Store Them On Disk`
`VERSION: 1.00`
`DATE:    January 1, 1992`
	Documentation remarks.

108 *Command-line enhancements*

6-5 Continued

Batch File Line	Explanation
`:TOP`	Label used to jump over the non-executing documentation remarks.
`IF (%1)==(/?) GOTO HELP` `IF (%1)==(?) GOTO HELP`	If the user starts the batch file with a request for help, jump to a section to display that help.

`SET BATCMD=`
`SET TOEDIT=`
`SET EDIT=NO`
	Reset the environmental variables used by this batch file.

`FOR %%J IN (1 2 3 4 5) DO IF EXIST` `    C:\JUNK%%J.BAT DEL C:\JUNK%%J.BAT`	Delete JUNK1.BAT through JUNK5.BAT in the root directory of the C drive.
`:1`	Beginning of the section to get input and handle editing of the first command.
`BATCMD GE Enter First Command:`	Use Batcmd to have the user enter the command. Batcmd stores the input in the environment under the name BATCMD.

`IF (%BATCMD%)==() ECHO Nothing Entered`
`IF (%BATCMD%)==() ECHO Exiting Program`
`IF (%BATCMD%)==() GOTO END`
	If the user doesn't enter the first command, assume he doesn't want to enter commands. Explain what has happened to the user and exit the batch file.

`ECHO @%BATCMD% > C:\JUNK1.BAT`	Pipe the first command to a batch file and append a @ to the beginning to turn off command-echoing.
`SET BATCMD=`	Reset the environmental variable used by Batcmd.
`IF %EDIT%==YES GOTO DONENTER`	These sections do double duty, handling both initial entry and editing. When used for editing, this line causes control to return to the edit routine without you having to edit the other variables.
`:END_1`	Label marking the end of this section.

`:2`
`BATCMD GE Enter Second Command:`
`IF (%BATCMD%)==() GOTO DONENTER`
`ECHO @%BATCMD% > C:\JUNK2.BAT`
`SET BATCMD=`
`IF %EDIT%==YES GOTO DONENTER`
`:END_2`
	Section to handle the second variable.

Batch File Line	Explanation

``
:3
BATCMD GE Enter Third Command:
IF (%BATCMD%)==() GOTO DONENTER
ECHO @%BATCMD% > C:\JUNK3.BAT
SET BATCMD=
IF %EDIT%==YES GOTO DONENTER
:END_3
``
	Section to handle the third variable.

``
:4
BATCMD GE Enter Fourth Command:
IF (%BATCMD%)==() GOTO DONENTER
ECHO @%BATCMD% > C:\JUNK4.BAT
SET BATCMD=
IF %EDIT%==YES GOTO DONENTER
:END_4
``
	Section to handle the fourth variable.

``
:5
BATCMD GE Enter Fifth Command:
IF (%BATCMD%)==() GOTO DONENTER
ECHO @%BATCMD% > C:\JUNK5.BAT
SET BATCMD=
IF %EDIT%==YES GOTO DONENTER
:END_5
``
	Section to handle the fifth variable.

``` :DONENTER ```	Label marking the beginning of the section that controls editing once the user has entered the commands.
``` CLS ```	Clear the screen.
``` ECHO You Have Entered The Following IF EXIST C:\JUNK1.BAT ECHO Command #1 IF EXIST C:\JUNK1.BAT ECHO ---------- IF EXIST C:\JUNK1.BAT TYPE C:\JUNK1.BAT BATCMD SL ```	Display the current value of the first command.
``` IF EXIST C:\JUNK2.BAT ECHO Command #2 IF EXIST C:\JUNK2.BAT ECHO ---------- IF EXIST C:\JUNK2.BAT TYPE C:\JUNK2.BAT BATCMD SL ```	Display the current value of the second command.
``` IF EXIST C:\JUNK3.BAT ECHO Command #3 IF EXIST C:\JUNK3.BAT ECHO ---------- IF EXIST C:\JUNK3.BAT TYPE C:\JUNK3.BAT BATCMD SL ```	Display the current value of the third command.
``` IF EXIST C:\JUNK4.BAT ECHO Command #4 IF EXIST C:\JUNK4.BAT ECHO ---------- IF EXIST C:\JUNK4.BAT TYPE C:\JUNK4.BAT BATCMD SL ```	Display the current value of the fourth command.

Batch File Line	Explanation

`IF EXIST C:\JUNK5.BAT ECHO Command #5`
`IF EXIST C:\JUNK5.BAT ECHO ----------`
`IF EXIST C:\JUNK5.BAT`
`    TYPE C:\JUNK5.BAT`
`BATCMD SL`
	Display the current value of the fifth command.

`ECHO Enter # Of Command To Reenter`
`ECHO Enter 0 To Run These Commands`
`ECHO Enter 9 To Exit Batch File`
`:GETNO`
`BATCMD GN Enter Selection # (0-5,9)`
	Ask the user what to do next.

`IF ERRORLEVEL 0` `    IF NOT ERRORLEVEL 1 GOTO RUNTHEM`	If the user entered a zero, jump to a section to run the commands.
`IF ERRORLEVEL 9 GOTO EXIT`	If the user entered a nine, jump to a section to handle exiting the batch file without running the commands.
`IF ERRORLEVEL 6 GOTO GETNO`	The only acceptable value of six or larger was nine and if the user entered a nine the batch file has already jumped to a different section. An errorlevel value of six or larger here, therefore, indicates the user entered an invalid number, so jump to the top of this section and ask again.
`:END_GETNO`	Label marking the end of the Getno section. If the batch file reaches this point, the user entered a 1-5 to edit that command.
`FOR %%J IN (1 2 3 4 5) DO IF` `    ERRORLEVEL %%J SET TOEDIT=%%J`	Find the errorlevel and store it to the environmental variable TOEDIT.
`SET EDIT=YES`	Set the environmental variable EDIT to YES so the entry/editing routines will know the user is editing commands and not entering them.
`GOTO %TOEDIT%`	Jump to the section to edit the command requested by the user.
`:END_DONENTER`	Label marking the end of the Donenter section.

Batch File Line	Explanation
`:RUNTHEM`	Label marking the beginning of the section that actually runs the commands.

`IF EXIST C:\JUNK1.BAT`
`    CALL C:\JUNK1.BAT`
`IF EXIST C:\JUNK2.BAT`
`    CALL C:\JUNK2.BAT`
`IF EXIST C:\JUNK3.BAT`
`    CALL C:\JUNK3.BAT`
`IF EXIST C:\JUNK4.BAT`
`    CALL C:\JUNK4.BAT`
`IF EXIST C:\JUNK5.BAT`
`    CALL C:\JUNK5.BAT`
	Run the commands. MULTI4.-BAT calls the batch files containing the commands so it can regain control when they terminate.

`GOTO END`	Exit the batch file.
`:END_RUNTHEM`	Label marking the end of the Runthem section.
`:EXIT`	Label marking the beginning of the section to handle the user requesting to exit the batch file without running the commands he entered.

`CLS`
`ECHO You Selected Exit`
`ECHO Is This What You Want (Y/N)?`
	Clear the screen and explain the option he selected.

`BATCMD GF yYnN`	Use Batcmd to get a response from the user.
`IF NOT ERRORLEVEL 3 GOTO END` `GOTO DONENTER`	If the user selects yes, exit the batch file; otherwise, jump back to the editing routine.
`:END_EXIT`	Label marking the end of the Exit section.

`:HELP`
`ECHO MULTI4.BAT Allows You To Enter`
`ECHO Five Commands For It To Execute`
`BATCMD SL`
`ECHO MULTI4.BAT Stores The Commands In`
`ECHO Five Batch Files Named JUNK1.BAT`
`ECHO To JUNK5.BAT In C:\`
`BATCMD SL`
`ECHO Once Done, MULTI4.BAT Deletes`
`ECHO These Working Batch Files`
`GOTO END`
`:END_HELP`
	Section that displays help when the user starts the batch file with a /? or a ? as the first replaceable parameter.

`:END`	Label marking the end of the batch file.

6-5 Continued

Batch File Line	Explanation

`SET BATCMD=`
`SET TOEDIT=`
`SET EDIT=`
	Reset the environmental variables used by MULTI4.BAT.

`FOR %%J IN (1 2 3 4 5) DO IF EXIST` `    C:\JUNK%%J.BAT DEL C:\JUNK%%J.BAT`	Delete the temporary batch files used by MULTI4.BAT.

6-6 USEOVER.BAT stores a single command in an environmental variable so you can use it over and over.

Batch File Line	Explanation
`@ECHO OFF`	Turn command-echoing off.

`REM NAME:     USEOVER.BAT`
`REM PURPOSE: Use A Command Over`
`            And Over`
`REM VERSION: 1.02`
`REM DATE:    August 3, 1991`
	Documentation remarks.

`IF (%1)==(/?) GOTO HELP` `IF (%1)==(?)  GOTO HELP`	If the user starts the batch file with a request for help, jump to a section to display that help.
`IF (%1)==() GOTO JUSTCMD`	If the user didn't enter a command on the command line, jump to the section that enters the command already stored in an environmental variable.
`REM Construct Command in` `REM Environmental Variable`	Documentation remarks.
`SET COMMAND=`	Reset the environmental variable.
`:TOP`	Label marking the top of a loop.
`SET COMMAND=%COMMAND% %1`	Add the next replaceable parameter onto the existing command. The first time through the loop, this will begin constructing the command but will add a space to the beginning. The extra space has no impact on the command.
`SHIFT`	Move all replaceable parameters down one level.
`IF (%1)==() GOTO JUSTCMD`	If there are no more parts of the command, jump to the section that issues the command.
`GOTO TOP`	Continue looping.
`:END_TOP`	Label marking the end of the TOP section that constructs the command from the replaceable parameters.

Batch File Line	Explanation
`:JUSTCMD`	Label marking the top of the section to issue the command.
`%COMMAND%`	Issue the command.
`GOTO END`	Exit the batch file.
`:END_JUSTCMD`	Label marking the end of the JUSTCMD section.

`:HELP`
`ECHO Running USEOVER.BAT With`
`ECHO A Command Following Its`
`ECHO Name Runs That Command And`
`ECHO Stores It In The`
`ECHO Environment For Reuse`
`ECHO Running USEOVER.BAT`
`ECHO Without A Command After`
`ECHO Its Name Runs The Command`
`ECHO Stored In The Environment`
`GOTO END`
`:END_HELP`
	Section that displays help when the user starts the batch file with a /? or a ? as the first replaceable parameter.

`:END`	Label marking the end of the batch file.

6-7 With MACRO.BAT, you can define up to four macros, run them from the command line, and change them on the fly.

Batch File Line	Explanation
`@ECHO OFF`	Turn command-echoing off.

`REM NAME:     MACRO.BAT`
`REM PURPOSE: Simulate Macros`
`REM VERSION: 2.00`
`REM DATE:     November 4, 1991`
	Documentation remarks.

`IF (%1)==(/?) GOTO HELP` `IF (%1)==(?)  GOTO HELP`	If the user starts the batch file with a request for help, jump to a section to display that help.
`IF (%1)==() GOTO ERROR1`	If the user did not enter a macro number, then jump to an error-handling routine.

`IF %1==1 GOTO OK`
`IF %1==2 GOTO OK`
`IF %1==3 GOTO OK`
`IF %1==4 GOTO OK`
	If the user entered a correct macro number, continue with the batch file.

`GOTO ERROR2`	The user entered an invalid macro number, so jump to an error-handling routine.

Batch File Line	Explanation
`:OK`	Label marking the beginning of the macro processing section.
`IF (%2)==() GOTO RUN`	If there's no second parameter the user simply wants to run a macro, so jump to the section to handle that.
`SHIFT`	Move the replaceable parameters down one level so the macro number becomes %0. This allows the macro to include one additional command word at the end without additional complexity.

`IF %0==1 SET A=%1 %2 %3 %4 %5 %6`
`              %7 %8 %9`
`IF %0==2 SET B=%1 %2 %3 %4 %5 %6`
`              %7 %8 %9`
`IF %0==3 SET C=%1 %2 %3 %4 %5 %6`
`              %7 %8 %9`
`IF %0==4 SET D=%1 %2 %3 %4 %5 %6`
`              %7 %8 %9`
	Define the macro to the appropriate letter.

`SHIFT`	Move the replaceable parameters down one level.
`IF (%9)==() GOTO END`	If %9 contains anything, then the command word was not included in the macro definition. If %9 is blank, exit the batch file; otherwise, warn the user.

`ECHO Only Nine "Words" Are Allowed`
`ECHO In The Macro So Everything`
`ECHO After the %8 Was Lost`
`GOTO END`
`:END_OK`
	Explain the problem to the user and exit.

`:ERROR1`
`ECHO You Must Specify The Macro`
`ECHO To Run Or The Macro To Define`
`ECHO On The Command Line.`
`ECHO The First Replaceable Parameter`
`ECHO Must Be The Macro Number 1-4.`
`ECHO If No Other Information Is`
`ECHO Entered And That Macro Already`
`ECHO Exists, MACRO.BAT Runs It.`
`ECHO To Define A Macro, Enter Its`
`ECHO Commands After The Macro Name.`
`GOTO END`
`:END_ERROR1`
	This section handles explaining the error when the user enters nothing on the command line. After explaining the problem, it exits the batch file.

Batch File Line	Explanation

`:ERROR2`
`ECHO The First Replaceable Parameter`
`ECHO Must Be The Macro Number 1-4.`
`ECHO If No Other Information Is`
`ECHO Entered And That Macro Already`
`ECHO Exists, MACRO.BAT Runs It.`
`ECHO To Define A Macro, Enter Its`
`ECHO Commands After The Macro Name.`
`GOTO END`
`:END_ERROR2`
	This section explains the problem when the user enters an invalid macro number. After explaining the problem, it exits the batch file.

`:RUN`
`IF %1==1 IF NOT (%A%)==() %A%`
`IF %1==2 IF NOT (%B%)==() %B%`
`IF %1==3 IF NOT (%C%)==() %C%`
`IF %1==4 IF NOT (%D%)==() %D%`
`GOTO END`
`:END_RUN`
	Select the correct macro to run, run it, and then exit the batch file.

`:HELP`
`ECHO Entering MACRO # Runs The`
`ECHO Macro Stored Under That Number`
`ECHO ----------------------------`
`ECHO Entering MACRO # Commands`
`ECHO Stores The Specified Commands`
`ECHO Under The Macro Number`
`ECHO This Does *NOT* Run The Macro`
`ECHO ----------------------------`
`ECHO Valid Macro Numbers Are 1-4`
`GOTO END`
`:END_HELP`
	Section that displays help when the user starts the batch file with a /? or a ? as the first replaceable parameter.

`:END`	Label marking the end of the batch file.

6-8 MACRO2.BAT works similarly to MACRO.BAT; however, it stores its macros in a batch file rather than in the environment.

Batch File Line	Explanation
`@ECHO OFF`	Turn command-echoing off.

`REM NAME:      MACRO2.BAT`
`REM PURPOSE: Run Macros From File`
`REM VERSION: 1.00`
`REM DATE:      November 6, 1991`
	Documentation remarks.

`IF (%1)==(/?) GOTO HELP` `IF (%1)==(?)   GOTO HELP`	If the user starts the batch file with a request for help, jump to a section to display that help.
`IF NOT EXIST C:\MACRO2\*.*` `    MD C:\MACRO2`	If the macro storage subdirectory doesn't exist, create it.

Batch File Line	Explanation
`IF (%1)==() GOTO MISSING`	If the user didn't enter any instructions, jump to an error-handling routine.
`IF (%1)==(D) GOTO DISPLAY` `IF (%1)==(d) GOTO DISPLAY`	If the user entered a D as the first replaceable parameter, display the existing macros.
`IF (%2)==() GOTO RUN`	If the second replaceable parameter is blank the user can't define a macro, so jump to a section that figures out which macro to run.

`IF (%1)==(0) GOTO DEFINE`
`IF (%1)==(1) GOTO DEFINE`
`IF (%1)==(2) GOTO DEFINE`
`IF (%1)==(3) GOTO DEFINE`
`IF (%1)==(4) GOTO DEFINE`
`IF (%1)==(5) GOTO DEFINE`
`IF (%1)==(6) GOTO DEFINE`
`IF (%1)==(7) GOTO DEFINE`
`IF (%1)==(8) GOTO DEFINE`
`IF (%1)==(9) GOTO DEFINE`
	If the first replaceable parameter is 0-9 then the user wants to define that macro, so jump to a macro definition section.

`GOTO ERROR1`	If the user wanted to define a macro but the first replaceable parameter wasn't 0-9, an error has occurred so jump to an error-handling routine.

`:ERROR1`
`ECHO You Entered An Invalid Code On`
`ECHO The Command Line`
`ECHO`
`GOTO MISSING`
`:END_ERROR1`
	Error-handling section for when the user enters an invalid code. It displays an error message and then jumps to another error-handling section to display more information. Note: The ECHO by itself echos an Alt-255 to display a blank space.

`:ERROR2`
`ECHO The Command You Entered Was Too`
`ECHO Long And Everything After The`
`ECHO %9 Is Missing From The Macro`
`ECHO`
`ECHO MACRO2 Allows Only 9 Commands`
`ECHO After the Macro Number`
`ECHO Try Avoiding Spaces Between`
`ECHO Programs And Switches Or`
`ECHO Otherwise Shorten The Command`
`GOTO END`
`:END_ERROR2`
	To simplify the batch file, it allows only nine replaceable parameters in the command. When the user exceeds that, the batch file jumps to this error-handling routine to warn him.

Batch File Line	Explanation

`:ERROR3`
`ECHO The Macro You Selected (%1)`
`ECHO Does Not Exist`
`ECHO`
`GOTO MISSING`
`:END_ERROR3`
	When the user tries to run a macro that doesn't exist, the batch file jumps to this error-handling routine to display an error message, and then jumps to another error-handling routine to display additional information.

`:RUN`	Label marking the beginning of the section that runs an existing macro.
`IF NOT EXIST C:\MACRO2\%1.BAT` `    GOTO ERROR3`	If the macro requested by the user doesn't exist, jump to an error-handling routine.

`IF (%1)==(0)  CALL C:\MACRO2\0.BAT`
`IF (%1)==(1)  CALL C:\MACRO2\1.BAT`
`IF (%1)==(2)  CALL C:\MACRO2\2.BAT`
`IF (%1)==(3)  CALL C:\MACRO2\3.BAT`
`IF (%1)==(4)  CALL C:\MACRO2\4.BAT`
`IF (%1)==(5)  CALL C:\MACRO2\5.BAT`
`IF (%1)==(6)  CALL C:\MACRO2\6.BAT`
`IF (%1)==(7)  CALL C:\MACRO2\7.BAT`
`IF (%1)==(8)  CALL C:\MACRO2\8.BAT`
`IF (%1)==(9)  CALL C:\MACRO2\9.BAT`
`GOTO END`
`:END_RUN`
	Run the macro requested by the user, and then exit the batch file. MACRO2.BAT stores macros in batch files so it runs them by running the associated batch file. Using the CALL command allows MACRO2.BAT to regain control when the macro batch file terminates.

`:MISSING`
`ECHO To Define A Macro, Enter The`
`ECHO Number Followed By The Macro`
`ECHO`
`ECHO Numbers 0-9 Are Allowed`
`ECHO`
`ECHO To Run An Existing Macro, Enter`
`ECHO The Number Of That Macro`
`ECHO`
`ECHO The Available Macros Are:`
`GOTO DISPLAY`
`:END_MISSING`
	Display a message telling the user how to use MACRO2.BAT, and then jump to another error-handling routine to display the available macros.

`:DISPLAY` `:0EXIST`	Label marking the beginning of the section that displays the available macros.
`IF NOT EXIST C:\MACRO2\0.BAT` `    GOTO 1EXIST`	If this macro doesn't exist, skip to the next one. Because macros don't have to be assigned sequentially, the batch file must check the all.
`ECHO --0--`	Display the macro number.

Batch File Line	Explanation
`TYPE C:\MACRO2\0.BAT |` `    FIND /V "@ECHO OFF"`	Type the batch file and pipe it to the DOS FIND program. Each batch file consists of two lines. The first one is @ECHO OFF and the second is the actual command. The /V switch causes FIND to display only the line not containing @ECHO OFF.
`ECHO`	Display a blank line by echoing Alt-255.
`:END_0EXIST`	Label marking the end of the 0EXIST section.
The remaining macros are displayed in a similar fashion	
`GOTO END`	After displaying all the macros, exit the batch file.
`:DEFINE`	Label marking the beginning of the section to define a macro.
`SHIFT`	Move the replaceable parameters down one level, making the macro name %0. This allows the maximum room for macro definitions.
`ECHO @ECHO OFF > C:\MACRO2\%0.BAT`	Begin the batch file with an @ECHO OFF command. Using the > pipe overwrites the file if it exists.
`ECHO %1 %2 %3 %4 %5 %6 %7 %8` `    %9 >> C:\MACRO2\%0.BAT`	Add the macro commands to the batch file. Using the > > pipe causes the commands to be written to the bottom.
`SHIFT`	Move the replaceable parameters down one level.
`IF NOT (%9)==() GOTO ERROR2`	If this replaceable parameter exists it was left out of the macro, so jump to an error-handling routine to warn the user.
`GOTO END` `:END_DEFINE`	Go to the end of the batch file.

`:HELP`
`ECHO MACRO2.BAT Allows You To Define`
`ECHO Up To Ten Macros (0-9) That Are`
`ECHO Stored On Disk So They Do Not`
`ECHO Use Any Memory`
`GOTO END`
`:END_HELP`
	Section that displays help when the user starts the batch file with a /? or a ? as the first replaceable parameter.

`:END`	Label marking the end of the batch file.

Batch File Line	Explanation
`@ECHO OFF`	Turn command-echoing off.

`REM NAME:    CL.BAT`
`REM PURPOSE: Store/Reuse Commands`
`REM VERSION: 2.00`
`REM DATE:    November 6, 1991`
	Documentation remarks.

`IF (%1)==(/?) GOTO HELP` `IF (%1)==(?)  GOTO HELP`	If the user starts the batch file with a request for help, jump to a section to display that help.
`IF (%1)==()   GOTO MISSING`	If the user does not enter a replaceable parameter, jump to an error-handling routine.
`IF (%1)==(D) GOTO DISPLAY` `IF (%1)==(d) GOTO DISPLAY`	If the user enters a D, jump to a section to display available commands.

`IF (%1)==(1) GOTO RUN1`
`IF (%1)==(2) GOTO RUN2`
`IF (%1)==(3) GOTO RUN3`
`IF (%1)==(4) GOTO RUN4`
	If the user enters one of four numbers, jump to a section to run the appropriate command.

`GOTO STORE`	If the user doesn't want to display the available macros or run one of them, jump to a section to create a command.
`:STORE`	Label marking the section that stores the command in the environment.
`SHIFT`	Move the replaceable parameters down one level to allow the maximum length for the command.

`IF (%W%)==() GOTO USEW`
`IF (%X%)==() GOTO USEX`
`IF (%Y%)==() GOTO USEY`
`IF (%Z%)==() GOTO USEZ`
	Jump to the first available variable to store the command. Unlike macros, commands are stored sequentially, so the command is always stored in the next available slot.

`GOTO ALLFULL` `:END_STORE`	If all four variables are full, jump to a routine to handle that.
`:USEW`	Label marking the beginning of the section to store a command in the first slot.
`SET W=%0 %1 %2 %3 %4 %5 %6 %7 %8 %9`	Store the command.
`%W%`	Unlike macros, commands are executed after they're, stored so execute the command.

Batch File Line	Explanation
GOTO END :END_USEW	After executing the command, exit the batch file.
Commands are stored in the other three variables in the same fashion.	
:ALLFULL	Label marking the section to handle storing the command when all available slots are full.
SET W=%X% SET X=%Y% SET Y=%Z%	Move all the commands down one variable. This has the effect of discarding the first command to be entered.
SET Z=%0 %1 %2 %3 %4 %5 %6 %7 %8 %9	Store the command in the last variable.
%Z%	Run the command.
GOTO END :END_ALLFULL	Exit the batch file.
:MISSING ECHO You Did Not Enter Anything ECHO After The Name So CL Does ECHO Not Know What To Do! ECHO GOTO EXPLAIN :END_MISSING	Section to display an error message when the user doesn't enter any replaceable parameter on the command line. After that, jump to another section to display additional information. Note: the ECHO command that appears by itself echoes an Alt-255 to create a blank line.
:EXPLAIN ECHO Enter CL D To Display The ECHO Existing Command Lines ECHO ECHO Enter CL # To Reuse One Of ECHO The Existing Command Lines ECHO Where # Is The Number Of ECHO The Command Line To Reuse ECHO GOTO DISPLAY :END_EXPLAIN	Explain how to use the batch file and then jump to a section to display the available commands.
:DISPLAY ECHO The Four Available ECHO Commands Are: ECHO 1: %W% ECHO 2: %X% ECHO 3: %Y% ECHO 4: %Z% GOTO END :END_DISPLAY	Section to display the available commands and then exit the batch file.

Batch File Line	Explanation

`:RUN1`
`%W%`
`GOTO END`
`:END_RUN1`
	Section to run the first command and then exit the batch file.

`:RUN2`
`%X%`
`GOTO END`
`:END_RUN2`
	Section to run the second command and then exit the batch file.

`:RUN3`
`%Y%`
`GOTO END`
`:END_RUN3`
	Section to run the third command and then exit the batch file.

`:RUN4`
`%Z%`
`GOTO END`
`:END_RUN4`
	Section to run the fourth command and then exit the batch file.

`:HELP`
`ECHO CL.BAT Stores The Command Line`
`ECHO To The Environment And Then`
`ECHO Executes That Command`
`ECHO Up To Four Commands Are Stored`
`ECHO CL.BAT Can Also Display And Run`
`ECHO The Stored Commands`
`GOTO END`
`:END_HELP`
	Section that displays help when the user starts the batch file with a /? or a ? as the first replaceable parameter.

`:END`	Label marking the end of the batch file.

6-10 CL2.BAT works similarly to CL.BAT; however, it stores its command lines in a batch file rather than in the environment.

Batch File Line	Explanation
`@ECHO OFF`	Turn command-echoing off.

`REM NAME:     CL2.BAT`
`REM PURPOSE: Store Command Lines`
`REM          Using Files, Not Memory`
`REM VERSION: 1.00`
`REM DATE:    November 6, 1991`
	Documentation remarks.

`IF (%1)==(/?) GOTO HELP` `IF (%1)==(?)  GOTO HELP`	If the user starts the batch file with a request for help, jump to a section to display that help.
`IF (%1)==()    GOTO MISSING`	If the user doesn't enter a replaceable parameter, jump to an error-handling section.
`IF (%1)==(D)  GOTO DISPLAY` `IF (%1)==(d)  GOTO DISPLAY`	If the user enters a D, jump to a section to display the available commands.

Batch File Line	Explanation

`IF (%1)==(1)   GOTO RUN`
`IF (%1)==(2)   GOTO RUN`
`IF (%1)==(3)   GOTO RUN`
`IF (%1)==(4)   GOTO RUN`
`IF (%1)==(5)   GOTO RUN`
`IF (%1)==(6)   GOTO RUN`
`IF (%1)==(7)   GOTO RUN`
`IF (%1)==(8)   GOTO RUN`
`IF (%1)==(9)   GOTO RUN`
	If the user enters the number of a command, jump to a section to run that command.

`IF NOT EXIST   C:\CL2\1.BAT GOTO USE1`
`IF NOT EXIST   C:\CL2\2.BAT GOTO USE2`
`IF NOT EXIST   C:\CL2\3.BAT GOTO USE3`
`IF NOT EXIST   C:\CL2\4.BAT GOTO USE4`
`IF NOT EXIST   C:\CL2\5.BAT GOTO USE5`
`IF NOT EXIST   C:\CL2\6.BAT GOTO USE6`
`IF NOT EXIST   C:\CL2\7.BAT GOTO USE7`
`IF NOT EXIST   C:\CL2\8.BAT GOTO USE8`
`IF NOT EXIST   C:\CL2\9.BAT GOTO USE9`
`GOTO ALLUSED`
	Jump to the first free slot to store the command. If none are free, jump to a special section.

`:RUN`	Label marking the beginning of the section to run a command.
`CALL C:\CL2\%1.BAT`	Run the requested command.
`GOTO END` `:END_RUN`	Exit the batch file.
`:USE1`	Label marking the beginning of the section to store the command in the first slot.
`SHIFT`	Move the replaceable parameters down one level to store the maximum amount of the command.
`ECHO %0 %1 %2 %3 %4 %5 %6 %6 %7` `    %8 %9 > C:\CL2\1.BAT`	Echo the commands into a batch file.
`C:\CL2\1.BAT`	Run the batch file containing the command.
`GOTO END` `:END_USE1`	Exit the batch file.
Commands are stored in the remaining eight slots in the same fashion.	
`:ALLUSED`	Label marking the beginning of the section that handles storing the command when there are no free slots.
`DEL C:\CL2\1.BAT`	Delete the first batch file.

Batch File Line	Explanation
REN C:\CL2\2.BAT 1.BAT REN C:\CL2\3.BAT 2.BAT REN C:\CL2\4.BAT 3.BAT REN C:\CL2\5.BAT 4.BAT REN C:\CL2\6.BAT 5.BAT REN C:\CL2\7.BAT 6.BAT REN C:\CL2\8.BAT 7.BAT REN C:\CL2\9.BAT 8.BAT	Rename the remaining batch files to move each one down one level.
GOTO USE9 :END_ALLUSED	The last slot is now free, so jump to the section that stores the command in the last slot.
:DISPLAY	Label marking the beginning of the section to display the available commands.
IF NOT EXIST C:\CL2\1.BAT GOTO END	If this command doesn't exist there are no more to display, so exit the batch file.
ECHO 1: ECHO ----------	Display the command number with a line below it to separate it from the command.
TYPE C:\CL2\1.BAT	The batch file will have only one line, so type it to the screen.
BATCMD SL	Display a blank line using Batcmd.
The remaining commands (stored in 2.BAT - 9.BAT) are displayed in a similar fashion.	
GOTO END :END_DISPLAY	After displaying the available commands, exit the batch file.
:MISSING ECHO You Did Not Enter Anything ECHO After The Name So CL Does ECHO Not Know What To Do! BATCMD SL GOTO EXPLAIN :END_MISSING	Section that displays an error message when the user doesn't enter anything on the command line.
:EXPLAIN ECHO Enter CL D To Display The ECHO Existing Command Lines BATCMD SL ECHO Enter CL # To Reuse One Of ECHO The Existing Command Lines ECHO Where # Is The Number Of ECHO The Command Line To Reuse BATCMD SL GOTO DISPLAY :END_EXPLAIN	Section that explains how to use the batch file.

Batch File Line	Explanation
:HELP ECHO Enter CL D To Display The ECHO Existing Command Lines BATCMD SL ECHO Enter CL # To Reuse One Of ECHO The Existing Command Lines ECHO Where # Is The Number Of ECHO The Command Line To Reuse BATCMD SL GOTO END :END_HELP	Section that displays help when the user starts the batch file with a /? or a ? as the first replaceable parameter.
:END	Label marking the end of the batch file.

7
Making DOS run smoothly

This chapter will show you how to create batch files to make DOS and therefore your computer run more smoothly.

A more intelligent AUTOEXEC.BAT file

It seems that lately more and more users are trying to wring out every possible byte of free memory so they can give their programs the maximum amount of memory possible to operate in. If your AUTOEXEC.BAT file loads memory-resident programs, you might be able to significantly reduce their memory usage.

Any time DOS loads a program, including memory-resident ones, it passes that program a full copy of the environment. Most memory-resident programs don't use the environment, so they discard the space but retain any information already stored in it.

The trick, then, is to load all your memory-resident programs first, before the environment contains much information. That means you should load them before you set the path, before you change the prompt, and before you create any environmental variables.

One difficulty in doing this is, because your path hasn't yet been set, you can't simply enter the name of the program to load it. You must first access the drive and subdirectory that contain the program, or specify the full path to the program in a batch file. However, the memory you save with this approach is worth it.

Unloading memory-resident programs

Many memory-resident programs include an option that unloads them from memory. Of course, you must unload the programs in reverse order, starting by unloading the last program loaded into memory.

One of the programs I sometimes use requires a lot of memory to run. My original approach was to have the batch file that starts it unload all my memory-resident programs, run the application, and then reload the memory-resident program. However, when I started the application using this batch file, I didn't have enough memory!

The reason is the way DOS handles memory. Because a portion of the batch file is loaded into memory after the memory-resident programs are loaded, the memory being freed by unloading the memory-resident programs isn't available until the batch file that unloads them terminates.

My solution was to create three batch files. The first unloads your memory-resident programs, the second runs the "memory hog" application, and the third reloads the memory-resident programs. (I could have combined the second and third.)

Shelling out to DOS

Many programs allow you to temporarily exit to DOS (called a DOS *shell*) but users often forget they have a program running and try to start another program, or even the same program a second time. Sometimes the program starts but runs very slow due to low memory, and other times it fails to load because of inadequate memory.

I've seen this problem a lot with Windows. When Windows allows you to shell out to DOS, it provides DOS with enough memory to run large applications—so you don't have the protection of having only a small quantity of memory like you do with other applications. I've even seen users running two copies of Windows as a result of shelling out of the first copy!

To avoid this problem, you need a way to remind users that they have another program in memory. This is very easy if you start your programs with a batch file or with a menu program that allows you to issue multiple DOS commands. Just change the prompt from the regular one to something like Type EXIT to return to Lotus$_$p$g just before the application starts, and change it back to your normal prompt after the application terminates. That way the prompt is a constant reminder that a program is loaded in memory. Notice that the prompt contains both the name of the program and instructions on how to return to that program. To do this, you need a custom prompt for each application. Figure 7-1 shows an example of a batch file using this technique that starts Lotus.

The technique in Fig. 7-1 doesn't prevent the user from trying to run a second program while shelled to DOS, it just displays an explanatory prompt to tell the user that one program is already in memory. If you start all your applications with batch files and you're willing to occasionally surprise your users, there's a way to prevent the user from loading a second program while shelled to DOS. This method uses the fact that the EXIT command will unload a second copy of COMMAND.COM (which programs load to shell to DOS) but has absolutely no impact on the first copy of COMMAND.COM.

By including EXIT near the top of each batch file, as shown in Fig. 7-2, you prevent the program from being loaded under a second copy of COMMAND.COM. If the batch file is run under the first copy of COMMAND.COM, the EXIT command is ignored. If it's run under a second copy of COMMAND.COM, the EXIT command will unload the second copy of COMMAND.COM. In doing so, it causes DOS not to execute the remaining portion of the batch file. Not only that, but it immediately returns to the original program.

This technique can surprise a new or even an experienced user. Imagine the surprise if a user shells from Microsoft Word and then runs LOTUS.BAT expecting to load Lotus. Instead, LOTUS.BAT gives the EXIT command and appears to load Microsoft Word.

While this technique works fine with batch files, it won't work with all menu programs. Some menu programs run under a second copy of COMMAND.COM and the EXIT command can unload them or cause other problems. Only experimentation will tell you if this technique works with your menu program.

You can use either or both of these methods. Of course, they'll work only when users start their programs with batch files or menu programs that allow you to issue multiple DOS commands for each selection.

Running inflexible programs

At my office, we have one computer that we use for all our communications. One of the things we do is log onto a remote database, which provides us with custom communications software. One limitation of this software is that it stores the account number, password, and other information in a file called MENU.INF. We have two people who use this database, and they both have different account numbers, passwords, and so on. This communications software can't handle multiple users. The vendor suggested keeping two versions in two different subdirectories, but I created a batch file as a better solution.

When the first user ran the configuration program to create MENU.INF with his information, I copied MENU.INF to a file called RONNY.INF. When the second user ran the configuration program, we once again copied MENU.INF to a file—this time DAVID .INF. MENU.INF is the only file that differs for different users. The batch file in Fig. 7-3 copies the appropriate one to MENU.INF, depending on which user is accessing the database.

You can use this same technique with any program that stores the defaults values in a special file. For example, Microsoft Word for DOS stores the document you're working on, your place, and several optional settings in a file called MW.INI. Figure 7-4 shows a batch file that both Ronny and David could use to maintain their own versions of MW.INI. There's only one major difference between the batch files in Figs. 7-3 and 7-4. Because Microsoft Word allows you to change the defaults while running Word, each user's defaults are copied back to the holding file when that user exits the program. The /L switch is required to force Word to use some of the defaults from the MW.INI file.

Several readers of an earlier version of this book have told me that they use the same method with Ventura Publishing and multiple copies of its VP.INI file. However, rather than using this trick for multiple users, they use it to store multiple configurations of Ventura for a single user.

I've started using the same approach to run Lotus 1-2-3, version 2.3 with different add-in sets. Specifically, I work with one massive worksheet that requires an add-in called SQZ!. SQZ! compresses the worksheet when you save it to disk and uncompresses it when you load it into memory. Lotus stores its add-in loading list in 123.CNF and you can't specify a different one to use on the command line—making it perfect for this approach.

Running commands occasionally

In chapter 12, you'll see how you can have your computer perform a backup only when it's booted on a Wednesday or Friday. The advantage of this approach is that backups are performed automatically without you having to remember to perform them. If you don't use the computer on the assigned day, however, the backup gets missed. Another approach is to occasionally back up the computer.

Most people think of batch files as being either the AUTOEXEC.BAT file, which is run every time you turn your computer on, or a stand-alone batch file that's run only when you enter its name. However, there are some things you want your computer to perform occasionally, like make a backup.

OCCASION.BAT in Fig. 7-5 illustrates this concept. To run this from your AUTOEXEC.BAT file, you would have the statement CALL OCCASION.BAT if you use DOS 3.3 or later, or COMMAND/C OCCASION.BAT if you run an earlier version of DOS.

This batch file maintains a counter in the form of a file. When the batch file first starts, it creates COUNT.00. The next time it runs, it renames this file COUNT.01, the next time it renames it COUNT.02, and so on. When it encounters COUNT.09, it renames it COUNT.00 and performs the task it's supposed to perform occasionally— backing up the computer. That gives this batch file a period of ten.

The batch file counts reboots, not days. If you're working with problem software that frequently locks up, you could end up running a backup several times a day. If you leave your computer on for days at a time, ten reboots could end up being several weeks.

OCCASION.BAT has two interesting tricks in it. The first trick is the counter test on line 2. The batch file needs to perform ten IF EXIST COUNT.00 GOTO 00 tests. Because these tests will be exactly the same except for the digit used, all ten tests are combined into a single FOR command. The second trick is the zero-length file it creates. These zero-length files are discussed in chapter 19.

Occasional batch files have applications outside of performing tasks occasionally when you boot. For example, my disk-testing program has two levels of testing. The first is the quick mode, which takes only a few minutes to run. The complete mode spots more errors but takes much longer to run. The batch file that runs the program normally runs it in quick mode, but it occasionally runs it in complete mode. You can have as many different occasional batch files as you need; the only trick is to remember to use a different name for each counter.

OCCASION.BAT in Fig. 7-5 has to have at least three separate lines for every possible value it tests for. While that works fine for a few possible values, like the ten in OCCASION.BAT, it quickly becomes tedious for a lot of values.

CNTBOOTS.BAT in Fig. 7-6 solves that problem by using only a few lines to find the counter value, and a few more generic lines to increment the counter. After that, it needs lines only for those counter values where it will perform some action. This results in much shorter batch files. OCCASION.BAT has 45 lines to handle ten possible counter values, while CNTBOOTS.BAT has 47 lines to handle fifty possible counter values.

CNTBOOTS.BAT's approach is to use Batcmd's addition ability to loop through all fifty possible counter values. Like OCCASION.BAT, CNTBOOTS.BAT stores the counter value between sessions as the extension of a zero-length file in the root directory.

The approach in CNTBOOTS.BAT isn't limited to fifty possible values for the counter. In fact, it's possible to have one thousand (000−999) when using the extension, and one billion (00000000−99999999) if the name is used rather than the extension. However, the batch file is really too slow for more than fifty. When testing for just fifty values, CNTBOOTS.BAT is slow enough to significantly slow down the booting of my 386/20 machine. Users with a slower machine would want to use even fewer possible values for CNTBOOTS.BAT.

Running under different versions of DOS

For the most part, batch files don't really care which version of DOS they run under. There simply haven't been that many changes to the batch "language" across the different versions. Most of the changes that have occurred happened in DOS 3.3 or earlier, so you can generally assume your users have a DOS version that will run your batch files.

The two specific problems you might run into are using the @ symbol and the CALL command. The @ symbol causes a line in a batch file not to echo, even if echo is on. Most batch files use it once in the @ECHO OFF command that starts the batch file. The CALL command calls a second batch file but leaves the first batch file in memory, so it regains control when the second batch file terminates.

The only time this is a problem is when you're writing batch files that are likely to be run under versions of DOS both before and after version 3.3, and you don't want to take the time to write separate batch files for both systems. In this case, my first suggestion would be to have your pre-3.3 DOS users upgrade to DOS 5.0. The upgrade is inexpensive and DOS 5.0 is good enough that there's simply no reason not to upgrade.

If your users can't or won't upgrade, then it's possible to use a batch file to help reduce the problems. The problems you'll face are:

- Under DOS 3.3 and later, you want to start the batch file with @ECHO OFF, while under earlier versions you need to start them with ECHO OFF. Of course, you can avoid this problem by simply starting all your batch files with ECHO OFF.
- Under DOS 3.3 and later, you want to call a second batch file with the CALL *batch file* command, while under earlier versions you need to call it with COMMAND/C *batch file*. You can minimize this problem by using COMMAND/C for all batch files where CALL isn't absolutely necessary.
- Certain batch files simply won't run under earlier versions of DOS, so you want to have those batch files abort. Any batch file that calls a second batch file where that second batch file must write information to the environment won't work using COMMAND/C because the second batch file gets a second copy of the environment that's lost—along with its changes—when the second batch file terminates. VERSION.BAT in Fig. 7-7 helps solve this problem.

This batch file creates three environmental variables (@, CALL, and VERSION) for addressing each of these problems. Originally, it configures these three variables to contain the following:

Variable	Contains
@	Nothing, so the variable doesn't exist.
CALL	COMMAND/C, only it uses the COMSPEC variable to specify the full path to COMMAND.COM.
VERSION	2.0

VERSION.BAT then calls itself using the CALL command. If it's running under a DOS version that doesn't support the CALL command, this action will abort with a *Bad command of file name* error message, and the value of the variables won't be changed. If it's running under a DOS version that does support the CALL command, then it calls itself with a unique replaceable parameter that causes VERSION.BAT to jump to a special section of the batch file. This section resets the variables to these values:

Variable	Contains
@	@
CALL	CALL
VERSION	3.3

Now the three previous problems can be addressed by @ECHO OFF being replaced with a %@%ECHO OFF command. Under earlier versions of DOS, the @ variable doesn't exist, so the command automatically becomes ECHO OFF. Under later versions of DOS, the value of the @ variable is @ so the command automatically becomes @ECHO OFF. If the user has failed to run VERSION.BAT, then the @ variable won't exist and the command will default to the universally acceptable ECHO OFF.

Any lines in the batch file that call another batch file with the command CALL *batch file* and COMMAND/C *batch file* will work and can be replaced with %CALL% *batch file*. Under earlier versions of DOS, the value of the CALL variable is equal to COMMAND/C, so the command automatically becomes COMMAND/C. Under later versions of DOS, the CALL variable is equal to CALL, so the command automatically becomes CALL *batch file*.

If the user has failed to run VERSION.BAT, then the command will default to the specified batch file, which will call the second batch file in a fashion so that control doesn't return to the first batch file—with results that depend on the logic of the specific batch files involved. To protect against this, each batch file using this approach should first test to make sure the CALL variable actually exists, and abort if it doesn't.

If a batch file requires DOS 3.3 or later in order to operate, it can test on the contents of the VERSION variable (which will either be 2.0, 3.3, or blank if the user failed to run VERSION.BAT) and run it only if it finds a value of 3.3.

Summary

- Loading your memory-resident programs before storing information in the environment can reduce their memory requirements.
- When a batch file unloads a memory-resident program, the memory associated with that program might not be available until after the unloading batch file terminates.
- Having a batch file change the prompt before starting an application and resetting it after exiting the application will remind users that the application is still in memory if they shell out to DOS.
- Including an EXIT at the top of a batch file will prevent that batch file from being used to start an application while shelled out of another application.

- When a program stores configuration information in a file, you can have a batch file activate different configurations by copying the configuration file "on top of" the active version before starting the program.
- By tracking the number of times the computer reboots, the AUTOEXEC.BAT file can perform different tasks occasionally as the reboot tracker reaches a specific count.
- If your batch files must run under different versions of DOS and you don't want to create different batch files for different DOS versions, you can use environmental variables as commands where those variables issue different commands for different versions of DOS.

7-1 LOTUS.BAT changes the prompt to one that will remind Lotus users who exit to DOS using /S that Lotus is still in memory.

Batch File Line	Explanation
`@ECHO OFF`	Turn command-echoing off.

`REM NAME:      LOTUS.BAT`
`REM PURPOSE: Start Lotus`
`REM VERSION: 1.00`
`REM DATE:      April 15, 1991`
	Documentation remark.

`IF (%1)==(/?) GOTO HELP` `IF (%1)==(?)   GOTO HELP`	If the user starts the batch file with a request for help, jump to a section to display that help.
`C:`	Make sure the computer is logged onto the C drive.
`CD\123`	Change to the Lotus subdirectory.
`PROMPT=Type EXIT to return to` `    Lotus$_$p$g`	Change the prompt so if a user shells out of Lotus (using the /System command) he'll know that Lotus is still loaded into memory and will have a visual reminder of how to return to Lotus.
`123`	Start Lotus.
`PROMPT=$p$g`	Reset the prompt once the user exits Lotus.
`GOTO END`	Exit the batch file.

`:HELP`
`ECHO Demonstration Batch File`
`ECHO That Starts Lotus And`
`ECHO Changes The Prompt So`
`ECHO Users Who Shell Out Of`
`ECHO Lotus Will Be Reminded`
`ECHO Of That`
`GOTO END`
`:END_HELP`
	Section that displays help when the user starts the batch file with a /? or a ? as the first replaceable parameter.

`:END`	Label marking the end of the batch file.

7-2 LOTUS1.BAT is a modified version of LOTUS.BAT that won't let you load Lotus under a second copy of COMMAND.COM. By making similar modifications to all your batch files that start applications, you avoid the problem of loading a second application while the first is in memory.

Batch File Line	Explanation
`@ECHO OFF`	Turn command-echoing off.

`REM NAME:      LOTUS1.BAT`
`REM PURPOSE: Start Lotus But`
`REM          Not As 2nd Program`
`REM VERSION: 1.00`
`REM DATE:     April 15, 1991`
	Remark giving the name of the batch file.

`IF (%1)==(/?) GOTO HELP` `IF (%1)==(?)  GOTO HELP`	If the user starts the batch file with a request for help, jump to a section to display that help.
`EXIT`	If the user is running this batch file for the first time, this command has no effect. If the user runs this batch file to try and restart Lotus after shelling out of Lotus, it will return him to Lotus and cause the remainder of the batch file not to execute. If he uses this batch file to start Lotus while shelled out of another program (Escape Library Run in Microsoft Word, for example) then this batch file will return him to that application and causes the remainder of the batch file not to execute.
`C:`	Make sure the computer is logged onto the C drive.
`CD\123`	Change to the Lotus subdirectory.
`PROMPT=Type EXIT to return to` `    Lotus$_$p$g`	Change the prompt so if a user shells out of Lotus (using the /System command) he will know that Lotus is still loaded into memory and will have a visual reminder of how to return to Lotus.
`123`	Start Lotus.
`PROMPT=$p$g`	Reset the prompt once the user exits Lotus.
`GOTO END`	Exit the batch file.

Batch File Line	Explanation
:HELP ECHO Demonstration Batch File ECHO That Starts Lotus And ECHO Changes The Prompt So ECHO Users Who Shell Out Of ECHO Lotus Will Be Reminded ECHO Of That ECHO It Also Prevents Lotus ECHO From Being Loaded While ECHO You Are Shelled Out Of ECHO Another Program GOTO END :END_HELP	Section that displays help when the user starts the batch file with a /? or a ? as the first replaceable parameter.
:END	Label marking the end of the batch file.

7-3 STARTDATA.BAT activates different setups for an application program by means of a batch file.

Batch File Line	Explanation
@ECHO OFF	Turn command-echoing off.
REM NAME: STARTDATA.BAT REM PURPOSE: Allow Two Users To REM Access Database REM VERSION: 1.00 REM DATE: April 15, 1991	Documentation remark.
IF (%1)==(/?) GOTO HELP IF (%1)==(?) GOTO HELP	If the user starts the batch file with a request for help, jump to a section to display that help.
IF (%1)==() GOTO NOTHING	If the user didn't enter a replaceable parameter, jump to an error-handling section.
IF %1==DAVID GOTO OK IF %1==David GOTO OK IF %1==david GOTO OK IF %1==RONNY GOTO OK IF %1==Ronny GOTO OK IF %1==ronny GOTO OK GOTO ERROR	David and Ronny are the only acceptable inputs to the batch file. These lines test for the more common capitalizations and assume that anything that doesn't match them is an error.
:NOTHING	Beginning of section to handle the error of the user not entering his name.
ECHO Enter Your Name After ECHO The STARTDAT Command	Tell the user what happened.
GOTO END :END_NOTHING	Exit the batch file.

Batch File Line	Explanation
`:ERROR`	Beginning of section to handle an invalid name.
`ECHO Invalid User Name` `ECHO Try Again Or See Manager`	Tell the user what happened.
`GOTO END` `:END_ERROR`	Exit the batch file.
`:OK`	Section marking the beginning of the section of the batch file that handles running the application.
`COPY %1.INF MENU.INF`	Two different files exist with setup information, DAVID.INF and RONNY.INF. This line copies the right one for the current user to the name MENU.INF, which the program requires to run.
`MENU /1200/5551212`	This line starts the program. It tells the program the computer has a 1200-baud modem and the phone number to call is 555-1212.
`GOTO END` `:END_OK`	Exit the batch file.

`:HELP`
`ECHO This Batch File Allows Ronny`
`ECHO Or David To Access Remote`
`ECHO Database`
`BATCMD SL`
`ECHO Enter STARTDAT RONNY/DAVID`
`ECHO To Start The Database`
`GOTO END`
`:END_HELP`
	Section that displays help when the user starts the batch file with a /? or a ? as the first replaceable parameter.

`:END`	Label marking the end of the batch file.

7-4 STARTWORD.BAT activates different setups for Microsoft Word by means of a batch file. After exiting Word, the settings are saved for later reuse.

Batch File Line	Explanation
`@ECHO OFF`	Turn command-echoing off.

`REM NAME:      STARTWORD.BAT`
`REM PURPOSE: Allow Two Users To Store`
`REM          Custom Word Configuration`
`REM VERSION: 1.00`
`REM DATE:    April 15, 1991`
	Documentation remarks.

`IF (%1)==(/?) GOTO HELP` `IF (%1)==(?)  GOTO HELP`	If the user starts the batch file with a request for help, jump to a section to display that help.

Batch File Line	Explanation

```IF (%1)==() GOTO NOTHING```
```IF %1==DAVID GOTO OK```
```IF %1==David GOTO OK```
```IF %1==david GOTO OK```
```IF %1==RONNY GOTO OK```
```IF %1==Ronny GOTO OK```
```IF %1==ronny GOTO OK```
```GOTO ERROR```
	David and Ronny are the only acceptable inputs to the batch file. These lines test for the more common capitalizations and assume that anything that doesn't match them is an error.

```:NOTHING```	Beginning of section to handle the error of the user not entering his name.
```ECHO Enter Your Name After``` ```ECHO The STARTWOR Command```	Tell the user what happened.
```GOTO END``` ```:END_NOTHING```	Exit the batch file.
```:ERROR```	Beginning of section to handle an invalid name.
```ECHO Invalid User Name``` ```ECHO Try Again Or See System Manager```	Tell the user what happened.
```GOTO END``` ```END_ERROR```	Exit the batch file.
```:OK```	Beginning of the section to run Word.
```CD\WORD```	Change to the Word subdirectory.
```COPY %1.INI MW.INI```	Two different files exist with setup information, DAVID.INI and RONNY.INI. This line copies the right one for the current user to the name MENU.INF, which the program requires to run.
```WORD/L %2```	This line starts Microsoft Word. The /L is required to force Word to use some of the information in MW.INI. The %2 allows the user to enter a file on the command line to edit.
```COPY MW.INI %1.INI```	The user can make changes to the defaults while in Word (these are stored in MW.INI), so the contents of MW.INI could be different now than when the application started. This copies the new defaults to the storage file under the user's name.

Batch File Line	Explanation
GOTO END :END_OK	Exit the batch file.
:HELP ECHO This Batch File Allows Ronny ECHO Or David To Use Microsoft Word BATCMD SL ECHO Enter STARTWOR RONNY/DAVID ECHO To Start The Program GOTO END :END_HELP	Section that displays help when the user starts the batch file with a /? or a ? as the first replaceable parameter.
:END	Label marking the end of the batch file.

7-5 OCCASION.BAT runs a backup once for every ten times the computer is rebooted.

Batch File Line	Explanation
@ECHO OFF	Turn command-echoing off.
REM NAME: OCCASION.BAT REM PURPOSE: Run Programs Occasionally REM VERSION: 1.00 REM DATE: April 15, 1991	Documentation remarks.
IF (%1)==(/?) GOTO HELP IF (%1)==(?) GOTO HELP	If the user starts the batch file with a request for help, jump to a section to display that help.
FOR %%J IN (00 01 02 03 04 05 06 07 08 09) DO IF EXIST COUNT.%%J GOTO %%J	This batch file uses a zero-length counter file called COUNT.00, COUNT.01, and so on to keep track of the last time it ran. This FOR loop figures out which version of the counter exits and jumps to the appropriate place in the batch file.
GOTO NOFILE	If all the above tests fail, then the counter file doesn't exist. This command causes the batch file to jump to a section to handle that.
:00	This section handles the situation where COUNT.00 exists--so none of the other versions exists.
REM All Work Done Here	Documentation remark.
BACKUP C:\ A:	The command performs a full backup.

Batch File Line	Explanation
`REN COUNT.00 COUNT.01`	Increments the counter by one by changing the name of the counter file.
`GOTO END` `:END_00`	Exits the batch file.
`:01`	This section handles the situation where COUNT.01 exists.
`REN COUNT.01 COUNT.02`	Increments the counter by one. Because the batch file performs a backup only when the counter is named COUNT.00, there's nothing else to do in this section.
`GOTO END` `:END_01`	Exit the batch file.

`:02`
`REN COUNT.02 COUNT.03`
`GOTO END`
`:END_02`
	This section handles the situation where the counter is named COUNT.02.

`:03`
`REN COUNT.03 COUNT.04`
`GOTO END`
`:END_03`
	This section handles the situation where the counter is named COUNT.03.

`:04`
`REN COUNT.04 COUNT.05`
`GOTO END`
`:END_04`
	This section handles the situation where the counter is named COUNT.04.

`:05`
`REN COUNT.05 COUNT.06`
`GOTO END`
`:END_05`
	This section handles the situation where the counter is named COUNT.05.

`:06`
`REN COUNT.06 COUNT.07`
`GOTO END`
`:END_06`
	This section handles the situation where the counter is named COUNT.06.

`:07`
`REN COUNT.07 COUNT.08`
`GOTO END`
`:END_07`
	This section handles the situation where the counter is named COUNT.07.

`:08`
`REN COUNT.08 COUNT.09`
`GOTO END`
`:END_08`
	This section handles the situation where the counter is named COUNT.08.

`:09`
`REN COUNT.09 COUNT.00`
`GOTO END`
`:END_09`
	This section handles the situation where the counter is named COUNT.09.

Batch File Line	Explanation
`:NOFILE`	Label marking the beginning of the section that handles a missing counter file.
`REM Restore Counter File` `REM Then Restart Process`	Documentation remark.
`TYPE NOFILE > COUNT.00`	Create the zero-length counter file.
`GOTO 00` `:END_NOFILE`	Jump to the section of the batch file that performs the backup.

`:HELP`
`ECHO OCCASION.BAT Demonstrates How`
`ECHO Commands Can Be Run Occasionally`
`ECHO By Performing A Backup Every`
`ECHO Tenth Time It Is Run`
`GOTO END`
`:END_HELP`
	Section that displays help when the user starts the batch file with a /? or a ? as the first replaceable parameter.

`:END`	Label marking the end of the batch file.

7-6 When you want to cycle through more than a few rebootings, the technique in CNTBOOTS .BAT works better than the technique in OCCASION.BAT.

Batch File Line	Explanation
`@ECHO OFF`	Turn command-echoing off.

`REM NAME:     CNTBOOTS.BAT`
`REM PURPOSE: Count Bootings &`
`          Perform Tasks Based On`
`          Boot Count`
`REM VERSION: 2.00`
`REM DATE:    December 24, 1991`
	Documentation remarks.

`IF (%1)==(/?) GOTO HELP` `IF (%1)==(?)  GOTO HELP`	If the user starts the batch file with a request for help, jump to a section to display that help.
`SET MATH=0`	Create a counter variable to be used by Batcmd.
`:LOOPTOP`	Label marking the top of the loop.
`BATCMD AD`	Increase the counter variable by one.
`IF EXIST CNTBOOTS.%MATH% SET` `      BOOTCOUNT=%MATH%`	If the zero-length file exists with the extension of the current counter variable, store that count to a second variable.
`IF EXIST CNTBOOTS.%MATH% GOTO` `      OUTLOOP`	Once the counter variable exists, exit the loop.

Batch File Line	Explanation
`IF %MATH%==50 GOTO NOFILE`	If the counter makes it to fifty without encountering a match, exit the loop and jump to a special section to handle this.
`GOTO LOOPTOP` `:END_LOOPTOP`	Continue looping.
`:OUTLOOP`	Label marking the beginning of the section that handles incrementing the counter when it's successfully identified.
`BATCMD AD`	Increase the MATH variable by one to find the next value of the counter.
`REN CNTBOOTS.%BOOTCOUNT%` `    CNTBOOTS.%MATH%`	Change the extension of the counter zero-length file from the old value to the new value.
`IF %MATH%==51 REN CNTBOOTS.51` `    CNTBOOTS.1`	If the counter has increased to 51, drop its value to 1.
`GOTO WORK` `:END_OUTLOOP`	Once the counter has been identified and incremented, jump to the section of the batch file that operates based on this counter.
`:NOFILE`	Label marking the beginning of the section that deals with not finding a counter file.
`TYPE NOFILE > CNTBOOTS.1`	Create a zero-length file with a counter value of one, which would be the value of the counter after zero is increased by one.
`SET BOOTCOUNT=0`	Set the BOOTCOUNT memory variable to represent the counter's current value of zero.
`GOTO WORK` `:END_NOFILE`	Jump to the working section of the batch file.
`:WORK`	Label marking the section of the batch file that works based on the counter value.
`IF %BOOTCOUNT%==10 GOTO INCREMENT`	If the counter is 10, perform an incremental backup.
`IF %BOOTCOUNT%==20 GOTO INCREMENT`	If the counter is 20, perform an incremental backup.

Batch File Line	Explanation
`IF %BOOTCOUNT%==25 GOTO DISKTEST`	If the counter is 25, perform a disk test.
`IF %BOOTCOUNT%==30 GOTO INCREMENT`	If the counter is 30, perform an incremental backup.
`IF %BOOTCOUNT%==40 GOTO INCREMENT`	If the counter is 40, perform an incremental backup.
`IF %BOOTCOUNT%==50 GOTO FULL`	If the counter is 50, perform a full backup.
`GOTO END` `:END_WORK`	If the counter isn't equal to one of these six values, exit the batch file without doing anything.

`:INCREMENT`
`ECHO Perform Incremental Backup Here`
`GOTO END`
`:END_INCREMENT`
	Section that performs an incremental backup. The batch file has been disabled, so it acknowledges only that it's time to perform the incremental backup.

`:FULL`
`ECHO Perform Full Backup Here`
`GOTO DISKTEST`
`:END_FULL`
	Section that performs a full backup. The batch file has been disabled, so it acknowledges only that it's time to perform the full backup. Because the disk is to be tested every 25 counters and 50 is in that scheme, jump to the section to perform the disk test.

`:DISKTEST`
`CHKDSK/F`
`ECHO Run Other Disk Test Program`
`Here`
`GOTO END`
`:END_DISKTEST`
	Section that performs the disk test. The batch file has been disabled, so it acknowledges only that it's time to perform the disk test.

`:HELP`
`ECHO CNTBOOTS.BAT Is A Demonstration`
`ECHO Batch File That "Occasionally"`
`ECHO Performs An Incremental And`
`ECHO Full Backup, As Well As A`
`ECHO Disk Test`
`GOTO END`
`:END_HELP`
	Section that displays help when the user starts the batch file with a /? or a ? as the first replaceable parameter.

`:END`	Label marking the end of the batch file.

7-7 VERSION.BAT helps you write batch files that will run smoothly under different versions of DOS.

Batch File Line	Explanation
`ECHO OFF`	Turn command-echoing off. This batch file is designed to run under both pre- and post-DOS 3.3, so it doesn't use the @ECHO OFF command.

`REM NAME:     VERSION.BAT`
`REM PURPOSE: Deal With Different`
`           DOS Versions`
`REM VERSION: 1.00`
`REM DATE:    December 20, 1991`
	Documentation remarks.

`IF (%1)==(/?) GOTO HELP` `IF (%1)==(?)  GOTO HELP`	If the user starts the batch file with a request for help, jump to a section to display that help.
`IF (%1)==(XYZ123ABC) GOTO CALLED`	VERSION.BAT calls itself as a subroutine. When it does this, it uses the unlikely replaceable parameter of XYZ123ABC to tell VERSION.BAT to run as a subroutine.
`SET VERSION=2.0`	Start off assuming it's running on a pre-DOS 3.3 version, which is labeled DOS 2.0.
`SET @=`	Under pre-DOS 3.3 versions this command doesn't work, so set the environmental variable to nul.
`SET CALL=%COMSPEC% /C`	Under pre-DOS 3.3 versions, a batch file must call another batch file by loading a second copy of COMMAND.COM if the calling batch file needs to regain control.
`CALL VERSION.BAT XYZ123ABC`	VERSION.BAT tries to call itself as a subroutine. Under pre-DOS 3.3 version CALL is not a valid batch command, so it will try to find a program called CALL.EXE or CALL.COM to run. When it fails to find one, it will display a *Bad command or file name* error message. VERSION.BAT is never called as a subroutine in this case, so the contents of the above environmental variables are never changed.
`GOTO END`	Exit the batch file.
`:CALLED`	Label marking the portion of the batch file that serves as the subroutine.

Batch File Line	Explanation

`SET VERSION=3.3`
`SET @=@`
`SET CALL=CALL`
	If the batch file reaches this point then it's running under a post-DOS 3.3 version, so the environmental variable is set accordingly.

`GOTO END` `:END_CALLED`	Exit the subroutine.

`:HELP`
`ECHO VERSION.BAT Creates The`
`ECHO Memory Variables @, CALL,`
`ECHO And VERSION And Enters`
`ECHO Different Values Depending`
`ECHO On The DOS Version`
`GOTO END`
`:END_HELP`
	Section that displays help when the user starts the batch file with a /? or a ? as the first replaceable parameter.

`:END`	Label marking the end of the batch file.

8

Working with subdirectories

This chapter will provide you with different ways to control and manipulate subdirectories.

Changing subdirectories

Many users have a very complex directory structure, several levels deep. They often need to leave one subdirectory to check something in another subdirectory and later switch back, and are looking for a way to automate this. There are actually a couple of different ways to attack this problem. The best way is to use a quick directory changing program like NCD in the Norton Utilities or the shareware program, QC, from Steven Flores.

With these types of programs, you simply enter the subdirectory name and they'll specify the entire path of that subdirectory for you. Their advantage over DOS is that you don't have to enter the entire path every time you want to change subdirectories.

A custom batch file for each subdirectory

If you need or want to tackle the problem with batch files, you have a couple of alternatives. If you're always switching between just a couple of subdirectories, you can write a custom batch file to change to each subdirectory. For example, you could write a batch file called 0-9.BAT, containing the single command:

```
CD \ D \ LOTUSFIG \ 0-9
```

to change to that subdirectory. I use this method to change back to my home directory on the network at the office, because entering CD \ D \ USERS \ MKTEVAL \ RICHARDS is a lot to type, and I issue that command a lot.

Returning home

Of course, this can become a complex solution if you have a lot of subdirectories to change between. You can write a batch file to partially solve this problem. This batch file will mark the current directory as home and build a second batch file to always return you to that home directory. The next time you run this batch file, it will create a new home directory and a new batch file to put you there.

This batch file, RETURN.BAT, is shown in Fig. 8-1. It first copies a file called RETURN to the batch file named RETURNTO.BAT. RETURN contains a single line with CD ^z, where ^z is an end-of-file marker. Because there's no return in the file, when the next line of RETURN.BAT pipes in the subdirectory it gets added to the same line as the CD. The result is a line similar to:

CD C: \ D \ LOTUSFIG \ 0-9

Because the batch file must be in a subdirectory that's in the path to work, RETURN.BAT is configured to always use the C: \ BAT subdirectory. For that reason, every time you run RETURN.BAT it overwrites RETURNTO.BAT with a new version. You can expand RETURN.BAT to handle multiple subdirectories by using a replaceable parameter on the command line and creating RETURN1.BAT, RETURN2.BAT, and so on.

If you don't want to create a custom batch file, you can use the batch file RETURN2 .BAT in Fig. 8-2. Because there's no way to pipe the current subdirectory into the environment, this batch file requires you to manually issue the command at the C: prompt:

SET HOME = C: \ D \ LOTUSFIG \ 0-9

to tell RETURN2.BAT which subdirectory is home. The only real drawback to RETURN2.BAT is that you have to manually type the home subdirectory into the environment. You can, however, avoid that—as shown in RETURN3.BAT in Fig. 8-3. Using RETURN3.BAT to change to a subdirectory (which you have to do anyway) records that subdirectory into the environment automatically. When you use RETURN3.BAT without a subdirectory, it changes back to the last subdirectory you changed to, using RETURN3 .BAT with a subdirectory name. Like RETURN1.BAT, you can modify RETURN3.BAT to record multiple home subdirectories in the environment.

Quick changes

Another approach is to write a batch file that duplicates much of the function of the NCD program within the batch file itself. To do that, you need a batch file where you enter an abbreviation of the subdirectory name on the command line and it changes to that subdirectory. RCD.BAT (short for Ronny's change directory) in Fig. 8-4 does just that. It's not as advanced as NCD because you have to manually program in every subdirectory name you want to use and the full path to that subdirectory. However, it does allow you to use nicknames where NCD doesn't. Unless you use NCD to change to a lot of subdirectories or if you frequently update your hard disk structure, RCD.BAT should work almost as well for you as NCD.

Personally, I've started using RCD.BAT a lot even though I have (and use) NCD. Symantec has expanded the functions of NCD so much that its requires much more memory than it used to. That isn't a problem when running NCD directly from DOS. It does, however, prevent NCD from running when I shell out of a program to quickly check something. In those cases, the original program takes up so much memory that there isn't enough left for the expanded version of NCD to work. In those cases, I use RCD.

Quick change with a partial filename

One of the advantages of NCD is you can change to a subdirectory when you remember only a fragment of its name, no matter how deeply nested that subdirectory is. For example, on my system, I can change to the N: \ D \ USERS \ MKTEVAL \ RICHARDS \ BALER subdirectory with a simple NCD BALE command.

This same feature is also available in a batch file. CHKDSKCD.BAT in Fig. 8-5 performs the same task. It runs the command CHKDSK/V, which displays all the subdirectories and pipes the information to a FIND filter, which searches for the text you specify. If it finds a match, it pipes that information to C: \ BAT \ JUNK.BAT. Each line of this file is in the format DIRECTORY *subdirectory*, where *subdirectory* matches your search specification. The batch file then runs JUNK.BAT, which immediately runs DIRECTOR.BAT in Fig. 8-6, while passing it the name of the subdirectory to change to.

Several notes are in order. First, because JUNK.BAT runs DIRECTOR.BAT without the CALL command, control doesn't return to JUNK.BAT, so DIRECTOR.BAT always changes to the first subdirectory that matches the search criteria. Second, with NCD you can add a drive letter to the command, so NCD N:Baler would be a valid command if you had another drive currently specified. CHKDSKCD.BAT works only on the current drive. Finally, NCD requires that you begin entering text from the beginning, so NCD LER wouldn't find the N: \ D \ USERS \ MKTEVAL \ RICHARDS \ BALER subdirectory. CHKDSKCD.BAT doesn't suffer from this limitation, so CHKDSKCD LER would find the N: \ D \ USERS \ MKTEVAL \ RICHARDS \ BALER subdirectory if it were the first subdirectory containing the LER text string.

Quick change with no backslashes

Changing subdirectories on a laptop is a real pain! Every laptop or notebook computer I've ever used has the backslash key in a different spot. The only thing they ever have in common is that it's always some out-of-the-way spot. Even on a desktop computer with a standard keyboard, there's simply no reason to have to type a backslash after every subdirectory, and a colon after drive letters.

QCD.BAT in Fig. 8-7 allows you to type in drive letters and subdirectories without the colons and backslashes. To use, enter:

QCD *drive subdirectory1 subdirectory2, etc.*

If the first replaceable parameter is an A−D, QCD adds a colon after it and changes to that drive. That means you have to be sneaky to change to a subdirectory like C: \ A because if you entered QCD A, it would assume you wanted to change to the A drive. When the first subdirectory is a single-letter name that could be mistaken for a drive, just enter both the drive and subdirectory. So, to change to C: \ A, just enter QCD C A.

When entering subdirectories, you must enter the full path from the root directory. So, to change to the \ PENDING \ CONTRACT \ BILL subdirectory, you would enter QCD PENDING CONTRACT BILL. QCD doesn't test to make sure a subdirectory exists, it just tries to change to it. If you're interested, you might want to add a bit of logic to this batch file.

Quick change to a new subdirectory

When I'm working with files, I often want to create a new subdirectory, change to it, and then move files into it. Sometimes I create the subdirectory but forget to change to it before I start copying files. When I do that, I end up with a mess. RMD.BAT (short for Ronny's make directory) in Fig. 8-8 corrects this problem by automatically creating a subdirectory and then changing to it.

Finding files

While not as flexible as some commercial programs, the program Attrib lets you write a fast file-searching batch file if you have DOS 3.3 or later. DOS 3.0 introduced Attrib (short for attribute) to change the archive and read-only status of files. The original version worked only in the current subdirectory. With DOS 3.3, however, it was upgraded to work across subdirectories using a /s switch.

Running Attrib without any switches to change the status of the archive and read-only bits will cause it to list all the files it finds, and the /s switch will cause it to search subdirectories. Combining these two will cause it to find files. FASTFIND.BAT in Fig. 8-9 is the resulting batch file.

Summary

- Using a different batch file for each subdirectory is a quick way to change between a couple of subdirectories.
- You can use RETURN.BAT and RETURNTO.BAT to store the name of the current subdirectory and easily change back to it.
- RETURN2.BAT can store the name of a subdirectory in the environment and later return you to that subdirectory.
- When RETURN3.BAT is used to change to a subdirectory, it stores the name of that subdirectory in the environment for quick return to that subdirectory.
- RCD.BAT can quickly change to any subdirectory you have programmed into it.
- CHKDSKCD.BAT will scan the current hard disk for the subdirectory you specify. If it finds it, it will change to it.
- QCD.BAT can quickly change drives and subdirectories without a colon or back-slash.
- RMD.BAT creates a subdirectory and then automatically changes to it.
- FASTFIND.BAT can quickly locate a file or files on your hard disk.

8-1 RETURN.BAT constructs a batch file to return you to a specific subdirectory.

Batch File Line	Explanation
`@ECHO OFF`	Turn command-echoing off.

`REM NAME:     RETURN.BAT`
`REM PURPOSE: Return To A Subdirectory`
`REM VERSION: 1.00`
`REM DATE:    April 15, 1991`
	Documentation remarks.

Batch File Line	Explanation
`IF (%1)==(/?) GOTO HELP` `IF (%1)==(?)  GOTO HELP`	If the user starts the batch file with a request for help, jump to a section to display that help.
`COPY C:\BAT\RETURN C:\BAT\RETURNTO.BAT`	Copy the file RETURN to the file RETURNTO.BAT. RETURN contains the line CD\ and nothing more.
`CD >> C:\BAT\RETURNTO.BAT`	Pipe the current subdirectory to RETURNTO.BAT. If the current subdirectory were \BAT, the last two lines would result in RETURNTO.BAT containing the line CD\BAT.
`GOTO END`	Exit the batch file.

`:HELP`
`ECHO This Batch File Creates Another`
`ECHO Batch File Called RETURNTO.BAT`
`ECHO That Will Return To The`
`ECHO Subdirectory Automatically`
`GOTO END`
`:END_HELP`
	Section that displays help when the user starts the batch file with a /? or a ? as the first replaceable parameter.

`:END`	Label marking the end of the batch file.

8-2 RETURN2.BAT returns you to a subdirectory stored in the environment.

Batch File Line	Explanation
`@ECHO OFF`	Turn command-echoing off.

`REM NAME:    RETURN2.BAT`
`REM PURPOSE: Change To Directory`
`REM          In Environment`
`REM VERSION: 1.00`
`REM DATE:    January 3, 1991`
	Documentation remarks.

`IF (%1)==(/?) GOTO HELP` `IF (%1)==(?)  GOTO HELP`	If the user starts the batch file with a request for help, jump to a section to display that help.
`CD %HOME%`	Change to the subdirectory stored in the environmental variable HOME.
`GOTO END`	Exit the batch file.

Batch File Line	Explanation

`:HOME`
`ECHO Changes To The Subdirectory`
`ECHO Stored In The Environment`
`ECHO Under The Name HOME`
`GOTO END`
`:END_HOME`
	Section that displays help when the user starts the batch file with a /? or a ? as the first replaceable parameter.

`:END`	Label marking the end of the batch file.

8-3   RETURN3.BAT lets you not enter the home subdirectory into the environment by recording it when you originally change to the home subdirectory.

Batch File Line	Explanation
`@ECHO OFF`	Turn command-echoing off.

`REM NAME:     RETURN3.BAT`
`REM PURPOSE: Change To & Return`
`REM         To A Subdirectory`
`REM VERSION: 1.00`
`REM DATE:    April 15, 1991`
	Documentation remark.

`IF (%1)==(/?) GOTO HELP` `IF (%1)==(?)  GOTO HELP`	If the user starts the batch file with a request for help, jump to a section to display that help.
`IF (%1)==() GOTO GOHOME`	If the user did not enter a subdirectory on the command line, then jump to a section that changes to the subdirectory currently stored in an environmental variable.
`CD\%1`	Change to the subdirectory entered on the command line.
`SET HOME=%1`	Store the subdirectory entered on the command line in the environmental variable HOME so the batch file can use it again later.
`GOTO END`	Exit the batch file.
`:GOHOME`	Label marking the beginning of the section to change subdirectories.
`CD %HOME%`	Change to the subdirectory the batch file stored earlier in the environmental variable HOME.
`GOTO END`	Exit the batch file.

Batch File Line	Explanation

`:HELP`
`ECHO RETURN3 Subdirectory`
`ECHO Stores That Subdirectory`
`ECHO In The Environment And`
`ECHO Changes To It`
`BATCMD SL`
`ECHO Entering RETURN3 By Itself`
`ECHO Changes Back To The Last`
`ECHO Subdirectory Stored In`
`ECHO The Environment`
`GOTO END`
`:END_HELP`
	Section that displays help when the user starts the batch file with a /? or a ? as the first replaceable parameter.

`:END`	Label marking the end of the batch file.

8-4 RCD.BAT duplicates much of the function of the Norton Utilities' NCD program.

Batch File Line	Explanation
`@ECHO OFF`	Turn command echoing.

`REM NAME:     RCD.BAT`
`REM PURPOSE: Ronny's Change Directory`
`REM VERSION: 1.00`
`REM DATE:    November 15, 1991`
	Documentation remarks.

`IF (%1)==(/?) GOTO HELP` `IF (%1)==(?)  GOTO HELP`	If the user starts the batch file with a request for help, jump to a section to display that help.

`ECHO If You See The Error Message`
`ECHO Label Not Found`
`ECHO Then You Selected A Subdirectory`
`ECHO Not Stored In RCD.BAT`
	Tell the user what will happen if he enters an invalid label or no label at all.

`GOTO %1`	Jump to the label matching the first replaceable parameter.
`:BAT`	Label marking the section to jump to the batch file subdirectory.
`C:`	Change to the right drive.
`CD\BAT`	Change to the right subdirectory.
`GOTO END` `:END_BAT`	Exit the batch file.

`:SYSLIB`
`:DOS`
`C:`
`CD\SYSLIB`
`GOTO END`
`:END_SYSLIB`
	Section of the batch file that handles jumping to the DOS subdirectory. Note that the batch file can have as many of these sections as you need to handle all of the subdirectories you routinely change between.

Batch File Line	Explanation
Other subdirectories are handled in a similar fashion.	

`:HELP`
`ECHO RCD Nickname`
`ECHO Changes To That Subdirectory`
`BATCMD SL`
`ECHO RCD.BAT Must Be Preconfigured`
`ECHO To Use The Nickname`
`GOTO END`
`:END_HELP`
	Section that displays help when the user starts the batch file with a /? or a ? as the first replaceable parameter.

`:END`	Label marking the end of the batch file.

8-5 CHKDSKCD.BAT runs CHKDSK/V and searches for the text you enter. It passes that information to DIRECTOR.BAT using C: \ BAT \ JUNK.BAT as a temporary file.

Batch File Line	Explanation
`@ECHO OFF`	Turn command-echoing off.
`GOTO TOP`	Skip over the documentation remarks that follow.

`NAME:     CHKDSKCD.BAT`
`PURPOSE: Use Chkdsk To Change Subdirectory`
`VERSION: 1.00`
`DATE:     December 31, 1991`
	Documentation remarks.

`:TOP`	Label used to jump over the nonexecuting documentation remarks.
`IF (%1)==(/?) GOTO HELP` `IF (%1)==(?)  GOTO HELP`	If the user starts the batch file with a request for help, jump to a section to display that help.
`IF (%1)==()   GOTO NOTHING`	If the user doesn't enter any text to search for, the batch file can't run, so jump to an error-handling routine.
`CHKDSK /V	FIND "Directory"	FIND "%1" /I` ` > C:\BAT\JUNK.BAT`	Run CHKDSK in the verbose mode to display all the subdirectories. Pipe this to the FIND filter to search for the requested text and pipe this to a batch file.

Batch File Line	Explanation
`C:\BAT\JUNK.BAT`	Run the batch file. If the text is found, it will start off with the word *DIRECTORY*, so when JUNK.BAT is run it will immediately run DIRECTOR.BAT.
`GOTO END`	Control never returns to this batch file so this line is never executed. It's just in here as a safety feature.

`:NOTHING`
`ECHO Subdirectory To Change To`
`ECHO Not Specified On Command Line`
`GOTO END`
`:END_NOTHING`
	Section to display an error message and exit if the user fails to enter text to search for.

`:HELP`
`ECHO CHKDSKCD.BAT Uses CHKDSK To`
`ECHO Display All The Subdirectories`
`ECHO Then Uses FIND To Find The`
`ECHO Text You Specify On The Command`
`ECHO Line And Then Runs DIRECTOR.BAT`
`ECHO To Change To That Subdirectory`
`GOTO END`
`:END_HELP`
	Section that displays help when the user starts the batch file with a /? or a ? as the first replaceable parameter.

`:END`	Label marking the end of the batch file.

8-6 DIRECTOR.BAT changes to the subdirectory passed to it by CHKDSKCD.BAT.

Batch File Line	Explanation
`@ECHO OFF`	Turn command-echoing off.
`GOTO TOP`	Skip over the documentation remarks that follow.

`NAME:     DIRECTOR.BAT`
`PURPOSE: Change To Subdirectory`
`         When Called By CHKDSKCD.BAT`
`VERSION: 1.00`
`DATE:    December 31, 1991`
	Documentation remarks.

`:TOP`	Label used to jump over the nonexecuting documentation remarks.

Batch File Line	Explanation

`IF (%1)==(/?) GOTO HELP`
`IF (%1)==(?) GOTO HELP`
`IF (%1)==() GOTO HELP`
	If the user starts the batch file with a request for help, jump to a section to display that help. It also shows help if the user runs the batch file without any replaceable parameters because the batch file isn't designed to run from the command line.

`CD %1`	When the user runs CHKDSKCD.BAT, it pipes its results to C:\BAT\JUNK.BAT and then runs that batch file. JUNK.BAT contains the results of a search for text with the CHKDSK/V command as input. If a match is found, that line starts with *DIRECTORY,* followed by the name of the subdirectory. When JUNK.BAT is run, it runs this batch file and passes it the subdirectory to change to as a replaceable parameter.
`DEL C:\BAT\JUNK.BAT`	Delete the temporary batch file.
`GOTO END`	Exit the batch file.

`:HELP`
`ECHO DIRECTOR.BAT Is Designed To Be`
`ECHO Called By CHKDSKCD.BAT`
`ECHO **DO NOT RUN DIRECTLY**`
`GOTO END`
`:END_HELP`
	Section that displays help when the user starts the batch file with a /? or a ? as the first replaceable parameter.

`:END`	Label marking the end of the batch file.

8-7 QCD.BAT allows you to change drives without the colon and subdirectories without the backslash. It's especially useful on laptop and notebook computers.

Batch File Line	Explanation
`@ECHO OFF`	Turn command-echoing off.

`REM NAME:    QCD.BAT`
`REM PURPOSE: Speed Directory Changes`
`REM VERSION: 1.00`
`REM DATE:    December 20, 1991`
	Documentation remarks.

`IF (%1)==(/?) GOTO HELP` `IF (%1)==(?) GOTO HELP`	If the user starts the batch file with a request for help, jump to a section to display that help.

Batch File Line	Explanation
`SET DIR=NO`	Make sure the environmental variable used by the batch file starts off empty.
`IF (%1)==() GOTO ERROR1`	If the user failed to enter a drive or subdirectory to change to, jump to an error-handling section.
`FOR %%J IN (a A b B c C d D) DO` `    IF (%1)==(%%J) SET DIR=YES`	If the first replaceable parameter was A-D, assume it was a drive to change to and set a flag accordingly.
`IF %DIR%==NO GOTO SKIP`	If the drive-indicator flag wasn't set, skip the section to change to a different drive.
`%1:`	Because the first replaceable parameter is a letter A-D, add a colon to it and issue that as a command to change to that drive.
`SHIFT`	Shift to discard the drive letter as a replaceable parameter.
`IF (%1)==() GOTO END`	If the user didn't enter a subdirectory to go along with the drive letter, exit the batch file.
`:SKIP`	Label marking the beginning of the section to change subdirectories.
`SET DIR=`	Reset the environmental variable in case the user entered a drive letter.
`:TOPLOOP`	Label marking the top of a loop.
`SET DIR=%DIR%\%1`	Add a backslash and the subdirectory stored in the first replaceable parameter to the environmental variable containing the subdirectory to change to.
`SHIFT`	Discard the current replaceable parameter.
`IF NOT (%1)==() GOTO TOPLOOP`	If there are more replaceable parameters, continue looping.

File Line	Explanation
`%DIR%`	Change to the subdirectory stored in the environmental variable that was constructed. Interested users could add a test here to make sure that a subdirectory exists before changing to it.
`GOTO END` `:END_TOPLOOP`	Jump to the end of the batch file.

`:ERROR`
`ECHO No Drive / Subdirectory Specified`
`ECHO Use QCD {Drive} {Subdirectory 1}`
`     {Sub 2} {So On}`
`ECHO Without A Colon Or Backslash`
`GOTO END`
`:END_ERROR`
	Section that displays an error message if the user fails to enter a drive or subdirectory on the command line.

`:HELP`
`ECHO QCD.BAT Will Change Drives And`
`ECHO Subdirectories Without Entering`
`ECHO The Colon After The Drive Or The`
`ECHO Backslash Between The`
`ECHO Subdirectories`
`BATCMD SL`
`ECHO Enter: QCD {Drive} {Sub1} {Sub2}`
`GOTO END`
`:END_HELP`
	Section that displays help when the user starts the batch file with a /? or a ? as the first replaceable parameter.

`:END`	Label marking the end of the batch file.

8-8 RMD.BAT creates a subdirectory and then changes to it.

Batch File Line	Explanation
`@ECHO OFF`	Turn command-echoing off.

`REM NAME:     RMD.BAT`
`REM PURPOSE: Make & Change Subdirectory`
`REM VERSION: 1.00`
`REM DATE:    December 20, 1991`
	Documentation remarks.

`IF (%1)==(/?) GOTO HELP` `IF (%1)==(?)  GOTO HELP`	If the user starts the batch file with a request for help, jump to a section to display that help.
`IF (%1)==() GOTO ERROR`	If the user failed to enter the name of a subdirectory to create, jump to an error-handling section.

Batch File Line	Explanation
IF NOT (%2)==() GOTO ERROR	If the user entered two subdirectory names, jump to an error-handling section.
MD %1	Create the subdirectory.
CD %1	Change to the subdirectory.
GOTO END	Exit the batch file.
:ERROR ECHO Either You Failed To Enter ECHO A Subdirectory Name To Create ECHO Or You Entered Two Subdirectory ECHO Names While RMD Can Handle Just One GOTO END END_ERROR	Section to display error-messages when the user fails to enter a subdirectory name or enters two subdirectory names.
:HELP ECHO Entering: RMD Subdirectory ECHO Creates That Subdirectory And Then ECHO Changes To It GOTO END :END_HELP	Section that displays help when the user starts the batch file with a /? or a ? as the first replaceable parameter.
:END	Label marking the end of the batch file.

8-9 FASTFIND.BAT uses Attrib to create a very fast file-searching program—if you use DOS 3.3 or later.

Batch File Line	Explanation
@ECHO OFF	Turn command-echoing off.
REM NAME: FASTFIND.BAT REM PURPOSE: Find A File REM VERSION: 2.00 REM DATE: April 15, 1991	Documentation remarks.
IF (%1)==(/?) GOTO HELP IF (%1)==(?) GOTO HELP	If the user starts the batch file with a request for help, jump to a section to display that help.
IF (%1)==() GOTO NOFILE	Jump to an error-handling section if the user does not enter a filename on the command line.
GOTO FILE	Jump to a section to handle finding the file.
:NOFILE	Label marking the beginning of the section to handle the user not entering a filename.

Batch File Line	Explanation
ECHO No File Entered On Command Line ECHO Syntax Is C>FASTFIND file, ECHO Where file Is The File You ECHO Want To Find	Explain the problem to the user.
GOTO END :END_NOFILE	Exit the batch file.
:FILE	Label marking the beginning of the section that handles finding the file.
ATTRIB \%1 /S | MORE	Use the DOS ATTRIB program to list all the files matching the replaceable parameter and pipe to MORE to handle the display. Note that the backslash before the %1 forces ATTRIB to begin its search in the root directory and the /S forces it to search all the subdirectories. NOTE: This method requires DOS 3.3, as the /S option was not available earlier. Unlike the method used in FILEFIND.BAT of piping CHKDSK/V through a FIND filter, this method works with wildcards. It's also much faster.
GOTO END :END_FILE	Exit the batch file.
:HELP ECHO Entering: FASTFIND file ECHO Will Search The Entire Hard ECHO Disk Looking For That File ECHO Wildcards Are Allowed GOTO END :END_HELP	Section that displays help when the user starts the batch file with a /? or a ? as the first replaceable parameter.
:END	Label marking the end of the batch file.

9

DOS-based virus protection

With all the computer viruses making news today, it makes sense to protect yourself, and it makes especially good sense to take protection measures that don't require you to spend any money.

I'll leave it to others to explain "safe" computing; I'm only going to show you how DOS and batch files can help protect your computer and your work from damage. While the three steps outlined in this chapter don't offer as much protection as anti-viral software, they use DOS so they're free, and they're all fairly unobtrusive. That is, they rarely get in the way. That's important. If the anti-viral procedures you use generate too many false alarms, you're going to deactivate them. The three DOS-based anti-viral procedures are:

- Write-protecting your program files
- Hiding COMMAND.COM
- Testing your critical program files to make sure they haven't been altered

Writing program protection files

DOS has a program called Attrib that lets you mark files as read-only. While a smart virus can bypass this, it will stop some viruses. Not only that, it will protect you against accidently erasing program files yourself. The command to mark files as read-only is:

    ATTRIB file +r

Attrib accepts wildcards, so you can mark more than one file at a time. You can also use a /s switch to mark all the files in the current path. (This requires DOS 3.3 or later.) You should be able to mark all your program files (∗.EXE and ∗.COM) files as read-only without any problem. If you later need to erase a file, you can turn off the read-only setting with the following command:

    ATTRIB file −r

159

You might occasionally run into a minor problem when write protecting your program files. A few programs, like the original version of Sidekick, are *self-modifying*, meaning that the program modifies itself. Most programs, like Sidekick, modify themselves only when you install them or change an option. A few programs, like the Compute utility from *PC Magazine*, modify themselves every time they run. If a program is write protected, then its attempts to modify itself will fail.

For programs like Sidekick that modify themselves only during installation or option changes, you can leave them write protected and just turn the protection off manually before changing options. For programs like Compute that continually modify themselves, you can't write protect them at all.

Hiding COMMAND.COM

Viruses hit COMMAND.COM more than any other file, primarily because almost every computer has COMMAND.COM and runs it every time the computer runs. Because COMMAND.COM runs every time the computer boots, infecting it gives the virus the best opportunity to be running when other disks are available for infection.

Most computers have COMMAND.COM in the root directory, so some viruses won't take the time to look elsewhere. Beginning with DOS 3.0, you can put COMMAND .COM into any subdirectory you like. On my system, I have it in the \SYSLIB (system library) subdirectory. To move COMMAND.COM to another subdirectory, follow these easy steps:

1. Create a disk you can boot from in case you run into a problem. That way, you can boot from a floppy disk to correct the problem. The technique for doing this is explained in chapter 19. Be sure to read the portion of chapter 19 describing how to create a boot disk before you continue with this chapter.
2. Perform a backup of your hard disk. You probably won't need to, but frequent backups are a good idea and, if you do need the backup, you'll have it.
3. Copy COMMAND.COM to the subdirectory on your hard disk where you store your DOS files.
4. Leave a copy in the root directory as a sacrificial lamb. DOS won't be using that copy, so it doesn't matter if it becomes infected.
5. Add the following line to your CONFIG.SYS file:

    SHELL = C:\ *subdirectory* \ COMMAND.COM /P
6. Add the following line to your AUTOEXEC.BAT file:

    SET COMSPEC = C:\ *subdirectory* \ COMMAND.COM

In step 5, you must specify /P or DOS won't run your AUTOEXEC.BAT. If you need to expand the size of your environment, follow the directions in chapter 16.

This is by no means a fool-proof method. First, your COMSPEC variable points to your real COMMAND.COM, so any virus can check its contents and infect COM-MAND.COM no matter where it's located or what it's named. There is a second, though less obvious, problem. You have to make sure that your PATH statement doesn't point to the root directory or you could end up running the wrong copy of COMMAND.COM. For example, when Microsoft Word shells you to the DOS prompt it runs a second copy of the command processor. If your root directory is in your path and comes before the directory containing the used COMMAND.COM, Word will run the fake version. No matter how your path is set, Word will run the fake version if you're accessing the root directory when you issue this command.

Testing your critical files

You can test COMMAND.COM against a known good copy in a batch file. This requires that you have a known good copy stored under a different name available for testing. The COMP command won't work because it doesn't return a DOS errorlevel setting. Some versions of DOS include a program called FC that does return the errorlevel of one if the two files are different. The batch file in Fig. 9-1 shows how to perform this test. Notice that here the good copy can (and should) have a different name. You could add this to your AUTOEXEC.BAT file to test COMMAND.COM every time you boot. You could also run the comparison only occasionally, as explained in chapter 7.

This test isn't restricted to COMMAND.COM or even program files. You could have the batch file test any or all critical files on your hard disk. That would require a lot of room, however, because you need a second copy of any files you're testing. Also, this test takes about ten seconds on my 386/20, so doing more than one or two tests in the AUTOEXEC.BAT file could significantly slow down booting. For multiple tests, you might want to create a separate batch file that you run once a day or even once every few days.

DOS 5.0

While DOS 5.0 includes the FC program, its ability to report its results through the errorlevel has been removed. Therefore, the errorlevel testing in TESTCOMM.BAT won't work. Luckily, you can modify it to work under DOS 5.0.

The FC program under DOS 5.0 displays an *FC: no differences encountered* message when it tests two files that are identical. TESTCOM5.BAT in Fig. 9-2 first pipes the results of the FC comparison to the FIND filter. The FIND filter then searches for the *FC: no differences encountered* message and pipes the results of its search to a file. The resulting file is a zero-length file if the two tested files are different. If the files are the same, the resulting file contains text.

Next, TESTCOM5.BAT copies the resulting file to a new subdirectory and deletes the original copy. Next, it tries to copy the file back to the original location and deletes the copy in the alternative location. Two outcomes are possible, depending on the results of running FC:

No differences in the two versions If the two COMMAND.COM files are the same, the results file will contain text, so it's copied to the new location properly and copied back properly.

Differences in the two versions If the original FIND filter doesn't find the *FC: no differences encountered* message, the original results file is a zero-length file. As a result, it isn't copied to the new location and isn't available to copy back.

If the results file still exists after all this copying, the two versions of COMMAND.COM are the same, so TESTCOM5.BAT terminates. If it doesn't exist, the two versions were different and TESTCOM5.BAT displays an error message. Users running TESTCOM-5.BAT from their AUTOEXEC.BAT file might want to use Batcmd to set an errorlevel (Batcmd EX 255) so the AUTOEXEC.BAT can react to TESTCOM5.BAT finding a virus.

TESTCOM5.BAT requires two copies of COMMAND.COM, the one you boot from and a good copy. It also needs to freely create and delete a results file, and a location it can try and copy this results file to. Rather than hard-coding these values into TESTCOM-5.BAT, I've stored them in environmental variables so they can be used in all the commands. Users with a different configuration from mine can simply change the contents of the SOURCE, COPY, LOC1, and LOC2 environmental variables in TESTCOM5.BAT.

While TESTCOM5.BAT is designed to work only with DOS 5.0, users with any other version of DOS that comes with FC can easily modify TESTCOM5.BAT to work with their version of DOS. Simply compare two identical files, see what message FC displays, and change the message that the FIND filter in TESTCOM5.BAT searches for. In changing the message, pay particular attention to the capitalization because the batch file doesn't use the ignore-case FIND switch.

Summary

- Making COMMAND.COM and other program files read-only might stop a simple virus. It will certainly make it less likely that you'll accidently erase a program file.
- Hiding COMMAND.COM in a subdirectory and even changing its name might stop some viruses.
- You can compare COMMAND.COM and other mission-critical programs against good copies to see if they've been modified.

None of these methods are as good as running a good anti-viral software package, but users with only a low chance of infection might find these measures adequate.

9-1 TESTCOMM.BAT tests COMMAND.COM against a good copy.

Batch File Line	Explanation
`@ECHO OFF`	Turn command-echoing off.

`REM NAME:     TESTCOMM.BAT`
`REM PURPOSE: Verify COMMAND.COM Good`
`REM VERSION: 1.00`
`REM DATE:    April 15, 1991`
	Documentation remarks.

`IF (%1)==(/?) GOTO HELP` `IF (%1)==(?)  GOTO HELP`	If the user starts the batch file with a request for help, jump to a section to display that help.

Batch File Line	Explanation
REM Simple Anti-Viral Program REM To Test COMMAND.COM REM I Have COMMAND.COM Stored In REM My \SYSLIB Subdirectory Rather REM Than In My Root Directory REM There Is An Identical REM Copy In My \MISC Subdirectory REM Under The Name TEST.TXT	Documentation remarks.
FC \SYSLIB\COMMAND.COM \MISC\TEST.TXT	Run the program File Compare and test COMMAND.COM against a copy stored in a subdirectory under a different name.
IF ERRORLEVEL 1 GOTO VIRUS	If the FC program reports an error, jump to an error-handling routine.
GOTO END	If the batch file reaches this point there was no error, so exit the batch file.
:VIRUS	Label marking the beginning of the error-handling routine.
ECHO COMMAND.COM MODIFIED! ECHO Find Problem Before Continuing	Tell the user what happened.
PAUSE GOTO END :END_VIRUS	Pause execution of the batch file so the user will have time to read the message and exit the batch file.
:HELP ECHO TESTCOMM.BAT Compares The ECHO Existing COMMAND.COM With A ECHO Version Known To Be Good And ECHO Reports The Results BATCMD SL ECHO Requires A Version Of FC That ECHO Sets The Errorlevel GOTO END :END_HELP	Section that displays help when the user starts the batch file with a /? or a ? as the first replaceable parameter.
:END	Label marking the end of the batch file.

Batch File Line	Explanation
`@ECHO OFF`	Turn command-echoing off.
`GOTO TOP`	Skip over the documentation remarks that follow.

`NAME:      TESTCOM5.BAT`
`PURPOSE: Verify COMMAND.COM Good`
`         Under DOS 5 Without Errorlevel`
`VERSION: 1.00`
`DATE:      April 15, 1991`
 	
`Simple Anti-Viral Program`
`To Test COMMAND.COM`
`I Have COMMAND.COM Stored In`
`My \SYSLIB Subdirectory Rather`
`Than In My Root Directory`
`There Is An Identical`
`Copy In My \MISC Subdirectory`
`Under The Name TEST.TXT`
	Documentation remarks.

`:HELP`
`ECHO TESTCOM5.BAT Compares The Working`
`ECHO Copy Of COMMAND.COM With A Second`
`ECHO Copy To Make Sure COMMAND.COM Has`
`ECHO Not Been Modified`
`BATCMD SL`
`ECHO TESTCOM5.BAT Requires A Good`
`ECHO Copy Of COMMAND.COM To Be Stored`
`ECHO On The Hard Disk`
`BATCMD SL`
`ECHO It Also Requires Configuration`
`ECHO See The Text For Details`
`BATCMD SL`
`ECHO In Addition, TESTCOM5.BAT Works Only`
`ECHO With DOS 5.0`
`GOTO END`
`:END_HELP`
	Section that displays help when the user starts the batch file with a /? or a ? as the first replaceable parameter.

`:TOP`	Label used to jump over the nonexecuting documentation remarks.
`IF (%1)==(/?) GOTO HELP` `IF (%1)==(?)  GOTO HELP`	If the user starts the batch file with a request for help, jump to a section to display that help.

`SET SOURCE=C:\SYSLIB\COMMAND.COM`
`SET COPY=C:\MISC\TEST.TXT`
`SET LOC1=C:\COM_TEST`
`SET LOC2=C:\MISC\COM_TEST`
	Store the location of the primary and test copy of COMMAND.COM and the original and copy-to location of the file. The results are piped to an environmental variable so users can change these values easily.

Batch File Line	Explanation
IF NOT EXIST %SOURCE% ECHO Batch File Configured Improperly IF NOT EXIST %SOURCE% ECHO Source COMMAND.COM Missing IF NOT EXIST %SOURCE% GOTO END	If the source copy of COMMAND.COM doesn't exist, inform the user and exit the batch file.
IF NOT EXIST %COPY% ECHO Test Copy Of COMMAND.COM Missing IF NOT EXIST %COPY% GOTO END	If the good copy of COMMAND.COM doesn't exist, inform the user and exit the batch file.
IF EXIST %LOC2% DEL %LOC2%	If a copy of the piped file already exists, delete it.
FC %SOURCE% %COPY% | FIND "FC: no differences encountered" > %LOC1%	Perform the comparison using the DOS FC program and pipe the results to a file.
COPY %LOC1% %LOC2%	Copy the results file to a new location. If the copies did not match, then this is a zero-length file and won't copy.
DEL %LOC1%	Delete the original copy of the results file.
COPY %LOC2% %LOC1%	Try to copy the file back. This copy of the file will exist only if the file is not a zero-length file.
IF EXIST %LOC2% DEL %LOC2%	If this copy exists, delete it.
IF EXIST %LOC1% GOTO END	If this copy exits then all the copying was successful, so the file was not a zero-length file. That means that the FC: no differences encountered string was found, indicating the two versions of COMMAND.COM were the same, so exit the batch file.
GOTO VIRUS	Go to a section to tell the user that the versions weren't the same.
:VIRUS ECHO COMMAND.COM MODIFIED! ECHO Find Problem Before Continuing PAUSE :END_VIRUS	Explain the problem to the user and exit the batch file.

Batch File Line	Explanation
`:END`	Label marking the end of the batch file.

`IF EXIST %LOC1% DEL %LOC1%`
`SET SOURCE=`
`SET COPY=`
`SET LOC1=`
`SET LOC2=`
	Before exiting, delete the results file and reset the environmental variables.

10

Miscellaneous batch files

This chapter contains batch files to accomplish various functions.

A floppy-disk catalog

You can use batch files to catalog disks, and this method will work fairly well if you have only a few disks. If you have more than a few, however, you're probably better off buying one of the many shareware disk-cataloging programs because a batch-file method will prove to be fairly slow and lacks important error checking.

CATALOG.BAT in Fig. 10-1 creates the catalog. It makes sure that the user enters a drive name and then uses the FOR command to cycle through all the files in the root directory of that drive. As it echoes each filename, it adds two tab characters (^I) to make formatting with a word processor easier. It also adds an Alt−255 (which looks like a space) for use by the removal batch file.

CATALOG.BAT processes only the files in the root directory of a floppy disk. If you routinely create subdirectories on your floppy disks, you can use ATTRIB B: \ *.* /S to list all the files on your floppy disk—no matter how many subdirectories there are. However, this method gives you no way to add the name of the disk on the line after the name of the file. You could pipe that into the file first so it would be at the top of the list. Because REMOVE.BAT uses that name to delete lines, however, the removal portion of this batch file won't work if you use the ATTRIB command. As a result, this cataloging method is best reserved for those floppy disks without subdirectories.

REMOVE.BAT in Fig. 10-2 removes entries from the catalog. It also lacks much error checking, but it's impossible to add enough error checking with batch commands. The basic problem is using the FIND command to select lines to delete. If you start the batch file with the replaceable parameter OFFICE, it will delete not only the lines with the added label OFFICE, but also the file OFFICE.TAX and any other line containing the word OFFICE. For this reason, this cataloging method must be used with a great deal of care and frequent backups.

What little error checking is available is there because CATALOG.BAT also adds an Alt−255 (which looks like a space but is treated differently by DOS) to the front of the name. Because it's unlikely you would use Alt−255 in a filename, adding it to the name and having REMOVE.BAT automatically include it in the name search will reduce the change of unexpected matches.

Notice the /I switch being used with the FIND command. This is a recent addition to the command that causes it to ignore capitalization. However, due to a bug in DOS 5.0 it doesn't always work properly. If the text in the file has unusual capitalization, like *tEXt tO fInD*, a search for *text to find* with the /I switch will fail to find it.

As you can see, this floppy-disk cataloging system is fairly limited. It's limited to floppy disks without subdirectories. It can delete entries but it can't show you the entries it plans on deleting for you to approve first.

Stopping your batch files

Under some versions of DOS, your batch files can run into problems if they end with a label, e.g., :END, followed immediately by an end-of-file marker. Under DOS 3.3, if you don't reach the label with a GOTO command, the command before the label will be executed twice. Other versions of DOS will generate an error message.

There are two different solutions to this problem. First, the problem won't occur if the label is followed by the carriage return and line-feed characters, so you can avoid the problem by making sure that labels at the end of your batch file are followed by a return. Second, the problem won't occur if you reach the label via a GOTO command, even if the label is immediately followed by the end-of-file marker. So ending your batch files with the following will also correct the problem.

```
GOTO END
:END
```

Note that DOS 5.0 does not exhibit this problem.

Making CHKDSK smarter

Most computers need to have CHKDSK run fairly often to correct the minor problems that seem to creep into every hard disk. This can be a special problem for users who are fairly new to computers because the messages CHKDSK uses to report its problems aren't very understandable. In addition, CHKDSK doesn't set the errorlevel, so writing an intelligent batch-file interface to CHKDSK is difficult.

SMARTCHK.BAT in Fig. 10-3 overcomes this problem. It pipes the results of running CHKDSK to a file, uses FIND to search this file for specific strings, and then copies the output files as a method of determining if the text was actually found. It also uses Batcmd to set the errorlevel so you can use that to branch and perform additional actions.

As written, SMARTCHK.BAT needs some minor modifications. The CHKDSK error messages aren't consistent. In some versions *cross-linked* is hyphenated, and in others it isn't. There are also capitalization inconsistencies. You need to examine the version you use to see exactly how it phrases its error messages, and modify SMARTCHK.BAT accordingly. In addition, you'll want to modify its own error messages to something your users are likely to understand.

Not all of the errors found by CHKDSK can be handled this way. If you try to run CHKDSK on a drive created by the SUBST (substitute) command or assigned with the ASSIGN command, CHKDSK will display an error message to the screen and abort. This error message can't be piped to a file and, because CHKDSK aborts, the log file ends up being a zero-length file and SMARTCHK.BAT will incorrectly report that no errors were found.

Counting backup files

If you use the DOS BACKUP program to perform a backup, you're at a disadvantage when performing an incremental backup because BACKUP has no command to estimate how many files need to be backed up. So you have no way to estimate how much time the backup will take.

CNTFILES.BAT in Fig. 10-4 overcomes this problem. It begins by displaying every file on the specified drive (or default drive if a drive isn't specified) that currently needs to be backed up. After that, it counts those files and displays a total. While CNTFILES.BAT can't compute their size or the number of disks required, you're at least given more information that you get under DOS.

Summary

- If you're dealing with only a few floppy disks, you can use batch files to manage your floppy-disk catalog.
- Ending the last line of your batch file with an end-of-file marker in place of the normal CR/LF characters can cause problems under certain versions of DOS.
- SMARTCHK.BAT can make the error-reporting facilities of CHKDSK much smarter.
- The DOS BACKUP program won't display the number of files that need to be backed up, but CNTFILES.BAT will.

10-1 CATALOG.BAT creates a catalog of files on a floppy disk.

Batch File Line	Explanation
`@ECHO OFF`	Turn command-echoing off.

`REM NAME:     CATALOG.BAT`
`REM PURPOSE: Cataloging Floppy Disks`
`REM VERSION: 2.00`
`REM DATE:     November 15, 1991`
	Documentation remarks.

`REM Assumes You're Using The B Drive`
`REM For The Floppies And The C Drive`
`REM For The Catalog.`
	Documentation remarks.

`IF (%1)==(/?) GOTO HELP` `IF (%1)==(?)  GOTO HELP`	If the user starts the batch file with a request for help, jump to a section to display that help.

Batch File Line	Explanation
`IF (%1)==() GOTO NONAME`	If the user did not enter a replaceable parameter as a name for the disk, jump to an error-handling routine.
`C:` `CD\CATALOG`	Change to the appropriate drive and subdirectory for the catalog.

`ECHO Insert Disk To Catalog In A Drive`
`ECHO And Press Any Key When Ready`
`PAUSE>NUL`
	Tell the user what to do.

`FOR %%j in (B:\*.*) DO ECHO %%j ^I ^I`
`   %1 %2 %3 %4 %5 %6 %7 %8 %9 >>`
`   C:CATALOG.TXT`
	Pipe the name of each file, two tab characters (^I), an Alt-255, and the name of the disk into the catalog. While you can't see the Alt-255, its presence in the front of the name makes it easier to prevent errors in REMOVE.BAT.

`GOTO END`	Exit the batch file.

`:NONAME`
`ECHO You Must Enter CATALOG Name`
`ECHO Where Name Describes The Disk`
`GOTO END`
`:END_NONAME`
	Section to display an error message if the user fails to enter the name of the disk to catalog.

`:HELP`
`ECHO Creates A Catalog In The`
`ECHO C:\CATALOG Subdirectory That`
`ECHO Lists All The Files In The`
`ECHO B Drive Along With The Name You`
`ECHO Enter On The Command Line`
`GOTO END`
`:END_HELP`
	Section that displays help when the user starts the batch file with a /? or a ? as the first replaceable parameter.

`:END`	Label marking the end of the batch file.

10-2 REMOVE.BAT removes entries from the floppy-disk catalog.

Batch File Line	Explanation
`@ECHO OFF`	Turn command-echoing off.

`REM NAME:     REMOVE.BAT`
`REM PURPOSE: Removes Entries From`
`           Floppy Catalog`
`REM VERSION: 2.00`
`REM DATE:    November 15, 1991`
	Documentation remarks.

`IF (%1)==(/?) GOTO HELP` `IF (%1)==(?)  GOTO HELP`	If the user starts the batch file with a request for help, jump to a section to display that help.

Batch File Line	Explanation
IF (%1)==() GOTO NoName	If the user didn't enter text to delete, jump to an error-handling routine.
SET SPACE=	Store a space to an environmental variable.
SET FIND=	Reset the environmental variable used to construct the string of text to search the file and add an Alt-255 to the front. CATALOG.BAT adds an Alt-255 to the front of the name to help prevent errors in REMOVE.BAT.
:TOPLOOP	Label marking the top of the loop.
SET FIND=%FIND%%1	Add the current replaceable parameter on to the end of the string of text to search for.
SHIFT	Move the replaceable parameters down one level.
IF NOT (%1)==() SET FIND=%FIND%%SPACE%	If more replaceable parameters exist, add a space to the end of the string of text to search file because this process strips off all spaces.
IF NOT (%1)==() GOTO TOPLOOP :END_TOPLOOP	If more replaceable parameters exist, continue looping.
ECHO All Catalog Entries Containing ECHO %FIND% Will Be Deleted ECHO If Not OK, Press Ctrl-Break ECHO Otherwise, Press Any Other Key PAUSE>NUL	Tell the user what to do next.
C: CD\CATALOG	Change to the proper drive and subdirectory.
COPY CATALOG.TXT CATALOG.BAK	Create a backup file of the catalog.
TYPE CATALOG.TXT | FIND/V/I "%FIND%" > JUNK.TMP	Type the catalog, pipe the output to a temporary file, and delete those lines that contain the specified text.
DEL CATALOG.TXT	Delete the original catalog.
REN JUNK.TMP CATALOG.TXT	Rename the temporary file so it replaces the catalog.

Batch File Line	Explanation
GOTO END	Exit the batch file.
:HELP ECHO This Batch File Deletes The ECHO Entries From The Disk Catalog In ECHO The C:\CATALOG Subdirectory That ECHO Contain The Name You Enter On The ECHO Command Line GOTO END :END_HELP	Section that displays help when the user starts the batch file with a /? or a ? as the first replaceable parameter.
:END	Label marking the end of the batch file.

10-3 SMARTCHK.BAT runs CHKDSK and then reports the errors in a more understandable format.

Batch File Line	Explanation
@ECHO OFF	Turn command-echoing off.
REM NAME: SMARTCHK.BAT REM PURPOSE: Run CHKDSK And Report Results REM VERSION: 1.00 REM DATE: January 11, 1992	Documentation remarks.
IF (%1)==(/?) GOTO HELP IF (%1)==(?) GOTO HELP	If the user starts the batch file with a request for help, jump to a section to display that help.

IF (%1)==(A:) GOTO OK
IF (%1)==(a:) GOTO OK
IF (%1)==(B:) GOTO OK
IF (%1)==(b:) GOTO OK
IF (%1)==(C:) GOTO OK
IF (%1)==(c:) GOTO OK
IF (%1)==(D:) GOTO OK
IF (%1)==(d:) GOTO OK
IF (%1)==()   GOTO OK
	If the user entered a valid drive or didn't enter a drive (so it will use the default), jump to a section to continue processing.

GOTO INVALID	If the batch file reaches this point the user entered an invalid drive specification, so jump to an error-handling routine.
:INVALID ECHO You Entered An Invalid Drive ECHO Only Drives A-D Are Supported GOTO END :END_INVALID	If the user enters an invalid drive specification, display an error message and exit.

Batch File Line	Explanation
:HELP ECHO Enter SMARTCHK *drive* To Run CHO The Batch File Runs CHKDSK ECHO And Can React To Its ECHO Error Messages GOTO END :END_HELP	Section that displays help when the user starts the batch file with a /? or a ? as the first replaceable parameter.
:OK	Label marking the beginning of the processing section.
SET SUB1=C:\ SET SUB2=D:\ SET INFILE=IN-TEMP SET OUTFILE=OUTTEMP	Store the names of the files and subdirectories used to environmental variables so they can be easily changed.
CHKDSK %1 > %SUB1%%INFILE%	Run CHKDSK and pipe its output to a file.

TYPE %SUB1%%INFILE% | FIND "non-cont"
    > %SUB1%%OUTFILE%1
TYPE %SUB1%%INFILE% | FIND "lost clu"
    > %SUB1%%OUTFILE%2
TYPE %SUB1%%INFILE% | FIND "cross li"
    > %SUB1%%OUTFILE%3
	Type the file and search for three different error messages. Pipe the results of that search to different files.

:COPYTO	Label marking the beginning of the section to copy the files from one location to another.
FOR %%J IN (1 2 3) DO COPY %SUB1%%OUTFILE%%%J %SUB2% > NUL	Copy the three files from their current location to a second subdirectory. Those that are zero-length files won't copy successfully, a fact the batch file uses to determine if the files contain the specified text.
FOR %%J IN (1 2 3) DO DEL %SUB1%%OUTFILE%%%J > NUL	Delete the original versions of the files.
:END_COPYTO	Label marking the end of this section.
:COPYFROM	Label marking the beginning of the section to copy the files back.

FOR %%J IN (1 2 3) DO IF EXIST
    %SUB2%%OUTFILE%%%J COPY
    %SUB2%%OUTFILE%%%J %SUB1% > NUL
	Copy the files back from the second subdirectory if they exist.

FOR %%J IN (1 2 3) DO IF EXIST
    %SUB2%%OUTFILE%%%J DEL
    %SUB2%%OUTFILE%%%J > NUL
	If the files exist in the second subdirectory, delete them.

:END_COPYFROM	Label marking the end of this section.

Batch File Line	Explanation
`:ISOK`	Label marking the beginning of the section to test to see if the files exist.
`IF EXIST %SUB1%%OUTFILE%1 ECHO` `   Non_Contiguous Files Found!`	If the first file exists, display an appropriate error message.
`IF EXIST %SUB1%%OUTFILE%1 BATCMD EX 1`	If the first file exists, use Batcmd to set the errorlevel.
`IF EXIST %SUB1%%OUTFILE%2 ECHO Lost` `   Clusters Found!`	If the second file exists, display an appropriate error message.
`IF EXIST %SUB1%%OUTFILE%2 BATCMD EX 2`	If the second file exists, use Batcmd to set the errorlevel.
`IF EXIST %SUB1%%OUTFILE%3 ECHO Cross-` `Linked Files Found!`	If the third file exists, display an appropriate error message.
`IF EXIST %SUB1%%OUTFILE%3 BATCMD EX 3`	If the third file exists, use Batcmd to set the errorlevel.
`IF NOT EXIST %SUB1%%OUTFILE%? ECHO No` `   Errors Found`	If none of the files exist, tell the user no problems were found.
`IF EXIST %SUB1%%OUTFILE%? DEL` `   %SUB1%%OUTFILE%?`	Delete any files that exist.
`GOTO END` `:END_ISOK`	Exit the batch file.
`:END`	Label marking the end of the batch file.
`IF EXIST %SUB%%INFILE%` `   DEL %SUB1%%INFILE%`	Delete the input file before exiting.

`SET SUB1=`
`SET SUB2=`
`SET INFILE=`
`SET OUTFILE=`
	Reset the environmental variables before exiting.

10-4 CNTFILES.BAT counts the number of files that need to be backed up.

Batch File Line	Explanation
`@ECHO OFF`	Turn command-echoing off.

`REM NAME:      CNTFILES.BAT`
`REM PURPOSE: Show Files Needing Backup`
`REM VERSION: 1.00`
`REM DATE:      January 11, 1992`
	Documentation remarks.

`IF (%1)==(/?) GOTO HELP` `IF (%1)==(?)  GOTO HELP`	If the user starts the batch file with a request for help, jump to a section to display that help.

174 *Miscellaneous batch files*

Batch File Line	Explanation

IF (%1)==() GOTO OK
IF (%1)==(A:) GOTO OK
IF (%1)==(a:) GOTO OK
IF (%1)==(B:) GOTO OK
IF (%1)==(b:) GOTO OK
IF (%1)==(C:) GOTO OK
IF (%1)==(c:) GOTO OK
IF (%1)==(D:) GOTO OK
IF (%1)==(d:) GOTO OK
	If the user enters a valid drive or doesn't enter a drive (to use the default), jump to a section to continue processing.

GOTO INVALID	If the batch file reaches this point the user entered an invalid drive specification, so jump to an error-handling routine.
:INVALID ECHO You Have Entered An Invalid Drive ECHO Only Drives A-D Are Accepted GOTO END :END_INVALID	If the user enters an invalid drive specification, display an error-message and exit.
:OK	Label marking the beginning of the processing section.
ECHO Working! ECHO Please Wait	This takes several seconds to let the user know something is happening.
ATTRIB %1*.* /S | FIND "A "	Run the DOS ATTRIB program to display the attribute of all the files on the requested drive. Pipe that information to FIND to look for an *A* with a space after it, indicating a file with the archive bit on.
BATCMD SL	Skip a line.
ECHO Counting These Files ECHO Please Wait	The next command also takes several seconds, so again let the user know something is happening.
ATTRIB %1*.* /S | FIND "A " /C	Find the files with the archive bit on, but this time use the /C switch to just count the files.
ECHO Files Need To Be Backed Up	Tell the user what the number means.
GOTO END	Exit the batch file.
:END_OK	Label marking the end of this section.

Batch File Line	Explanation
| ```
:HELP
ECHO CNTFILES drive
ECHO Displays All The Files On
ECHO That Drive That Need To Be
ECHO Backed Up
GOTO END
:END_HELP
``` | Section that displays help when the user starts the batch file with a /? or a ? as the first replaceable parameter. |
| ```
:END
``` | Label marking the end of the batch file. |

PART FOUR
Configuring
DOS

11
Custom configurations

The two files that determine the configuration of your computing environment are the CONFIG.SYS and AUTOEXEC.BAT files. If you're lucky, you have one of each that handles all your programs. However, the nature of programs and their memory demands on your computer can change so rapidly that one do-it-all environment is rarely possible.

For example, the computer at my office usually loads Novell network software. However, when I want to run Ventura Publisher or when the network is down, I have to boot without the network.

If your computer has expanded or extended memory, you might face similar difficulties. Some programs, like Lotus 2.3, want expanded memory, so you need to load an expanded memory simulator in your CONFIG.SYS file. Other programs, like Lotus 3.1, want extended memory, so you have to skip the expanded memory simulator.

Between running with and without the network and using extended or expanded memory, my office computer needs four different configurations. If you have one application with a lot of memory-resident software and another without, you quickly have a lot of different configurations to deal with.

The basic approach

The basic approach to this problem is fairly simple. You need to maintain a set of configuration files (AUTOEXEC.BAT and CONFIG.SYS) for each of your configurations. When you want to change configurations, you run a batch file that copies the new set of configuration files to the root directory and then reboots the computer.

Before I explain this further, let's look at some ways to reduce the work necessary to maintain this system. No matter which configuration you boot from, there are some basic functions your AUTOEXEC.BAT file is going to have to perform. These include setting the path, prompt, and environmental variables. It's unlikely that these functions will vary between your different configurations.

Let's assume, for example, that you have eight different configurations, which means that you have eight different AUTOEXEC.BAT files (as well as eight different CONFIG.SYS files). Further, let's assume that you go out and buy a copy of the SuperWiz utili-

SuperWiz utilities, they install themselves in the C: \ SWIZ
~~enting a little, you find that you really love the SuperWiz utili-~~
~~to~~ your path statement so you can run them from anywhere on

~~a~~ a lot of work. Because you have eight AUTOEXEC.BAT files,
~~ght~~ different path statements to include the SuperWiz utilities in
~~the~~ SuperWiz utilities for a while, you come across a portion of
~~how~~ you can make the utilities run much faster by setting up an
~~alled~~ SWIZER that points to a temporary subdirectory SuperWiz
can use ~~for p~~   Once again, you've got to go in and edit all eight of your
AUTOEXEC.BAT files to add a line to create the SWIZER environmental variable. There
has to be a better way!

There is! On my system, I have three different batch files, SETS.BAT, SET-
PATH.BAT and NEWPROMPT.BAT. Three lines in each of my AUTOEXEC.BAT files
are:

```
CALL C: \ BAT \ SETS
CALL C: \ BAT \ SETPATH
CALL C: \ BAT \ NEWPROMPT
```

That way, when I need to change the environment, path, or prompt, I have to make the
change in only one location to have it effective in all my AUTOEXEC.BAT files. Two of
my four configurations log onto a network, so I have a NETWORK.BAT to handle that so
I can maintain changes to my network logon procedures in only one location.

You could combine all of these batch files into one and save a little space, but there's a
good reason not to. An additional advantage of these batch files is that batch files other than
your AUTOEXEC.BAT files can access them. For example, my normal prompt is a fairly
long ANSI.SYS escape sequence. When I run a program, like Lotus, that allows you to shell
out to DOS, I have the batch file change the prompt to something like *Running Under
Lotus$__$p$g* so I'll know Lotus is loaded in memory when I shell out. I don't want to have
to type in that long ANSI.SYS escape sequence in every batch file to reset the prompt after
the application terminates, so I simply have the batch file call NEWPROMPT.BAT.

The process of copying new configuration files on top of existing ones and rebooting
is fairly simple. AUTOBOOT.BAT in Fig. 11-1 handles the process nicely. And if you
want a method to reboot the computer, BatCmd has an option to do just that.

There's one drawback to this method. Any modifications you make to the AUTO-
EXEC.BAT and CONFIG.SYS file are lost the next time you run AUTOBOOT.BAT
because it just copies new configuration files on top of existing ones and reboots. You can
avoid this by being careful to either make changes to the files used by AUTOBOOT.BAT
or, once the changes to the AUTOEXEC.BAT and CONFIG.SYS files are complete, copy
them back to the appropriate AUTOBOOT.BAT files.

Putting it together

Putting together a system to handle eight different configurations is fairly straightforward.
First, create a subdirectory called C: \ RECONFIG. In that subdirectory, create eight sets

of configuration files, called AUTOEXEC.1 to AUTOEXEC.8 and CONFIG.1 to CONFIG.8. Sets of files with the same extension will be used together. Each set of files should contain a different configuration.

Once these files are created, copy RECONFIG.BAT in Fig. 11-2 into either the C: \ RECONFIG subdirectory or your normal batch subdirectory. Whichever you select will need to be in your path. Then you need to edit the text in RECONFIG.BAT to describe the configurations you've selected to use. Finally, you might want to make a backup copy of your existing AUTOEXEC.BAT and CONFIG.SYS files in case you want to revert to them.

That's all there is to it. Run RECONFIG.BAT by entering RECONFIG at the command line and it will prompt you for the number of the configuration you want to use. In addition to rebooting with the new configuration, RECONFIG.BAT creates a zero-length flag file in the root directory of the C drive called FLAG.1 to FLAG.8 to indicate which configuration is currently in place. This can be combined with the environmental surveying methods described in the following section to change the configuration automatically when your current configuration and a program you select to run aren't well matched.

Environmental surveying

The method of copying new configuration files on top of the old ones and rebooting, described in the previous section, works, but it's reactive rather than proactive. First you have to remember when an application takes a different configuration than the one that's currently in use. Then you have to remember which configuration the application needs and run AUTOBOOT.BAT to provide that configuration. That's a lot to remember!

Knowing which configuration is in force and which configuration an application needs isn't just a limitation of these batch files. Most commercial programs for changing the configuration, such as DynaBoot and Syscfg, suffer from this same limitation.

A better way to solve this problem is to develop several custom sets of CONFIG.SYS and AUTOEXEC.BAT files under different names. This time, rather than running a batch file yourself to change the environment, have the batch files you use to start programs figure out if the proper environment is in place. If it is, they can run the application. If not, they need to copy the proper boot files into place, reboot, and then run the application.

For this example, assume that CONFIG.001 and AUTOEXEC.001 are files that will configure the environment to give a program the maximum amount of memory possible. They do this by minimizing the DOS environmental space, lowering the buffers, and not loading any memory-resident software. Further, assume that CONFIG.002 and AUTOEXEC.002 create a more user-friendly environment, with a larger environment, more buffers, and several memory-resident programs. This second configuration, however, requires more memory. As a result, some memory-intensive programs might not run. For this example, the two applications are BigApp and TinyApp. The batch file 01.BAT in Fig. 11-3 runs BigApp, while 02.BAT in Fig. 11-4 runs TinyApp.

You want the batch file for each application to survey the environment and start the application if the environment is the proper one. If not, you want the batch file to copy the correct set of files over the current CONFIG.SYS and AUTOEXEC.BAT files, reboot the system, and then start the application automatically. This is a straightforward process except for two problems—figuring out which environment is running and starting the application automatically after booting.

The first problem is easier to handle than the second. You can create a flag file on the hard disk and maintain its extension where it always matches the current environment. The batch file that changes the environment also changes this file if necessary. If the flag doesn't exist, the batch file assumes the wrong environment is being used. It also creates a zero-length file to mark the type of environment being set up.

The second problem uses a similar solution, but this time the pending flag file is temporary. When DOS reboots, it checks for all possible pending flag files. If it finds one, it deletes the pending flag file and runs the associated application. It deletes the pending flag file so it won't run the same application the next time you reboot.

This is complex, so let's work through an example. Assume that CONFIG.002 and AUTOEXEC.002 are in effect and you want to run BigApp. Because this is the first time you've used the system, FLAG.002 won't exist. Simply enter 01 at the DOS prompt and the batch file will take over. When the computer reboots, it processes the new CONFIG.SYS file then the new AUTOEXEC.BAT file. The last line in the AUTOEXEC.BAT file calls STARTAPP.BAT, in Fig. 11-5.

As you can see from the batch file listing in Fig. 11-3, 01.BAT reboots the computer only if the wrong configuration files were used to initially boot the computer. Thus, the computer reboots only when the environment is the inappropriate environment or if it's not sure which environment is in effect. While this example uses two environments and two applications, the actual number you can implement is limited only by your needs.

Conditionally loading memory-resident software

Do you find yourself constantly editing your AUTOEXEC.BAT file to change the memory-resident programs (also called TSRs, for terminate and stay resident) you load when the computer boots? There's a better way! Instead of modifying your AUTOEXEC.BAT file, have it ask you if you want to load each TSR program. To do that, perform the following:

Modify your AUTOEXEC.BAT file to where it prompts you before loading each TSR program. The program you use to do this can be the BatCmd program included on the disk or any similar program. Have the batch file skip over the commands to load the TSR package unless you request the AUTOEXEC.BAT file to load the program.

Figure 11-6 shows a sample AUTOEXEC.BAT file called AUTOASK.BAT. It asks prior to loading each of three TSR packages: Superkey, PrintCache, and Sidekick. You can choose to load all of them, any two, any single program, or none of them—all without modifying the AUTOEXEC.BAT file. Because they're always loaded in the only order that works—Superkey, PrintCache, then Sidekick—you don't have to worry about conflicts caused by skipping one or more of them.

DR DOS is even better

As you've seen, under MS-DOS you can minimize the changes necessary to your AUTOEXEC.BAT by calling other batch files to handle tasks like setting the prompt and path. That way you don't have to make changes to every version of your AUTOEXEC

.BAT files when you modify the contents of your hard disk. Because MS-DOS lacks the ability to call other files from the CONFIG.SYS file, however, this same sort of savings isn't possible there.

While MS-DOS offers nothing to save time in dealing with multiple configurations in the CONFIG.SYS file, beginning with version 5.0, DR DOS offers two enhancements that make dealing with multiple configurations a breeze. First, if you precede any line in your CONFIG.SYS file with a question mark and a prompt inside quotation marks, DR DOS will display that prompt while booting. If you press N, it will skip that line and if you press Y, it will process the remainder of the line. Second, your main CONFIG.SYS file can call other files and those files will function as though they were part of the original CONFIG.SYS file.

As a result, running multiple configurations is much easier. First, create a CON-FIG.SYS file for every configuration, only call the different files CONFIG .001, CONFIG.002, and so on. Next, have your main CONFIG.SYS file ask you which one you want to load. That way you can decide which CONFIG.SYS file to process at boot time.

The AUTOEXEC.BAT file has always had the ability to ask questions and branch based on the results (using a utility like BatCmd to ask the question and set the errorlevel), so all that remains is to modify the AUTOEXEC.BAT file to ask which configuration you want and branch to a different batch file depending on your response.

As close as MS-DOS can come

While MS-DOS doesn't have the power to use multiple CONFIG.SYS files the way DR DOS does, with some careful coding you can write a batch file that allows you to boot with different CONFIG.SYS files "on the fly" using MS-DOS.

The approach is different from RECONFIG.BAT (discussed previously) because you won't be storing multiple versions of the CONFIG.SYS file. Rather, you'll be constructing a custom CONFIG.SYS each time you select this option.

Begin by listing all the different statements you might want to include in a CON-FIG.SYS file when you reboot. Once you have all these, group them into one of five groups:

Always load   These would be statements like BREAK=ON that you always want to be in the CONFIG.SYS file.

Different choices, independent items   These are items like the environment size or the number of FILES and BUFFERS, where you might want to select a low value when maximizing memory and a higher value otherwise. The value you select for these items shouldn't affect other items in the CONFIG.SYS file.

Independent conditional items   These are items you might not always load, but loading them or not loading them has no effect on other statements. For example, it's not likely that loading or leaving out your mouse driver will affect any other line in your CON-FIG.SYS file.

Dependent conditional items   These are items where your choice for one line affects other lines. For example, if your trackball and mouse drivers conflict, you would want to load one and automatically skip the other.

Grouped items   These are lines that can be grouped together under one question. For example, if your network requires two different drivers, you could either load both or skip both with a single question asking if you want to log onto the network.

Once you have these listed, the hard part begins. Create a batch file similar to CONFIG.BAT in Fig. 11-7 that asks about each option and echoes the appropriate text to the CONFIG.SYS file when you answer Yes. Once the new CONFIG.SYS file is complete, CONFIG.BAT will reboot the computer so the new CONFIG.SYS file can take effect.

There's one major consideration in writing CONFIG.BAT and it's the reason for the command grouping above. The CONFIG.SYS file is processed prior to COMMAND .COM, so you can't break out of it with Ctrl-Break as you can in AUTOEXEC.BAT file if there's an error. If the error is serious enough, you won't be able to boot from the computer, and will have to boot from a floppy disk to correct the problem.

For that reason, you must review CONFIG.BAT to make sure that no combination of answers given will lead to a problem CONFIG.SYS file. If you group as many commands together as is logical, you should be able to see if there are problems. If this review process becomes too complex, you're better off limiting yourself to eight configurations and using RECONFIG.BAT rather than CONFIG.BAT.

Summary

- If you have to maintain multiple versions of your AUTOEXEC.BAT file, then you can save time by performing common functions, like setting the path and prompt, using a separate batch file that each version of the AUTOEXEC.BAT file calls as needed.
- Booting under different configurations is as simple as copying the new configuration files to the root directory under the proper name and rebooting. AUTOBOOT .BAT illustrates this and RECONFIG.BAT automates the process for eight configurations.
- If you have your AUTOEXEC.BAT set a flag, batch files can determine the environment they're running under, change the configuration files, and reboot when the current environment isn't the right one for the appropriate application. START-APP.BAT illustrates this.
- If the only difference you plan between different configurations is different memory-resident programs, then the AUTOEXEC.BAT file can handle that by prompting you whether or not to load the programs each time you boot. AUTOASK.BAT illustrates this.
- Beginning with version 5.0, DR DOS makes it easy to boot under multiple configurations by allowing the CONFIG.SYS to ask questions and respond differently depending on the response.
- CONFIG.BAT will create a custom CONFIG.SYS file for you each time you run it.

11-1 AUTOBOOT.BAT allows you to reconfigure the computer system by means of a batch file.

Batch File Line	Explanation
`@ECHO OFF`	Turn command-echoing off.

`REM AUTOBOOT.BAT`
`REM PURPOSE: Boot Custom Configuration`
`REM VERSION: 1.00`
`REM DATE:    March 1, 1991`
	Documentation remarks.

`IF (%1)==(/?) GOTO HELP` `IF (%1)==(?)  GOTO HELP`	If the user starts the batch file with a request for help, jump to a section to display that help.
`REM Test For Missing Parameter And Branch` `IF (%1)==() GOTO NOTHING`	Check for missing replaceable parameter and skip to an error routine if needed.
`REM Now Test For Proper Parameters.` `REM If Found, Copy Files And Branch`	Documentation remarks.

`IF %1==001 COPY AUTOEXEC.001 AUTOEXEC.BAT`
`IF %1==001 COPY CONFIG.001    CONFIG.SYS`
`IF %1==001 GOTO BOOT`
	If the user specifies 001, copy those configuration files into place and jump to the rebooting section.

`IF %1==002 COPY AUTOEXEC.002 AUTOEXEC.BAT`
`IF %1==002 COPY CONFIG.002    CONFIG.SYS`
`IF %1==002 GOTO BOOT`
	Handling user selecting 002.

`IF %1==003 COPY AUTOEXEC.003 AUTOEXEC.BAT`
`IF %1==003 COPY CONFIG.003    CONFIG.SYS`
`IF %1==003 GOTO BOOT`
	Handle user selecting 003.

`REM Must Be Wrong Parameter.` `REM Branch To Message`	Documentation remark.
`GOTO WRONG`	Jump to the section to handle the user entering an invalid replaceable parameter.
`:BOOT`	Reboot the computer.
`BATCMD RB`	Run a program to reboot the computer. Of course, this will stop the batch file.

`REM Computer Reboots, So Rest Of This`
`REM Batch File Not Executed`
`GOTO END`
`:END_BOOT`
	Documentation remark.

`:NOTHING`
`ECHO No Parameter Entered After AUTOBOOT`
`GOTO MESSAGES`
`:END_NOTHING`
	Section to handle the user not entering a replaceable parameter.

`:WRONG`
`ECHO Wrong parameter after AUTOBOOT`
`GOTO MESSAGES`
`:END_WRONG`
	Section to handle user entering an unacceptable replaceable parameter.

	Explanation
| ```
      ...ter 001
ECHO ---------
ECHO No memory-resident software
ECHO Enter 002
ECHO ---------
ECHO Writing memory-resident software
ECHO Enter 003
ECHO ---------
ECHO Database memory-resident software
GOTO END
:END_MESSAGES
``` | Section that displays the possible parameters. |
| ```
:HELP
ECHO Enter: AUTOBOOT #
BATCMD SL
ECHO To Reboot With That Configuration
ECHO The Possible Configurations Are:
GOTO MESSAGE
:END_HELP
``` | Section that displays help when the user starts the batch file with a /? or a ? as the first replaceable parameter. |
| ```
:END
``` | Label marking the end of the batch file. |

11-2 RECONFIG.BAT allows you to select from one of eight different configurations. Once you've selected, it copies those configuration files into place and reboots the computer.

Batch File Line	Explanation
`@ECHO OFF`	Turn command-echoing off.
`GOTO TOP`	Skip over the documentation remarks that follow.
| ```
NAME:    RECONFIG.BAT
PURPOSE: Reboot With 1 Of 8 Configurations
VERSION: 1.00
DATE:    January 2, 1992
``` | Documentation remarks. |
| `:TOP` | Label used to jump over the nonexecuting documentation remarks. |
| ```
IF (%1)==(/?) GOTO HELP
IF (%1)==(?)  GOTO HELP
``` | If the user starts the batch file with a request for help, jump to a section to display that help. |
| ```
C:
CD\RECONFIG
``` | Change to the proper drive and subdirectory. |

Batch File Line	Explanation
CLS ECHO 0. Exit Without Taking Any Action ECHO 1. Load Maximum Memory ECHO 2. Load Expanded Memory ECHO 3. Load Extended Memory ECHO 4. Load Network And Expanded Memory ECHO 5. Load Network And Extended Memory ECHO 6. Load All TSR Programs ECHO 7. Load CD ROM Drivers/Expanded Memory ECHO 8. Load CD ROM Drivers/Extended Memory ECHO 9. Reboot With Same Configuration BATCMD SL	Clear the screen and show the available options.
IF NOT EXIST C:\FLAG.? ECHO Unable To Determine Configuration IF NOT EXIST C:\FLAG.? GOTO NOSHOW	If no flag file exists in the root directory, then tell the user that the batch file can't determine the current configuration and skip the routines to determine the configuration.
SET MATH=0	Set the math variable used by Batcmd to zero. Users needing to keep a value in this variable should store its contents prior to this routine and restore it afterwards.
FOR %%J IN (1 2 3 4 5 6 7 8) DO IF EXIST C:\FLAG.%%J BATCMD AD	Loop through the possible configurations and count the number of configuration files that exist.
IF %MATH%==1 FOR %%J IN (1 2 3 4 5 6 7 8) DO IF EXIST C:\FLAG.%%J ECHO Current Configuration Is #%%J	If only one configuration exists, loop through the configurations again in order to tell the user which configuration is currently in force.
IF NOT %MATH%==1 ECHO Unable To Determine Configuration	If multiple configurations are in force, inform the user that the current configuration can't be determined.

Batch File Line	Explanation
`:NOSHOW`	Label used to skip the routines that determine the current configuration when no configuration file exists.
`BATCMD SL` `BATCMD GN Please Enter Your Selection`	Use Batcmd to get a selection from the user. Batcmd with the GN option allows only the user to enter a 0-9 and those are all valid options, so no error-checking is required on the user's input.
`FOR %%J IN (0 1 2 3 4 5 6 7 8 9) DO` `   IF ERRORLEVEL %%J SET SELECT=%%J`	Store the errorlevel value (and therefore the user's selection) to the environmental variable SELECT.
`IF %SELECT%==0 GOTO END`	If the user selected to exit the batch file, jump to the end of the batch file.
`IF %SELECT%==9 GOTO BATCMD RB`	If the user selected to reboot using the current configuration, reboot the computer. Because the computer reboots, none of the rest of the batch file executes.
`GOTO REST` `:END_NOSHOW`	The remaining selections can all be handled the same way, so jump to a section to do that.
`:REST`	Label marking the beginning of the section to put the new configuration into place and reboot the computer.
`BATCMD YN Please Confirm Overwriting` `   Current AUTOEXEC.BAT And CONFIG.SYS Files`	Give the user one last chance to reboot before the existing configuration files are overwritten.

Batch File Line	Explanation
`IF NOT ERRORLEVEL 1 GOTO END`	If the user didn't confirm overwriting the files, exit the batch file.

`IF NOT EXIST AUTOEXEC.%SELECT% ECHO`
`    C:\RECONFIG\AUTOEXEC.%SELECT% Missing!`
`IF NOT EXIST CONFIG.%SELECT%    ECHO`
`    C:\RECONFIG\CONFIG.%SELECT%    Missing!`
	If either of the configuration files for the selected option is missing, warn the user.

`IF NOT EXIST AUTOEXEC.%SELECT% GOTO END` `IF NOT EXIST CONFIG.%SELECT%    GOTO END`	If either of the configuration files for the selected option is missing, exit the batch file without performing any action.
`XCOPY AUTOEXEC.%SELECT% C:\*.BAT`	Copy the new AUTOEXEC.BAT file into place.
`IF ERRORLEVEL 1 GOTO NOCOPY`	If there was a copy problem, jump to a section to handle that.
`XCOPY CONFIG.%SELECT%    C:\*.SYS`	Copy the new CONFIG.BAT file into place.
`IF ERRORLEVEL 1 GOTO NOCOPY`	If there was a copy problem, jump to a section to handle that.
`FOR %%J IN (1 2 3 4 5 6 7 8) DO IF EXIST` `    C:\FLAG.%%J DEL C:\FLAG.%%J`	If any flag files currently exist, delete them.
`TYPE NOFILE C:\FLAG.%SELECT%`	Create a new zero-length flag file in the root directory of the C drive, indicating the current configuration.
`BATCMD RB`	Reboot the computer so the new configuration will take effect. Because the computer reboots, the rest of this batch file won't execute.
`:END_REST`	Label marking the end of the Rest section.

Batch File Line	Explanation

`:NOCOPY`
`ECHO Failure To Copy Either AUTOEXEC.BAT`
`ECHO Or CONFIG.SYS File!`
`BATCMD SL`
`ECHO Suggest You Check To Make Sure These`
`ECHO Files Are Not Marked Read-Only`
`BATCMD SL`
`ECHO RECONFIG.BAT Aborting`
`GOTO END`
`:END_NOCOPY`
	When there's a problem copying the AUTOEXEC.BAT or CONFIG.SYS file, this section displays an error message and then exits the batch file.

`:HELP`
`ECHO RECONFIG.BAT Allows You To Reboot`
`ECHO With One Of Eight Different`
`ECHO Configurations. It Does This By`
`ECHO Storing Eight Configurations In`
`ECHO The C:\RECONFIG Subdirectory Under`
`ECHO The Names AUTOEXEC.1 To AUTOEXEC.8`
`ECHO And CONFIG.1 To CONFIG.8 And Copying`
`ECHO The Selected Ones Over The`
`ECHO C:\AUTOEXEC.BAT And C:\CONFIG.SYS`
`ECHO Files When A New ECHO Configuration`
`ECHO Is Requested.`
`GOTO END`
`:END_HELP`
	Section that displays help when the user starts the batch file with a /? or a ? as the first replaceable parameter.

`:END`	Label marking the end of the batch file.
`SET SELECT=`	Reset the environmental variable used by this batch file before exiting.

11-3 01.BAT runs BigApp.

Batch File Line	Explanation
`@ECHO OFF`	Turn command-echoing off.

`REM NAME:    01.BAT`
`REM PURPOSE: Run BigApp`
`REM VERSION: 1.00`
`REM DATE:    March 1, 1991`
`REM Runs BIGAPP, A Program That`
`REM Needs A Lot Of Memory`
	Documentation remarks.

`IF (%1)==(/?) GOTO HELP` `IF (%1)==(?)  GOTO HELP`	If the user starts the batch file with a request for help, jump to a section to display that help.
`IF EXIST FLAG.001 GOTO OK`	If the flag file FLAG.001 exists, the computer was booted with the proper configuration files and the batch file will skip to the OK label.

Batch File Line	Explanation
`IF EXIST FLAG.002 GOTO 002`	If the flag file FLAG.002 exists, the computer was booted with the wrong configuration files and the batch file will skip to an area that handles this.

`REM At This Point, Flag Does`
`REM Not Exist`
`REM Will Assume Files Wrong`
`REM Will Create Flag File`
`REM Copy Over`
`REM Proper Files And Reboot`
	Documentation lines.
	
	If the batch file reaches this point, then neither flag file exists and the batch file will assume the wrong configuration was used.

`TYPE NOFILE > FLAG.002`	Create a zero-length flag file flagging that the computer was booted under CONFIG.002--the wrong one in this case.
`:002`	A label marking the section of the batch file that handles resetting the computer when the wrong configuration is in effect.
`COPY CONFIG.001 CONFIG.SYS`	Replace the current CONFIG.SYS file with the minimum memory one stored under the name CONFIG.001. There's no need to store the old one because it's stored under the name CONFIG.002.
`COPY AUTOEXEC.001 AUTOEXEC.BAT`	Replace the current AUTOEXEC.BAT file with the minimum memory one stored under the name AUTOEXEC.001.
`REN FLAG.002 FLAG.001`	Rename the flag file to indicate that the computer was rebooted using the minimum memory configuration files.
`REM Create Marker File`	Documentation remark.
`TYPE NOFILE > START.001`	Create a zero-length file that tells the AUTOEXEC.BAT file that a program is pending to be run.
`BATCMD RB` `:END_02`	Reboot the computer using Batcmd. The balance of this batch file doesn't present a problem for this segment of code because rebooting causes this batch file to stop execution. Otherwise, you would need a GOTO command to skip over the next section of code.

`:HELP`
`ECHO This Demonstration Batch`
`ECHO File Runs BigApp`
`ECHO Will Change Configuration`
`ECHO Files And Reboot The`
`ECHO Computer If Needed`
`GOTO END`
`:END_HELP`
	Section that displays help when the user starts the batch file with a /? or a ? as the first replaceable parameter.

Batch File Line	Explanation
:OK	Label marking the section of code that runs BigApp if the computer has the proper configuration without rebooting.
CD\BIGAPP	Change to the BigApp subdirectory.
BIGAPP :END_OK	Run the BigApp application. You might also want to add another line to restart the menu.
:END	Label marking the end of the batch file.

11-4 02.BAT runs TinyApp.

Batch File Line	Explanation
@ECHO OFF	Turn command-echoing off.
REM NAME: 02.BAT REM PURPOSE: Run TinyApp REM VERSION: 1.00 REM DATE: March 1, 1991 REM TinyApp Does Not REM Need A Lot Of Memory	Documentation remarks.
IF (%1)==(/?) GOTO HELP IF (%1)==(?) GOTO HELP	If the user starts the batch file with a request for help, jump to a section to display that help.
IF EXIST FLAG.002 GOTO OK	If flag file FLAG.002 exists, then the computer was booted in the proper configuration and will run the application.
IF EXIST FLAG.001 GOTO 001	If flag file FLAG.001 exists, the computer was booted in the wrong configuration and will jump to a section to handle this.
REM At This Point, Flag Does REM Not Exist REM Will Assume Files Wrong REM Will Create Flag File REM Copy Over REM Proper Files and Reboot	Documentation remarks.
TYPE NOFILE > FLAG.001	If the batch file reaches this point, no flag file exists. It creates one and then continues as though the wrong configuration were in force. 001 is used rather than a .002 so the REN command below will work properly.
:001	Label marking the section that handles resetting the configuration files and rebooting.
COPY CONFIG.002 CONFIG.SYS	Replace the CONFIG.SYS file with the proper one.

Batch File Line	Explanation
`COPY AUTOEXEC.002 AUTOEXEC.BAT`	Replace the AUTOEXEC.BAT file with the proper one.
`REN FLAG.001 FLAG.002`	Rename the configuration file to flag the appropriate configuration.
`REM Create Marker File`	Documentation remark.
`TYPE NOFILE > START.002`	Create a marker indicating TinyApp is pending to run.
`BATCMD RB` `:END_001`	Reboot the computer using BatCmd.

`:HELP`
`ECHO This Demonstration Batch`
`ECHO File Runs TinyApp`
`ECHO Will Change Configuration`
`ECHO Files And Reboot The`
`ECHO Computer If Needed`
`GOTO END`
`:END_HELP`
	Section that displays help when the user starts the batch file with a /? or a ? as the first replaceable parameter.

`:OK`	Label marking the section that runs TinyApp if the configuration is correct.
`CD\TINYAPP`	Change to the proper subdirectory.

`TINYAPP`
`GOTO END`
`:END_OK`
	Run the application and exit the batch file.

`:END`	Label marking the end of the batch file.

11-5 STARTAPP.BAT runs from AUTOEXEC.BAT and decides if a program is pending to run.

Batch File Line	Explanation
`@ECHO OFF`	Turn command-echoing off.

`REM NAME:    STARTAPP.BAT`
`REM PURPOSE: Decides If Program`
`REM         Is Pending To Run`
`REM VERSION: 1.00`
`REM DATE:    March 1, 1991`
	Documentation remarks.

`IF (%1)==(/?) GOTO HELP` `IF (%1)==(?)  GOTO HELP`	If the user starts the batch file with a request for help, jump to a section to display that help.
`IF EXIST START.001 GOTO 001`	If the file START.001 exists it's a flag telling the batch file which program to run, so jump to the appropriate section.
`IF EXIST START.002 GOTO 002`	If the file START.002 exists it's a flag telling the batch file which program to run, so jump to the appropriate section.

Batch File Line	Explanation
GOTO END	If neither flag file exists no application is pending to run, so exit the batch file.
:HELP ECHO This Demonstration Batch ECHO File Decides If An ECHO Application Is Pending And ECHO Runs It If It Is BATCMD SL ECHO Do Not Run This Batch File ECHO From The Command Line GOTO END :END_HELP	Section that displays help when the user starts the batch file with a /? or a ? as the first replaceable parameter.
:001	Label marking the section to run the first application.
DEL START.001	Delete the flag file so the batch file won't start the application the next time the computer is rebooted.
1 :END_001	Run the application by running another batch file. The batch file doesn't use the CALL command, so control never returns to this batch file.
:002 DEL START.002 2 :END_002	Section to handle the second application identically to the way the above section handled the first application.
:END	Label marking the end of the batch file.

11-6 AUTOASK.BAT is a version of the AUTOEXEC.BAT file that will ask before loading memory-resident programs.

Batch File Line	Explanation
@ECHO OFF	Turn off command-echoing.
REM NAME: AUTOASK.BAT REM PURPOSE: AUTOEXEC.BAT Illustrating REM Conditional TSR Loading REM VERSION: 1.00 REM DATE: March 1, 1991	Documentation remarks.
BATCMD YN Do You Want to Load APP1 (Y/N)	Ask the user a question and use BatCmd to obtain a response.
IF NOT ERRORLEVEL 1 GOTO SKIP1	If the user answers no, skip loading APP1.
CD\APP1	Change to the APP1 subdirectory.

Batch File Line	Explanation
APP1	Load APP1.
CD\	Change back to the root directory.
:SKIP1	Label marking the end of the APP1 section.

BATCMD YN Do You Want to Load APP2 (Y/N)
IF NOT ERRORLEVEL 1 GOTO SKIP2
   CD\APP2
   APP2
  CD\
:SKIP2
	Conditionally load APP2 if the user answers yes to the prompt.

BATCMD YN Do You Want to Load APP3 (Y/N)
IF NOT ERRORLEVEL 2 GOTO SKIP3
   CD\APP3
   APP3
  CD\
:SKIP3
	Conditionally load APP3 if the user answers yes to the prompt.

REM Rest of AUTOEXEC.BAT File Goes Here	The rest of AUTOEXEC.BAT would go here.

11-7 CONFIG.BAT allows you to boot with a custom CONFIG.SYS file under MS-DOS.

Batch File Line	Explanation
@ECHO OFF	Turn command-echoing off.
GOTO TOP	Skip over the documentation remarks that follow.
NAME: CONFIG.BAT PURPOSE: Create A Custom CONFIG.SYS File VERSION: 1.00 DATE: January 2, 1992	Documentation remarks.
:TOP	Label used to jump over the nonexecuting documentation remarks.
IF (%1)==(/?) GOTO HELP IF (%1)==(?) GOTO HELP	If the user starts the batch file with a request for help, jump to a section to display that help.
DEL C:\CONFIG.SYS	Delete the old CONFIG.-SYS file.

Batch File Line	Explanation
ECHO REM Custom CONFIG.SYS Created By CONFIG.BAT >> C:\CONFIG.SYS ECHO REM CONFIG.BAT Copyright (c) 1992 Windcrest Books >> C:\CONFIG.SYS ECHO REM You May Use CONFIG.BAT On All The Machines >> C:\CONFIG.SYS ECHO REM You Own Or Use, But You May Not Give A >> C:\CONFIG.SYS ECHO REM Copy To Other Users >> C:\CONFIG.SYS	Pipe a copyright message into the new CONFIG.-SYS file.
BATCMD YN Do You Want To Load HIMEM.SYS?	Ask the user if he wants to load HIMEM.SYS.
IF ERRORLEVEL 1 ECHO DEVICE=C:\HIMEM.SYS >> C:\CONFIG.SYS	If the user answers yes, pipe the appropriate code to the CONFIG.SYS file.
BATCMD YN Do You Want To Load EMM386.SYS?	Ask the user if he wants to load EMM386.SYS.
IF ERRORLEVEL 1 ECHO DEVICE= C:\WINDOWS\EMM386.SYS 2500 D=32 X=D800-DBFF >> C:\CONFIG.SYS	If the user answers yes, pipe the appropriate code to the CONFIG.SYS file.
BATCMD YN Do You Want To Load SETVER?	Ask the user if he wants to load SETVER.EXE.
IF ERRORLEVEL 1 ECHO DEVICE= C:\SYSLIB\SETVER.EXE >> C:\CONFIG.SYS	If the user answers yes, pipe the appropriate code to the CONFIG.SYS file.
BATCMD YN Do You Want To Load ANSI.SYS?	Ask the user if he wants to load ANSI.SYS.
IF ERRORLEVEL 1 ECHO DEVICE= C:\SYSLIB\ANSI.SYS >> C:\CONFIG.SYS	If the user answers yes, pipe the appropriate code to the CONFIG.SYS file.
BATCMD YN Do You Want To Expand The Environment?	Ask the user if he wants to expand the environment.
IF ERRORLEVEL 1 ECHO SHELL=C:\SYSLIB\ COMMAND.COM C:\SYSLIB\ /E:600 /P >> C:\CONFIG.SYS	If the user answers yes, pipe the appropriate code to the CONFIG.SYS file.
IF NOT ERRORLEVEL 1 ECHO SHELL=C:\SYSLIB\ COMMAND.COM /P >> C:\CONFIG.SYS	Even if the user doesn't want to expand the environment, this system requires a SHELL statement because COMMAND.COM has been relocated.

Batch File Line	Explanation
ECHO BREAK=ON >> C:\CONFIG.SYS	CONFIG.BAT doesn't ask about this statement, so it will appear in all the CONFIG.SYS files it creates.
BATCMD YN Do You Want To Expand Files And Buffers?	Ask the user if he wants to expand the FILES and BUFFERS statements.

IF ERRORLEVEL 1 ECHO BUFFERS=50
   >> C:\CONFIG.SYS
IF ERRORLEVEL 1 ECHO FILES=60
   >> C:\CONFIG.SYS
	If the user answers yes, pipe the appropriate code to the CONFIG.SYS file.

IF NOT ERRORLEVEL 1 ECHO BUFFERS=20
   >> C:\CONFIG.SYS
IF NOT ERRORLEVEL 1 ECHO FILES=20
   >> C:\CONFIG.SYS
	If the user answers no, pipe the code for the smaller values into the CONFIG.SYS file.

ECHO LASTDRIVE=D >> C:\CONFIG.SYS	CONFIG.BAT doesn't ask about this statement, so it will appear in all the CONFIG.SYS files it creates.
BATCMD YN Do You Want To Load The Mouse Driver?	Ask the user if he wants to load ANSI.SYS.
IF ERRORLEVEL 1 ECHO DEVICE= C:\MOUSE\MOUSE.SYS /Y >> C:\CONFIG.SYS	If the user answers yes, pipe the appropriate code to the CONFIG.SYS file.
BATCMD YN Do You Want To Load SMARTDRIV.SYS?	Ask the user if he wants to load ANSI.SYS.
IF ERRORLEVEL 1 ECHO DEVICE=C:\WINDOWS\ SMARTDRV.SYS 1048 256 >> C:\CONFIG.SYS	If the user answers yes, pipe the appropriate code to the CONFIG.SYS file.
BATCMD RB :END_TOP	Reboot the computer so the new configuration can take effect.
:HELP ECHO This Batch File Deletes The CONFIG.SYS ECHO File, Asks A Series Of Questions To ECHO Construct A New CONFIG.SYS File, Then ECHO Reboots The Computer GOTO END :END_HELP	Section that displays help when the user starts the batch file with a /? or a ? as the first replaceable parameter.
:END	Label marking the end of the batch file.

12

Accessing global information

Certain information about the computing environment, such as the date or volume label, should be accessible to all batch files. However, in most cases DOS makes it hard to get to this information. In this chapter, we'll look at how to obtain and use information about the computing environment.

Date and time

One limitation of DOS is that a batch file can't directly access the date and time. This makes it tricky to run a batch file only at a certain date or time. If DOS had access to the date, you could automatically run a backup batch file every Friday when you started the computer. The following set of batch files shows how to construct a system to give batch files access to this information. You can expand this methodology to run any program or set of programs on specific dates.

First add these two lines to the end of your AUTOEXEC.BAT file:

```
ECHO | MORE | DATE > STOREDATE.BAT
STOREDATE
```

The first line creates a batch file called STOREDATA.BAT with the output of the DATE prompt. The ECHO | MORE is used to supply the return needed so you don't have to answer the DATE question. STOREDATA.BAT will contain the following two lines:

```
Current date is Mon 10-14-1991
Enter new date (mm-dd-yyyy):
```

The last line of the AUTOEXEC.BAT file runs STOREDAT.BAT. STOREDAT.BAT runs a batch file you create called CURRENT.BAT, and passes five parameters. Those five parameters are:

Parameter	Contains
%0	Current
%1	date
%2	is

| %3 | Mon (This will change each time the batch file is run.) |
| %4 | 10-14-1991 (This will change each time the batch file is run.) |

Finally, Fig. 12-1 shows CURRENT.BAT configured to automatically back up the hard disk every Friday and automatically perform an incremental backup every Wednesday. Additional commands can be added to conditionally run other programs. You can make the day and date available to other batch files by adding these lines to include the date and time in the environment:

```
SET DAY = %3
SET DATE = %4
```

One drawback to this method is that CURRENT.BAT gets run every time you boot your computer. This isn't a problem if you never have to reboot; however, if computer problems sometimes cause you to reboot then this can be a significant problem. The reason for running a batch file occasionally is that you don't want to have to fool with it. As written, CURRENT.BAT would run a backup every time the computer was rebooted on Friday.

You can eliminate this problem by having the batch file create a dummy file after a successful backup. If it tests to see if the dummy file exists prior to the backup, it won't make two backups on Friday. Of course, the batch file would need to delete the dummy file after Friday was over. CURRENT1.BAT in Fig. 12-2 does just this.

Volume label

The basic trick in using the DATE and TIME is to pipe the output of these commands to a file and then run the resulting file. This places the rest of the line into replaceable parameters that the batch file can access. You can use the same trick with the volume label.

The batch file GETVOL.BAT in Fig. 12-3 gets the volume label and pipes it to the file STOREVOL.BAT. Notice that ¦ MORE is missing. Because the VOL command doesn't expect an input, you don't need to echo a return. The file STOREVOL.BAT in Fig. 12-4 shows the typical contents of this file. The second line was added in DOS 4.0, so you might not see this line in your own files. Its presence won't affect the procedure.

The batch file VOLUME.BAT actually places the volume label into the environment. Figure 12-5 shows this file. The steps in the process are:

1. Run GETVOL.BAT, shown in Fig. 12-3. This file first pipes the volume label into the file STOREVOL.BAT and then runs STOREVOL.BAT. The CALL command isn't used, so control never returns to GETVOL.BAT.
2. STOREVOL.BAT, shown in Fig. 12-4, runs and enters the single command VOL UME to run VOLUME.BAT. The word *in* is passed as %1, *drive* is passed as %2, *C* is passed as %3, *is* is passed as %4, and the volume label is passed as %5. The CALL command isn't used, so control never returns to STOREVOL.BAT.
3. VOLUME.BAT, shown in Fig. 12-5, runs and places the contents of the volume label into an environmental variable.

So far the process has been fairly simple, but there's a major complication you might have to consider. Many utilities allow you to enter a volume label with a space in it. In fact, your volume label could be *A B C D E F*, which has five spaces in it. Using the process above, only the *A* part of the volume label would be placed into the environment. Although GETVOL.BAT and STOREVOL.BAT can remain the same, VOLUME.BAT must be modified to handle volume labels with spaces.

Figure 12-6 shows VOLUME1.BAT, which is VOLUME.BAT with the necessary modifications. A couple of comments are in order:

- The most difficult volume label you can have is six individual characters separated by a single space each. This fills up the entire eleven spaces allocated for the volume label. When this happens, the replaceable parameters out to %9 are one short of the necessary six parameters. A single SHIFT command changes this.
- The %SPACE% variable contains a single space, so the batch file requires a space after the equal sign and before the return.
- The lack of spaces on the last line is crucial. If you include spaces, DOS will incorporate those spaces into the environmental variable as well. While this line looks confusing, DOS handles it properly.

Of course, once you get the volume label into the environment, you need something to do with it. The typical thing is to test to see if it matches some predefined value. You can do this using a typical IF test. It's important to remember that many after-market utilities allow volume labels with lowercase letters, so you can't make any assumptions about the capitalization.

Serial number

Since DOS 4.0, DOS adds a unique serial number to each disk when it's formatted. Even disks created with DISKCOPY have a different serial number than the one they were copied from. It's possible for a batch file to access this serial number in much the same fashion as it accesses the volume label. The advantage of writing a batch file to access the serial number is that the serial number never has a space in it so you don't have to deal with that complexity.

The first step is to use the VOL command to display the volume label and serial number. That display is processed by the FIND filter to look for the line containing the word *Serial*. Then the line is piped to a temporary batch file. SERIAL.BAT in Fig. 12-7 handles all this. The last step is to run the temporary batch file, which is called JUNK.BAT. JUNK.BAT will contain the single line, *Volume Serial Number is ####-####*.

Using Batcmd

While getting date and time information using batch files is possible, the process is somewhat clumsy. This is one area where utility programs are very useful. GET-TIME.BAT in Fig. 12-8 quickly finds the date and time using Batcmd. While GET-TIME.BAT just displays the information, it could also be left in the environment for other batch files to access.

Calling technical support

I write about and use a lot of software, so I'm occasionally forced to call technical support lines. I have to be ready to answer any questions they have about my system, but sometimes I'm not actually in front of my computer. To aid me in answering these questions, I wrote TECH-AID.BAT in Fig. 12-9.

TECH-AID.BAT uses a number of features specific to DOS 5.0, so if you use a different version of DOS you'll need to modify the batch file. In addition, if you have a utility like SI in the Norton Utilities, you'll want to add that command to the batch file to take advantage of its information.

As written, TECH-AID.BAT creates a text file called C:\TECH-AID.TXT, which contains its results. This file is configured by an environmental variable at the top of TECH-AID.BAT, so it's easy to change the name. If you want the information to go directly to your printer, change the name to LPT1 or LPT2, depending on how your printer is connected.

Summary

- It's possible for a batch file to access the date, as CURRENT.BAT illustrates.
- It's possible for a batch file to access the volume label, as GETVOL.BAT illustrates.
- It's possible for a batch file to access the serial number, as SERIAL.BAT illustrates.
- TECH-AID.BAT uses DOS 5.0 to create a text file describing your computing environment.

12-1 CURRENT.BAT is a batch file configured to do backups on Wednesdays and Fridays.

Batch File Line	Explanation
`@ECHO OFF`	Turn command-echoing off.

`REM NAME:     CURRENT.BAT`
`REM PURPOSE: Backup On Wednesday`
`REM          And Friday`
`REM VERSION: 1.00`
`REM DATE:    April 15, 1991`
	Documentation remarks.

`IF (%1)==(/?) GOTO HELP` `IF (%1)==(?)  GOTO HELP`	If the user starts the batch file with a request for help, jump to a section to display that help.

`IF (%1)==() GOTO END`
`IF (%2)==() GOTO END`
`IF (%3)==() GOTO END`
`IF (%4)==() GOTO END`
	Exit the batch file if all four of the replaceable parameters it expects aren't entered.

`REM Jump To Testing Section`	Documentation remark.
`GOTO TESTS`	Jump down to the section of the batch file that tests the parameters.

Batch File Line	Explanation

`:BACKUP`
`BACKUP C:\ A: /S`
`GOTO ENDBACK`
`:END_BACKUP`
	Perform a full backup and exit this section of the batch file.

`:PARTBACK`
`BACKUP C:\ A: /S/M`
`GOTO ENDPART`
`:END_PARTBACK`
	Perform an incremental backup and exit this section of the batch file.

`REM Other Operations Here` `REM Jump To Them Using Tests`	This batch file is a simple illustration. You could have many more sections to perform different operations on different days.
`:TESTS`	The section of the batch file that decides what to do each day.
`IF %3==Fri GOTO BACKUP`	If it's Friday, perform a full backup. A trick described in the book sends the day of the week to this batch file.
`:ENDBACK`	The full backup jumps back to this label so the batch file can test to see if it needs to perform any other operations today.
`IF %3==Wed GOTO PARTBACK`	If it's Wednesday, the batch file performs an incremental backup.
`:ENDPART`	The incremental backup returns to this point.
`REM Other Tests Here` `GOTO END`	This batch file is for illustration and performs only two tests on the day of the week. You might also want to optimize the hard disk on certain days or perform other tasks.

`:HELP`
`ECHO This Batch File Uses The Day`
`ECHO Of The Week To Decide What`
`ECHO Actions To Perform`
`ECHO Do Not Run From The Command`
`ECHO Line`
`GOTO END`
`:END_HELP`
	Section that displays help when the user starts the batch file with a /? or a ? as the first replaceable parameter.

`:END`	A label marking the end of the batch file.

12-2 CURRENT1.BAT is a modified version of CURRENT.BAT that will perform a backup only the first time a computer is booted on the assigned day.

Batch File Line	Explanation
`@ECHO OFF`	Turn command-echoing off.

`REM NAME:      CURRENT1.BAT`
`REM PURPOSE: Perform Tasks On A`
`REM          Specific Day`
`REM VERSION: 1.00`
`REM DATE:    April 15, 1991`
	Documentation remarks.

`IF (%1)==(/?) GOTO HELP` `IF (%1)==(?)  GOTO HELP`	If the user starts the batch file with a request for help, jump to a section to display that help.

`IF (%1)==() GOTO END`
`IF (%2)==() GOTO END`
`IF (%3)==() GOTO END`
`IF (%4)==() GOTO END`
	Exit if the batch file doesn't receive the appropriate replaceable parameter. A trick discussed in the book sends DOS information from the TIME command to this batch file.

`REM Notice That In The GOTO`
`REM Statement Below I Use The`
`REM %3 Variable As The Basis Of`
`REM The GOTO. This Assumes That`
`REM The Batch File Is Never Run`
`REM From The Command Line.`
`REM I Could Avoid This By`
`REM Testing On Each Day`
`REM Value Of %3 Separately.`
	Documentation remarks.

`GOTO %3`	The day of the week comes into the batch file as the third replaceable parameter. This line uses that to jump to a section to handle the specific day.
`:SUN`	The section to handle the Sunday commands.
`REM Sunday Commands`	Whatever commands you want to perform every Sunday would go here. If they take a long time, you would need a flag file like FLAGWED to make sure they're not repeated if you reboot on Sunday.
`IF EXIST FLAGFRI DEL FLAGFRI` `IF EXIST FLAGWED DEL FLAGWED`	If any of the flag files exist, delete them.
`GOTO END`	Exit the batch file to avoid processing the other days.

`:MON`
`REM Monday Commands`
`IF EXIST FLAGFRI DEL FLAGFRI`
`IF EXIST FLAGWED DEL FLAGWED`
`GOTO END`
`:END_MON`
	Perform the tasks for Monday.

Batch File Line	Explanation

`:TUE`
`REM Tuesday Commands`
`IF EXIST FLAGFRI DEL FLAGFRI`
`IF EXIST FLAGWED DEL FLAGWED`
`GOTO END`
`END_TUE`
	Perform the tasks for Tuesday.

`:WED`	Perform the tasks for Wednesday.
`REM Wednesday Commands`	Documentation remark.
`IF NOT EXIST FLAGWED BACKUP C:\` `    A: /S`	If the file FLAGWED doesn't exist, perform a full backup. Once this backup is completed, the batch file will create FLAGWED to signal that the Wednesday backup has been completed. That way, if the computer is rebooted on Wednesday, it isn't backed up twice on the same day. Tomorrow, or the next day the computer is used, FLAGWED will be deleted because the backup will no longer be current.
`REM Create Flag File`	Documentation remark.
`TYPE Nofile > FLAGWED`	This command creates a zero-length flag file that doesn't take up any disk space. Note that NOFILE must *not* exist. This is explained in more detail in the book.
`IF EXIST FLAGFRI DEL FLAGFRI`	Because it isn't Friday, the batch file deletes the Friday flag.
`GOTO END` `:END_WED`	Exit the batch file.

`:THU`
`REM Thursday Commands`
`IF EXIST FLAGFRI DEL FLAGFRI`
`IF EXIST FLAGWED DEL FLAGWED`
`GOTO END`
`:END_THU`
	Perform the tasks for Thursday.

`:FRI`
`REM Friday Commands`
`IF NOT EXIST FLAGFRI BACKUP`
`    C:\ A: /S/M`
`TYPE Nofile > FLAGFRI`
`IF EXIST FLAGWED DEL FLAGWED`
`GOTO END`
`:END_FRI`
	Perform the Friday tasks, including an incremental backup and creating a flag file as discussed previously.

`:SAT`
`REM Saturday Commands`
`IF EXIST FLAGFRI DEL FLAGFRI`
`IF EXIST FLAGWED DEL FLAGWED`
`GOTO END`
`:END_SAT`
	Perform the tasks for Saturday.

Batch File Line	Explanation
:HELP ECHO This Batch File Performs ECHO Different Tasks On ECHO Different Days ECHO It Is *NOT* Intended To ECHO Run From The Command Line GOTO END :END_HELP	Section that displays help when the user starts the batch file with a /? or a ? as the first replaceable parameter.
:End	Label marking the end of the batch file.

12-3 GETVOL.BAT gets the volume label and pipes it to a file.

Batch File Line	Explanation
@ECHO OFF	Turn command-echoing off.
REM NAME: GETVOL.BAT REM PURPOSE: First Step To Get REM Volume Label REM VERSION: 1.00 REM DATE: April 15, 1991	Remark giving the name of the batch file.
IF (%1)==(/?) GOTO HELP IF (%1)==(?) GOTO HELP	If the user starts the batch file with a request for help, jump to a section to display that help.
VOL > STOREVOL.BAT	Pipe the volume into a file named STOREVOL.BAT.
STOREVOL	Run STOREVOL.BAT for additional processing.
GOTO END	Exit the batch file.
:HELP ECHO This Batch File Pipes The ECHO Volume Label To The Batch ECHO File STOREVOL.BAT And Then ECHO Runs That Batch File GOTO END :END_HELP	Section that displays help when the user starts the batch file with a /? or a ? as the first replaceable parameter.
:END	Label marking the end of the batch file.

12-4 STOREVOL.BAT contains the volume label along with the rest of the messages DOS displays for the VOL command.

Batch File Line	Explanation
`Volume in drive C is Richardson`	Note that this batch file is created by another batch file issuing a VOL command and piping the results to STOREVOL.BAT. When this batch file is run, it runs VOLUME.BAT and passes the following parameters: %1 in %2 drive %3 C %4 is %5 Richardson and thus VOLUME.BAT has access to the volume label. As explained in the text, %5 cannot contain all the volume.
`Volume Serial Number is 2F47-0FE7`	This line contains the serial number of the disk for later versions of DOS, but there's no way to access this information in this batch file because the first time VOLUME.BAT runs, it never returns control to this batch file.

12-5 VOLUME.BAT actually places the volume label into the environment.

Batch File Line	Explanation
`@ECHO OFF`	Turn command-echoing off.
`GOTO TOP`	Skip over the documentation remarks that follow.

`NAME:    VOLUME.BAT`
`PURPOSE: Store Volume Or Serial Number`
`VERSION: 2.00`
`DATE:    April 15, 1991`
	Documentation remarks.

`:TOP`	Label used to jump over the non-executing documentation remarks.
`IF (%1)==(in) SET VOLUME=%5`	If the batch file was passed the volume label string, store the volume label to the environment.

Batch File Line	Explanation
`IF (%1)==(Serial) SET SERIAL=%4` `IF (%1)==(Serial) DEL JUNK.BAT`	If the batch file was passed the serial number string, store the serial number to the environment and delete the temporary batch file that called it.
`IF (%1)==(/?) GOTO HELP` `IF (%1)==(?)  GOTO HELP`	If the user starts the batch file with a request for help, jump to a section to display that help.
`GOTO END`	Exit the batch file.

`:HELP`
`ECHO VOLUME.BAT Stores Volume Or`
`ECHO Serial Number In Environment`
`ECHO Must Be Called By Another`
`ECHO Program`
`BATCMD SL`
`ECHO Cannot Run From Command Line`
`GOTO END`
`:END_HELP`
	Section that displays help when the user starts the batch file with a /? or a ? as the first replaceable parameter.

`:END`	Label marking the end of the batch file.

12-6 VOLUME1.BAT is a version of VOLUME.BAT that will handle spaces in the volume label properly.

Batch File Line	Explanation
`@ECHO OFF`	Turn command-echoing off.

`REM NAME:     VOLUME1.BAT`
`REM PURPOSE: Stores Volume In`
`REM          Environment`
`REM VERSION: 2.00`
`REM DATE:    December 24, 1991`
	Documentation remarks.

`IF (%1)==(/?) GOTO HELP` `IF (%1)==(?)  GOTO HELP`	If the user starts the batch file with a request for help, jump to a section to display that help.
`IF (%5)==() SET VOLUME=No Volume Label` `IF (%5)==() GOTO END`	If no volume label was passed to the batch file, create an appropriate entry and exit the batch file.
`SET SPACE=`	Create an environmental variable called SPACE containing a single space.
`SHIFT` `SHIFT` `SHIFT` `SHIFT`	Move the first character of the volume label down to %1.

Batch File Line	Explanation
SET VOLUME=%1	Store the first character of the volume label to the environmental variable VOLUME.
:TOPLOOP	Label marking the top of a loop.
SHIFT	Move the components of the volume label down one level.
IF (%1)==() GOTO END	When there are no more components to the volume label, exit the batch file.
SET VOLUME=%VOLUME%%SPACE%%1	Store the current portion of the volume label, a space, and the next component of the volume label to the VOLUME environmental variable.
GOTO TOPLOOP :END_TOPLOOP	Continue looping.
:HELP ECHO VOLUME1.BAT Stores Volume ECHO In Environment ECHO Must Be Called By Another ECHO Program BATCMD SL ECHO Cannot Run From Command Line GOTO END :END_HELP	Section that displays help when the user starts the batch file with a /? or a ? as the first replaceable parameter.
:END	Label marking the end of the batch file.
SET SPACE=	Delete the temporary environmental variable.

12-7 SERIAL.BAT calls VOLUME.BAT to store the serial number in the environment.

Batch File Line	Explanation
@ECHO OFF	Turn command-echoing off.
GOTO TOP	Skip over the documentation remarks that follow.
NAME: SERIAL.BAT PURPOSE: Get Serial Number VERSION: 1.00 DATE: January 7, 1992	Documentation remarks.
:TOP	Label used to jump over the nonexecuting documentation remarks.

Batch File Line	Explanation
`IF (%1)==(/?) GOTO HELP` `IF (%1)==(?)  GOTO HELP`	If the user starts the batch file with a request for help, jump to a section to display that help.
`VOL | FIND "Serial" >JUNK.BAT`	Display the volume label/serial number display, search for the line containing *Serial* and pipe that line to a temporary batch file.
`JUNK`	Run the temporary batch file.
`GOTO END`	The line above runs the temporary batch file without using the CALL command, so command doesn't return to this batch file and this command is never executed.

`:HELP`
`ECHO Stores Serial In`
`ECHO Environment`
`GOTO END`
`:END_HELP`
	Section that displays help when the user starts the batch file with a /? or a ? as the first replaceable parameter.

`:END`	Label marking the end of the batch file.

12-8 GET-TIME.BAT gets date and time information using the Batcmd utility program.

Batch File Line	Explanation
`@ECHO OFF`	Turn command-echoing off.

`REM NAME:    GET-TIME.BAT`
`REM PURPOSE: Get Date/Time Using Batcmd`
`REM VERSION: 1.00`
`REM DATE:    December 21, 1991`
	Documentation remarks.

`IF (%1)==(/?) GOTO HELP` `IF (%1)==(?)  GOTO HELP`	If the user starts the batch file with a request for help, jump to a section to display that help.
`IF NOT (%1)==(XYZ123ABC) GOTO START`	GET-TIME.BAT calls itself as a subroutine and uses XYZ123ABC as a replaceable parameter to flag when it's being called as a subroutine. This tells it to jump to a special section when acting like a regular batch file and to stay at the top when acting like a subroutine.

Batch File Line	Explanation

`FOR %%J IN (0 1 2 3 4 5 6 7 8 9 10) DO`
`    IF ERRORLEVEL %%J SET ERROR=%%J`
`FOR %%J IN (11 12 13 14 15 16 17 18) DO`
`    IF ERRORLEVEL %%J SET ERROR=%%J`
`FOR %%J IN (19 20 21 22 23 24 25 26) DO`
`    IF ERRORLEVEL %%J SET ERROR=%%J`
`FOR %%J IN (27 28 29 30 31 32 33 34) DO`
`    IF ERRORLEVEL %%J SET ERROR=%%J`
`FOR %%J IN (35 36 37 38 39 40 41 42) DO`
`    IF ERRORLEVEL %%J SET ERROR=%%J`
`FOR %%J IN (43 44 45 46 47 48 49 50) DO`
`    IF ERRORLEVEL %%J SET ERROR=%%J`
`FOR %%J IN (51 52 53 54 55 56 57 58) DO`
`    IF ERRORLEVEL %%J SET ERROR=%%J`
`FOR %%J IN (59 60 61 62 63 64 65 66) DO`
`    IF ERRORLEVEL %%J SET ERROR=%%J`
`FOR %%J IN (67 68 69 70 71 72 73 74) DO`
`    IF ERRORLEVEL %%J SET ERROR=%%J`
`FOR %%J IN (75 76 77 78 79 80 81 82) DO`
`    IF ERRORLEVEL %%J SET ERROR=%%J`
`FOR %%J IN (83 84 85 86 87 88 89 90) DO`
`    IF ERRORLEVEL %%J SET ERROR=%%J`
`FOR %%J IN (91 92 93 94 95 96 97 98) DO`
`    IF ERRORLEVEL %%J SET ERROR=%%J`
	This subroutine section finds the errorlevel value and stores it to an environmental variable. It does this by testing repeatedly from 0-98. As long as the test value is less than or equal to the errorlevel, each IF test is passed so the value of the environmental variable is updated each time. Once the test value exceeds the actual value, each IF test will fail, so the environmental variable is no longer updated. Thus, when this routine finishes it contains the proper value.

`GOTO END`	When functioning as a subroutine, finding the errorlevel is the only task this batch file needs to perform, so after doing that it exits, returning control to the calling batch file, or GET-TIME.BAT in this case.
`:START`	Label marking the start of the nonsubroutine section of the batch file.
`BATCMD SH`	Use the Batcmd utility to get the hour and store it in error-level.
`CALL GET-TIME XYZ123ABC`	Call GET-TIME.BAT as a subroutine to store the error-level value in an environmental variable.
`SET HOUR=%ERROR%`	Transfer the contents of the ERROR environmental variable to another variable.

`BATCMD SM`
`CALL GET-TIME XYZ123ABC`
`SET MINUTE=%ERROR%`
	Repeat the process to get the minute.

Batch File Line	Explanation
BATCMD SS CALL GET-TIME XYZ123ABC SET SECOND=%ERROR%	Repeat the process to get the second.
ECHO The Time Is %HOUR%:%MINUTE%:%SECOND%	Display the time.
SET HOUR= SET MINUTE= SET SECOND=	Reset the environmental variables used so far.
BATCMD SY CALL GET-TIME XYZ123ABC SET YEAR=%ERROR%	Repeat the process to get the year.
BATCMD SO CALL GET-TIME XYZ123ABC SET MONTH=%ERROR%	Repeat the process to get the month.
BATCMD SD CALL GET-TIME XYZ123ABC SET DAY=%ERROR%	Repeat the process to get the day.
ECHO The Date Is %MONTH%/%DAY%/%YEAR%	Display the date.
SET DAY= SET MONTH= SET YEAR= SET ERROR=	Reset the environmental variables.
GOTO END :END_START	Exit the batch file.
:HELP ECHO This Batch File Uses Batcmd To Store ECHO The Date And Time In The Environment GOTO END :END_HELP	Section that displays help when the user starts the batch file with a /? or a ? as the first replaceable parameter.
:END	Label marking the end of the batch file.

12-9 TECH-AID.BAT will create a text file containing a description of your computing environment.

Batch File Line	Explanation
@ECHO OFF	Turn command-echoing off.
GOTO MAIN	Skip over the documentation remarks that follow.
NAME: TECH-AID.BAT PURPOSE: Document System Attributes VERSION: 1.00 DATE: December 26, 1991	Documentation remarks.
:MAIN	Label used to jump over the non-executing documentation remarks.

Batch File Line	Explanation
`IF (%1)==(/?) GOTO HELP` `IF (%1)==(?) GOTO HELP`	If the user starts the batch file with a request for help, jump to a section to display that help.
`SET A=C:\TECH-AID.TXT`	Create an environmental variable to store the name of the ASCII file to use. This way, commands are shorter and the user can easily modify the batch file to use a different name or subdirectory.
`IF EXIST %A% GOTO EXIST`	If the file already exists, jump to a section to warn the user.
`:CONTINUE`	Label used by the section that warns about the file already existing to reenter the processing section at the proper point.
`ECHO *****Working*****`	This batch file takes a while to work, so put something on the screen to let the user know it has started.
`ECHO TECH-AID.TXT Created By` `     TECH-AID.BAT > %A%`	Pipe a message to the file indicating the source of the file.
`ECHO  >> %A%`	Pipe a blank line to the file by echoing an ALT-255 to the file.

`ECHO TECH-AID.BAT Copyright (C) 1992`
`     Tab Books >> %A%`
`ECHO Written by Ronny Richardson >>`
`     %A%`
`ECHO >> %A%`
`ECHO You Can Use It On All The`
`     Machines You >> %A%`
`ECHO Own Or Personally Use But You`
`     Cannot >> %A%`
`ECHO Give Copies To Anyone Else >> %A%`
`ECHO >> %A%`
`ECHO >> %A%`
	Pipe copyright information into the file.

`ECHO Processing System Files`	Tell the user what's happening.

`ECHO ^I^I System Configuration >> %A%`
`ECHO ^I^I -------------------- >> %A%`
`ECHO    >> %A%`
	Pipe an overall header into the file. Note that ^I is the tab character and moves the text to the right several spaces.

Batch File Line	Explanation

ECHO DOS VERSION >> %A%
ECHO ----------- >> %A%
VER >> %A%
ECHO Unless The Above Is 5.00 Or
     Higher >> %A%
ECHO This File Will Be Incomplete
     >> %A%
ECHO >> %A%
	Pipe the DOS version and supporting information into the file.

ECHO CONFIG.SYS File >> %A%
ECHO --------------- >> %A%
IF EXIST C:\CONFIG.SYS TYPE
     C:\CONFIG.SYS >> %A%
IF NOT EXIST C:\CONFIG.SYS ECHO No
     CONFIG.SYS File >> %A%
ECHO >> %A%
	Pipe the CONFIG.SYS file and supporting information into the file.

ECHO AUTOEXEC.BAT File >> %A%
ECHO ---------------- >> %A%
IF EXIST C:\AUTOEXEC.BAT TYPE
     C:\AUTOEXEC.BAT >> %A%
IF NOT EXIST C:\AUTOEXEC.BAT ECHO No
     AUTOEXEC.BAT File >> %A%
ECHO >> %A%
	Pipe the AUTOEXEC.BAT file and supporting information into the file.

ECHO Processing Memory	Tell the user what's happening.

ECHO SYSTEM MEMORY (PROGRAMS IN
     MEMORY) >> %A%
ECHO -----------------------------------
     >> %A%
MEM/P >> %A%
ECHO >> %A%
ECHO SYSTEM MEMORY (STATUS OF PROGRAMS
     ETC.) >> %A%
ECHO ------------------------------------
     ------ >> %A%
MEM/D >> %A%
ECHO >> %A%
ECHO SYSTEM MEMORY (CLASSIFIED BY
     MEMORY USE) >> %A%
ECHO ------------------------------
     ------- >> %A%
MEM/C >> %A%
ECHO >> %A%
	Pipe the memory and supporting information into the file.

ECHO ENVIRONMENT >> %A% ECHO ----------- >> %A% SET >> %A% ECHO >> %A%	Pipe the environment into the file.
ECHO Processing Other	Tell the user what's happening.
ECHO SETVER ASSIGNMENTS >> %A% ECHO ------------------ >> %A% SETVER >> %A% ECHO >> %A%	Pipe the SETVER information into the file.

Batch File Line	Explanation

`ECHO MODE ASSIGNMENTS >> %A%`
`ECHO ---------------- >> %A%`
`MODE >> %A%`
`ECHO  >> %A%`
	Pipe the MODE information into the file.

`ECHO ***END*** >> %A%`	Place an END at the end of the file.
`GOTO END`	Jump to the end of the file.
`:END_MAIN`	Label marking the end of the MAIN section.
`:EXIST`	Label marking the beginning of the section to tell the user that C:\TECH-AID.TXT already exists.
`ECHO %A% Already Exists`	Tell the user the file already exists.
`BATCMD YN Overwrite?`	Use Batcmd to see if he wants to overwrite the file.
`IF ERRORLEVEL 1 GOTO CONTINUE`	If he answers yes, jump to a section to continue processing.
`GOTO END`	If he answers no the batch file will reach this point, so exit the batch file.
`:END_EXIST`	Label marking the end of the EXIST section.

`:HELP`
`ECHO TECH-AID.BAT Creates A File`
`ECHO Called C:\TECH-AID.TXT That`
`ECHO Contains Information You Might Be`
`ECHO Asked For When Calling`
`ECHO Software Technical Support`
`BATCMD SL`
`ECHO TECH-AID.BAT **REQUIRES** DOS 5.0`
`BATCMD SL`
`ECHO Without DOS 5.0, The File Created`
`ECHO By TECH-AID.BAT Will Be`
`ECHO Incomplete And The Batch File`
`ECHO Will Generate "Bad Command`
`ECHO Or File Name" Error Messages`
`GOTO END`
`:END_HELP`
	Section that displays help when the user starts the batch file with a /? or a ? as the first replaceable parameter.

`:END`	Label marking the end of the batch file.
`SET A=`	Reset the environmental variable before exiting the batch file.

13

Working with your path

Your path is nothing more than a list of subdirectories for DOS to look through when you issue a command that isn't an internal command and not a program in the current subdirectory. You can see what your path is by issuing a PATH or SET command by themselves.

Both the PATH and SET commands are bi-modal DOS commands. That is they perform two functions, depending on how they're used. Used alone, both commands display information. When followed by a series of subdirectories, the PATH command places a new path into the environment. When followed by a variable and its contents, the SET command stores that variable in the environment. For example:

```
PATH = C: \ ;..;C: \ BAT;C: \ EDITOR;C: \ DATABASE;C: \ 123
SET USER = Richardson
```

The command to set the path must begin with a PATH= statement and the DOS command line is limited to 127 characters, so the path itself is limited to 122 characters.

Both the PATH and SET commands display the path as a continuous string of subdirectories that's hard to read and interpret. SP.BAT in Fig. 13-1 overcomes this limitation by listing the subdirectories one per line and numbering them.

SP.BAT accesses the path by calling itself and passing the path as a replaceable parameter, something you can't do from the command line. It's important that you don't rename SP.BAT, especially to a longer name like SHOWPATH.BAT. SP.BAT calls itself and passes your entire path as a replaceable parameter. As discussed above, your path can contain as many as 122 characters. For SP.BAT to obtain the entire path on the command line, its name can't exceed four characters because a 122-character path plus a 4-character name and a space between the batch file name and path reaches the DOS command-line limit of 127 characters.

The only way DOS allows you to construct a path is to enter everything on the command line following a PATH= command. Not only do you have to remember all the subdirectories, you have to remember to enter semicolons between them. SETPATH.BAT in Fig. 13-2 overcomes this limitation by prompting you for the subdirectories one at a time, and it adds the semicolons for you.

Once you've entered all the subdirectories, SETPATH.BAT gives you the option of making the path you've just entered the current path. It also gives you the option of creating a batch file (C:\NEWPATH.BAT) so you can reuse the path without having to rerun SETPATH.BAT. If C:\NEWPATH.BAT exists, it will warn you before overwriting it.

SETPATH.BAT requires Batcmd for all its operations. If the new path you enter doesn't include the subdirectory containing Batcmd and you elect to activate that path, SETPATH.BAT won't operate properly. To be entirely safe, you should have SET-PATH.BAT and Batcmd in a common subdirectory and modify SETPATH.BAT to change to that subdirectory at the top of the batch file. That way, Batcmd will always be available to SETPATH.BAT.

When you create or modify your path, DOS makes no effort to make sure all the subdirectories entered in your path are valid. In fact, the only time DOS will display an error message telling you about an invalid subdirectory is when it has to search for a program and it doesn't find the program until it has searched far enough along the path that it reaches the invalid subdirectory entry. TP.BAT in Fig. 13-3 overcomes that limitation by testing your path to make sure all the entries are valid.

Adding to your path

Most people simply include every subdirectory they need DOS to search in the path for and forget it. There are occasions, however, when you might want to have two separate paths. For example, if you're testing a new program and don't want DOS to search anywhere other than the current subdirectory, if you've added a subdirectory for a special program and want it in the path for only a short period of time, or if you have so many subdirectories to search that you want to have a separate path for each task. The plan of attack is the same for each of these problems. The steps are:

1. Store the current path to a variable in the environment.
2. Replace the path with a new path or modify the existing path.
3. Restore the old path from the environment.

Figure 13-4 shows PATH1.BAT, which will replace the current path with one specified on the command line. Figure 13-5 shows PATH2.BAT, which returns the path to the value stored in the environment. Figure 13-6 shows PATH3.BAT, which will append a new value onto the existing path. Then you could use PATH2.BAT to return to the old path. PATH4.BAT in Fig. 13-7 allows you to easily switch between three paths.

Deleting from your path

A batch file can also remove subdirectories, but the process is a little tricky. A batch file has access to the %PATH% environmental variable, but it has no way to strip it into its component parts. The different subdirectories in a path, however, are separated by semicolons, which DOS treats as legal dividers for replaceable parameters. If you issue the command

BATCH %PATH%

and have DOS treat %PATH% as the environmental variable, then the first subdirectory in the path would be %1, the second would be %2, and so on. Unfortunately, you can't use environmental variables on the command line in this fashion. Luckily, batch files can—so, if one batch file invokes another with this exact same command, the subdirectory components are passed as separate replaceable parameters just as you'd expect.

This method takes one more piece of information to work. The two batch files doing the work (EDITPATH.BAT and EDIT1.BAT in Figs. 13-8 and 13-9) need to know how much of the path to keep. They expect you to enter the number of subdirectories to keep on the command line. The batch files keep this many subdirectories from the front of the path and discard the remaining. You're limited to keeping the first eight but, with the addition of a SHIFT command, you can keep as many as you like. It would also be a simple modification to delete subdirectories from the front of the path rather than from the end. You might also want to modify the batch files to delete a single subdirectory where you specify the number of the subdirectory to delete. Of these two batch files, EDITPATH.BAT performs all the error checking and EDIT1.BAT has none.

While all these forward and backward deleting methods are quite useful, they're very inflexible if you want to delete a single subdirectory in the middle of your path. On the other hand, EDITPAT2.BAT in Fig. 13-10 is very flexible. It calls EDIT2.BAT in Fig. 13-11, which prompts you whether you want to keep each of your subdirectories, one by one. Using this method, you can easily delete one subdirectory in the middle of your path. EDIT2.BAT uses Batcmd to ask a question and set the errorlevel accordingly.

Notice that EDIT2.BAT first decides which subdirectories to keep and then constructs the new path. With this approach, there's no need to reset the path first, so all programs in your path will continue to work while EDIT2.BAT runs.

EDIT2.BAT doesn't attempt to construct the new path using a command like PATH=%PATH%;%1. If you use this approach, you have to test each time to see if the path contains anything because you don't want to add the semicolon before %1 the first time or the path will start with a semicolon. However, as the path expands, the following test

```
IF (%PATH%) = = ( ) SET PATH = %1
```

has the potential to exceed the 127-character limit DOS sets on the command line. To avoid this problem, EDIT2.BAT takes the approach of waiting until you've selected all the subdirectories to retain before constructing the path.

As written, EDIT2.BAT is limited to 20 subdirectories in the new path. In the unlikely event that you select more than twenty subdirectories to retain in the new path, EDIT2.BAT will abort without changing the path. Because the entire path statement is also limited to DOS's 127-character limit, this is unlikely to occur. If you have longer paths, you might want to expand EDIT2.BAT to handle the necessary number of subdirectories.

Summary

- Because the path is an environmental variable, batch files can work with it and manipulate it like any other environmental variable.

- SP.BAT will show your path in a much more usable format than DOS.
- SETPATH.BAT makes setting the path easier than DOS, and can create a batch file for you.
- TP.BAT will test your path to make sure all the entries are valid, something DOS doesn't do until it uses the path.
- PATH1.BAT through PATH4.BAT allow you to switch between different paths.
- EDITPATH.BAT and EDITPAT2.BAT let you edit your path.

13-1   SP.BAT will give you a nice listing of the subdirectories in your path.

Batch File Line	Explanation
`@ECHO OFF`	Turn command-echoing off.

`REM NAME:     SP.BAT`
`REM PURPOSE: Show Nice Path`
`REM VERSION: 1.00`
`REM DATE:    January 11, 1992`
	Documentation remarks.

`IF (%1)==(/?) GOTO HELP` `IF (%1)==(?)  GOTO HELP`	If the user starts the batch file with a request for help, jump to a section to display that help.
`IF NOT (%1)==() GOTO TOP`	If anything is entered on the command line, assume it's the path and jump to a processing section. This could cause problems if the user runs SP.BAT with a replaceable parameter, but it's necessary because having SP.BAT call itself with a subroutine flag would cause the command line to exceed 127 characters for users with a long path.
`SP %PATH%`	If the batch file reaches this point the user ran it without a replaceable parameter, so it runs itself, passing itself the path on the command line.
`:TOP`	Label marking the top of the section that processes the path.
`SET MATH=0`	Set a counter variable to zero.
`:TOPLOOP`	Label marking the top of the loop that displays the path.
`BATCMD AD`	Increase the counter variable by one.
`ECHO %MATH%:   %1`	Display the counter variable and the first replaceable parameter. (When the path was passed to SP.BAT on the command line DOS treated the semicolon as a divider, so each subdirectory entry is treated as a separate replaceable parameter.)
`SHIFT`	Move the replaceable parameters down one level.

13-1 Continued

Batch File Line	Explanation
`IF NOT (%1)==() GOTO TOPLOOP`	If there are more replaceable parameters, continue looping.
`GOTO END` `:END_TOPLOOP`	If there are no more replaceable parameters, exit the batch file.

`:HELP`
`ECHO Batch File Shows Path`
`ECHO Using A Nice Format`
`GOTO END`
`:END_HELP`
	Section that displays help when the user starts the batch file with a /? or a ? as the first replaceable parameter.

`:END`	Label marking the end of the batch file.

13-2 SETPATH.BAT makes it easy to write a new path and create a batch file to store that path.

Batch File Line	Explanation
`@ECHO OFF`	Turn command-echoing off.

`REM NAME:      SETPATH.BAT`
`REM PURPOSE: Interactive Path Building`
`REM VERSION: 1.00`
`REM DATE:      January 12, 1992`
	Documentation remarks.

`IF (%1)==(/?) GOTO HELP` `IF (%1)==(?)  GOTO HELP`	If the user starts the batch file with a request for help, jump to a section to display that help.

`SET MATH=0`
`SET NEWPATH=`
`SET FIRST=YES`
`SET BATCMD=`
	Configure some environmental variables used by the batch file.

`CLS`	Clear the screen.

`ECHO Enter Subdirectories`
`ECHO *WITHOUT* Leading Semicolon`
`ECHO For Example, Enter C:\BAT As`
`ECHO C:\BAT *NOT* ;C:\BAT`
`ECHO Press Return When Done`
	Give the user instructions.

`:TOPLOOP`	Label marking the top of a loop.
`BATCMD AD`	Increase the counter variable by one.
`IF NOT (%BATCMD%)==() ECHO` `    Added: %BATCMD%`	The first time through this batch file the environmental variable BATCMD doesn't exist, so the batch file skips this step. After that, this line displays the subdirectory that was last added to the path.

Batch File Line	Explanation
`BATCMD GE Enter #%MATH% Subdirectory` `    For Path`	Use Batcmd to obtain the next subdirectory to be added to the path. Batcmd stores this information to the environment using the variable name BATCMD.
`IF (%BATCMD%)==()    GOTO DONE`	If the user just pressed return, jump to the DONE section.
`IF (%FIRST%)==(YES) GOTO FIRST`	If this is the first subdirectory added to the path, jump to a special section to handle it.
`ECHO @PATH=%%PATH%%;%BATCMD% >>` `    C:\JUNK.BAT`	If this isn't the first subdirectory, pipe the command necessary to add this subdirectory to the path into the temporary batch file.
`GOTO TOPLOOP` `:END_TOPLOOP`	Continue looping.
`:FIRST`	Label marking the beginning of the section to handle the first subdirectory added to the path.
`IF (%BATCMD%)==() GOTO END`	If the user just pressed enter, exit the batch file.
`ECHO @ECHO OFF > C:\JUNK.BAT`	Start off by piping an @ECHO OFF command into the temporary batch file. A single pipe bracket is used, so this command will overwrite the temporary file if it exists.

`ECHO REM NAME:    JUNK.BAT Or`
`    NEWPATH.BAT >> C:\JUNK.BAT`
`ECHO REM PURPOSE: Set Path >>`
`    C:\JUNK.BAT`
`ECHO REM        Created By`
`    SETPATH.BAT >> C:\JUNK.BAT`
`ECHO REM        Copyright (c) 1992`
`    Tab Books >> C:\JUNK.BAT`
`ECHO REM VERSION: 1.00 >> C:\JUNK.BAT`
	Pipe some header information into the file.

`ECHO @PATH=%BATCMD% >> C:\JUNK.BAT`	Pipe the command that begins creating the new path into the file.
`SET FIRST=NO`	Reset the first entry flag so the remaining subdirectories will be handled differently.
`GOTO TOPLOOP` `:END_FIRST`	Continue looping.

Batch File Line	Explanation
:HELP ECHO This Batch File Prompts You ECHO For Subdirectories To Include In ECHO Your Path And Then Builds The ECHO Path For You BATCMD SL ECHO It Will Also Optionally Build ECHO A Batch File To Set That Path ECHO For You Automatically GOTO END :END_HELP	Section that displays help when the user starts the batch file with a /? or a ? as the first replaceable parameter.
:DONE	Label marking the beginning of the section to continue processing after the user is done entering subdirectories.
BATCMD YN Make The Path You Just Entered The "Real" Path?	Ask the user about switching to this new path.
IF ERRORLEVEL 1 CALL C:\JUNK.BAT	If the user answers yes, call the temporary batch file to change the path.
BATCMD YN Write Out Batch File Containing Path?	Ask the user about creating a batch file containing the commands to set this path.
IF ERRORLEVEL 1 GOTO WRITEIT	If the user answers yes, jump to another section.
GOTO END :END_DONE	If the user answered no to writing out the path to a batch file, exit this batch file.
:WRITEIT	Label marking the beginning of the section to handle creating a permanent batch file to set this path.
IF EXIST C:\NEWPATH.BAT GOTO WRITEIT2	If the file already exists, jump to another section.
COPY C:\JUNK.BAT C:\NEWPATH.BAT GOTO END :END_WRITEIT	If the file doesn't exist, create it and exit the batch file.
:WRITEIT2	Label marking the beginning of the section to deal with the batch file already existing.
ECHO C:\NEWPATH.BAT Exists! BATCMD YN Overwrite This File?	Warn the user and ask for permission to overwrite the existing file.

Batch File Line	Explanation
`IF NOT ERRORLEVEL 1 GOTO END`	If the user doesn't grant permission to overwrite the file, exit the batch file.

`COPY C:\JUNK.BAT C:\NEWPATH.BAT`
`GOTO END`
`:END_WRITEIT2`
	If the user does grant permission to overwrite the file, create it and exit the batch file.

`:END`
`SET NEWPATH=`
`SET FIRST=`
`SET MATH=`
`IF EXIST C:\JUNK.BAT DEL C:\JUNK.BAT`
	Label marking the end of the batch file. Reset the environmental variables used by the batch file and delete the temporary file used by the batch file before exiting.

13-3 TP.BAT will test your path to see if it has any invalid entries.

Batch File Line	Explanation
`@ECHO OFF`	Turn command-echoing off.

`REM NAME:     TP.BAT`
`REM PURPOSE: Test Path`
`REM VERSION: 1.00`
`REM DATE:     January 12, 1992`
	Documentation remarks.

`IF (%1)==(/?) GOTO HELP` `IF (%1)==(?)  GOTO HELP`	If the user starts the batch file with a request for help, jump to a section to display that help.
`IF NOT (%1)==() GOTO USEASSUB`	If anything is entered on the command line, assume it's the path and jump to a processing section. This could cause problems if the user runs TP.BAT with a replaceable parameter, but it's necessary because having TP.BAT call itself with a subroutine flag would cause the command line to exceed 127 characters for users with a long path.
`TP %PATH%`	If the batch file reaches this point the user ran it without a replaceable parameter, so it runs itself, passing itself the path on the command line.

Batch File Line	Explanation
`:USEASSUB`	Label marking the portion of the batch file that functions as a subroutine when it calls itself.
`SET TESTPATH=`	Reset an environmental variable used by the batch file.

`ECHO Testing The Following Path`
`ECHO ----------------------------`
`ECHO %PATH%`
	Show the user the path to be tested. The path is echoed on a separate line, so long paths will be displayed without being truncated.

`:TESTPATH`	Label marking the top of the section that tests the path.
`IF (%1)==() GOTO DONE`	Once all the subdirectories have been tested, jump to the next section.
`IF (%1)==(C:\) GOTO SKIP`	The testing method append a \NUL to the subdirectory, and C:\\NUL is an invalid entry. However, we know C:\ is a valid entry, so skip the testing for this entry.
`IF (%1)==(D:\) GOTO SKIP`	The D:\ is skipped for the same reason as the C:\ entry. Users without a D drive should delete this line.
`IF (%1)==(..) GOTO SKIP`	The double dot always references the subdirectory one level closer to the root directory. This is always a valid entry, so the testing can be skipped for this entry. The test for ..\NUL will work as long as the batch file isn't running from the root directory. When it's running from the root directory, ..\NUL is the same as C:\\NUL, which is invalid.

Batch File Line	Explanation
IF NOT EXIST %1\NUL ECHO %1 Invalid Entry	The test for %1\NUL is a valid DOS test that's true if the subdirectory exists. When a subdirectory doesn't exist the test for %1\NUL is false, so preceding it with a NOT makes it true. When a subdirectory doesn't exist, therefore, display an error message.
IF NOT EXIST %1\NUL BATCMD BE	If a subdirectory doesn't exist, use Batcmd to beep the speaker.
IF NOT EXIST %1\NUL SET TESTPATH= INVALID	If the subdirectory doesn't exist, set a flag environmental variable.
:SKIP	Label used above to skip testing for certain entries.
SHIFT	Move the replaceable parameters down one level.
GOTO TESTPATH :END_TESTPATH	Continue looping.
:DONE	Label marking the section that handles processing once all the subdirectories have been tested.
IF (%TESTPATH%)==() ECHO All Entries Valid	If the invalid entry flag was never created, tell the user all the subdirectory entries were valid.
GOTO END :END_DONE	Exit the batch file.
:HELP ECHO Enter TP To Test Your Path ECHO To See If It Contains Any ECHO Invalid Entries GOTO END :END_HELP	Section that displays help when the user starts the batch file with a /? or a ? as the first replaceable parameter.
:END	Label marking the end of the batch file.

13-4 PATH1.BAT dynamically changes the path while storing the old path.

Batch File Line	Explanation
`@ECHO OFF`	Turn command-echoing off.

`REM NAME:     PATH1.BAT`
`REM PURPOSE: Store Current Path And`
`REM          Reset To Subdirectory`
`REM          On Command Line`
`REM VERSION: 1.00`
`REM DATE:    April 17, 1991`
	Documentation remarks.

`IF (%1)==(/?) GOTO HELP` `IF (%1)==(?)  GOTO HELP`	If the user starts the batch file with a request for help, jump to a section to display that help.
`IF (%1)==() GOTO NOPATH`	If the user didn't enter a replaceable parameter, jump to an error-handling routine.
`SET OLDPATH=%PATH%`	Set an environmental variable called OLDPATH equal to the current path. This allows for restoring the original path later.
`SET PATH=%1`	Set the current path to the value entered as a replaceable parameter. Because a semicolon on the command line is treated as a parameter divider, this is limited to setting the path equal to a single subdirectory.
`GOTO END`	Exit the batch file.

`:NOPATH`
`ECHO No Path Specified`
`GOTO END`
`:END_NOPATH`
	Section to handle the error of the user not entering a path on the command line.

`:HELP`
`ECHO Stores The Current Path In The`
`ECHO Environment And Sets The Path`
`ECHO Equal To The Single`
`ECHO Subdirectory Entered On The`
`ECHO Command Line`
`GOTO END`
`:END_HELP`
	Section that displays help when the user starts the batch file with a /? or a ? as the first replaceable parameter.

`:END`	Label marking the end of the batch file.

13-5 PATH2.BAT restores the path to the value stored by PATH1.BAT.

Batch File Line	Explanation
`@ECHO OFF`	Turn command-echoing off.

`REM NAME:    PATH2.BAT`
`REM PURPOSE: Reset Path To Stored Value`
`REM VERSION: 1.00`
`REM DATE:    April 17, 1991`
	Documentation remarks.

`IF (%1)==(/?) GOTO HELP` `IF (%1)==(?)  GOTO HELP`	If the user starts the batch file with a request for help, jump to a section to display that help.
`IF (%OLDPATH%)==() GOTO MISSING`	If the path is not stored in the environment, jump to an error-handling routine.
`SET PATH=%OLDPATH%` `GOTO END`	Restore the path to its original value after being changed by PATH1.BAT and exit the batch file.

`:MISSING`
`ECHO The Path Has Not Been Stored In The`
`ECHO Environment By PATH1.BAT`
`ECHO Batch File Aborting`
`GOTO END`
`:END_MISSING`
	Section to display an error message when the path isn't stored in the environment.

`:HELP`
`ECHO Restores The Path To The Value`
`ECHO PATH1.BAT Stores To The Environment`
`GOTO END`
`:END_HELP`
	Section that displays help when the user starts the batch file with a /? or a ? as the first replaceable parameter.

`:END`	Label marking the end of the batch file.

13-6 PATH3.BAT appends a subdirectory onto the current path.

Batch File Line	Explanation
`@ECHO OFF`	Turn command-echoing off.

`REM NAME:    PATH3.BAT`
`REM PURPOSE: Append Subdirectory To Path`
`REM VERSION: 1.00`
`REM DATE:    April 17, 1991`
	Documentation remarks.

`IF (%1)==(/?) GOTO HELP` `IF (%1)==(?)  GOTO HELP`	If the user starts the batch file with a request for help, jump to a section to display that help.

Batch File Line	Explanation
`IF (%1)==()    GOTO NOPATH`	Jump to an error-handling routine if the user didn't enter a subdirectory on the command line.
`SET OLDPATH=%PATH%`	Store the old path in an environmental variable.
`SET PATH=%PATH%;%1`	Add the subdirectory entered on the command line to the path.
`GOTO END`	Exit the batch file.

`:NOPATH`
`ECHO No Path Specified`
`GOTO END`
`:END_NOPATH`
	Error-handling routine.

`:HELP`
`ECHO Stores The Current Path In The`
`ECHO Environment And Adds The`
`ECHO Subdirectory Entered On The`
`ECHO Command Line To The Path`
`GOTO END`
`:END_HELP`
	Section that displays help when the user starts the batch file with a /? or a ? as the first replaceable parameter.

`:END`	Label marking the end of the batch file.

13-7 PATH4.BAT allows easy switching among three different paths.

Batch File Line	Explanation
`@ECHO OFF`	Turn command-echoing off.

`REM NAME:     PATH4.BAT`
`REM PURPOSE: Switch Between Three Paths`
`REM VERSION: 1.00`
`REM DATE:     April 17, 1991`
	Documentation remarks.

`IF (%1)==(/?) GOTO HELP` `IF (%1)==(?)  GOTO HELP`	If the user starts the batch file with a request for help, jump to a section to display that help.
`IF (%1)==()    GOTO NOPATH`	If the user didn't enter a number on the command line, jump to an error-handling routine.

Batch File Line	Explanation
| ```
IF %1==1 PATH=C:\WORD;C:\DOS;C:\BAT
IF %1==1 GOTO END
``` | If the user entered a one on the command line, set the path accordingly and exit the batch file. Note the addition of the C:\DOS and C:\BAT to the path for this application. C:\BAT is required so this batch file will run again to switch applications and C:\DOS allows most DOS tools to operate under any path. |
| ```
IF %1==2 PATH=C:\LOTUS;C:\DOS;C:\BAT
IF %1==2 GOTO END
``` | If the user entered a two on the command line, set the path accordingly and exit the batch file. |
| ```
IF %1==3 PATH=C:\DBASE;C:\DOS;C:\BAT
IF %1==3 TOTO END
``` | If the user entered a three on the command line, set the path accordingly and exit the batch file. |
| ```
GOTO ERROR
``` | If the batch file reaches this point the user entered an invalid selection, so jump to an error-handling section. |
| ```
:ERROR
ECHO ONLY 1-3 Are Valid Path Selections
GOTO END
:END_ERROR
``` | Section to handle invalid entries. |
| ```
:NOPATH
ECHO No Path Selected
GOTO END
:END_NOPATH
``` | Section to handle no input on the command line. |
| ```
:HELP
ECHO This Demonstration Batch File Will
ECHO Switch Between Three Different Paths
ECHO They Are:
ECHO --------
ECHO 1: PATH=C:\WORD;C:\DOS;C:\BAT
ECHO 2: PATH=C:\LOTUS;C:\DOS;C:\BAT
ECHO 3: PATH=C:\DBASE;C:\DOS;C:\BAT
GOTO END
:END_HELP
``` | Section that displays help when the user starts the batch file with a /? or a ? as the first replaceable parameter. |
| ```
:END
``` | Label marking the end of the batch file. |

13-8 EDITPATH.BAT is the first of two batch files used to remove extra subdirectories from your path.

Batch File Line	Explanation
`@ECHO OFF`	Turn command-echoing off.

`REM NAME:     EDITPATH.BAT`
`REM PURPOSE: Selectively Discard`
`REM         Subdirectories From Path`
`REM VERSION: 1.00`
`REM DATE:    May 10, 1991`
`REM Keep First n Elements Of Path`
	Documentation remarks.

`IF (%1)==(/?) GOTO HELP` `IF (%1)==(?)  GOTO HELP`	If the user starts the batch file with a request for help, jump to a section to display that help.
`IF (%1)==()   GOTO ERROR`	If the user does not enter a replaceable parameter, jump to an error-handling section.

`IF %1==1 GOTO OK`
`IF %1==2 GOTO OK`
`IF %1==3 GOTO OK`
`IF %1==4 GOTO OK`
`IF %1==5 GOTO OK`
`IF %1==6 GOTO OK`
`IF %1==7 GOTO OK`
`IF %1==8 GOTO OK`
`GOTO ERROR`
	This illustrates one way to make sure the user enters only the digits 1-8 as the first replaceable parameter.

`:ERROR`
`ECHO Number Of Elements To Retain Not`
`ECHO Specified Or Specified Improperly`
`GOTO END`
`:END_ERROR`
	Deal with the problem of the user entering an invalid replaceable parameter or not entering one at all.

`:OK`	Section that edits the path if the user runs the batch file appropriately.

`EDIT1 %1 %PATH%`
`GOTO END`
`:END_OK`
	Run EDIT1.BAT and pass the path as a series of replaceable parameters. Because EDIT1.BAT is run without the CALL command, control does not pass back to EDITPATH.BAT.

`:HELP`
`ECHO This Batch File Allows You To`
`ECHO Keep The First 1-8 Entries Of`
`ECHO Your Path By Specifying That`
`ECHO Number On The Command Line`
`GOTO END`
`:END_HELP`
	Section that displays help when the user starts the batch file with a /? or a ? as the first replaceable parameter.

`:END`	Label marking the end of the batch file.

13-9 EDIT1.BAT actually performs the work of changing your path, but it must be called by EDIT PATH.BAT.

Batch File Line	Explanation
`@ECHO OFF`	Turn command-echoing off.

`REM NAME:     EDIT1.BAT`
`REM PURPOSE: Perform Editing Passed`
`REM          By EDITPATH.BAT`
`REM VERSION: 1.00`
`REM DATE:    May 10, 1991`
	Documentation remarks.

`REM Reconstruct First n Elements Of`
`REM PATH. n Assumed To Be Less`
`REM Than Or Equal To Eight.`
	Documentation remarks.

`IF (%1)==(/?) GOTO HELP` `IF (%1)==(?)  GOTO HELP`	If the user starts the batch file with a request for help, jump to a section to display that help.
`PATH=%2`	Set the path to the second replaceable parameter. The first replaceable parameter stores the number of subdirectories to keep.
`IF %1==1 GOTO END`	If keeping just the first subdirectory, exit the batch file.
`PATH=%PATH%;%3`	Add the second subdirectory onto the existing path--which currently contains only the first subdirectory.
`IF %1==2 GOTO END`	If keeping just two subdirectories, exit the batch file.
Continues in a similar fashion through %8	
`IF %1==7 GOTO END`	If adding seven subdirectories, exit the batch file. If this test fails, the batch file assumes an eight was entered without testing for an invalid response.
`PATH=%PATH%;%9` `GOTO END`	Add the final subdirectory to the path.

`:HELP`
`ECHO This Batch File Must Be Called`
`ECHO By EDITPATH.BAT`
`ECHO *DO NOT RUN FROM COMMAND LINE*`
`GOTO END`
`:END_HELP`
	Section that displays help when the user starts the batch file with a /? or a ? as the first replaceable parameter.

`:END`	A label marking the end of the batch file.
`ECHO Path Now Set To %PATH%`	Tell the user what has happened before exiting.

13-10 EDITPAT2.BAT also lets you remove subdirectories from your path, but it's much more powerful than EDITPATH.BAT.

Batch File Line	Explanation
`@ECHO OFF`	Turn command-echoing off.

`REM NAME:     EDITPAT2.BAT`
`REM PURPOSE: Selectively Delete`
`REM          Subdirectories`
`REM VERSION: 1.00`
`REM DATE:    May 10, 1991`
	Documentation remark.

`IF (%1)==(/?) GOTO HELP` `IF (%1)==(?)  GOTO HELP`	If the user starts the batch file with a request for help, jump to a section to display that help.
`EDIT2 %PATH%` `GOTO END`	Run another batch file while passing the path as a series of replaceable parameters. A couple of notes are important: Because the batch file runs EDIT2.BAT without the CALL command, control never returns to EDITPAT2.BAT. The semicolons in the current path statement are treated as replaceable parameter dividers by DOS. This causes each subdirectory to become a separate replaceable parameter, but it also strips the semicolons out of the path so EDIT2.BAT has to add them back.

`:HELP`
`ECHO This Batch File Lets You`
`ECHO Review Each Subdirectory`
`ECHO And Decide If You Want To`
`ECHO Leave It In Your Path`
`GOTO END`
`:END_HELP`
	Section that displays help when the user starts the batch file with a /? or a ? as the first replaceable parameter.

`:END`	Label marking the end of the batch file.

13-11 EDIT2.BAT lets you decide if you want to keep your subdirectories, one by one, in your path.

Batch File Line	Explanation
`@ECHO OFF`	Turn command-echoing off.

`REM NAME:     EDIT2.BAT`
`REM PURPOSE: Selectively Delete`
`REM          Path Subdirectory`
`REM VERSION: 2.00`
`REM DATE:    December 24, 1991`
	Documentation remark.

Batch File Line	Explanation
IF (%1)==(/?) GOTO HELP IF (%1)==(?) GOTO HELP	If the user starts the batch file with a request for help, jump to a section to display that help.
SET MATH=0	Set a counter variable that will be used to count the number of subdirectories kept in the path.
:TOP	Label marking the top of a loop.
IF (%1)==() GOTO ENDLOOP	Once there are no more subdirectories to decide on, exit the loop.
BATCMD SL	Use Batcmd to display a blank line on the screen.
BATCMD YN Keep %1 in PATH (Y/N)	Use Batcmd to ask a question. The YN option causes Batcmd to accept only an n or y keystroke and set the errorlevel to zero for an n keystroke or one for a y keystroke.
IF NOT ERRORLEVEL 1 GOTO NOTSET	If the user responded no, skip saving the subdirectory.
BATCMD AD	Increment the MATH environmental variable by one.
IF %MATH%==1 SET A=%1 IF %MATH%==2 SET B=%1 Continues In A Similar Fashion C-R IF %MATH%==19 SET S=%1 IF %MATH%==20 SET T=%1	Store the subdirectory to keep in the next environmental variable in the series.
:NOTSET	Label used to skip saving the subdirectory if the user selects to discard a subdirectory.
SHIFT	Move the path elements down one level.
GOTO TOP	Continue looping.
:ENDLOOP	Label marking the end of the loop.

Batch File Line	Explanation
| ```
IF %MATH%==1  SET PATH=%A%
IF %MATH%==2  SET PATH=%A%;%B%

Continues In A Similar Fashion For 4-18

IF %MATH%==19 SET PATH=%A%;%B%;%C%;%D%
    ;%E%;%F%;%G%;%H%;%I%;%J%;%K%;%L%
    ;%M%;%N%;%O%;%P%;%Q%;%R%;%S%
IF %MATH%==20 SET PATH=%A%;%B%;%C%;%D%
    ;%E%;%F%;%G%;%H%;%I%;%J%;%K%;%L%
    ;%M%;%N%;%O%;%P%;%Q%;%R%;%S%;%T%
``` | Construct the new path. It isn't possible to construct the path incrementally using a statement like SET PATH= %PATH%;%1 because a very long path can cause the command line to exceed the 127-character limit DOS places on it. |
| ```
FOR %%J IN (A B C D E F G H I J K L M
    N O P Q R S T) DO SET %%J=
``` | Reset the environmental variables. |
| ```
ECHO PATH Now Set To:
PATH
``` | Display the new path for the user. This must be done on two lines because a long path will cause a single line to exceed the 127-character limit. |
| ```
GOTO END
``` | Exit the batch file. |
| ```
:HELP
ECHO This Batch File Is Used By
ECHO EDITPAT2.BAT To Edit The Path
ECHO **DO NOT RUN FROM COMMAND LINE**
GOTO END
:END_HELP
``` | Section that displays help when the user starts the batch file with a /? or a ? as the first replaceable parameter. |
| ```
:END
``` | Label marking the end of the batch file. |

14
Modifying DOS without version 5.0

This chapter will show you how to modify several DOS files in order to customize the way DOS works. Some of the illustrations show the modifications being made with The Norton Utilities. Any similar product that allows you to modify program files should work as well.

In addition, please note that this isn't my recommended method for modifying DOS. Except for changing the name used by DOS for configuration files, all of the modifications in this chapter can be made more easily, quickly, and safely using the DOSKEY program included with DOS 5.0. If you're interested in modifying the way DOS's internal commands operate, I suggest you upgrade to DOS 5.0 and use the directions in the next chapter to perform those modifications using DOSKEY.

A word of warning

Modifying DOS files is never risk-free. If you make a mistake, it's possible that you won't be able to boot off your disk. Less serious problems are also possible. You can reduce the risk of these problems with three steps:

1. Before you begin, back up your hard disk. Also, make a copy of your backup program on a floppy disk just in case you end up not being able to access the copy on your hard disk.
2. Before you begin, prepare a bootable floppy disk that contains every file you'll need in order to return the system to its original state if you make a mistake. These files should include a copy of the files you're modifying, a text editor, and your restoration program. Chapter 19 contains more details on this step. Read it before continuing.
3. As soon as you finish modifying a file, reboot and try various DOS operations to make sure they work properly. If they don't, the changes you made will be fresh in your mind so you can correct them.

With these precautions in mind, any knowledgeable user should be able to make these modifications with little difficulty.

Your AUTOEXEC.BAT and CONFIG.SYS files

The current trend in software is to have the installation program do everything for you. Generally, you type INSTALL and the software installation program will:

- Create a directory for the software files
- Copy all the files to this directory
- Add the directory to your PATH statement in your AUTOEXEC.BAT file
- Change the FILES= and BUFFERS= statements in your CONFIG.SYS file

It's the last two steps that I object to, especially when the package modifies these files without first asking permission. If your path is like that of most users, it's already near the 127-character DOS limit. Blindly tacking on another subdirectory can cause you to exceed this limit. You probably won't even know there's a problem until you reboot the computer. On some models under certain versions of DOS, a path that's too long will cause the computer to mysteriously lock up with no warning.

The problem is even worse with memory-resident software. Most memory-resident software on the market expects to be loaded either first or last. When that software installs itself, it will add itself as either the first or last line in your AUTOEXEC.BAT file. If the new software conflicts with existing software, you end up with an AUTOEXEC.BAT file that locks up your computer. Again, you have no indication that the new software is the problem or how to correct the problem. Additionally, if your AUTOEXEC.BAT file loads a menu system, any lines added after the command to load the menu system might never even be processed.

Some software automatically modifies your CONFIG.SYS file or adds device drivers. Changing a BUFFERS= or FILES= statement is no big deal. You can always edit the file and return it to its original value. A new number won't do any damage. And if you have reasonable values (BUFFERS=20 and FILES=20), as a general rule, the installation software won't change the values.

Adding device drivers is another matter. Device drivers can cause all the memory problems of memory-resident software, with the additional drawback that they're loaded so early in the boot process that you can't use Ctrl-Break to stop their loading. Fortunately, device driver conflicts are uncommon.

Because I can't stop self-installing software from modifying my AUTOEXEC.BAT and CONFIG.SYS files, I prevent it by using DOS. There are three ways to protect your AUTOEXEC.BAT file and two ways to protect your CONFIG.SYS file.

The easiest way to protect your AUTOEXEC.BAT file is with a single line in the AUTOEXEC.BAT file that calls a second batch file. This second batch file serves as your "real" AUTOEXEC.BAT file. This method has the advantage that you can examine your "fake" AUTOEXEC.BAT file after installing software to see how it was modified. You can then incorporate those changes into the real AUTOEXEC.BAT file if you think they'd be useful.

Because the CONFIG.SYS file has no command to call another file, You can't use this method for a CONFIG.SYS file under MS-DOS. However, DR DOS can call other files from the CONFIG.SYS file, so this method works fine with DR DOS. Every file has four attributes that DOS tracks:

Archive   This flag indicates if the file has changed since the last time it was backed up.

System   This flag indicates that the file is a special DOS file.

Hidden   This flag indicates a file you don't see when you perform a directory. These are usually special DOS files.

Read only   This flag indicates a file that can be read by any program, but can't be modified.

By making the AUTOEXEC.BAT and CONFIG.SYS files read-only, you can prevent installation programs from modifying them. If you have DOS 3.0 or later, you can make a file read-only with the following command:

```
ATTRIB + R AUTOEXEC.BAT
```

This method has one drawback. Some software installation programs will crash when they try to modify the AUTOEXEC.BAT or CONFIG.SYS file and fail. The only way to install those programs is to remove the read-only protection and reinstall them normally.

Changing DOS

The Norton Utilities allow you to edit any file, so it's a good program to use in order to edit your DOS files. When you're editing a file, you'll see hexadecimal values on the left side of your screen and ASCII values on the right. You can make changes on one side, and they'll be reflected on the other side.

DOS must know which file to load as the CONFIG.SYS file and which file to load as the AUTOEXEC.BAT file. This isn't automatic; the names are stored in DOS. You could change the name of CONFIG.SYS to START1.SYS. If you then change the name in your DOS files, DOS would treat START1.SYS as CONFIG.SYS. You could rename AUTOEXEC.BAT as START-UP.BAT and change the DOS files, and START-UP.BAT would function as your AUTOEXEC.BAT file.

If you make these changes, the CONFIG.SYS and AUTOEXEC.BAT filenames will have no special meaning outside of your modified version of DOS. As a result, when installation software creates or modifies the CONFIG.SYS or AUTOEXEC.BAT file, it won't change how the system works.

One special note: START1.SYS and START-UP.BAT have the same number of letters in their names and extensions as do CONFIG.SYS and AUTOEXEC.BAT. This is important. You can use any names and extensions you like, but they must have exactly the same length as the ones they're replacing.

Because CONFIG.SYS is loaded and processed prior to loading the command processor, its name is stored in the IBMBIO.COM (or equivalent MS-DOS) file. Edit this file. Scroll through the file until you see the ASCII text *CONFIG.SYS* on the right side of the screen, as shown in Fig. 14-1. Move the cursor to the ASCII file and replace CONFIG.SYS with the name of the file you've selected. Remember that:

- The name must have six characters and must be typed over CONFIG.
- The extension must have three characters and be typed on top of SYS.

Save your modified file and exit The Norton Utilities. This change will take effect the next time you boot the computer. Remember to rename your existing CONFIG.SYS file to the new name you just selected.

The AUTOEXEC.BAT file is processed after the command processor is loaded, so its name is stored in COMMAND.COM file. Edit this file the same way you edited CONFIG.SYS. Scroll through the file until you see the ASCII text *AUTOEXEC.BAT* on the right side of the screen (shown in Fig. 14-2). Move the cursor to the ASCII file and replace AUTOEXEC.BAT with the name of the file you've selected. Remember that:

- The name must have eight characters and be typed over AUTOEXEC.
- The extension must have three characters and must be typed over BAT.
- The extension doesn't have to be BAT, but if it is you can run it from the DOS prompt.

Save your modified file and exit The Norton Utilities. This change will take effect the next time you reboot the computer. Remember to rename your existing AUTOEXEC.BAT file to the new name you just selected.

If you're so inclined, you can make these changes with the Debug program that comes with your DOS disk. Figure 14-3 shows how to change the name of the CONFIG.SYS file using Compaq DOS 3.2 and Fig. 14-4 shows how to change the name of the AUTO-EXEC.BAT file. Other versions of DOS should work similarly.

Changing commands

The same technique can be used for an even more powerful purpose. DOS stores the name of all its internal commands in the COMMAND.COM file. You can change the names of these commands just like the CONFIG.SYS and AUTOEXEC.BAT filenames. The new command names must also be the same length as the existing command name. In addition, the name must not conflict with other command names and must not contain illegal characters. Figure 14-5 shows using the Norton utilities to modify the name of an internal command.

If you're just trying to prevent common mistakes, you can replace DEL, ERASE, and other troublesome commands with batch files. These batch files can be very powerful. Consider the batch file DEL.BAT in Fig. 14-6. Because the DEL command was renamed to XXX, there's no internal command named DEL, so it's a valid batch file name. This batch file is much more useful than the naked DEL command.

Summary

- You can change the name of the configuration files by editing DOS programs.
- You can change the name of internal commands and substitute batch files by editing COMMAND.COM.

14-1 Screen display of patching IBMBIO.COM to cause DOS to get its configuration from a file other than CONFIG.SYS when booting, using the Norton Utilities.

```
ibmbio.com                                              Hex format
  Cluster 3,647, Sectors 14,869-14,872        File offset 31,595, hex 7B6B
83C705EB 0383C729 E2EBF9EB 0B3C0175 0347EB04 26C47D01  ‚╟╟•╪╪‚▐)Γδ·δδ<╚u♥Gδ♦&─)Θ
59C350B8 0042F9CD 21597209 33D233F6 B43FF9CD 21C3561E  Y▐P┐.B•─↑Yro3▄╗3+↑?•─↑│U▲
061F07E8 31007206 0A044646 EB06B419 CD210441 2EA2E930  ♠▼•░1.r♠♦↑FFδ↕│↓─↑♦A.θΘ8
BFEC300A 043C5C74 092E3A06 2F007402 EB014FE8 1F00BFE9  ┐ Θδ♦<\to.:♦/.tθδ╚Θ▌V•┐θ
381E061F 075EC350 003C4172 0D003C5A 7700007C 013A7502  8▲♠▼.^ ┤PG<Ar┌╦G<Zw┤C│Θ:u8
EB01F958 C3A4007C FF0075F9 C30E070B F2BA373C BBF43B0E  δθ•X├┤G│..u•┤┐•Y2┤7<╗┌:▐
1FE81F00 268A140A D27407B4 02CD2146 EBF28BD3 E80C002E  ▼δ▼.╚Θ┤╬▄.t•┤•θ↑Fδ2Y╖δΘ.
003EA909 017403E8 15F5C3B4 09CD21C3 E81C0073 07BACD30  Ç>─.╚tθ♣SJ ┤o─↑╠─.s•┤θ
E81400C3 8BD033C0 B444CD21 F6C28075 F2B43ECD 21EBE6B4  3¶.├Y↓3┴↓D─↑╦u2┤>─↑δ╟┤
3DF9CD21 C3B003CF 49424D20 444F5320 56657273 696F6E20  =•─↑├╫•┴IBM DOS Version
342E3030 20284329 436F7079 72696768 74204942 4D20436F  4.00 (C)Copyright IBM Co
72702031 39383312C 31393838 4C696E65 204D6174  rp 1981,1988Licensed Mat
65726961 6C202D20 50726F67 72616D20 50726F70 65727479  erial - Program Property
206F6620 49424D4E 554C0043 4F4E0041 55580050 524E005C   of IBMNUL.CON.AUX.PRN.\
434F4E46 49472E53 59530041 3A5C434F 554E5452 592E5359  CONFIG.SYS A:\COUNTRY.SY
53000000 00000000 00000000 00000000 00000000 00000000  S...┬.................
00000000 00000000 00000000 00000000 00000000 00000000  .....│................
00000000 0000FF43 4F554E54 52590000 5C434F4D 4D414844  .......COUNTRY..\COMMAND
2E434F4D 00000000 00000000 00000000 00000000 00000000  .COM.................
00000000 00000000 00000000 00000000 00000000 00000000  .....................
00000000 00000000 00000000 00000000 00000000 00000000  .....................
00000000 00000000          Press Enter to continue      ........
```

14-2 Screen display of patching COMMAND.COM to cause DOS to process a different file rather than the AUTOEXEC.BAT file, using the Norton Utilities.

```
command.com                                             Hex format
  Cluster 147, Sectors 869-872                 File offset 9,040, hex 2350
BF6416E8 5700BF35 15E84900 07B82E12 B2099090 8D3EBF08  ┐d─☒W.┐5§8I.•┐.‡║o£έ}>┐█
CD2FEB30 BF6417E8 3B00BF2C 1A093E7A 10EB2100 3EA22401  ═/δ0┐d‡8:,.↑♠>z├θδ!Ç§◙
750BC606 220E02BA 0200E8AF FEB82E12 B2038B3E 97248E06  u♂├♠"┌θ█.θ╗•↑.‡♥Y)ù$Å♠
9924CD2F E816005F 5A5A071F C3B82E12 B203CD2F C3B82E12  Ö$─/θ↑─_ZX•▼┤.‡╗─/┤.‡
B201CD2F C3505352 06573309 8EC133FF B82E12B2 00CD2F0C  ▓θ─/┤PSR♠W3┴Å3.┐.‡█─/î
06591309 3E5713B0 2E12B202 CD2F0C06 6113093E 5F13B02E  ♠Y‼♠>W‼║.↑▓Θ═/♀♠a‼♠>_‼║.
12B204CD 2F0C0671 13093E6F 13B02E12 B206CD2F 0C065513  ‡▓♦═/♀♠q‼♠>o‼║.‡▲─/îΘ‼
893E5313 B82E12B2 00CD2F0C 06791309 3E7713E8 06EF893E  ë>S‼╗.‡█─/î♠y‼♠>w‼θ♠∩ë>
7B13E8A3 02893E7F 13E80DF3 893E8313 E857F209 3E8713E8  {‼θú☻ë>⌂‼θ♪≤ë>â‼θW≥♠>â‼θ
38F6893B 8B13E813 0051E827 00720059 5F075A5B 58E80403  8╦ë;Y‼θ‼.Qθ'.r.Y_•Z[Xθ♦♥
C40CF9C3 50561EB0 0063CD21 1E071F72 0089369F 130C06A1  ─♀•┤PUA┐.c─↑▼•▼r░6f‼î♀║
135E50C3 B430CD21 3D040075 03F8E80E BBFFFFB0 0100B900  ‼^P┤┤0─↑=♦.u•┤θ♪├    θ┤.
00B200B6 FFF9C300 00000000 00000000 2F444556 2F434F4E  .▓.¶ •┤.........../DEV/CON
00000000 000000.........  .......COMMAND.COM...:\
4155544F 455845...   Change AUTOEXEC.BAT here   →AUTOEXEC.BAT.J. .:\KAUTOEX
452E4241 54000D[.                          E.BAT.J.....┌G..c%...╖.C
4F4D5358 45433D3D 617A2F5C 20434100 00000000 00000000  OMSPEC==az∕\ CA.........
000000DE 47000000 000000AA 24000001 BC2406C5  .......─$...Θ║│$♠├
24D124DD 24E92402 250E2500 01020100 1C252425 00000002  $┬$é$☻%♫%.☺☻☺.∟%$%...■
001C2524 25012F50 00000002 001C2524 25012F46 00000002  .∟%$%♣/P...■.∟%$%♣/F...■
001C2524 25012F44 00000000 001C25F5 24012F45 00010101  .∟%$%♣/D...Ç.∟%✦$♣/E.☺☺☺
```

14-3 Screen display of patching IBMBIO.COM to cause DOS to get its configuration from a file other than CONFIG.SYS when booting, using Debug.

Command	Meaning
`DEBUG IBMBIO.COM`	Edit IBMBIO.COM. DEBUG.COM must be in the current directory or in your path. Note that Debug will edit IBMBIO.COM even though it's a hidden file.
`-RCX`	Debug command to display the length of the file.
`CX 406A` `:`	Debug responding with length of file in hexadecimal. Press Return again at the colon prompt to return to the dashed Debug prompt. The size of the file (406A) will vary depending on the version of DOS you're modifying.
`-S 100 406A "CONF"`	Command telling Debug to search for the text CONF. Be sure to replace the 406A with the number from the RCX command.
`420E:3F11`	Debug response telling you where the text was located. Ignore the first four numbers and use the 3F11. Remember to replace 3F11 with the number you got.
`-E 3F11 "START1.SYS"`	Edit the file and replace CONFIG.SYS with START1.SYS. Be sure to replace 3F11 with the number you got.
`-D 14B1`	Display the changes to make sure you didn't make a mistake. Be sure to replace 14B1 with the number you got.
`-W`	Write your changes to disk. Before the W command, nothing has been on the disk. Quitting without saving will discard all your changes if you make a mistake.
`-Q`	Quit Debug. You won't be prompted to save.

14-4 Screen display of patching COMMAND.COM to cause DOS to process a different file rather than the AUTOEXEC.BAT file, using Debug.

Command	Meaning
`DEBUG COMMAND.COM`	Edit COMMAND.COM. DEBUG.COM must be in the current directory or in your path.
`-RCX`	Debug command to display the length of the file.
`CX 5D2F` `:`	Debug responding with length of file in hexadecimal. Press Return again at the colon prompt to return to the Debug prompt. The size of the file (5D2F) will vary depending on the version of DOS you're modifying.
`-S 100 5D2F "AUTO"`	Command telling Debug to search for the text AUTO. Be sure to replace the 5D2F with the number you got from the RCX command.

Command	Meaning
`6880:14B1`	Debug response telling you where the text was located. Ignore the first four numbers, and use the 14B1. Remember to replace 14B1 with the number you got.
`-E 14B1 "START-UP.BAT"`	Edit the file and replace AUTOEXEC.BAT with START-UP.BAT. Be sure to replace 14B1 with the number you got.
`-D 14B1`	Display the changes to make sure you didn't make a mistake. Be sure to replace 14B1 with the number you got.
`-W`	Write your changes to disk. Before the W command, nothing has been on the disk. Quitting without saving will discard all your changes if you make a mistake.
`-Q`	Quit Debug. You won't be prompted to save.

14-5 Screen display of patching COMMAND.COM to change the name of internal commands with the Norton Utilities.

14-6 DEL.BAT is a batch file to replace the renamed internal DEL command.

Batch File Line	Explanation
`@ECHO OFF`	Turn command-echoing off.

`REM NAME:     DEL.BAT`
`REM PURPOSE: Replace DEL Command`
`REM VERSION: 2.00`
`REM DATE:     January 12, 1992`
	Documentation remarks.

Batch File Line	Explanation
IF (%1)==(/?) GOTO HELP IF (%1)==(?) GOTO HELP	If the user starts the batch file with a request for help, jump to a section to display that help.
IF (%1)==() GOTO NO-FILES	Quit if a replaceable parameter is not entered.
:TOP	Label marking the top of a loop.
FOR %%J IN (%1) DO ECHO To Be Deleted......%%J	Tell the user which files will be deleted.
BATCMD YN Delete These Files	Ask if the user wants to delete the specified files.

IF ERRORLEVEL 1 IF (%1)==(*.*)
    ECHO Y | XXX %1
IF ERRORLEVEL 1 IF (%1)==(.)
    ECHO Y | XXX %1
	If the user answered yes and specified all the files so that DOS will prompt the user with an *Are you sure (Y/N)?* message, pipe the answer to DOS to avoid the user having to answer the question twice. Notice that the new DEL command (XXX) is used.

IF ERRORLEVEL 1 IF NOT (%1)==(*.*) IF NOT (%1)==(.) XXX %1	If the user answered yes and did not specify all the files, go ahead and delete the files.
SHIFT	Move the replaceable parameters down one level.
IF (%1)==() GOTO END	If there are no more files to delete, exit the batch file.
GOTO TOP :END_TOP	If the user specified more than one set of files to delete, continue looping.
:NO-FILES ECHO No Files To Delete Specified GOTO END :END_NO-FILES	Section to display an error message if the user runs the batch file without specifying the files to delete.
:NOTHERE ECHO You Specified Deleting %1 ECHO However, Files Matching This ECHO Do Not Exist SHIFT IF (%1)==() GOTO END GOTO TOP :END_NOTHERE	If the user specifies a file that doesn't exist or a wildcard specification that doesn't match any files, this section will display an error message. If the user specifies additional files to delete, this section continues that processing.

Batch File Line	Explanation

`:HELP`
`ECHO This Demonstrations Batch File`
`ECHO Requires DOS Be Modified To`
`ECHO Replace The DEL Command With XXX`
`ECHO See Book For Details`
`GOTO END`
`:END_HELP`
	Section that displays help when the user starts the batch file with a /? or a ? as the first replaceable parameter.

`:END`	Label marking the end of the batch file.

15
Modifying DOS 5.0 with DOSKEY

If you've upgraded to DOS 5.0, then you have a copy of DOSKEY. DOSKEY is a memory-resident program that comes with DOS 5.0 that allows you to change the operation of any of the DOS commands. Let's begin by seeing just how powerful DOSKEY is.

If you don't have DOSKEY loaded, change to your DOS subdirectory and enter DOSKEY at the command line. Now change to your batch subdirectory and create this simple batch file:

```
@ECHO OFF
FOR %%J IN (%1) DO ECHO %%J...To Be Deleted
BATCMD YN Do You Wish To Delete These Files?
IF NOT ERRORLEVEL 1 GOTO END
DEL %1
:END
```

Give the batch file the name of KEYDEL.BAT. KEYDEL.BAT uses Batcmd, so it will need to be in the path.

Create a temporary subdirectory and some temporary files in that subdirectory called JUNK.1 through JUNK.9. Now enter the following command:

```
DOSKEY DEL = KEYDEL $1
```

at the command line. Now enter the command DEL JUNK.? on the command line. As you can see, DOS will run your macro rather than using its internal DEL command.

If you look at the KEYDEL.BAT file, you'll see that it uses the DEL command to perform the actual deletion, yet DOSKEY was supposed to replace the DEL command with KEYDEL.BAT! That's the real advantage of DOSKEY over editing COMMAND.COM to change the names of internal commands, as explained back in chapter 14.

When you change the command inside COMMAND.COM, the command changes everywhere, so you have to modify all your batch files. When you change the command with DOSKEY, it changes only for the command line, so your batch files behave normally. So when you enter the DEL command from the command line DOSKEY maps it into KEYDEL.BAT, but when a batch file uses the DEL command, including KEYDEL.BAT, it isn't mapped and can therefore access the actual DOS internal command.

Before we continue, I need to let you know about one problem. There's a bug in DOS 5.0 that prevents the /P switch from working when you alias a command. Whether it's built into the batch file or passed to the batch file as a parameter, the batch file will abort the first time the user answers Yes to the prompt and the file won't be erased.

Now, let's see more about how DOSKEY operates.

DOSKEY basics

If you've read this far in the book, it's a safe bet that you're pretty familiar with batch files. Well, a DOSKEY macro is very much like a batch file. Some of the symbols you use, however, are different. Those differences include:

$1-$9   In a batch file, the replaceable parameters are represented by %0 − %9, where %0 is the name of the batch file and %1 − %9 are the first nine replaceable parameters entered on the command line after the name of the batch file. In a DOSKEY macro, the name of the macro isn't available and the replaceable parameters are represented by $1 − $9. But they work the same.

$*   This stands for the entire command line after the macro name, making it easy to pass long command lines through DOSKEY.

Piping   You can't include DOS piping in a DOSKEY command directly because DOS processes the pipe before it gets to DOSKEY. To overcome that, DOSKEY allows you to replace the pipes with symbols not processed by DOS. The greater-than pipe (>) becomes $G, the less-than pipe (<) becomes %L, and the vertical bar pipe (¦) becomes $B. DOSSKEY, however, still has problems with pipes so that many times a properly written macro containing pipes will execute but the pipe won't work.

You can make a DOSKEY assignment with a command like:

    DOSKEY command = replacement [parameters]

where *command* is the item you type on the command line, *replacement* is what you want DOSKEY to replace it with, and *parameters* are any parameters you want DOSKEY to pass from the command line to the replacement.

What can you do with DOSKEY?

DOSKEY has three different functions: command shortening, command name changing, and function changes. Let's take a look at how each of these works.

Shortening commands

This is actually the easiest way to use DOSKEY. You simply define the "shorthand" you plan to use on the command line. For example, if you're cleaning up your hard disk and plan on repeatedly entering a directory command, you could use the following DOSKEY command:

```
DOSKEY D = DIR $1 /P /OE
```

This way, if you enter D on the command line by itself you'll get a directory of all the files in the current subdirectory. Entering D *.TXT would give you just the text files.

Changing command names

This allows you to change the names of commands or programs to something the user is more likely to remember. For example, you might use the following to make a system more friendly:

```
DOSKEY KILL = DEL $* /P
DOSKEY GONE = DEL $* /P
DOSKEY DESTROY = DEL $* /P
```

This allows users to use commands they're more likely to remember to perform common tasks. It also illustrates that the term *command name changing* is a little misleading. While it does allow you to access the command under a new name, or even several new names, as shown above, the old name also works.

Changing functions

You've already seen this one in action with KEYDEL.BAT. Here, you can write a batch file (or even a .EXE or .COM program) to perform a task in place of a DOS internal command and then use DOSKEY to map the DOS internal command onto the batch file.

Occasionally, you might have a command remapped using DOSKEY but want to access the original command. For example, you might have the DEL command remapped to execute a batch file. All you need to do is enter a space on the command line before the command. Spaces before commands don't effect DOS but they fool DOSKEY's remapping, so the DOS command will work.

Putting it together

When you load DOSKEY, it loads with the default size of 512 bytes for its storage area. While 512 bytes is large enough to demonstrate the power of DOSKEY, it's too small to be really useful. To increase the size of the DOSKEY storage space, load it with a command like this:

```
DOSKEY /BUFSIZE = 2000
```

where 2,000 is the size (in bytes) that DOSKEY allocates for storage. DOSKEY uses this space to store both macros and old command lines. I use 2,000 on my system and I rarely run out of space.

If you've been following along with this chapter by working with your computer, then you've already loaded DOSKEY with the default buffer size. That's too small for what you'll be doing next. DOSKEY lacks an unload command, so you'll have to reboot to remove it from memory. Then load a second copy and give it a larger storage space with the following command:

```
DOSKEY /REINSTALL BUFSIZE = 2000
```

To show you the power of DOSKEY, run KEYASSGN.BAT in Fig. 15-1. This batch file creates a number of new commands and modifies the way several commands operate. Table 15-1 summarizes these new commands. Several of them run one of two batch files, KEYERASE.BAT in Fig. 15-2 and MOVEIT.BAT in Fig. 15-3. The commands relying on KEYERASE.BAT just change the way existing commands work, while the commands relying on MOVEIT.BAT create entirely new commands. Creating entirely new commands is something that you can't use the techniques in chapter 14 to do. You might also notice how KEYERASE.BAT avoids the problem associated with using the /P switch in a DOSKEY macro.

Table 15-1   The new commands created by KEYASSGN.BAT.

New or Modified Command	Function
DEL	Runs KEYERASE.BAT instead of functioning as an internal command.
ERASE	Runs KEYERASE.BAT instead of functioning as an internal command.
GONE	A new command to erase files.
KILL	A new command to erase files.
MOVE	Moves files to a new location by copying them to the new location and then deleting them from the original location. It has extensive error checking.
NUKE	A new command to erase files.
ZAP	A new command to erase files.
RELOCATE	Moves files to a new location by copying them to the new location and then deleting them from the original location. It has extensive error checking.
NEWDIR	Moves files to a new location by copying them to the new location and then deleting them from the original location. It has extensive error checking.

Table 15-1   Continued.

New or Modified Command	Function
CHECK	Runs CHKDSK.
MACROS	Displays the currently assigned DOSKEY macros.
MACRO	Displays the currently assigned DOSKEY macros.
DIR	Automatically includes the /P switch.
FILES	Displays a list of files.
FF1	Sends a formfeed to LPT1.
FF2	Sends a formfeed to LPT2.
FORMFEED1	Sends a formfeed to LPT1.
FORMFEED2	Sends a formfeed to LPT2.
HIDE	Changes a file's attribute to hidden.
UNHIDE	Turns off a file's hidden attribute.
READONLY	Turns on a file's read-only attribute.
RO	Turns on a file's read-only attribute.
UNREADONLY	Turns off a file's read-only attribute.
UNRO	Turns off a file's read-only attribute.
LINES25	Sets the text mode of the screen to display 25 lines. Requires loading ANSI.SYS in the CONFIG.SYS file.
LINES43	Sets the text mode of the screen to display 43 lines. Requires loading ANSI.SYS in the CONFIG.SYS file. Also requires an EGA screen.
LINES50	Sets the text mode of the screen to display 50 lines. Requires loading ANSI.SYS in the CONFIG.SYS file. Also requires a VGA screen.
LIST	Types files to the screen and pipes the output through the MORE filter.
FILEFIND	Locate files on the current drive only.

Command-line recall

DOSKEY stores your command lines so you can reuse them. Just press the up arrow to scroll back through your commands, one at a time. When you get to one you want to reuse, just press Return to run it.

If you know how the command started, just type in the first few letters of the command and press F8. That will take you back to the last command that started with the letters you entered. If that isn't the command you wanted, press F8 again to cycle back to the command before that starting with the letter you entered.

If you want to review all the commands you've entered, just press F7. It lists all your commands with line numbers to the left of them. If there's more than will fit on one screen, it will show them one screen at a time and wait for you to press a key before showing the next screen. You can use the numbers it shows to select a command by pressing F9 and entering the number. This will bring the command to the command line so you can make sure you want to run it. If you do, just press Return.

It's easy to purge the command line storage and macros from DOSKEY. Pressing Alt−F7 purges all the command lines, and pressing Alt−F10 purges the macros. You can purge a single DOSKEY macro with the command:

DOSKEY *macro* =

where *macro* is the name of the macro to purge and nothing follows the equal sign.

Summary

- DOSKEY allows you to have DOS automatically translate commands you enter on the command line into different commands before running them.
- DOSKEY also allows you to map commands onto batch files and pass the contents of the command line to that batch file.
- Having DOSKEY map a command onto a batch file can cause that command to behave far differently than its normal DOS operation.
- DOSKEY allows you to easily recall old command lines.
- You can easily purge DOSKEY macros and command from memory.
- Once you see how powerful DOSKEY is, I'm sure it'll be one of the programs you load into your system with AUTOEXEC.BAT!

15-1 KEYASSGN.BAT can create a number of useful DOSKEY commands.

Batch File Line	Explanation
`@ECHO OFF`	Turn command-echoing off.

`REM NAME:     KEYASSGN.BAT`
`REM PURPOSE: Make DOSKEY Assignments`
`REM VERSION: 1.00`
`REM DATE:     December 25, 1991`
`REM Batch Assignment`
	Documentation remarks.

Batch File Line	Explanation
`IF (%1)==(/?) GOTO HELP` `IF (%1)==(?) GOTO HELP`	If the user starts the batch file with a request for help, jump to a section to display that help.
`REM Batch Files` `REM ===========`	Documentation remarks.
`ECHO Attaching Batch Files` `ECHO Please Wait`	This batch file takes several seconds to run with nothing showing on the screen, so tell the user it's running.
`DOSKEY DEL=KEYERASE $*` `DOSKEY ERASE=KEYERASE $*`	Remap the DEL and ERASE commands to KEYERASE.BAT.

`DOSKEY NUKE=KEYERASE $*`
`DOSKEY GONE=KEYERASE $*`
`DOSKEY KILL=KEYERASE $*`
`DOSKEY ZAP=KEYERASE $*`
	Remap four new keywords to KEYERASE.BAT. Because they're remapped to the same batch file, these new commands will function identically to the DEL and ERASE commands.

`DOSKEY MOVE=MOVEIT $*`
`DOSKEY RELOCATE=MOVEIT $*`
`DOSKEY NEWDIR=MOVEIT $*`
	Create three new commands by mapping them to a batch file. If only one command accesses this batch file, it would be easier just to give the batch file the name of the new command and include it in a subdirectory in the path. Because these three names access the same batch file, however, they'll function identically.

`REM Commands` `REM ========`	Documentation remarks.

`BATCMD SL`
`ECHO Renaming Commands`
`ECHO Please Wait`
	Skip a line and let the user know the batch file is still running.

`DOSKEY CHECK=CHKDSK $*`	Remap the CHECK command to run CHKDSK. You could write a batch file called CHECK.BAT to do the same, but this approach uses no disk space.
`DOSKEY MACROS=DOSKEY /MACROS` `DOSKEY MACRO=DOSKEY /MACROS`	Remap these two commands to the DOSKEY command to show the macros that have been defined.
`DOSKEY DIR=DIR $1 /P`	Alter the way the DIR command operates by forcing it to include a /P switch.

Batch File Line	Explanation
`DOSKEY FILES=DIR $1 /P`	Add a new command that operates by running DIR.

`DOSKEY FF1=ECHO ^L $G LPT1`
`DOSKEY FF2=ECHO ^L $G LPT2`
`DOSKEY FORMFEED1=ECHO ^L $G LPT1`
`DOSKEY FORMFEED2=ECHO ^L $G LPT2`
	Create several formfeed commands that pipe a ^L (formfeed) character to the printer.

`DOSKEY HIDE=ATTRIB +H $1`	Replace the hard-to-understand ATTRIB +H command with an easy-to-understand replacement.

`DOSKEY UNHIDE=ATTRIB -H $1`
`DOSKEY READONLY=ATTRIB +R $1`
`DOSKEY RO=ATTRIB +R $1`
`DOSKEY UNREADONLY=ATTRIB -R $1`
`DOSKEY UNRO=ATTRIB -R $1`
	Replace several other ATTRIB commands with easy-to-understand and easy-to-remember replacements.

`DOSKEY LINES25=MODE CON: LINES=25`
`DOSKEY LINES43=MODE CON: LINES=43`
`DOSKEY LINES50=MODE CON: LINES=50`
	Add commands to change the display type. These commands require that you load ANSI.SYS in your CONFIG.SYS file.

`DOSKEY LIST=FOR %%J IN ($1) DO TYPE` `    %%J $b MORE`	Create a command to display text files using DOS commands.
`DOSKEY FILEFIND=ATTRIB \$1 /S`	Create a command to locate files anywhere on the current drive using DOS commands.

`BATCMD SL`
`ECHO Finished`
`GOTO END`
	Tell the user the batch file is finished and exit the batch file.

`:HELP`
`ECHO This Batch File Uses DOS 5.0's`
`ECHO DOSKEY To Make A Number Of`
`ECHO Useful Command Changes`
`GOTO END`
`:END_HELP`
	Section that displays help when the user starts the batch file with a /? or a ? as the first replaceable parameter.

`:END`	Label marking the end of the batch file.

15-2 KEYERASE.BAT replaces the DEL and ERASE commands once you've run KEYASSGN.BAT.

Batch File Line	Explanation
`@ECHO OFF`	Turn command-echoing off.

`REM NAME:     KEYERASE.BAT`
`REM PURPOSE: DOSKEY Erase Replacement`
`REM VERSION: 1.00`
`REM DATE:     December 25, 1991`
	Documentation remarks.

Batch File Line	Explanation
IF (%1)==(/?) GOTO HELP IF (%1)==(?) GOTO HELP	If the user starts the batch file with a request for help, jump to a section to display that help.
IF (%1)==(XYZ123ABC) GOTO PROMPT	When the batch file calls itself as a subroutine, jump to a section to handle that.
IF (%1)==() GOTO NOTHING	If the user fails to enter the name of any files to delete, jump to an error-handling section.
:TOP	Label marking the top of the main portion of the batch file.
FOR %%J IN (%1) DO ECHO %%J.... To Be Erased!	List the files to be deleted.
BATCMD YN Do You Want To Erase These Files?	Ask the user about deleting these files.
IF NOT ERRORLEVEL 1 GOTO END	If the users says no, exit the batch file.
BATCMD YN Do You Want To Be Asked Individually?	Ask the user about prompting for each file individually.
IF NOT ERRORLEVEL 1 DEL %1 IF NOT ERRORLEVEL 1 GOTO NEXT	If the user doesn't want individual prompting, delete the files and jump to a section called NEXT.
:TOPLOOP	Label marking the top of a section to individually delete the files. The user reaches this point only by answering yes to the above prompt asking about individual deletion.
FOR %%J IN (%1) DO CALL KEYERASE XYZ123ABC %%J	Loop through all the files to be deleted. For each file, call this batch file as a subroutine and pass it a subroutine flag and the name of the batch file to delete.
GOTO NEXT :END_TOP	Go to the NEXT section to continue looping.
:NEXT SHIFT IF NOT (%1)==() GOTO TOP GOTO END :END_NEXT	Section to check to see if the user specified another set of files to delete. If so, jump back to the processing section of the batch file.

Batch File Line	Explanation
:NOTHING ECHO Did Not Specify Files To Erase! ECHO The Format For The Command Is: BATCMD SL ECHO ERASE *.BAK ECHO DEL *.TXT BATCMD SL ECHO Where You Replace *.BAK or *.TXT ECHO With The File You Want To Erase GOTO END :END_NOTHING	Section to handle the problem when the user fails to specify any files to erase.
:PROMPT BATCMD YN Delete %2? IF ERRORLEVEL 1 DEL %2 GOTO END :END_PROMPT	Subroutine section that handles asking about deleting a single file. Note the use of %2, because %1 is the subroutine flag.
:HELP ECHO This Batch File Is An Intelligent ECHO Replacement For The DEL And ERASE ECHO Commands Designed To Be Mapped To ECHO Those Commands Using DOSKEY ECHO OK To Run From Command Line GOTO END :END_HELP	Section that displays help when the user starts the batch file with a /? or a ? as the first replaceable parameter.
:END	Label marking the end of the batch file.

15-3 MOVEIT.BAT adds several new commands to DOS, including a MOVE command.

Batch File Line	Explanation
@ECHO OFF	Turn command-echoing off.
REM NAME: MOVEIT.BAT REM PURPOSE: DOSKEY Move Command REM VERSION: 1.00 REM DATE: January 12, 1992	Documentation remarks.
IF (%1)==(/?) GOTO HELP IF (%2)==(?) GOTO HELP	If the user starts the batch file with a request for help, jump to a section to display that help.
IF (%1)==() GOTO NOSOURCE	If the user did not enter the name of a file to move, jump to an error-handling routine.
IF (%2)==() GOTO NOTARGET	If the user did not enter the name of a subdirectory to move the files to, jump to an error-handling routine.

Batch File Line	Explanation
`IF NOT EXIST %1 GOTO NOFILES`	If the files the user wants to move don't exist, jump to an error-handling routine.
`IF NOT EXIST %2\NUL GOTO DIRGONE`	If the target subdirectory doesn't exist, jump to an error-handling routine.
`IF EXIST %2\%1 GOTO ALREADY`	If the files already exist in the target subdirectory, jump to an error-handling routine.
`XCOPY %1 %2\*.*`	Copy the files.
`IF ERRORLEVEL 1 GOTO OOPS`	If there's a copy error, jump to an error-handling routine.
`DEL %1`	Delete the original files.
`GOTO END`	Exit the batch file.

`:OOPS`
`BATCMD BE 5`
`ECHO A Copy Error Has Occurred`
`ECHO Source Files *NOT* Erased`
`GOTO END`
`:END_OOPS`
	When XCOPY reports an error, display an error message and exit the batch file.

`:ALREADY`
`ECHO Files Named %2\%1 Already Exist`
`ECHO This Routine Will *NOT*`
`ECHO Overwrite Files`
`ECHO You Must Delete The %2\%1 Files`
`ECHO In Order To Use This Routine`
`GOTO END`
`:END_ALREADY`
	If the files already exist in the target subdirectory, display an error message and exit the batch file.

`:DIRGONE`
`ECHO You Specified Moving The %1`
`ECHO Files Into The %2 Subdirectory`
`ECHO However, The %2 Subdirectory`
`ECHO Does Not Exist`
`ECHO (Must Be Entered As C:\BAT`
`ECHO *NOT* C:\BAT\)`
`BATCMD SL`
`GOTO SYNTAX`
`:END_DIRGONE`
	If the specified target subdirectory doesn't exist, display an error message and jump to a routine to display the proper syntax before exiting the batch file.

`:NOFILES`
`ECHO You Specified Moving The`
`ECHO %1 Files, But None Of`
`ECHO These Files Exist`
`GOTO SYNTAX`
`:END_NOFILES`
	If the source files don't exist, display an error message and jump to a routine to display the proper syntax before exiting the batch file.

Batch File Line	Explanation
:NOSOURCE ECHO Source Files Not Specified GOTO SYNTAX :END_NOSOURCE	If the user doesn't specify the source files to move, display an error message and jump to a routine to display the proper syntax before exiting the batch file.
:SYNTAX ECHO Enter MOVEIT {Source} {Target} ECHO Where {Source} Is The Files ECHO To Move And {Target} Is The ECHO Location To Move Them To BATCMD SL ECHO DOSKEY Users Can Enter The ECHO Command As MOVE {Source} {Target} ECHO Although The MOVEIT Command ECHO Will Also Work GOTO END END_SYNTAX	This section displays the proper syntax for the command and then exits the batch file. It's called by several other error sections.
:NOTARGET ECHO Target Subdirectory Not Specified GOTO SYNTAX :END_NOTARGET	When the user specifies a target subdirectory that doesn't exist, display an error message and jump to a routine to display the proper syntax before exiting the batch file.
:HELP ECHO MOVEIT.BAT Moves Files From One ECHO Location To Another With ECHO Extensive Error Checking BATCMD SL ECHO Designed To Work With DOSKEY ECHO However It Can Also Be Run ECHO As A Stand-Alone Batch File GOTO END :END_HELP	Section that displays help when the user starts the batch file with a /? or a ? as the first replaceable parameter.
:END	Label marking the end of the batch file.

PART FIVE
The environment

16

The DOS environment

Using the DOS environment, you can create a set of variables that can be accessed by any batch file and by any program. This environment is useful for passing parameters between programs and batch files and for supplying batch files with often-used information without having to enter it on every command line.

In spite of these advantages, the DOS environment is under-utilized. There are a couple of reasons. First, it's poorly documented. In fact, the %variable% function was undocumented until just recently. While undocumented, it works with DOS 2.0 and later. A second limitation is space. Using a long path and a complex prompt will fill up your environment! Don't worry, this chapter will show you how to expand its size.

A final problem is that programs have access to only a copy of the environment, not the original. So a program can use the environment as temporary storage or as a source of direction, but it can't use it to pass information to other programs. While programs files (.COM and .EXE) have access to only a copy of the environment, however, batch files have access to the original. So this limitation doesn't apply to batch files.

What is the environment?

The DOS environment is a section of RAM (random-access memory) that DOS sets aside for specific information. The following three pieces of information are always stored in the environment:

- The location of COMMAND.COM
- The path, if one has been set
- The prompt, if it has been changed from the default

You can see the contents of your environment by entering the command SET followed by an Enter. Note that some of the information might be so wide that it wraps to a second line of the screen.

This original copy of the environment, also called the master copy, is "owned" by COMMAND.COM, and COMMAND.COM is the only program that can modify its contents without tricks. You can modify its contents from either the DOS prompt or with batch files, but other programs can't generally modify this original environment. Any time you run a program, that program gets a copy of the environment from COMMAND .COM if you run it from the DOS prompt, or from another program if you shell out of one program to run another.

A few batch file utilities and batch file compilers are able to modify the master copy of the environment. They do this by searching through memory to find the master copy. When they find it, they write to that section of memory directly.

The contents of the environment has important implications for memory-resident programs (TSRs, for terminate and stay resident). When you load a TSR program, it gets a copy of the environment from COMMAND.COM. Most TSRs will release the unused environmental space but will retain the portion of the environment that contains data. For this reason, you should load your TSRs before storing information in the environment. See chapter 7 for more details.

When a program terminates, its copy of the environment is also terminated. Any changes to the environment made to that copy are lost forever. For example, if you're running Lotus 1-2-3 and you use the /S command to shell to DOS to change your prompt, the new prompt will be lost as soon as you return to Lotus. (Lotus loads a second copy of COMMAND.COM to let you shell out. That copy of COMMAND.COM has an environment attached to it and your new prompt is stored there. When you use the EXIT command to return to Lotus, the EXIT command unloads this copy of COMMAND.COM and terminates its environment.)

The SET command

DOS stores each piece of information in the environment as a string. As you'll see later, this allows you to enter absolutely anything you want into the environment. The general syntax for placing information into the environment is:

    SET variable = value

The only space should be between the set and the variable name. DOS will actually accept other spaces, for example before or after the equal sign. These are treated as part of the variable name or the value, however, and make working with them difficult. The command

    SET TEMP = C:\JUNK

will actually create a variable named TEMP(space) containing the value (space)C:\ JUNK. You'll avoid a lot of problems by not using extra spaces in the SET command.

The keywords COMSPEC, PATH, and PROMPT have special meaning in DOS. They're the ways you change default values in the environment. The general syntax for these is also

    SET COMSPEC = value
    SET PATH = value
    SET PROMPT = value

however, DOS allows you to drop the SET in front of these. Warning: Changing COMSPEC is dangerous and can cause your computer to lock up. If the command isn't just right, you'll get the dreaded *Cannot load COMMAND, system halted* error message. You must reboot when you get this message. When experimenting, make sure to save everything first.

In addition to the three entries placed into the environment automatically, DOS allows you to store your own information there. This custom information can be accessed by programs and accessed and modified by batch files. You can remove a variable from memory using the

    SET *variable* =

command. Be sure not to enter any spaces after the equal sign or you'll set the variable equal to spaces. You can check to be sure the variable was removed by entering the SET command by itself.

SET PROMPT

The default DOS prompt is C >, which tells you almost nothing. The C indicates the current drive. You can use the PROMPT command, however, to create a wide range of prompts. The PROMPT command is normally just used in the AUTOEXEC.BAT file. When used by itself, PROMPT resets the prompt to C >.

Any printable character string can be included in the PROMPT command. In fact, one of the first tricks most computer users learn is to include their name or company name in the prompt. One of the most popular prompts is

    SET PROMPT = pg

which adds the current subdirectory to the default disk display.

It's important to remember that any prompt you develop is stored in the environmental space, along with the PATH and SET variables. Long PROMPT, PATH, and SET variables might require you to expand your environmental space, as explained later in this chapter.

SET COMSPEC

COMSPEC is short for *command specification*. It tells DOS where to find COMMAND .COM so it can be reinstalled after it's overwritten by a program. DOS takes up a lot of memory. When your computer is short of memory, because you either have less than 640K or have a lot of memory-resident software, this can be a problem. A lack of memory might prevent some programs from running or limit the size of others. DOS solves this problem by making part of itself provisionally resident (or transient) in memory. You need this part to enter DOS commands but not to run application programs. If a program needs this space, it can overwrite the transient portion of DOS.

When you exit a program that has overwritten the transient portion of DOS, DOS is less than complete. If you were to use this version, you wouldn't be able to enter most internal commands. DOS replenishes itself by rereading portions of COMMAND.COM into memory. (Note: this is why COMMAND.COM isn't a hidden file like the other two system files.) DOS usually reloads itself from the drive it booted from. Using

    SET COMSPEC = C: \ COMMAND.COM

you can force DOS to reload itself from some other place. You can also change COM-SPEC with the SHELL command in the CONFIG.SYS file.

Many RAM-disk users copy COMMAND.COM to their RAM disk and then use the SET COMSPEC command to reload COMMAND.COM from the RAM disk. This is noticeably faster than reloading from disk.

One note: while available in series 2 of DOS, the SET COMSPEC command doesn't work reliably in versions of DOS prior to 3.0.

SET PATH

There are four types of commands DOS will accept: internal commands, .EXE program names, .COM program names, and .BAT file names. Every time DOS receives a command, it first checks to see if it's an internal command, like ERASE. If so, it executes the command. If the command isn't an internal command, DOS next checks the current subdirectory for a .EXE file by that name, then a .COM file, and finally a .BAT file. If DOS finds a program with the correct name, it executes that program. If DOS doesn't find a file in the current directory, it searches the path for a .COM, .EXE, or .BAT file. If it finds a program in the path with the correct name, it executes that program. Otherwise, DOS returns the *Bad command or file name* error message.

So the path is nothing more than a list of subdirectories for DOS to search when a program isn't in the current subdirectory. The syntax is:

PATH = C: \ ;subdirectory1;subdirectory2;...;subdirectory-last

If your path is

PATH = C: \ ; \ SYSLIB; \ DATABASE; \ WORDPROCESSOR

then DOS will search only those subdirectories on the default disk. This is normally what you want. However, if you're working on the A drive, then the path is really

PATH = C: \ ;A: \ SYSLIB;A: \ DATABASE;A: \ WORDPROCESSOR

because A is the default drive. So you're better off specifying the full path, like this

PATH = C: \ ;C: \ SYSLIB;C: \ DATABASE;C: \ WORDPROCESSOR

A problem is that the PATH command can contain only the same 127 characters as other DOS commands. Before DOS 3.0, there was simply no way to have a path longer than 127 characters. While DOS 3.0 retained the 127-character command-line limit, it introduced the SUBST, or substitute, command. SUBST allows you to substitute a drive letter for a subdirectory, so

SUBST D: C: \ SYSLIB \ LEVEL1 \ LEVEL2

allows you to use D: anywhere you would have used C: \ SYSLIB \ LEVEL1 \ LEVEL2. This allows you to make your PATH command like this

PATH = C: \ ;D: \

instead of

PATH = C: \ ;C: \ SYSLIB \ LEVEL1 \ LEVEL2

which makes the path command shorter as well as easier to read.

Generally speaking, you won't have set the path before using the SUBST command. Therefore, either SUBST.EXE must be in the root directory or you must change to the directory containing it before you issue the SUBST command. The following is an example of SUBST.EXE in the C: \ SYSLIB directory:

```
CD \ SYSLIB
SUBST D: C: \ SYSLIB \ LEVEL1 \ LEVEL2
```

If you enter the PATH command with nothing after it, DOS will display the current path. If you enter the PATH command followed by a semicolon and nothing else, DOS will reset the path to nothing. This causes DOS to search only the default directory for programs and batch files. If you specify a path incorrectly, DOS won't find the error until it needs to search the path. If you enter an invalid directory in the path, DOS will ignore that entry.

Using SET variables in batch files

As explained above, SET variables are variables you've placed into the environment using the SET command, or that DOS placed in the environment with a default value. A batch file can use these variables by adding a percent before and after their name.

Increasing the size of the environment

Most Microsoft compilers use one or more SET variables to point to their libraries. In fact, a couple of them use the same variables to point to different libraries! I once got a frantic call from a developer using two Microsoft products. He didn't know how to deal with this problem. I told him to construct two batch files, one to start each compiler. He could then have each batch file custom set the variables for that compiler. He called me back even more frantic because it wouldn't work. I had him type SET at the DOS prompt and read the contents back to me. It turned out that he hadn't expanded the environment and, with his long path and prompt, there just wasn't enough room to store all the information he was trying to shove into the environment. I walked him through the procedure to expand the environment and everything worked properly.

The default size of the environment is 160 bytes, which means it can store 160 characters. This 160-character storage space must store the COMSPEC value, the path, the prompt, and any variables you want to enter. If this isn't enough room, you need to expand the environment.

Users of DOS 3.0 and later have it easy. For them, adding one of the following lines as the first line of their CONFIG.SYS file will expand the environment:

DOS version	Command
3.0	SHELL=C: \ COMMAND.COM /e:*xx* /p
3.1	SHELL=C: \ COMMAND.COM /e:*xx* /p
3.2	SHELL=C: \ COMMAND.COM /e:*yy* /p
3.3	SHELL=C: \ COMMAND.COM /e:*yy* /p
4.0	SHELL=C: \ COMMAND.COM /e:*yy* /p
5.0	SHELL=C: \ COMMAND.COM /e:*yy* /p

If you're running off floppies, then change the C: \ to an A: \. The *xx* is a number between 10 and 62. It represents the number of 16-byte segments to use for the environment. So a 20 will give you a 320-byte environmental space. The maximum value is 992 bytes, which is an *xx* of 62. Beginning with version 3.2, you can create a much larger environment. The *yy* is a number from 160 to 32,768 and represents the number of bytes to use for the environment. This allows an environmental space up to 32K! The /p switch is required to force COMMAND.COM to automatically run the AUTOEXEC.BAT file. Because the SHELL command is in the CONFIG.SYS file and the CONFIG.SYS file is processed prior to the AUTOEXEC.BAT file, without the /p switch the AUTOEXEC.BAT file will be bypassed.

In this example SHELL statement, the /e and /p aren't SHELL switches; they're COMMAND.COM switches. The full set of switches are:

/C This tells COMMAND.COM to run the command listed after the /c switch.

/D This causes COMMAND.COM not to run the AUTOEXEC.BAT file. It's used in conjunction with the /p switch.

/E This switch to change the environment size first appeared in DOS 3.0, but wasn't documented until DOS 3.1. Also, it works differently in DOS 3.0 and 3.1 than it does in latter versions.

/F This switch first appeared in DOS 3.1. It causes DOS to automatically respond with a Fail anytime it displays the *Abort, retry or fail* or *Abort, ignore, retry or fail* error messages. You'll still see the error message on the screen, along with DOS's response.

/P This tells COMMAND.COM to load in permanent mode and set a couple of switches internally. One switch causes it not to unload when you issue an EXIT command. Another switch causes it to run the AUTOEXEC.BAT file after loading.

Note that the syntax includes the .COM on the end of COMMAND.COM. This is required. These changes won't take effect until you reboot. Make sure you have a bootable system disk in case you make a mistake. Some mistakes will hang the computer. If this happens, reboot from the floppy and switch over to the hard disk to edit the problem CONFIG.SYS. As a precaution, you should make a copy of your CONFIG.SYS file before trying this change.

If you use DOS 2.*x*, then you must change the COMMAND.COM program in order to increase the environment. The example shown in Fig. 16-1 expands the environment to 992 bytes. Series-2 DOS includes a routine that limits the environment to a maximum of 992 bytes regardless of how COMMAND.COM is patched. It expands the environment in 16-byte increments. If you enter an odd increment, it's rounded up to the nearest 16 bytes.

To edit the COMMAND.COM program, use Debug. DEBUG.COM is a program editor that comes with DOS. The first step is to format a floppy disk as a system disk and make your changes to this disk, even if you have a hard disk. Once you're sure that everything works, you can copy COMMAND.COM from the modified floppy disk to your hard disk. After formatting a system disk, copy DEBUG.COM to the floppy. Finally, change over to the A drive and perform the steps in Fig. 16-1.

Note: I've tested this patch on IBM's PC DOS versions 2.0 and 2.1 and Compaq's MS-DOS versions 2.0 and 2.1. While it should work on most compatible versions of

DOS, some vendors rewrite parts of COMMAND.COM for specific operating systems. It's possible that this could prevent the patch from working. If you have trouble, check with the manufacturer of your computer or upgrade to DOS 5 where you won't have this problem.

After you patch COMMAND.COM, reboot from the new floppy disk and run the batch file TESTENVI.BAT, shown in Fig. 16-2. If the environment is expanded, the patch worked and you can copy COMMAND.COM to other floppy disks or to your hard disk. Otherwise, you need to reformat the diskette and try again, contact the manufacturer for information on how to patch his version of COMMAND.COM, or upgrade to DOS 5.0.

Testing the environment

As you begin to use the environment more, you'll begin incorporating it into your batch files. If you're concerned about your batch files running out of environmental space, you can test for the amount of free space first. ENV_SIZE.BAT in Fig. 16-3 shows the general approach.

In ENV_SIZE.BAT, the length of the first variable name (48_BYTE) is 7. The length of the string it contains, which is *This String (Including Name) Is 47 Bytes*, is 39. Thus, the space required for this string is 7+39+2, or 48. The second variable (SET A=B) has a length of 1+1+2, or 4. As a result, this test actually tests to see if the environment contains (48+4) 52 bytes.

When I write batch files, I tend to ignore this slight over-testing of the environment. My feeling is that, if the environment is so tight that the couple of extra bytes involved will cause the test to fail, then the environment needs to be expanded anyway.

Summary

This chapter has presented a discussion of the usefulness of the DOS environment and explained how to expand the environment by patching COMMAND.COM (series-2 DOS) or by including the SHELL command in your CONFIG.SYS file.

16-1 Patching COMMAND.COM to enlarge the environmental space under DOS 2.x.

Command	Explanation
A:<Return>	Change to the A drive. The modification will be made to a floppy disk (formatted as a system disk) and later transferred to the hard disk once the change is tested.
DEBUG COMMAND.COM	DOS command to start Debug (a DOS program editor) and edit COMMAND.COM.
-	The dash is the Debug prompt. When you see a dash, Debug is waiting for a command.

Command	Explanation
-s 100 L 1000 bb 0a 00	This is the command to search for the part of COMMAND.COM that stores the size of the environment. That location will be different on different versions of DOS. NOTE: This command is case-sensitive. You must enter the command exactly as shown. Also, the 0s are zeros and not letters.
XXXX:YYYY	When Debug finds the correct string, it will display this information as two numbers separated by a colon. The numbers are in hexadecimal so they might also contain letters. That's ok. You'll be using the second number.
-e YYYY bb 3e 00	This is the Debug command to edit COMMAND.COM so it will allocate more space for the environment. The 0a 00 two lines above is the default 160 bytes in hexadecimal. This command changes that to 992 bytes (3e 00 in hexadecimal.) NOTE: Do not use YYYY. Replace the YYYY with the second number from the line above. Do not enter YYYY.
-w	Write the change to disk. You should see the message Writing *n* bytes where *n* is a number.
-q	Quit Debug. Now reboot from the floppy disk and test it for proper operation.

16-2 TESTENVI.BAT is a batch file to test the success of the COMMAND.COM patch to DOS 2.0.

Batch File Line	Explanation
ECHO OFF	Turn command-echoing off.
REM NAME: TESTENVI.BAT REM PURPOSE: Test Environment REM VERSION: 1.10 REM DATE: January 12, 1992	Remark giving the name of the batch file.

Batch File Line	Explanation
ECHO Use This Variable To Test Your ECHO Environment. The Last Line In ECHO This Batch File Will Display ECHO The Environment. Count The ECHO Characters You See Before The ECHO Variable 1. Be Sure To Count ECHO The Variable Names And The Equal ECHO Sign. Then Add 50 For Each ECHO Numeric Variable Except The Last. ECHO Because The Last Variable Might ECHO Have Been Cut Short, You Must ECHO Count Those Characters. The ECHO Resulting Number Is The Current ECHO Size Of The Environment. ECHO NOTE: If You See All 19 ECHO Variables, Then Your Environment ECHO Is Too Large To Measure Using ECHO This Batch File.	Tell the user what will happen.
IF (%1)==(/?) GOTO END IF (%1)==(?) GOTO END	The above text is always displayed and is adequate as help text, so exit the batch file after displaying it if the user requests help.
SET 1=4567890123456789012345678901234567890123456789012345678901234567890	Define an environmental variable. Including the SET 1=, this line contains 50 characters, counting the ASCII code zero that DOS adds after the definition of each environmental variable.
SET 2=4567890123456789012345678901234567890123456789012345678901234567890	Define an environmental variable.
The batch file continues in similar fashion for variables 3-18.	
SET 19=4567890123456789012345678901234567890123456789012345678901234567890	Define an environmental variable.
SET	Display the contents of the environment.
:END	Label marking the end of the batch file.

16-3 ENV_SIZE.BAT verifies that the environment has 50 bytes of free space. Generally, this code would precede code that required the environment to operate.

Batch File Line	Explanation
`@ECHO OFF`	Turn command-echoing off.

`REM NAME:     ENV_SIZE.BAT`
`REM PURPOSE: Check For Adequate`
`REM          Environmental Space`
`REM          (Assume 50 Bytes)`
`REM VERSION: 1.00`
`REM DATE:    December 17, 1991`
	Documentation remarks.

`IF (%1)==(/?) GOTO HELP` `IF (%1)==(?)  GOTO HELP`	If the user starts the batch file with a request for help, jump to a section to display that help.
`SET 48_BYTE=This String (Including` `          Name) Is 47 Bytes`	Store a 47-byte string into the environment. (Please see technical note in chapter.)

`REM Please Forgive The Poor English`
`REM I had To Make The Statement`
`REM An Exact Length And That`
`REM Took Its Toll On The English`
	Documentation remarks.

`SET A=B`	Create a second variable.
`IF (%A%)==() GOTO ERROR`	If the second variable wasn't created successfully the environment is out of space, so jump to an error-handling routine.
`GOTO OK`	The environment contains enough space if the batch file reaches this point, so jump to a section to tell the user the results.

`:ERROR`
`ECHO Environment Lacks 50 Bytes Free`
`GOTO END`
`:END_ERROR`
	Display an error message and then exit the batch file.

`:OK`
`ECHO Environment Has 50 Bytes Free`
`GOTO END`
`:END_OK`
	Tell the user the environment contains enough space and exit. Normally, this batch file would perform some useful function before exiting.

`:HELP`
`ECHO This Demonstration Batch File`
`ECHO Tests The Environment To See If`
`ECHO It Has 50 Bytes Free`
`GOTO END`
`:END_HELP`
	Section that displays help when the user starts the batch file with a /? or a ? as the first replaceable parameter.

`:END`	Label marking the exit point of the batch file.

Batch File Line	Explanation
| ```
SET 48_BYTE=
SET A=
``` | Before exiting the batch file, delete the environmental variables it used. If this batch file went on to perform some useful purpose, these would need to be deleted first so the batch file would have the space to perform its intended task. |
```

17

The DOS errorlevel

The DOS environment is a very inhospitable place for programs to store information. Each program is provided a copy of the environment when it's first loaded. When it reads from or writes to the environment, it's dealing with its copy of the environment, not the original. When the program terminates, its copy of the environment, along with all the changes the program made to it, are erased.

The DOS errorlevel function was added in DOS 2.0 to overcome this problem. The errorlevel isn't stored in the environment, so changes made to it aren't lost when a program terminates. Unlike the environment, there's only one copy of the errorlevel, so every program changes the same errorlevel. The errorlevel changes under the following conditions:

When you start a program Every time DOS starts a program, it resets the errorlevel to zero.

When the program changes the errorlevel Some programs pass information back to DOS using the errorlevel.

When you reboot The errorlevel is stored in memory, so its contents are lost when you reboot or turn the computer off.

Because the errorlevel rarely changes, you can perform multiple tests on it. The errorlevel has room for only one byte, so only an ASCII value of 0 to 255 can be stored in the errorlevel. Using the:

```
IF ERRORLEVEL #
IF NOT ERRORLEVEL #
```

statements, a batch file can test the contents of the errorlevel and make decisions based on that content.

Unfortunately, the test isn't straightforward. The test IF ERRORLEVEL 5 doesn't test to see if the errorlevel value is currently equal to five. Rather it tests to see if the errorlevel is currently greater than or equal to five. As a result, any number from 5 to 255 will result in a true on this test. Therefore, you must always test from the highest possible errorlevel value to the lowest. In addition, you must branch away from the testing after the first match.

The brute-force approach

One approach to testing for the errorlevel value is to sequentially test for every possible errorlevel value. CHECKERR.BAT in Fig. 17-1 does just this. It begins by testing for an errorlevel value of 255, the maximum possible value. If the errorlevel is 255, it displays that value and exits. If the errorlevel isn't 255, it tests for 254, the next possible value. It continues in this fashion until it finds the errorlevel value.

Fortunately, this brute-force approach is easier to implement in most batch files because most programs use only a few of the possible errorlevel values. For example, in DOS 5.0 the XCOPY command will terminate with one of only five possible values.

Combining IF statements

CHECKERR.BAT is a long batch file, containing over 500 lines! Part 6 of this book will show you how to combine multiple IF statements on a single line. Using that technique, you can cut the number of lines in CHECKERR.BAT in half. CHECKER2.BAT in Fig. 17-2 shows how to do this.

The impact on running time depends on the value of the errorlevel. When the errorlevel is zero, CHECKERR.BAT takes 7.6 seconds on my computer, while CHECK-ER2.BAT takes only 4.3 seconds. CHECKERR.BAT has to process every one of its IF statements as does CHECKER2.BAT, and the two batch files have the same number of IF statements. CHECKER2.BAT, however, doesn't reach half of them because, when the first IF statement fails the batch file doesn't reach the second one.

When the errorlevel is 150, CHECKERR.BAT takes 3.5 seconds and CHECKER2 .BAT takes 4.6 seconds. CHECKERR.BAT runs faster because it has to process fewer of its IF statements before escaping by way of the GOTO statement. CHECKER2.BAT still has to process all the first IF statements and 150 of them pass, so on those lines the second IF statement is processed as well. All of this adds to the processing time.

The trend of CHECKERR.BAT's processing time decreasing and CHECKER2.BAT's time increasing continues when the errorlevel is 255. CHECKERR.BAT takes .9 second and CHECKER2.BAT requires 5 seconds.

Shorter errorlevel tests

An easier way to find the errorlevel is to test each of the three digits individually. First, find out if the left digit is a 0, 1, or 2. This takes only one FOR loop. DIGIT-1.BAT in Fig. 17-3 does this. Next, find out if the middle digit is between a 0 and 9. That takes only one FOR loop as well. DIGIT-2.BAT in Fig. 17-4 does this. DIGIT-2.BAT requires that DIGIT-1.BAT run first, but there's no error checking to enforce that. The reason for this is that DIGIT-3.BAT (see Fig. 17-5) will call both of these batch files and will always run DIGIT-1.BAT before DIGIT-2.BAT.

Notice that the variable ERROR is being built as you go, from left to right. Testing for the right digit will work the same way. DIGIT-3.BAT will find the right digit. Notice that it calls the two prior batch files to find their digits because it requires that information to run properly.

This method works properly for errorlevel values between 0 and 199, but not for errorlevel values over 200. There are no restrictions in the batch file, so when the first digit is a two, DIGIT-2.BAT and DIGIT-3.BAT end up testing for values 256−299. The maximum errorlevel value is 255, and DOS doesn't handle tests above 255 properly. As a result, you need some complex branching.

If the first digit is a two, the batch file must branch to a separate test to make sure the test on the second digit doesn't exceed five. If the second digit is a five, it must branch again to make sure the test on the final digit doesn't exceed a five. That way, the batch file never tests for an errorlevel greater than 255. In addition, there's no advantage in using separate batch files for each digit, so all three batch files can be combined into one. The resulting batch file is SAVE-ERR.BAT, in Fig. 17-6.

SAVE-ERR.BAT quickly tests the errorlevel values. For every errorlevel value, the test takes under a second. In addition to displaying the errorlevel value, SAVE-ERR.BAT also stores the value in the environment under the name ERROR. That allows you to retain the errorlevel value while running another program. It also makes testing the errorlevel value much easier. While the usual errorlevel test of IF ERRORLEVEL # is a greater-than-or-equal test, the test IF %ERROR% = = # is an equality test. This reduces the number of IF statements required to test for any value in half.

Programs that use errorlevel

Only a few DOS programs make use of the errorlevel. Tables 17-1 through 17-10 list the possible errorlevel values for those few DOS programs that do set the errorlevel. A few commercial programs also use the errorlevel, generally those that expect to be run from the command line, like compilers and backup programs. Check the program's documentation to find out the values it uses.

Table 17-1 BACKUP errorlevel values.

Value	Meaning
0	Normal completion.
1	No files were found.
2	There was a file-sharing conflict.
3	User terminated the restore process with a Ctrl-Break or a Ctrl-C.
4	The restore process terminated because of an error.

Table 17-2   DISKCOMP errorlevel values.

Value	Meaning
0	The two disks being compared are the same.
1	The two disks being compared are different.
2	User terminated the process with a Ctrl-Break or a Ctrl-C.
3	A hard error occurred.
4	An initialization error occurred.

Table 17-3   DISKCOPY errorlevel values.

Value	Meaning
0	The disk was copied correctly.
1	A nonfatal read or write error occurred.
2	User terminated the process with a Ctrl-Break or a Ctrl-C.
3	A fatal hard error occurred.
4	An initialization error occurred.

Table 17-4   FORMAT errorlevel values.

Value	Meaning
0	The disk was successfully formatted.
3	User terminated the process with a Ctrl-Break or a Ctrl-C.
4	Any error other than those that cause an errorlevel of 3 or 5 occurred.
5	The user answered N when asked *Proceed with Format (Y/N)?* by the program.

Table 17-5   GRAFTABL errorlevel values.

Value	Meaning
0	The requested character set was loaded and no previous code page was loaded.
1	The requested character set was loaded, replacing a code page that was already loaded.
2	A file error occurred.
3	The user specified an incorrect parameter and the program took no action.
5	An incorrect version of DOS is being used.

Table 17-6   KEYB errorlevel values.

Value	Meaning
0	The keyboard definition file was loaded.
1	The user specified an invalid keyboard code or otherwise used improper syntax.
2	The keyboard definition file is missing or invalid.
4	An error occurred communicating with the keyboard.
5	The requested code page hasn't been prepared.

Table 17-7   REPLACE errorlevel values.

Code	Meaning
0	Replace successfully replaced or added the files.
2	Replace couldn't find the source files.
3	Replace couldn't find the specified path.
5	Access to the source file was denied by the operating system.
8	Insufficient memory to complete the process.
11	An error on the command line--for example, using an invalid parameter.

Table 17-8 RESTORE errorlevel values.

Value	Meaning
0	The files were restored as requested.
1	No files were found to restore.
3	The user terminated the restore with a Ctrl-Break or a Ctrl-C.
4	The restore process terminated because of an error.

Table 17-9 SETVER errorlevel values.

Value	Meaning
0	SETVER was successful.
1	The user specified an invalid switch on the command line.
2	The user specified an invalid filename.
3	There wasn't enough memory to perform the requested task.
4	The user entered an invalid DOS version number.
5	SETVER couldn't find the specified entry in its internal tables.
6	SETVER couldn't find SETVER.EXE.
7	The user specified an invalid drive letter.
8	The user specified too many parameters on the command line.
9	The user didn't specify enough parameters on the command line.
10	SETVER encountered an error while reading SETVER.EXE.
11	SETVER.EXE has become corrupted.
12	This version of SETVER.EXE doesn't support a version table.
13	The SETVER.EXE table lacks space for another entry.
14	SETVER encountered an error while writing to SETVER.EXE.

Table 17-10 XCOPY errorlevel values.

Code	Meaning
0	The files were copied correctly.
1	No files were found to copy.
2	User pressed Ctrl-Break or Ctrl-C to stop the copy, or answered Abort to the *Abort, Retry, or Ignore* error message.
4	An initialization error occurred. Possible causes include not enough memory, not enough disk space, and an invalid drive name.
5	An error occurred while writing to the disk.

Summary

- Each program gets a copy of the DOS environment and that copy is deleted when that program terminates.
- There's only one copy of the errorlevel, so all programs have access to a common storage area. However, the errorlevel stores only one byte of information.
- The errorlevel test is a greater-than-or-equal test, making errorlevel testing complex.
- CHECKERR.BAT uses the brute-force approach to test for every possible errorlevel.
- Most programs only use a few errorlevel values, making errorlevel testing easier after running those programs.
- CHECKER2.BAT uses a fewer number of lines than CHECKERR.BAT by combining multiple IF tests on a single line.
- DIGIT-1.BAT tests for the hundreds digit of the errorlevel.
- DIGIT-2.BAT tests for the tens digit of the errorlevel. It lacks error checking to make sure that DIGIT-1.BAT is run first, but without running DIGIT-1.BAT first DIGIT-2.BAT returns the wrong answer.
- DIGIT-3.BAT first runs DIGIT-1.BAT and DIGIT-2.BAT to find the hundreds and tens digit; then it finds the ones digit of the errorlevel.
- DIGIT-2.BAT and DIGIT-3.BAT can report incorrect results when the hundreds digit of the errorlevel is a two.
- SAVE-ERR.BAT combines the functions of DIGIT-1.BAT through DIGIT-3.BAT while correcting the problem they have with errorlevel values of 200 and above.

17-1 CHECKERR.BAT uses a brute-force approach to test for every single errorlevel value so it can display the current value.

Batch File Line	Explanation
`@ECHO OFF`	Turn command-echoing off.

`REM NAME:    CHECKERR.BAT`
`REM PURPOSE: Show Errorlevel`
`REM VERSION: 1.00`
`REM DATE:    January 3, 1991`
	Documentation remarks.

`IF (%1)==(/?) GOTO HELP` `IF (%1)==(?)  GOTO HELP`	If the user starts the batch file with a request for help, jump to a section to display that help.
`IF ERRORLEVEL 255 ECHO 255`	If the errorlevel is 255, echo that fact to the screen. Because the errorlevel test is a greater-than-or-equal-to test, you must start testing at the highest value of interest and work your way to the lowest.
`IF ERRORLEVEL 255 GOTO END`	If the errorlevel is 255, skip to the end of the batch file. Once a match is found, you must exit the batch file because all the lower numbers will also match due to the greater-than-or-equal-to testing of the errorlevel test.
`IF ERRORLEVEL 254 ECHO 254` `IF ERRORLEVEL 254 GOTO END`	Test for an errorlevel of 254.
`IF ERRORLEVEL 253 ECHO 253` `IF ERRORLEVEL 253 GOTO END`	Test for an errorlevel of 253.
Continues through all the possible ASCII values with two lines per number	
`IF ERRORLEVEL    1 ECHO 1` `IF ERRORLEVEL    1 GOTO END`	Test for an errorlevel of 1.
`IF ERRORLEVEL    0 ECHO 0` `IF ERRORLEVEL    0 GOTO END`	Test for an errorlevel of 0. I used the same format for consistency. If the batch file reaches this point, then the errorlevel must equal zero.
`GOTO END`	Exit the batch file.

`:HELP`
`ECHO Display The Current`
`ECHO Errorlevel Value`
`GOTO END`
`:END_HELP`
	Section that displays help when the user starts the batch file with a /? or a ? as the first replaceable parameter.

`:END`	Label marking the end of the batch file.

17-2 CHECKER2.BAT cuts the number of lines in CHECKERR.BAT in half by combining IF statements. The two-line IF ERRORLEVEL commands are one line.

Batch File Line	Explanation
`@ECHO OFF`	Turn command-echoing off.

`REM NAME:    CHECKER2.BAT`
`REM PURPOSE: Show Errorlevel`
`REM VERSION: 1.00`
`REM DATE:    January 3, 1991`
	Documentation remarks.

`IF (%1)==(/?)  GOTO HELP` `IF (%1)==(?)   GOTO HELP`	If the user starts the batch file with a request for help, jump to a section to display that help.
`IF ERRORLEVEL 255 ECHO 255`	If errorlevel equals 255, it echoes that fact. Because 255 is the maximum possible value, only one test is required.
`IF ERRORLEVEL 254 IF NOT` `ERRORLEVEL 255 ECHO 254`	This multiple IF test overcomes the limitation of the greater-than-or-equal errorlevel test. All values greater than or equal to 254 pass the first test. Without the NOT, all values 255 or greater pass the second test and the NOT reverses it so only values less than 255 pass the test. The result is a test only 254 passes.
`IF ERRORLEVEL 253 IF NOT` `ERRORLEVEL 254 ECHO 253`	All values greater than or equal to 253 pass the first test. Without the NOT, all values 254 or greater pass the second test and the NOT reverses it so only values less than 254 pass the test. The result is a test only 253 passes.
`IF ERRORLEVEL 252 IF NOT` `ERRORLEVEL 253 ECHO 252`	Test for an errorlevel value of 252.
The batch file continues in a similar fashion for errorlevel values of 251-4	
`IF ERRORLEVEL   3 IF NOT` `ERRORLEVEL   4 ECHO   3`	Test for an errorlevel value of 3.
`IF ERRORLEVEL   2 IF NOT` `ERRORLEVEL   3 ECHO   2`	Test for an errorlevel value of 2.
`IF ERRORLEVEL   1 IF NOT` `ERRORLEVEL   2 ECHO   1`	Test for an errorlevel value of 1.
`IF ERRORLEVEL   0 IF NOT` `ERRORLEVEL   1 ECHO   0`	Test for an errorlevel value of 0.
`GOTO END`	Exit the batch file.

`:HELP`
`ECHO Display The Current`
`ECHO Errorlevel Value`
`GOTO END`
`:END_HELP`
	Section that displays help when the user starts the batch file with a /? or a ? as the first replaceable parameter.

`:END`	Label marking the end of the batch file.

17-3 DIGIT-1.BAT finds the left digit of the errorlevel.

Batch File Line	Explanation
`@ECHO OFF`	Turn command-echoing off.

`REM NAME:     DIGIT-1.BAT`
`REM PURPOSE: Show Errorlevel 100s`
`REM VERSION: 1.00`
`REM DATE:     January 3, 1991`
	Documentation remarks.

`IF (%1)==(/?) GOTO HELP` `IF (%1)==(?)  GOTO HELP`	If the user starts the batch file with a request for help, jump to a section to display that help.
`FOR %%J IN (0 1 2) DO IF ERRORLEVEL` `    %%J00 SET ERROR=%%J`	This line breaks down errorlevel into three categories, 0-99, 100-199, and 200-255. It also stores the first digit in the environment under the name ERROR.
`ECHO Left Digit Was %ERROR%`	Tell the user the results of running the batch file.
`GOTO END`	Exit the batch file.

`:HELP`
`ECHO Finds The Hundreds Digit Of`
`ECHO Errorlevel`
`ECHO Designed To Be Called By`
`ECHO DIGIT-3.BAT`
`GOTO END`
`:END_HELP`
	Section that displays help when the user starts the batch file with a /? or a ? as the first replaceable parameter.

`:END`	Label marking the end of the batch file.

17-4 DIGIT-2.BAT finds the second digit of the errorlevel. It lacks error checking to make sure DIGIT-1.BAT has run first to find the left errorlevel digit.

Batch File Line	Explanation
`@ECHO OFF`	Turns command-echoing off.

`REM NAME:     DIGIT-2.BAT`
`REM PURPOSE: Show Errorlevel 10s`
`REM VERSION: 1.00`
`REM DATE:     January 3, 1991`
	Documentation remarks.

`IF (%1)==(/?) GOTO HELP` `IF (%1)==(?)  GOTO HELP`	If the user starts the batch file with a request for help, jump to a section to display that help.

Batch File Line	Explanation

FOR %%J IN (0 1 2 3 4 5 6 7 8 9)
    DO IF ERRORLEVEL %ERROR%%J0 SET
ERROR=%ERROR%%J
	This line loops through the ten possible digits to find the middle digit of errorlevel. Although this batch file requires that DIGIT-1.BAT runs first, there is no error checking to enforce that.
	
	When ERROR has a value of 1, this line becomes:
	
	FOR %%J IN (0 1 2 3 4 5 6 7 8 9)
	    DO IF ERRORLEVEL 1%%J0
	    SET ERROR=1%%J

ECHO Left Two Digits Are %ERROR%	Tell the user the result of running the batch file.
GOTO END	Exit the batch file.
:HELP ECHO Finds The Tens Digit Of ECHO Errorlevel ECHO Designed To Be Called By ECHO DIGIT-3.BAT ECHO Must Run After DIGIT-1.BAT GOTO END :END_HELP	Section that displays help when the user starts the batch file with a /? or a ? as the first replaceable parameter.
:END	Label marking the end of the batch file.

17-5 DIGIT-3.BAT first calls DIGIT-1.BAT and DIGIT-2.BAT to find the first two digits of the errorlevel. Then DIGIT-3.BAT finds the third digit. When the errorlevel is 200 or larger, DIGIT-3.BAT might report the wrong answer.

Batch File Line	Explanation
@ECHO OFF	Turn command-echoing off.
REM NAME: DIGIT-3.BAT REM PURPOSE: Show Errorlevel 1s REM VERSION: 1.00 REM DATE: January 3, 1991	Documentation remarks.
IF (%1)==(/?) GOTO HELP IF (%1)==(?) GOTO HELP	If the user starts the batch file with a request for help, jump to a section to display that help.
SET ERROR=	Reset the environmental variable.

Batch File Line	Explanation
`CALL DIGIT-1` `CALL DIGIT-2`	Run the two batch files that must run first. (That's why DIGIT-2.BAT doesn't run DIGIT-1.BAT and lacks error checking.) There's no reason to separate the three main lines into separate batch files. I did it here only for illustration purposes.

`FOR %%J IN (0 1 2 3 4 5 6 7 8 9) DO`
`    IF ERRORLEVEL %ERROR%%%J SET`
`    ERROR=%ERROR%%%J`
	Test for the right-hand digit in errorlevel and add it to the environmental variable.

`ECHO ERRORLEVEL is %ERROR%`	Tell the user the results of running the batch file.
`GOTO END`	Exit the batch file.

`:HELP`
`ECHO Displays The Errorlevel And`
`ECHO Stores It To The Environment`
`ECHO Errorlevels 200 And Over`
`ECHO Could Be Reported Incorrectly`
`GOTO END`
`:END_HELP`
	Section that displays help when the user starts the batch file with a /? or a ? as the first replaceable parameter.

`:END`	Label marking the end of the batch file.

17-6 SAVE-ERR.BAT uses a FOR loop to quickly test errorlevel values. It also stores the errorlevel in the environment under the name ERROR for future use.

Batch File Line	Explanation
`@ECHO OFF`	Turn command-echoing off.

`REM NAME:    SAVE-ERR.BAT`
`REM PURPOSE: Show Errorlevel`
`REM VERSION: 1.00`
`REM DATE:    November 10, 1991`
	Documentation remarks.

`IF (%1)==(/?) GOTO HELP` `IF (%1)==(?)  GOTO HELP`	If the user starts the batch file with a request for help, jump to a section to display that help.
`SET ERROR=`	Reset the environmental variable to nul.

`FOR %%J IN (0 1 2) DO IF`
`    ERRORLEVEL %%J00 SET`
`    ERROR=%%J`
	Find out if
	ERRORLEVEL > 200,
	ERRORLEVEL > 100
	ERRORLEVEL > 0.

Batch File Line	Explanation
`IF %ERROR%==2 GOTO 2`	Jump to a special section if the errorlevel is 200 or larger. This is required because the maximum errorlevel is 255 and DOS doesn't handle errorlevel tests for numbers over 255 in a manner that will work with this batch file. When testing ERRORLEVEL 260 (for example) DOS subtracts increments of 256 until the number is less than 256, or 4 in this example.
`IF %ERROR%==0 SET ERROR=`	If the hundreds digit is a zero, remove it.
`FOR %%J IN (0 1 2 3 4 5 6 7 8 9) DO IF ERRORLEVEL %ERROR%%%J0 SET ERROR=%ERROR%%%J`	As complex as this looks, DOS understands it. If the value of ERROR was 1 coming into this test and the FOR loop was on 6, the test line would read: IF ERRORLEVEL 160 SET ERROR=16 This test sets the value of the tens digit.
`IF %ERROR%===0 SET ERROR=`	If the tens digit is a zero and there's no hundreds digit, remove the zero.
`FOR %%J IN (0 1 2 3 4 5 6 7 8 9) DO IF ERRORLEVEL %ERROR%%%J SET ERROR=%ERROR%%%J`	This test sets the value of the ones digit.
`GOTO END`	Jump to the end of the batch file.
`:2`	This marks the beginning of the section that handles errorlevels greater than or equal to 200.
`FOR %%J IN (0 1 2 3 4 5) DO IF ERRORLEVEL %ERROR%%%J0 SET ERROR=%ERROR%%%J`	Test for the tens digit. Because the maximum errorlevel value is 255, the test doesn't need to exceed 5.
`IF %ERROR%==25 GOTO 25`	If the errorlevel is 250 or larger, jump to a special section because the batch file needs to test only to five.
`FOR %%J IN (0 1 2 3 4 5 6 7 8 9) DO IF ERRORLEVEL %ERROR%%%J SET ERROR=%ERROR%%%J`	Test for the ones digit.
`GOTO END` `:END_2`	Exit the batch file.
`:25`	Label marking the section of the batch file to test errorlevel values greater than or equal to 250.

Batch File Line	Explanation
| ```
FOR %%J IN (0 1 2 3 4 5) DO
    IF ERRORLEVEL %ERROR%%%J
    SET ERROR=%ERROR%%%J
``` | Test for the ones digit. |
| ```
GOTO END
:END_25
``` | Exit the batch file. |
| ```
:HELP
ECHO Displays The Errorlevel
ECHO And Stores It To The
ECHO Environment
ECHO All Values Reported
ECHO Correctly
GOTO END
:END_HELP
``` | Section that displays help when the user starts the batch file with a /? or a ? as the first replaceable parameter. |
| ```
:END
``` | Label marking the end of the batch file. |

18
Working with ANSI

The device driver ANSI.SYS (ANSI for short) gives you an incredible amount of power over the appearance of the screen. By using that power, you can produce very attractive and eye-catching screens for your batch files. However, writing batch files for others using ANSI is asking for problems because so few users load ANSI, and nothing looks worse than seeing ANSI escape sequences stream across a screen when ANSI isn't running. The reason for ANSI's lack of popularity is that it's saddled with the worst user interface of any program on the market! Next to ANSI, Edlin looks downright friendly.

To use ANSI, you must first load it in your CONFIG.SYS file with a statement like:

```
DEVICE = C: \ DOS \ ANSI.SYS
```

Depending on the version of DOS you have, ANSI will use around 2K of additional memory. Actually, that's very little memory to give up for the power ANSI gives you. Before reading about ANSI, you might want to try a little experiment. Configure your computer to load ANSI and reboot. Once you've done that, run the ANSIDEMO.BAT batch file in Fig. 18-1.

If you have a color display, ANSIDEMO.BAT will give you a blue background with bright white letters for the text. At the top of the menu, there will be a flashing red title and at the bottom a bright yellow message. Now to see the real power of ANSI, issue a CLS command.

With other utilities that set the color of the display, CLS returns the display to white characters on a black background. However, ANSI color assignments are permanent, at least until you reboot or issue a new ANSI command, so the CLS command retains the blue background with bright white lettering. Because ANSIDEMO.BAT uses nothing but DOS and ANSI commands, this batch file will run on any computer that loads ANSI.

If you like what you saw, read on. What follows is a brief tutorial on ANSI. ANSI does much more than controlling the screen; it also lets you remap your keyboard, write keyboard macros, and change your prompt. But first a warning. ANSI is very difficult to learn to use. Plan on spending a lot of time studying this tutorial and your DOS manual, along with doing a lot of experimenting, before you can consider yourself an ANSI master.

An ANSI tutorial

Every single ANSI command starts with an escape followed by a left square bracket. The ANSI command to clear the screen, for example, is ESC[2J. (For all the commands and batch file listings that follow, I've used ESC to stand for the escape character, both in the text and the batch file listings. However, the batch file or command must have the escape character, which has an ASCII value of 27 and a hexadecimal value of 1b.) Because the first character in an ANSI command is always an escape, the commands are often called escape sequences.

From the above discussion, you should immediately see the first problem with ANSI. You can't enter any ANSI commands from the keyboard because, when you press the Escape key, DOS thinks you want to abort the current command. Typing Alt−27 on the number pad doesn't bypass this problem. I've included a second batch file called SEND-ANSI.BAT, as shown in Fig. 18-2, so you can experiment with ANSI without having to enter the escape character. Just enter the ANSI command you want to run without the escape and left bracket that begin the command. SENDANSI.BAT will add those two characters and issue the command. SENDANSI.BAT won't work with ANSI keyboard reassignment commands or any other ANSI commands that include a semicolon.

Many word processors and editors make it difficult to create batch files with ANSI commands. There's a trick to get around that. When you enter the CLS command, DOS responds with an ESC[2J command, even if ANSI isn't loaded. You can pipe that to a file with the command CLS>*filename*. Now you can edit that file with your word processor. While many word processors don't allow you to enter an escape, most will edit a file containing an escape without any problem. Just copy the escape character anywhere you need it.

The DOS 5.0 editor, Edlin, Wordstar, Microsoft Word, and WordPerfect all allow you to enter an escape character this way. With the DOS 5 editor, hold down the Control key and press P and then the Escape key. You'll see an arrow on the screen, the Escape symbol.

With Edlin, type Ctrl−V followed by a left bracket. You'll see ^V[on the screen. This is Edlin's symbol for Escape. You still need to type the left bracket that ANSI expects as part of its command. So in Edlin, the command to clear the screen looks like ^V[[2J.

With Wordstar, hold down the Control key and press P followed by Escape. You should see ^V on the screen. With Word and WordPerfect, hold down the Alt key and type 027 on the keypad. (Many, but not all, versions of DOS allow you to skip typing the zero.) You should see a left-pointing arrow on the screen. Beginning with Word 5.5, Word has some difficulty performing this task because Alt also accesses the pull-down menus. With Word 5.5, you must have the NumLock on and you might have to enter the keystrokes several times for it to work.

The most common ANSI command is the command to change colors, which is ESC [#m—where # is the number of the foreground or background color to use. The color numbers are all two digits, all foreground colors start with a three, and all background colors start with a four. The colors are:

Number	Color
0	Black
1	Red

2	Green
3	Yellow
4	Blue
5	Magenta
6	Cyan
7	White

So the command ESC[44mESC[37m sets the screen to white letters on a blue background, my personal favorite. Three notes are in order. First, these color numbers aren't the same as the IBM numbers you're used to using if you program in BASIC. Second, the clear screen command ends with an uppercase *J* while the color command ends with a lowercase *m*. Most ANSI commands are case-sensitive, so pay attention to case while writing ANSI commands. Third, an *m* ends every ANSI attribute setting command but you need only one per line. So the above command could be shortened to ESC[44;37m. The *m* terminates the command. You don't have to reissue the *ESC[* after the *44* because the ANSI command hasn't been terminated yet.

Being able to control screen colors leads to two somewhat useful utilities. BLANK.BAT, in Fig. 18-3, uses ANSI sequences to blank the screen at the DOS prompt by converting the screen to black text on a black background. This keeps amateur snoops from looking at your files. I should note that the blank screen is really only blank at DOS and the few programs that use ANSI color settings. Most programs will display fine while ANSI is set for a blank screen. Of course, you must first be able to load the program without seeing either the prompt or the commands you enter. Typing UNBLANK will run UNBLANK.BAT in Fig. 18-4. It uses ANSI commands to restore the screen to bright white letters on a blue background. (You have to, of course, run UNBLANK.BAT without being able to see the screen.)

While ANSI is loaded, all the text that's written to the screen through DOS is processed by ANSI, and ANSI watches for the ESC[sequence. Anything beginning with ESC[is treated as a command and anything else is sent to the screen. That gives you a number of ways to send ANSI sequences to the screen. For example, issue the following two commands:

```
CLS > TEMP.BAT
TYPE TEMP.BAT
```

If you look at the file TEMP.BAT with an editor, you'll see that it contains the text sequence ESC[2J. When you try to display it through DOS with the TYPE command, you'll discover that, because ANSI sees the sequence beginning with ESC[as a command, it also executed it. So in addition to echoing ANSI commands to the screen, you can put them in an ASCII file and type them to the screen. You can also copy them to the screen with the command:

```
COPY TEMP.BAT CON
```

Now, to continue with the experiment, load TEMP.BAT into an editor. Add SET TEMP = in front of the ANSI sequence so the line looks like SET TEMP = ESC[2J. Now, exit to DOS and run the batch file. Because you didn't turn command echoing off, DOS will try to echo the command to the screen, and again ANSI will intercept it and execute it. However, the environmental variable will be successfully created. Now enter the SET command. DOS will display the other environmental variables properly but, when it reaches the TEMP variable and tries to display its contents, ANSI will again intercept and execute the escape sequence. In addition to ECHO, TYPE, and COPY, this gives you a fourth way to issue ANSI commands. It also turns out that this is the easiest way.

Most environmental variables are rarely displayed. There is, however, one exception. The prompt is an environmental variable and it's displayed after every DOS command. The prompt is particularly useful for ANSI commands. The metacharacter $e issues an escape so you avoid the problem of having to get an escape into the sequence. In addition, the PROMPT command has other metacharacters to spice up a prompt. Table 18-1 lists them. You can see an example of the fancy prompts ANSI is capable of generating by running NICEPROM.BAT in Fig. 18-5.

**Table 18-1   The metacharacters
you can include in a prompt statement.**

Command	Action
$$	Displays a dollar sign
$_	Includes a carriage return and line feed
$b	Displays a vertical bar
$d	Displays the date
$e	Includes an escape (useful when ANSI.SYS is loaded)
$g	Displays a greater-than sign
$h	Displays a backspace (thus deleting the prior character)
$l	Displays a less-than sign
$n	Displays the current drive
$p	Displays the current subdirectory
$q	Displays an equal sign
$t	Displays the time
$v	Displays the DOS version

NICEPROM.BAT uses a couple of ANSI sequences I haven't yet discussed. They're as follows:

ESC[/#A   moves the cursor up the number of lines specified by the # symbol.

ESC[#B   moves the cursor down the number of lines specified by the # symbol.

ESC[#C   moves the cursor left the number of lines specified by the # symbol.

ESC[#D   moves the cursor right the number of lines specified by the # symbol.

ESC[6n reports the current cursor position.

ESC[K erases the current line from the cursor position right.

ESC[s stores the current cursor position.

ESC[u returns to the stored cursor position created by ESC[s.

There's one problem with using the prompt to send ANSI escape sequences in a batch file. Normally, the first command in a batch file is @ECHO OFF, to turn command-echoing off. However, this also causes DOS to stop displaying the prompt, which prevents ANSI escape sequences stored in the prompt from being sent to the screen and processed. The solution is to issue an ECHO ON when you want to send ANSI escape sequences with the prompt. After a command to display the prompt has been processed, you can turn echo back off so your batch file will execute cleanly. ANSIHIDE.BAT back in chapter 2 illustrates this.

I created a batch file called SENDANS2.BAT in Fig. 18-6 so you can experiment with all the combinations of ANSI commands you like. To run it, enter the command:

    SENDANS2 *command1 command2 . . .*

at the command line. SENDANS2.BAT adds the ESC[to the beginning of each command so you should leave it off all the commands. It builds a large environmental variable containing the entire command string and then issues it all at once, so there are no linefeeds between commands. However, that means your environment must be large enough to store all the commands you plan on issuing, plus the ESC[that SENDANS2.BAT adds to the beginning of each command. Finally, because SENDANS2 strips off one character from each parameter (the leading space) and adds two characters (ESC[), the environmental variable will be longer than the command you issue. If that causes it to exceed the 127-character limit DOS places on commands, the computer could lock, reboot, or misbehave in some unpredictable manner. If you keep your commands to 80 characters or less, this won't affect you. Like SENDANSI.BAT, SENDANS2.BAT can't be used to send ANSI commands containing a semicolon.

The keyboard

ANSI is also able to reconfigure your keyboard. The general format of the command is:

    ESC[*x;y*p

where x is the ASCII value of the key to reassign, and y is the ASCII value the key is to take on. If you like, you can enclose the actual value in double quotes. For example, most of the time in DOS you use parentheses more than brackets (although the left bracket gets a workout under ANSI). You can switch them in DOS using the commands:

    ECHO ESC[91;40p
    ECHO ESC[93;41p
    ECHO ESC[40;91p
    ECHO ESC[41;93p

The reassignment works under DOS but not in programs like Microsoft Word that bypass DOS for keystrokes. To reset the keyboard reassignments, issue the commands:

```
ECHO ESC[91;91p
ECHO ESC[93;93p
ECHO ESC[40;40p
ECHO ESC[41;41p
```

You could have started to remap these using the actual keystrokes, so the first command would have been:

```
ECHO ESC["[";"("p
```

But after remapping [and] to (and), you wouldn't be able to type them into the second two commands to map them to something else. Using ASCII values avoids this problem.

In addition to remapping standard keys, you can also remap extended keystrokes like Ctrl–F1. These keystrokes have a two-digit code that starts with 0; (the number zero, not the letter o). They're entered like any other keystroke, so, to remap Ctrl–F1 to issue a DIR command, issue the command:

```
ECHO ESC[0;94;"DIR";13p
```

You can't issue this command with SENDANSI.BAT or SENDANS2.BAT because DOS treats the semicolon as a divider between batch file parameters and doesn't pass them to the batch files. Table 18-2 shows many of the ASCII and extended keystrokes you can use.

Table 18-2 Extended keystrokes you can use with ANSI to remap the keyboard.

Keystroke	ANSI key code	Keystroke	ANSI key code	Keystroke	ANSI key code
Alt-;	0;131	Alt-L	0;38	Del	0;83
Alt-0	0;129	Alt-M	0;50	down arrow	0;80
Alt-1	0;120	Alt-N	0;49	End	0;79
Alt-2	0;121	Alt-O	0;24	F1	0;59
Alt-3	0;122	Alt-P	0;25	F10	0;68
Alt-4	0;123	Alt-Q	0;16	F2	0;60
Alt-5	0;124	Alt-R	0;19	F3	0;61
Alt-6	0;125	Alt-S	0;31	F4	0;62
Alt-7	0;126	Alt-T	0;20	F5	0;63
Alt-8	0;127	Alt-U	0;22	F6	0;64
Alt-9	0;128	Alt-V	0;47	F7	0;65

Table 18-2   Continued.

Keystroke	ANSI key code	Keystroke	ANSI key code	Keystroke	ANSI key code
Alt-A	0;30	Alt-W	0;17	F8	0;66
Alt-B	0;48	Alt-X	0;45	F9	0;67
Alt-C	0;46	Alt-Y	0;21	Home	0;71
Alt-D	0;32	Alt-Z	0;44	Ins	0;82
Alt-dash	0;130	Ctrl-F1	0;94	left arrow	0;75
Alt-E	0;18	Ctrl-left arrow	0;115	NUL	0;3
Alt-F	0;33	Ctrl-right arrow	0;116	PgDn	0;81
Alt-F1	0;104	Ctrl-End	0;117	PgUp	0;73
Alt-F10	0;113	Ctrl-F10	0;103	right arrow	0;77
Alt-F2	0;105	Ctrl-F2	0;95	Shift-F1	0;84
Alt-F3	0;106	Ctrl-F3	0;96	Shift-F10	0;93
Alt-F4	0;107	Ctrl-F4	0;97	Shift-F2	0;85
Alt-F5	0;108	Ctrl-F5	0;98	Shift-F3	0;86
Alt-F6	0;109	Ctrl-F6	0;99	Shift-F4	0;87
Alt-F7	0;110	Ctrl-F7	0;100	Shift-F5	0;88
Alt-F8	0;111	Ctrl-F8	0;101	Shift-F6	0;89
Alt-F9	0;112	Ctrl-F9	0;102	Shift-F7	0;90
Alt-G	0;34	Ctrl-Home	0;119	Shift-F8	0;91
Alt-H	0;35	Ctrl-PgDn	0;118	Shift-F9	0;92
Alt-I	0;23	Ctrl-PgUp	0;132	Shift-Tab	0;15
Alt-J	0;36	Ctrl-Print Screen	0;114	up arrow	0;72
Alt-K	0;37				

As you can see, ANSI gives you a great deal of control over the screen. It's also difficult to learn—but once you learn ANSI, it's fairly easy to use. Table 18-3 summarizes many frequently used ANSI commands.

Table 18-3   Common commands you can issue using ANSI.SYS.

ANSI command sequence	Function
ESC[#;#p	Reassigns the key defined by the first pound sign to the value of the second pound sign.
ESC[#A	Moves the cursor up the number of rows specified by the number that replaces the pound sign.
ESC[#B	Moves the cursor down the number of rows specified by the number that replaces the pound sign.
ESC[#C	Moves the cursor left the number of rows specified by the number that replaces the pound sign.
ESC[#D	Moves the cursor right the number of rows specified by the number that replaces the pound sign.
ESC[=7l	Turns line wrap off.
ESC[=7h	Turns line wrap on.
ESC[?7l	Turns line wrap off. When line wrap is off, once the cursor reaches the end of the line, each succeeding character is printed on top of the last one at the end of the line.
ESC[?7h	Turns line wrap on. This is needed only if line wrap has been turned off.
ESC[0h	Sets the display mode to 40x25 monochrome.
ESC[0l	Sets the display mode to 40x25 monochrome.
ESC[0m	Resets the screen display to white on black.
ESC[1h	Sets the display mode to 40x25 color.
ESC[1l	Sets the display mode to 40x25 color.
ESC[1m	Sets the foreground text to bold.
ESC[2h	Sets the display mode to 80x25 monochrome.
ESC[2J	Clears the screen.
ESC[2l	Sets the display mode to 80x25 monochrome.
ESC[30m	Sets foreground color to black.
ESC[31m	Sets foreground color to red.
ESC[32m	Sets foreground color to green.
ESC[33m	Sets foreground color to yellow.
ESC[34m	Sets foreground color to blue.
ESC[35m	Sets foreground color to magenta.
ESC[36m	Sets foreground color to cyan.
ESC[37m	Sets foreground color to white.
ESC[3h	Sets the display mode to 80x25 color.

Table 18-3   Continued.

ANSI command sequence	Function
ESC[31	Sets the display mode to 80x25 color.
ESC[40m	Sets background color to black.
ESC[41m	Sets background color to red.
ESC[42m	Sets background color to green.
ESC[43m	Sets background color to yellow.
ESC[44m	Sets background color to blue.
ESC[45m	Sets background color to magenta.
ESC[46m	Sets background color to cyan.
ESC[47m	Sets background color to white.
ESC[4h	Sets the display mode to 320x200 color graphics.
ESC[4l	Sets the display mode to 320x200 color graphics.
ESC[4m	Sets the foreground text to underlined on a monochrome display. On a color display, this sets the foreground to blue.
ESC[5A	Sets the foreground text to blinking.
ESC[5h	Sets the display mode to 320x200 monochrome graphics.
ESC[5l	Sets the display mode to 320x200 monochrome graphics.
ESC[6h	Sets the display mode to 640x200 monochrome graphics.
ESC[6l	Sets the display mode to 640x200 monochrome graphics.
ESC[6n	Reports the cursor position.
ESC[7m	Sets the display to reverse video, black text on a white background.
ESC[K	Erases the current line from the cursor position right.
ESC[r;cf	Positions the cursor on row number r and column number c.
ESC[r;cH	Positions the cursor on row number r and column number c.
ESC[s	Stores the current cursor position.
ESC[u	Returns to the cursor position stored by the ESC[s command.

Summary

- You can use ANSI escape sequences to change the foreground and background colors of the screen.
- When you use ANSI to change the color of the screen, a CLS command won't reset the colors to white on black.

- You can't enter ANSI commands from the keyboard because they start with the escape character.
- If your word processor can't enter an escape character in a file, pipe the CLS command to a file and incorporate the escape from that file into your document.
- ANSI processes any line sent to the screen that begins with an escape character followed by an open bracket, no matter how the characters are displayed.
- ANSI.SYS also allows you to remap the keyboard, although the remapping might not work with many programs that avoid DOS to get their keystrokes.

18-1 ANSIDEMO.BAT demonstrates some of the formatting power of ANSI.SYS. Before running ANSIDEMO.BAT, you must load ANSI.SYS in your CONFIG.SYS file.

Batch File Line	Explanation
`@ECHO OFF`	Turn command-echoing off.

`REM NAME:     ANSIDEMO.BAT`
`REM PURPOSE: Show ANSI.SYS Power`
`REM          To Control The Screen`
`REM VERSION: 2.00`
`REM DATE:    July 22, 1991`
	Documentation remarks.

`IF (%1)==(/?) GOTO HELP` `IF (%1)==(?)  GOTO HELP`	If the user starts the batch file with a request for help, jump to a section to display that help.
`REM Change The Screen Colors` `REM Bright White On Blue`	Documentation remarks.
`ECHO ESC[37m`	Send an ANSI sequence to set the foreground color to white. (Note: the batch file uses an ASCII 27 escape character, not ESC.)
`ECHO ESC[44m`	Send an ANSI sequence to set the background color to blue.
`ECHO ESC[1m`	Send an ANSI sequence to set the foreground color attribute to bright.

`REM Clear the Screen`
`REM Set Colors First So CLS`
`REM Will Use New Colors`
	Documentation remarks.

`ECHO ESC[2J`	Send an ANSI sequence to clear the screen.
`REM Change To Flashing Red` `REM Display Message And Reset`	Documentation remarks.

Batch File Line	Explanation

ECHO ESC[1;30HESC[31mESC[5mA Very
   Special MenuESC[0mESC[37mESC
   [44mESC[1m
	Send the following ANSI sequences:
	
	ESC[1;30H Position the cursor on row one and column thirty.
	
	ESC[31m Set the foreground color to red. This affects only the text that's written to the screen after this, not the existing text.
	
	ESC[5A Set the foreground text to blinking.
	
	At this point, a message is written to the screen.
	
	ESC[0m Reset the screen display to white on black. Again, this affects only future text and is used here to stop the blinking.
	
	ESC[37mESC[44mESC[1m Set the display to bright white on blue.

REM Position Cursor & Display Options	Documentation remark.
ECHO ESC[6;20H1. Run Word Processing	Position the cursor on row six at column twenty and write text.
ECHO ESC[7;20H2. Run Spreadsheet ECHO ESC[8;20H3. Run Database ECHO ESC[9;20H4. Play Games ECHO ESC[10;20H5. Format A Disk ECHO ESC[11;20H6. Backup Hard Disk To Floppies	Write the remaining menu options to the screen.

ECHO ESC[15;20HESC[33mPress The
   Number of The Program You
   WantESC[37m
	Position the cursor on row fifteen and column twenty, change the foreground color to yellow, write text to the screen, and reset the foreground color.

GOTO END	Exit the batch file.

Batch File Line	Explanation
:HELP ECHO This Batch File Is A ECHO Demonstration Of ANSI ECHO It Requires That You Load ECHO ANSI.SYS In Your CONFIG.SYS File GOTO END :END_HELP	Section that displays help when the user starts the batch file with a /? or a ? as the first replaceable parameter.
:END	Label marking the end of the batch file.

18-2 SENDANSI.BAT allows you to issue ANSI commands without preceding them with an Escape or left bracket. SENDANSI.BAT can issue only one ANSI command at a time.

Batch File Line	Explanation
@ECHO OFF	Turn command-echoing off.
REM NAME: SENDANSI.BAT REM PURPOSE: Let User Enter ANSI REM Command From Keyboard REM SYNTAX: SENDANSI Command REM Without Escape [REM VERSION: 1.00 REM DATE: July 22, 1991	Documentation remarks.
IF (%1)==(/?) GOTO HELP IF (%1)==(?) GOTO HELP	If the user starts the batch file with a request for help, jump to a section to display that help.
ECHO ESC[%1	Send an ESC[plus the user's command to ANSI. (Note: the batch file uses an ASCII-27 escape character, not ESC.)
GOTO END	Exit the batch file.
:HELP ECHO Sends A Single Command To ANSI ECHO Without The Leading ESC[ECHO Just Enter SENDANSI Command ECHO On The Command Line GOTO END :END_HELP	Section that displays help when the user starts the batch file with a /? or a ? as the first replaceable parameter.
:END	Label marking the end of the batch file.

18-3 BLANK.BAT uses ANSI commands to set the screen to black letters on a black background, effectively blanking the screen.

Batch File Line	Explanation
`@ECHO OFF`	Turn command-echoing off.

`REM NAME:      BLANK.BAT`
`REM PURPOSE: Blank Screen Using`
`                     ANSI`
`REM VERSION: 1.00`
`REM DATE:     July 22, 1991`
	Documentation remarks.

`IF (%1)==(/?)  GOTO HELP` `IF (%1)==(?)   GOTO HELP`	If the user starts the batch file with a request for help, jump to a section to display that help.
`ECHO ESC[0m`	Reset the display to normal. (Note: the batch file uses an ASCII 27 escape character, not ESC.)
`ECHO ESC[30m`	Set the foreground color to black.
`ECHO ESC[40m`	Set the background color to black.
`CLS`	Clear the screen.
`GOTO END`	Exit the batch file.

`:HELP`
`ECHO Uses ANSI To Blank The Screen`
`ECHO Run UNBLANK To Restore`
`GOTO END`
`:END_HELP`
	Section that displays help when the user starts the batch file with a /? or a ? as the first replaceable parameter.

`:END`	Label marking the end of the batch file.

18-4 UNBLANK.BAT returns the screen to normal after running BLANK.BAT, by setting the screen to white characters on a blue background.

Batch File Line	Explanation
`@ECHO OFF`	Turn command-echoing off.

`REM NAME:      UNBLANK.BAT`
`REM PURPOSE: Restore Screen`
`                     After BLANK.BAT`
`REM VERSION: 1.00`
`REM DATE:     July 22, 1991`
	Documentation remarks.

`IF (%1)==(/?)  GOTO HELP` `IF (%1)==(?)   GOTO HELP`	If the user starts the batch file with a request for help, jump to a section to display that help.

Batch File Line	Explanation
REM Change The Screen Colors REM To White On Blue	More documentation remarks.
ECHO ESC[37m	Set the foreground color to white. (Note: the batch file uses an ASCII-27 escape character, not ESC.)
ECHO ESC[44m	Set the background color to blue.
ECHO ESC[1m	Set the foreground attribute to bright.
CLS	Clear the screen.
GOTO END	Exit the batch file.
:HELP ECHO Restores The Screen After ECHO Running BLANK ECHO Requires ANSI GOTO END :END_HELP	Section that displays help when the user starts the batch file with a /? or a ? as the first replaceable parameter.
:END	Label marking the end of the batch file.

18-5 NICEPROM.BAT creates a very nice and useful prompt. It requires that ANSI be loaded first.

Batch File Line	Explanation
@ECHO OFF	Turn command-echoing off.
REM NAME: NICEPROMPT.BAT REM PURPOSE: Change Prompt To REM Nice ANSI Prompt REM VERSION: 1.01 REM DATE: July 23, 1991	Documentation remarks.
IF (%1)==(/?) GOTO HELP IF (%1)==(?) GOTO HELP	If the user starts the batch file with a request for help, jump to a section to display that help.

Batch File Line	Explanation
PROMPT=$e[s$e[1;1H$e[K$d $t pe[upg$e[44m$e[37m$e[1m	Send the following ANSI commands:
	$e[s Saves the current cursor position. Note that with the PROMPT command $e is a metacharacter that sends an escape.
	$e[1;1H Positions the cursor at the top left corner of the screen.
	$e[K Erases that line.
	$d Prompts metacharacter to display the date.
	$t Prompts metacharacter to display the time.
	$p Prompts metacharacter to display the current subdirectory.
	$e[u Returns the cursor to its original position.
	pg Prompts metacharacters to display the subdirectory and a > symbol.
	$e[44m$e[37m$e[1m Sets the color to bright white on blue.
GOTO END	Exit the batch file.
:HELP ECHO Displays A Fancy Prompt ECHO Requires ANSI GOTO END :END_HELP	Section that displays help when the user starts the batch file with a /? or a ? as the first replaceable parameter.
:END	Label marking the end of the batch file.

18-6 The metacharacters you can include in a PROMPT statement. For ANSI, $e is very useful because it issues an Escape.

Batch File Line	Explanation
@ECHO OFF	Turn command-echoing off.
REM NAME: SENDANS2.BAT REM PURPOSE: Send Multiple ANSI Commands REM VERSION: 1.11 REM DATE: July 23, 1991	Documentation remarks.

Batch File Line	Explanation
`IF (%1)==(/?) GOTO HELP` `IF (%1)==(?)  GOTO HELP`	If the user starts the batch file with a request for help, jump to a section to display that help.
`IF (%1)==() GOTO END`	If the user didn't enter any ANSI sequences, exit the program.
`SET ANSI=`	Reset the environmental variable the batch file uses to construct the command.
`:TOP`	Label marking the top of a loop.
`SET ANSI=%ANSI%ESC[%1`	Add the next replaceable parameter to the series of ANSI sequences. (Note: the batch file uses an ASCII-27 escape character, not ESC.)
`SHIFT`	Decrease all the replaceable parameters by one.
`IF (%1)==() GOTO SEND`	If there are no more replaceable parameters, exit the loop.
`GOTO TOP` `:END_TOP`	There are more replaceable parameters, so continue looping.
`:SEND`	Label marking the section where the ANSI command is issued.
`ECHO %ANSI%`	Issue the ANSI command.
`GOTO END` `:END_SEND`	Jump to the end of the batch file.
`:END`	Label marking the end of the batch file.

PART SIX
Documentation

PART SIX

Documentation

19
Advanced batch file techniques

The purpose of this chapter isn't to teach you how to write batch files. If you've made it this far in the book, then you're already well versed in writing batch files. This chapter is designed to document the advanced techniques you've seen. That way, when you're writing your own tough batch file and need a way to deal with a complex feature or command, you can quickly find the information without having to search through all the batch files in this book looking for one that deals with your problem.

List of techniques

The techniques are listed in alphabetical order. They are:

Case construction If you're used to programming in a high-level language, you're probably used to testing using the case method. It's possible to simulate this in batch files.

Creating a boot disk Several of the procedures in this book have the potential to cause significant problems if you make a mistake while carrying them out. Creating a bootable disk helps you recover from many of these problems.

Dealing with capitalization Sometimes, a batch file needs the user to enter information on the command line so it can operate properly. However, you can't always be sure that the information is going to be entered in the manner you expect. This section covers several techniques for coping with this problem.

Environmental variables You can create and delete environmental variables from the command line, but you can't access their contents. However, you can access that information in batch files by surrounding the variable name with percent signs.

FOR command tricks By loading multiple copies of COMMAND.COM, you can nest FOR loops. In some cases, this makes it much quicker to work through a lot of different cases that need to be tested.

Label testing Batch files like PHONE.BAT, in Fig. 19-1, deal with capitalization problems by using the GOTO command to jump to the label entered on the command line. If the user enters an invalid label, the batch file will abort with *Label not found*.

Nesting IF statements When a batch file needs to perform multiple IF tests, it's sometimes easier to perform all these tests at once—provided the length of the command line doesn't exceed the DOS limit of 127 characters.

Quotation marks Some programs expect either a single input or multiple inputs, surrounded by quotation marks. If you use a batch file to run this sort of application and it passes replaceable parameters to this type of program, your batch file has to be prepared to add quotation marks only when required.

Quicker than GOTO END Some of the batch files in this book are very long—some are in excess of 500 lines! When a batch file issues a GOTO command, DOS searches that batch file from top to bottom for the label to jump to. That's quick in a short batch file but can take a very long time in these 500-line monsters. In this case, it can be much quicker to run a dummy batch file.

Replacing commands with environmental variables When you use the same command over and over in a batch file, it might be possible to replace that command with an environmental variable. With long commands that are frequently repeated, the space savings can be amazing.

Subroutines in batch files A subroutine is a stand-alone batch file that generally performs some portion of the processing being performed by the batch file that called it. Diverting that function to a subroutine batch file allows the different functions of the calling batch file to be maintained separately, and makes it easier to reuse code.

Subroutine batch files inside the calling batch file While subroutines are nice, they do take up disk space and it's difficult to remember to copy all its subroutines when you want to transfer a batch file to another computer. One way to avoid these problems is to build the subroutine into the batch file itself.

Using reserved names in batch files If you name a batch file or program with an internal name like ERASE (resulting in ERASE.BAT) it appears to be impossible to run. Type in ERASE and DOS will give you an error message because you didn't tell it what to erase. Enter the command as ERASE.BAT and it will give you an error message something like the DOS 5.0 *Path not found* error message. With some care, you can still run ERASE-.BAT, but most other users will be unable to run it.

Writing batch files with a spreadsheet program When your batch file contains a lot of numbers, especially sequential numbers, it's often easier to write the batch file with the aid of a spreadsheet.

Zero-length files A zero-length file is a directory entry without an associated file. In most cases, it uses no space on the hard disk.

Case construction

Performing multiple tests on a variable in a batch file requires a series of complex IF statements. Many other languages use a much simpler case construct. With a case construct, you signal the start of a case test then just list all the cases and what to do if the situation matches that case. The batch language doesn't have a case construct, but it's possible to simulate one using the FOR statement.

Notice that the errorlevel tests in CASE.BAT in Fig. 19-2 are performed in ascending rather than the more common descending order. The reason for this is that, because the errorlevel test is a greater-than-or-equal-to test, this test passes until the test exceeds the errorlevel. Because the variable is reset each time, this results in the proper value. For example, if the errorlevel was three, the following would happen:

1. CASE.BAT tests for an errorlevel of 1. Because 3 is greater than or equal to 1, the test passes and sets NO equal to CASE1.
2. CASE.BAT tests for an errorlevel of 2. Because 3 is greater than or equal to 2, the test passes and it sets NO equal to CASE2. This removes the NO=CASE1 setting.
3. CASE.BAT tests for an errorlevel of 3. Because 3 is greater than or equal to 3, the test passes and it sets NO equal to CASE3. This removes the NO=CASE2 setting.
4. CASE.BAT tests for an errorlevel of 4. Because 3 isn't greater than or equal to 4, the test fails and the value of NO isn't reset. This doesn't remove the NO=CASE3 setting.

Thus, the batch file exits with the value for the environmental variable set properly for the errorlevel statement.

Creating a boot disk

Several of the procedures in this book, like moving COMMAND.COM to a subdirectory or changing the names of internal commands, have the potential to cause significant problems if you make a mistake. The worst part is that many of the resulting problems can cause your computer to become unbootable.

For example, several years ago I was updating the files on a Compaq running under DOS 3.3. I had a 40Meg hard disk partitioned into two 20Meg partitions. With Compaq DOS at that time, partitioning a hard disk required you to load device driver in your CONFIG.SYS file. I decided to move all the DOS files to the D drive. What I forgot was that the device driver was in the DOS subdirectory and DOS couldn't read the D drive until the device driver was loaded. When the computer tried to boot, it would reach the point in the CONFIG.SYS file where it tried to load the device driver and lock up. Because COMMAND.COM wasn't yet loaded, I couldn't press Ctrl-Break and get to a DOS prompt—so my computer was locked up.

Fortunately, I had a boot disk handy. I was able to boot off this floppy disk and correct the problem. This story also illustrates an important point about your boot disk—it must contain any device drivers your system requires to operate. The steps for creating a boot disk are:

1. Format a floppy disk using the /S option. If your computer uses two different disk sizes, the boot disk must be the correct one for the A drive. The /S option adds the DOS files necessary for the disk to be bootable.
2. Examine your CONFIG.SYS file to see if any of the device drivers are required to operate your system. For example, some add-on hard disks, like the Plus Develop-

ment Hardcard, require a device driver. You can ignore drivers like the mouse driver that are nice to have but not necessary to the operation of your system.

3. Copy the necessary device drivers you found in step 2 to the boot floppy disk.

4. Create a CONFIG.SYS file on the boot floppy that loads all these necessary device drivers. It should load them from the floppy disk and not from the hard disk. It should also set files and buffers to values you normally use.

5. Create an AUTOEXEC.BAT file on the boot floppy that specifies the path you normally use. It's best not to load any memory-resident software here. If you use this disk to troubleshoot, these will just get in the way.

6. Boot from your boot disk just to make sure it works. Don't just make sure you can get a directory of the C drive; go in and run your normal applications to make sure they work properly. If you have any problems, work through these steps again until you resolve all your problems.

7. Depending on how much room is left on this boot disk, copy some of your more useful recovery tools onto the disk. Some suggestions of what to include are: your backup program so you can restore from a backup, an editor so you can fix problems with the hard disk version of the CONFIG.SYS and AUTOEXEC.BAT file, and an unerasing program and the DOS SYS program so you can make the hard disk bootable if system files get erased.

Once you create this boot disk, it's a good idea to make one or two copies of it using the DISKCOPY program so the copies are also bootable. You also need to keep the DOS version current. Any time you upgrade DOS on your computer, you need to update the DOS versions on all your boot disks.

A few computers include a nasty "got you" in their setup program by allowing you to specify the drives to boot from. Generally, these computers can be configured to boot only from the C drive, but that isn't the default. With the computer configured in this fashion, it will be unusable if the hard disk fails or if you make an error in altering a configuration file that prevents the computer from booting from the hard disk. If you own a machine with this type of setup program, use this setting with a great deal of care!

Dealing with capitalization

Managing capitalization in batch files is a real pain. Consider the batch file CAPI-TAL1.BAT in Fig. 19-3. CAPITAL1.BAT is designed to run one of three programs (DAILY.EXE, MONTHLY.EXE, or ANNUAL.EXE) depending on the replaceable parameter you enter. The code to handle just the most likely capitalizations takes up nine lines, where three would work if capitalization weren't a problem.

Even this elaborate scheme won't respond properly to replaceable parameters such as DAIly. There are a number of ways of dealing with the capitalization problem quickly without a lot of extra code. Each method has unique advantages.

GOTO %1

The first way to avoid the capitalization problem is to use the replaceable parameter as a label for the GOTO command because labels are case-insensitive. Keep in mind that DOS always replaces the replaceable parameters with their value. Take a look at CAPI-TAL2.BAT in Fig. 19-4. If you run this batch file with the command line

CAPITAL2 daily

DOS replaces the GOTO %1 line with GOTO daily and the batch file runs properly.

Using the GOTO %1 method is only a partial solution. If you start the batch file with an invalid parameter, yearly for example, the batch file will abort on the GOTO yearly line with a *label not found* error message. There's a way to deal with this problem, however.

PHONE.BAT, back in Fig. 19-1, dials the phone for you. It uses the GOTO %1 trick to deal with capitalization. It also uses another interesting trick. The names of some of the companies I call contain more than one word and more than eight characters. Therefore, I had to shorten them to something that would work as a label. Thus, American Telephone and Telegraph became ATT. In addition, some of the people I call have more than one acceptable name. For example, to call my mother I might enter:

PHONE mom
PHONE mother
PHONE Dawn

Rather than trying to remember a specific value, I gave some of the sections multiple labels so the batch file would work with any of the names. Because batch files ignore labels except when executing a GOTO statement, the extra labels don't affect the operation of the batch file.

Environmental variables

A second method is to store the selected option in the environment as an environmental variable. Figure 19-5 illustrates this method. First, each possible environmental is deleted, and then the line SET %1 = YES creates a single environmental variable with the name of the replaceable parameter and a value of YES.

This method works well for most replaceable parameters and avoids the missing label problem associated with the GOTO %1 method, but has a minor problem of its own. If the replaceable parameter you enter is a number, the batch file will end up making unexpected tests. Suppose you wanted to use CAPITAL3.BAT to run Lotus 1-2-3; you would have to enter 123 as a replaceable parameter. The SET %1 = YES line would work properly. But in order to run Lotus, you would need a test line of IF %123% = = YES. DOS would translate the %1 as the first replaceable parameter.

PATH

PATH is the only environmental variable DOS converts to uppercase. You can use this to convert a replaceable parameter to uppercase by performing the following steps:

1. Store the current path under another variable name.
2. Set the path equal to the replaceable parameter. Note that you must use PATH = and not SET PATH = because some versions of DOS won't convert the path to uppercase using the SET PATH = method.

3. Store the replaceable parameter now stored under the path to another variable name.
4. Restore the proper path using the holding variable created in step 1.
5. Clear out the holding variable created in step 1.

CAPITAL4.BAT in Fig. 19-6 illustrates this method. It handles all possible inputs without problem, but requires the most environmental space because, when you store the path under a different name and before you store the replaceable parameter to the path variable, DOS must store two versions of the path in environmental memory at once.

One problem with CAPITAL4.BAT is that it stores the path in the environment. After storing the path to another variable but before using the original path to store the variable to be converted to all capital letters, there are two copies of the path in the environment. If you have a long path, this can use a lot of environmental space.

CAPITAL5.BAT in Fig. 19-7 avoids this problem by creating a temporary batch file to store the path. When it's time to restore the path, CAPITAL5.BAT runs the temporary batch file and then deletes it. Because most test strings to be converted are shorter than the path, this approach requires no additional environmental space.

Environmental variables

From the command line, you can do the following with environmental variables: view them with the SET command, create a new variable with a command like SET *variable* = *content*, and delete an existing variable with a command like SET *variable* = . Batch files can perform these three plus one additional action. When an existing environmental variable is used in a batch file with its name surrounded with percent signs, DOS will substitute the contents of that variable for its name.

As a result, in a batch file the command ECHO %PATH% would display the current path, and ECHO %COMSPEC% would display the path to the current command processor. This technique doesn't work from the command line.

FOR command tricks

Nested FOR statements

Normally, FOR statements can't be nested. If you enter the command

    FOR %I IN (0 1 2) DO FOR %J IN (0 1 2) DO ECHO %I%J

on the command line, you'll see the error message *FOR cannot be nested*. So FOR loops can't be nested—or can they?

The approach to tricking DOS into allowing nested FOR loops is fairly simple. Each version of COMMAND.COM can run only one FOR loop at a time, but you can nest the FOR loops by having each loop load a new copy of COMMAND.COM. When you load a second copy of COMMAND.COM, you can specify a command to run as long as you follow the COMMAND.COM with a /C. Thus, replacing the above line with the command

    FOR %I IN (0 1 2) DO COMMAND/C FOR %J IN (0 1 2) DO ECHO %I%J will work and produce the desired results. Instead of specifying a command following the COMMAND/C, you can also specify a batch file to run. While that batch file is running, it can execute its own FOR loop. When running a batch file in this fashion, it doesn't have access to the original loop variable (%I above) and the FOR loop executed from the command line. However, that variable can be passed to the batch file as a replaceable parameter if that's necessary. The batch files NUMBER1.BAT through NUMBER6.BAT in chapter 5 illustrate this.

Under some versions of DOS, a batch file executed in this fashion will need to have EXIT as its last command to unload the extra copy of COMMAND.COM. DOS 5.0 doesn't. If you have a different version, you'll have to experiment to see if EXIT is required with your version. It won't hurt to include it even if your DOS version doesn't require it.

Adding wildcard support

Most DOS commands, like DEL and COPY, support wildcards. You can, for example, enter

```
COPY*.* A:
```

rather than having to enter one COPY command for each file you want to copy. However, a few DOS commands, like TYPE, don't support wildcards. If you want to TYPE three files to the screen, you must enter three commands:

```
TYPE FILE1 | MORE
TYPE FILE2 | MORE
TYPE FILE3 | MORE
```

This process is long and cumbersome. You can automate it with the FOR command. The FOR equivalent of the above would be:

```
FOR %J IN (FILE?) DO TYPE %J | MORE
```

Running commands with a FOR loop

Every so often, a computer magazine "hint column" will have a tip from someone who has just discovered that the things you put in the list of variables for a FOR command can be commands themselves. The authors of these hints are excited because the batch file runs faster—because DOS processes batch files one line at a time and this puts more commands on a single line.

Don't be fooled. While the batch files are truly a little faster, this method has a couple of drawbacks that greatly outweigh the slight dose of speed. The biggest drawback is human readability. You and I could probably look at a batch file with the lines

```
DIR
CHKDSK
CD \
```

and tell exactly what it's supposed to do. However, the function of a batch file with the line

```
FOR %%j IN (DIR CHKDSK CD \) DO %%j
```

isn't nearly as clear. In the end, you'll waste more time writing and debugging such complex code than you'll save by stacking more commands on a single line.

This method has another drawback. You can't use this trick with any command that requires more than one word. For example, you might want to run CHKDSK and then beep the bell using Norton's batch enhancer, which requires the command BE BEEP. With two lines, you would enter the commands:

```
CHKDSK
BE BEEP
```

Using the FOR command, you would enter the command

```
FOR %%j IN (CHKDSK BE BEEP) DO %%j
```

but because of the space, DOS would actually try to run:

```
CHKDSK
BE
BEEP
```

The final drawback are the switches. Generally, you would run CHKDSK/F rather than CHKDSK, but under some versions of DOS the forward slash character, /, is treated as a divider in FOR, so the command CHKDSK/F in a FOR statement becomes two commands, CHKDSK and F. So while you can stack multiple commands in a FOR statement, there are some very good reasons not to.

Label testing

As discussed in an earlier section, using a GOTO %1 statement is an effective method of getting information from the user on the command line and using it without having to worry about capitalization. However, this approach has a significant drawback—if the user's entry has no corresponding label, the batch file will abort with a *Label not found* error message.

If you're willing to add extra code to the batch file and are willing to have it start much slower, then you can avoid this problem. The steps are:

1. Use a standard IF test to make sure a replaceable parameter was entered. If not, display an error message and abort the batch file.
2. Type the batch file and pipe the output of the TYPE command to the FIND filter. Have FIND search for the replaceable parameter entered by the user, with a colon added to the front of it. In performing this test, FIND must be configured to ignore capitalization or you're back to the original problem of dealing with capitalization.
3. Pipe the results from the FIND filter to a file. If FIND finds the text, this file will contain that line. If the label doesn't exist and FIND finds nothing, this will be a zero-length file.
4. Copy the file to another subdirectory. If the file contains text (meaning the label was found) DOS can copy it. If the file is a zero-length file (meaning the label wasn't found) DOS won't copy the file because there's nothing to copy.
5. Delete the file in the original subdirectory.

6. Try to copy the file back from the subdirectory it was copied to. At this point, the file will exist in both subdirectories if the label was found and in neither subdirectory if it wasn't found. Thus, you can test for a valid label using the IF EXIST command.

7. After testing, delete the files to keep the hard disk clean.

While it performs no useful function, TESTGOTO.BAT in Fig. 19-8 illustrates the technique in a working batch file.

Nesting IF statements

It's possible to place more than one IF statement on a line. The format is:

    IF condition1 IF condition2 . . . do this

For example:

    IF %1 = = BAK IF %2 = = OLD IF %3 = = TXT DEL *.%1

Generally, this isn't worth the confusing code that results. One place it's useful is when you have to make a lot of tests. Batch files make these tests very slow, and the fewer tests the better. Earlier, I introduced a batch file called CHECKERR.BAT for displaying the current value in the errorlevel. It has 510 lines of IF statements to test each possible value of errorlevel twice. One test displays its value and a second test jumps out of the testing when it passes because all smaller tests would pass as well.

By nesting two IF statements on one line, this batch file can be reduced to half its length. While it doesn't reduce the number of IF tests, the new arrangement runs faster and doesn't require any GOTO statements. CHECKER2.BAT back in chapter 17 is just such a batch file.

Under certain conditions, nesting IF statements can save a lot of testing. For example, the batch file fragment NEST1.BAT in Fig. 19-9 requires four lines to make sure that a Y or N is entered as the first replaceable parameter. (In this example, NEST1.BAT does nothing useful with %1 after testing it. In practice, after testing %1, the batch file would use it for some useful purpose.) These four tests can be reduced to one in NEST2.BAT, shown in Fig. 19-10.

Quicker than GOTO END

In many of the examples in this book, the batch file jumps to the end of the batch file with a GOTO END statement. Generally, the batch file has to test for several conditions. After successfully performing the task for a condition, the batch file will jump to the end of the file to avoid repeating the task for another condition.

Each time a batch file searches for a label, it searches the entire file from top to bottom. Exiting a batch file by going to the end forces the longest, and slowest, possible search because the batch file must be searched from top to bottom. A much faster way to exit a batch file is to run a second dummy batch file. Control never returns to the first batch file, so this is the same as an exit.

Every batch file that uses this technique can execute the same batch file. A good name to use is DUMMY.BAT. DUMMY.BAT doesn't even need to take up any space on your hard disk—all you need to do is create a zero-length file called DUMMY.BAT. To do that, issue the DOS command TYPE *nofile* > DUMMY.BAT, where *nofile* is the name of any file that doesn't exist. You might get an error message, but you can ignore it.

Quotation marks

Some programs like the Norton Text Search (TS.EXE) can accept a parameter with a space in it as part of an input. For example

    TS *.BAT "ECHO OFF"

would search through all the batch files in the current directory for the line ECHO OFF. Forget the quotes and it will ignore the OFF and just search for ECHO. Batch files don't have any trouble with quotes. If you were running this program with a batch file TEXT-FIND.BAT that just passed along replaceable parameters to the program and you entered

    TEXTFIND *.BAT "ECHO OFF"

the replaceable parameters would be:

    %1   *.BAT
    %2   "ECHO
    %3   OFF"

If you're like me, however, you often forget the quote marks. I set out to have the batch file add the quotes for me. It proved to be tougher than I had expected. My first attempt worked only some of the time. I tried passing TS the string ''%1 %2 %3 %4''. The problem was my selection of four replaceable parameters inside the quotes. If there were less than four, DOS still used the spaces between the replaceable parameters and spaces matter to a text-search program. If there were more than four words, then not all the text was used. My next attempt was to use more replaceable parameters inside the quotes and to remove the spaces. In this example, I had the batch file pass the string ''%1%2%3%4%5%6%7%8%9''. This didn't add any extra spaces before the final quote if I didn't use all the replaceable parameters, but it didn't add any spaces at all. For example, if I entered

    TEXTFIND *.BAT REM ECHO IS OFF

then the batch file issued the command

    TEXTFIND *.BAT "REMECHOISOFF"

which clearly didn't work. Those experiments made it clear that the batch file was going to have to intelligently construct the command.

At this point, I had two choices—the brute-force method or the finesse method. I decided to try both. TEXTFND4.BAT in Fig. 19-11 is the brute-force method. This batch file simply searches for the first blank replaceable parameter so it knows how many words were entered to search for. It then constructs a custom command line for that specific number of words. It has only one main drawback—it can't handle more than eight words to search for. If you enter more than that, it ignores all the words after the eighth. You could extend this to nine by adding a SHIFT command so the files to search become the %0 parameter rather than the %1.

The finesse method proved to be more difficult and ended up taking most of the afternoon to debug. TEXTFND5.BAT in Fig. 19-12 is the result. It works by looping through all the replaceable parameters and constructing a custom environmental variable containing the phrase to search for.

Both TEXTFND4.BAT and TEXTFND5.BAT, however, share a common problem— they require you to not enter the proper quotes. If you do, the batch files will work properly, but then the command passed to DOS will look something like this:

```
TS *.BAT ""REM ECHO IS OFF""
```

The basic technique presented by this series of batch files is the technique in TEXTFND-5.BAT—cycling through all the replaceable parameters and building a custom environmental variable based on their content.

Replacing commands with environmental variables

Some batch files end up being very long. For example, CHECKER2.BAT on the enclosed disk contains 12,916 bytes. When a batch file has a single command repeated a number of times, you can shorten the file by storing the command as an environmental variable and then replacing the command with %VARIABLE% in the batch file. Wherever the %VARIABLE% appears in the batch file, DOS replaces it with the contents of that variable.

If you frequently repeat several commands and if you have enough environmental space, you can replace each command with its own variable. Of course, to maximize your space savings in a batch file, you should use a variable with a single-character name.

There are some commands that can't be included in a variable in this fashion—specifically, piping symbols, equal signs, and replaceable parameter variables (%0–%9). When in doubt, experiment before changing your entire batch file.

Figure 19-13 shows SAVESPACE.BAT. This batch file is identical in function to CHECKER2.BAT, but contains only 6,477 bytes, a savings of almost 50%.

Of course, using this method makes it more difficult to debug the batch file, makes it run slightly slower, and requires additional environmental space. Therefore, you should use this only when space is at a premium on your system.

Subroutines in batch files

In programming, a subroutine is a special type of program. When a program calls a subroutine, control is passed to the subroutine. When the subroutine is finished, control is passed back to the calling program. The calling program continues from the point where it passed control to the subroutine. Figure 19-14 illustrates this graphically.

Prior to DOS version 3.3, batch files didn't support subroutines. With those older versions of DOS, once a batch file passed control to another batch file, control was never passed back to the original batch file.

This isn't how a batch file behaves when it passes control to a program. When that program finishes, control is passed back to the calling batch file. This fact can be used to trick pre-3.3 DOS into allowing one batch file to call another batch file and gain back control when the subroutine batch file finishes.

Tricking early DOS to run subroutines

Normally, you don't think of COMMAND.COM as a program. But it is. Entering COMMAND at the DOS prompt runs COMMAND.COM, which loads a second copy of the command processor into memory. The command to exit this second command processor is EXIT. This terminates the second command processor and returns control back to the first (and calling) command processor.

The trick involves invoking a second command processor, having that processor run the subroutine batch file, and then returning control to the calling batch file. The syntax to call the second batch file is:

COMMAND /C batch file name

The /C tells COMMAND.COM to run the following command, which in this case is a batch file. The last command of the subroutine batch file must be an EXIT. This returns control to the original batch file. Note that not all versions of DOS require the EXIT command, but it never hurts to have it.

DOS 3.3 and later

This trick isn't required in DOS 3.3 or later. DOS 3.3 adds the CALL batch file command. So you can have a batch file call another batch file with:

CALL < batch file >

The batch file being called doesn't have to end with an EXIT command.

Why use subroutines?

There are two basic advantages of a subroutine—function separation and code reuse. When you use subroutines, you keep program segments with different functions separate (at least in batch files) by physically having the program segments in different batch files. Subroutines also allow you to reuse your code because you can pass control to the subroutine batch file anytime you need to run that code.

The following example will illustrate these advantages. I routinely transfer a number of data files between different computers. To do this, I copy the files onto a floppy disk at the source computer and take that disk to the target computer. Rather than trying to remember where each file goes and issuing a bunch of COPY commands, I copy all the files into one subdirectory and run a batch file that moves them to their proper subdirectory.

For this system to work, I have to use fairly standard filenames. For example, all the files for my first book end with a 01 (as in CHAP0101.DOC for chapter 1 of my first book), all the files for my second book end with a 02, and so on. In addition to all these files with standardized names, some file types always go in a specific subdirectory. For example, all my Microsoft Word style sheets (*.STY) go in a common subdirectory, as do my batch files and Word for Windows dictionary files. Finally, there are about 50 files I update all the time. There's no naming scheme to them so I've simply built the names of these files into the batch file.

The batch file I run to move these files around is called FROM.BAT. Its basic function is to check my holding subdirectory to see if a file exists. If it does, it copies it to the proper subdirectory and then erases it from the holding subdirectory. It continues through a long list of filenames, checking to see if each one exists and moving it if it does.

Originally, I had all this built into one massive batch file. However, I realized there was a better approach. For each batch file in the holding subdirectory, FROM.BAT performs the following steps:

1. Uses XCOPY to copy the file to the proper subdirectory. It uses XCOPY rather than COPY because XCOPY sets the errorlevel and COPY doesn't.
2. Checks the errorlevel to see if an error has occurred. If it has, it displays an error message and aborts the batch file.
3. If an error didn't occur, it erases the original copy of the file from the holding subdirectory.

The second advantage of reusing code should now be clear. Rather than including all the lines in the original batch file necessary to perform these three tasks once for every filename, I wrote a subroutine batch file that accepts the name of the file and the name of the destination subdirectory as an input and takes care of everything else itself.

Once I had finished writing and debugging the subroutine, that separation of function made it much easier to keep the original batch file up-to-date. When I needed to add a new name to FROM.BAT, all I had to do was add two lines

```
IF EXIST D:\A\NEWNAME.DOC CALL FROM-SUB NEWNAME.DOC \ITS_SUB
IF ERRORLEVEL 1 GOTO END
```

and everything was taken care of. I didn't need to check and see if the file was copied properly because that function was separate and I hadn't modified it. Once FROM-SUB .BAT receives the name of the file and its subdirectory in the proper format, that data is in the hands of a fully tested batch file, so I know it will work properly.

Subroutine batch files
inside the calling batch file

Each batch file you write takes up a minimum of one cluster of disk space. Depending on several factors, that can be up to 8K and will most likely be at least 2K. If you're running short of hard disk space, that can seem like a large price to pay for a relatively small subroutine. You can avoid this by bundling all your subroutines within the main batch file.

The approach is fairly simple. A replaceable parameter functions as a signal to tell a batch file if it's being called from itself. When that signal is missing, the batch file knows that it's being called from the command line. A series of IF tests at the beginning of the batch file direct it to the appropriate section of the batch file, depending on the flag it receives as a replaceable parameter. That way, the batch file can contain more than one subroutine internally.

When you include subroutines inside of a batch file that calls the subroutines, the batch file is said to be *recursive*. In a sense, the batch file calls itself. Recursive batch files have two advantages over batch files that call separate batch files as subroutines. First, as discussed previously, the resulting batch file is generally smaller than the separate batch file and subroutines. This is generally true in spite of the requirement in the recursive batch file for additional IF tests to direct it to the appropriate spot in the batch file to continue processing. The reason it's smaller is the additional space that a separate subroutine batch file requires because it's allocated a full cluster of disk space no matter how small it is.

The second advantage of a recursive batch file is how easy it is to transfer to different systems. If you need to copy a recursive batch file, then the batch file is all you need to take to the new machine. If you want to transfer a batch file with external subroutines you have to copy all the files, and that's something I usually have trouble remembering to do.

There is, however, one very significant drawback to recursive batch files. The resulting batch file is longer and more complex and, without the proper approach, can be much more difficult to write. This additional complexity is an important consideration—one you shouldn't overlook.

The batch files NUMBER1.BAT through NUMBER6.BAT and NUMBER9.BAT in chapter 5 illustrate these points very well. NUMBER1.BAT is the first batch file in the group I wrote, and it calls NUMBER2.BAT through NUMBER6.BAT as subroutines. Because five subroutines waste a lot of space and are a lot of files to remember when copying, I combined them all into NUMBER9.BAT. As you can see, NUMBER9.BAT is more complex than any of the other batch files, but it takes up less space than the six individual files and is fully self-contained. Being self-contained was especially important here because NUMBER1.BAT doesn't call all the subroutines itself; some of them are called from other subroutines. That means you can't look at NUMBER1.BAT and see all the subroutines you need to take with you.

This example also illustrates the best approach to writing recursive batch files. Because the individual files approach is easier to write, that's what I did here. Only after that was finished did I begin working on the recursive batch file. I took NUMBER1.BAT, renamed it to NUMBER9.BAT, and added the logic to branch to a section to handle the functions of NUMBER2.BAT. Then I used the file-merging ability of my editor to incorporate the working code from NUMBER2.BAT into NUMBER9.BAT. Once I tested that and got it working, I bundled in NUMBER3.BAT. I continued in this fashion until all of the subroutines were bundled into NUMBER9.BAT.

Using reserve names in batch files

You can't normally run a batch file if you give it the same name as a DOS internal command like ERASE. If you try to run it with an ERASE command, DOS will abort with an error message like *Required parameter missing*. While the error message is different for different DOS versions, the effect is the same. When you enter a command, the first thing DOS checks is to see if it's an internal command. If it is, DOS won't check any further; it executes the appropriate internal command.

Beginning with DOS 3.0, DOS included the ability to add a path before a command. For example, if you want to run a program called INFO.EXE on the A drive, and the A drive isn't in your path, you could specify the full path to INFO.EXE using the command A:\INFO. It turns out that DOS is smart enough to know that, if you specify a path, you aren't running an internal command. As a result, it won't check its list of internal commands before searching for the program. Thus, the command C:\BAT\ERASE will run ERASE.BAT.

My first reaction to learning this was "So what!" While it worked, I didn't see any practical application for it. Then it hit me. A common approach to protecting your system against accidental hard disk formatting is to rename FORMAT.COM to something like XYZ.COM and then writing FORMAT.BAT to run XYZ.COM to handle formatting. This approach lets you make sure that no one formats your hard disk, but it has a flaw. If someone accesses the subdirectory list you have XYZ.COM in, they're going to see a program they never heard of . . . and what better way to find out what it does than to run it. Of course, running XYZ (really FORMAT) with no parameters is a sure way to format a hard disk. By renaming FORMAT.COM to RENAME.COM, no one can find out what it does by entering RENAME to run the program because DOS will execute its internal RENAME command. You can run it, however, by specifying the full path to RENAME .COM in a batch file—and thus you'll have even more protection against someone accidentally running FORMAT.COM. Next to erasing FORMAT.COM altogether, this is the best protection you can get.

Writing batch files with a spreadsheet program

Occasionally, a batch file needs to deal with a lot of numbers. MATH1.BAT and NUMBER.BAT back in chapter 5 are two such batch files. As you can imagine, typing in all of MATH1.BAT by hand would be time-consuming, and it would be too easy to make mistakes. Fortunately, you can save a significant amount of time, while preventing errors, by creating much of MATH1.BAT using a spreadsheet.

The top half of MATH1.BAT consists of two columns of numbers. The first column begins with 998 and decreases by one on each line. In your worksheet, go to cell B1 and enter 998. Then go to B2 and enter +B1−1. (These instructions are for Lotus. Readers with other spreadsheets might need to make slight modifications to the instructions.) Copy the formula in cell B2 down to B999. This will give you the numbers for the first column. Now go to cell A1 and enter %A%==. Copy this down the column to cell A999. Adjust the column width to minimize the space between the equal signs and the number.

Now go to cell C1 and enter %B%==. Again, copy this down the column through C999 and adjust the column width to minimize the extra space. Finally, the second column of numbers will always be one more than the first, so go to cell D1 and enter the formula +B1+1. Copy this down the column through cell D999. You can enter the numbers for the second half of MATH1.BAT in a similar fashion.

Now configure the spreadsheet for unformatted printing with a top, bottom, and left margin of zero, and then print the range A1 through D999 to a file called MATH1.BAT. Use the search and replace function of your editor to remove the undesired spaces and you'll have much of MATH1.BAT written.

Zero-length files

When DOS creates a file, the first thing it does is create a directory entry for that file. Once the file contains information, the file allocation table (FAT) will be updated and the directory entry will point to the first cluster in the file.

However, if the file contains no information, the FAT won't be updated and the directory won't point to any information, so the file takes up no space on the hard disk. (More on that later.)

Creating a zero-length file is as simple as issuing the command TYPE *nofile* > *zerofile* where *nofile* is the name of a file that doesn't exist and *zerofile* is the name of the zero-length file you want to create. While you can rename zero-length files, you can't copy them because there's nothing to copy. Therefore, you must recreate the file each time you need it.

Because files aren't erased when the computer reboots or is turned off, zero-length files are a nifty way to store small amounts of information you wish to retain between sessions. For example, you might have a zero-length file called BACK-00 that, each time the computer reboots, the AUTOEXEC.BAT renames to the next number. When the filename reaches BACK-10, a batch file will perform a backup and rename the zero-length file back to BACK-00.

Technical note: When DOS creates a subdirectory, it allocates enough directory space for 62 files. (Actually 64, but two of them are the dot and double dot files you see in subdirectories.) If the number of files exceeds 62, DOS must allocate additional space for directory information. If the first file to exceed the 62 available slots is the zero-length file, it will actually end up requiring space because DOS will still have to increase the space for the directory.

Summary

- If you use proper construction, it's possible to simulate a case construction with a batch file.
- Before you have trouble booting your computer, it's a good idea to create one or more floppy disks you can boot from so you can access the hard disk and resolve any problems.
- After creating a boot disk, it's a good idea to copy as many of your utility programs to that disk as will fit. An editor is an especially good tool to have on this disk.
- One way to deal with the unknown capitalization of a replaceable parameter is to use it as part of a GOTO statement. However, this method will cause the batch file to abort if the label doesn't exist.
- A second way to deal with the unknown capitalization of a replaceable parameter is to use the replaceable parameter as the name of an environmental variable. However, this method can cause unexpected results when a possible value for the replaceable parameter is a number.
- A third way to deal with the unknown capitalization of a replaceable parameter is to store it to the path environmental variable because the path is always converted to uppercase. This method, however, requires enough free environmental space to store two copies of the path.

- By surrounding an environmental variable name with percent signs, you can have a batch file access the contents of that variable.
- While you can't nest FOR loops directly, you can construct complex nestings by loading an additional copy of COMMAND.COM for each FOR loop.
- You can use FOR loops to add wildcard support to commands like TYPE that don't support wildcards.
- You can use a FOR loop to run multiple commands with one command on the command line. This isn't usually a good idea in a batch file, however, because it makes the batch file hard to read and won't work if any of the commands includes a space.
- By using a FIND filter, you can check to see if a batch file contains a specified label before trying to GOTO that label.
- Combining more than one IF test on a single line can make batch files much shorter—but also more difficult to write and debug.
- When you need to branch to the end of a long batch file, it might be quicker to execute a second dummy batch file rather than a GOTO END statement. Of course, you wouldn't use the CALL command because you don't want control to return to the original batch file.
- Multiple replaceable parameters can be combined inside quotation marks by a batch file, but the batch file must do this intelligently to avoid including extra spaces inside the quotation marks.
- When a batch file repeats the same command over and over again, like IF ERRORLEVEL, you can save space by storing the command in an environmental variable with a short name, like E, and replacing the command everywhere in the batch file with %E%. The portion of the command containing the replaceable parameter, piping, or equal sign can't be condensed in this fashion.
- You can run batch files (or programs) that have the same name as a DOS internal command by specifying the full path to the batch file. This allows you to rename dangerous programs to internal command names and run them from batch files that specify their full path—effectively preventing most users from running them from the command line.
- When your batch file needs to work through a lot of numbers, writing the batch file in a spreadsheet program and then translating it into ASCII can make the process easier.
- You can store information between rebootings in a zero-length file without taking up hard disk space—by changing its name to reflect the contents of the information.

19-1 PHONE.BAT dials the phone for you. Notice the use of multiple labels.

Batch File Line	Explanation
`@ECHO OFF`	Turn command-echoing off.

`REM NAME:     PHONE.BAT`
`REM PURPOSE: DIAL PHONE`
`REM VERSION: 2.20`
`REM DATE:     NOVEMBER 16, 1991`
	Documentation remarks.

Batch File Line	Explanation
`IF (%1)==(/?) GOTO HELP` `IF (%1)==(?) GOTO HELP`	If the user starts the batch file with a request for help, jump to a section to display that help.
`IF (%1)==() GOTO NOTHING`	If the user didn't enter a replaceable parameter, jump to an error-handling routine.
`GOTO %1`	Jump to the label represented by the first replaceable parameter.
`:MOM` `:MOTHER`	Labels marking the beginning of the section that handles dialing my mother.
`ECHO Mom`	Display a message indicating which number is being called.
`ECHO ATDT 1 (912) 555-1212 >COM1`	Dial the modem. ATDT is the modem command that causes it to dial the number that follows, and COM1 pipes the command to the port containing the modem. If your modem was connected to COM2, you would need to change this. Note: this isn't my mother's real phone number.
`PAUSE`	Pause the batch file while the modem dials.
`ECHO ATH>COM1`	Disconnect the modem. The user presses any key once the phone begins ringing. This command allows the user to talk over the phone without the modem interfering.
`GOTO END` `:END_MOM`	Exit the batch file.

`:FEDX`
`:FEDEX`
`ECHO Federal Express`
`ECHO ATDT  1 (800) 238-5355 > COM1`
`PAUSE`
`ECHO ATH > COM1`
`GOTO END`
`:END_FEDX`
	Section of the batch file for calling Federal Express.

`:NORTHGATE`
`ECHO ATDT 1 800 446 5037 > COM1`
`PAUSE`
`ECHO ATH > COM1`
`GOTO END`
`:END_NORTHGATE`
	Section of the batch file for calling Northgate Computers.

Batch File Line	Explanation
:NOTHING ECHO You Failed To Enter The Name ECHO Of The Number You Wanted The ECHO Batch File To Call ECHO Please Try Again GOTO END :END_NOTHING	Section to display an error message if the user fails to enter the name to call.
:HELP ECHO This Demonstration Batch File ECHO Will Dial The Phone For You ECHO You Must Modify It To Use ECHO Personal Phone Numbers First GOTO END :END_HELP	Section that displays help when the user starts the batch file with a /? or a ? as the first replaceable parameter.
:END	Label marking the end of the batch file.
EXIT	I often run this batch file while shelled out of another program. When this is the case, the command causes that program to reload. When I run the program but am not shelled out of another program, this command has no impact.

19-2 CASE.BAT illustrates the more readable case construct in a batch file.

Batch File Line	Explanation
@ECHO OFF	Turn command-echoing off.
REM NAME: CASE.BAT REM PURPOSE: Simulates Case Structure REM In A Batch File REM VERSION: 1.00 REM DATE: May 10, 1991	Documentation remarks.
IF (%1)==(/?) GOTO HELP IF (%1)==(?) GOTO HELP	If the user starts the batch file with a request for help, jump to a section to display that help.
:TOP	Label marking the top of the batch file.
CLS	Clear the screen.
ECHO NUMBER OPTION ECHO ====== ====== ECHO 1 Lotus ECHO 2 dBASE ECHO 3 Microsoft Word ECHO 4 Games	Display the menu.

Batch File Line	Explanation
SKIPLINE	Use the SkipLine program included on the disk to display one blank line.
BATCMD GF 1234 Press Option Number	Use Batcmd to request a number from the user.
REM I Am Adding The Logic To Handle REM Nonvalid Responses Even Though REM BatCmd Takes Care Of That REM Automatically	Documentation remarks.
SET NO=CASE0	Set the environmental variable NO equal to zero.
FOR %%j IN (1 2 3 4) DO IF ERRORLEVEL %%j SET NO=CASE%%j	Use a FOR loop to set the value of NO equal to the errorlevel plus a string. Because errorlevel is a greater-than test, NO will be set to four for all values of errorlevel greater than or equal to four.
GOTO %NO%	Jump to the label corresponding to the value of NO. The five possible values are CASE0, CASE1, CASE2, CASE3, and CASE4.
:CASE0 CLS ECHO Invalid Selection PAUSE GOTO TOP :END_CASE0	Section for handling an invalid response.
:CASE1 REM Commands To Run Lotus GOTO TOP :END_CASE1	Section for handling a response of 1.
The batch file repeats CASE1 for a response of 2, 3, and 4.	
:HELP ECHO This Batch File Demonstrates ECHO Case Programming In A Batch File GOTO END :END_HELP	Section that displays help when the user starts the batch file with a /? or a ? as the first replaceable parameter.
:END	Label marking the end of the batch file.

19-3 CAPITAL1.BAT tries to handle the most likely types of capitalization; however, unusual forms of capitalization will still pass by its tests.

Batch File Line	Explanation
`@ECHO OFF`	Turn command-echoing off.

`REM NAME:     CAPITAL1.BAT`
`REM PURPOSE: Accounting Control`
`REM          Program`
`REM VERSION: 1.00`
`REM DATE:    May 10, 1991`
	Documentation remarks.

`IF (%1)==(/?)     GOTO HELP` `IF (%1)==(?)      GOTO HELP`	If the user starts the batch file with a request for help, jump to a section to display that help.
`IF (%1)==()       GOTO NOTHING`	Jump to an error-handling section if the user did not enter a replaceable parameter.

`IF (%1)==(DAILY)   GOTO ONE`
`IF (%1)==(daily)   GOTO ONE`
`IF (%1)==(Daily)   GOTO ONE`
	Jump to the section to handle daily closings if any of these three common capitalizations of the replaceable parameter was entered.

`IF (%1)==(MONTHLY) GOTO TWO`
`IF (%1)==(monthly) GOTO TWO`
`IF (%1)==(Monthly) GOTO TWO`
	Jump to the monthly section if that is appropriate.

`IF (%1)==(ANNUAL)  GOTO THREE`
`IF (%1)==(annual)  GOTO THREE`
`IF (%1)==(Annual)  GOTO THREE`
	Jump to the annual section if that is appropriate.

`:NOTHING`
`ECHO This Batch File Requires`
`ECHO A Parameter. The Valid`
`ECHO Ways To Start It Are:`
`ECHO CAPITAL1 daily`
`ECHO CAPITAL1 monthly`
`ECHO CAPITAL1 annual`
`GOTO END`
`:END_NOTHING`
	Section that tells the user the batch file was run improperly and tells him how to run it properly.

`:ONE`
`DAILY`
`GOTO END`
`:END_ONE`
	Daily section.

`:TWO`
`MONTHLY`
`GOTO END`
`:END_TWO`
	Monthly section.

`:THREE`
`ANNUAL`
`GOTO END`
`:END_THREE`
	Annual section.

Batch File Line	Explanation

`:HELP`
`ECHO This Demonstration Batch File`
`ECHO Illustrates Dealing With Case`
`ECHO Problems In A Batch File`
`GOTO END`
`:END_HELP`
	Section that displays help when the user starts the batch file with a /? or a ? as the first replaceable parameter.

`:END`	Label marking the end of the batch file.

19-4 CAPITAL2.BAT uses a GOTO command to avoid the capitalization problem. However, this adds another problem—the batch file will abort with a *Label not found* error message if the user enters an invalid label.

Batch File Line	Explanation
`@ECHO OFF`	Turn command-echoing off.

`REM NAME:      CAPITAL2.BAT`
`REM PURPOSE: Use GOTO Statements To`
`REM          Overcome Capitalization`
`REM          Problems`
`REM VERSION: 1.00`
`REM DATE:    May 10, 1991`
	Documentation remarks.

`IF (%1)==(/?) GOTO HELP` `IF (%1)==(?)  GOTO HELP`	If the user starts the batch file with a request for help, jump to a section to display that help.
`IF (%1)==() GOTO NOTHING`	If the user did not enter a replaceable parameter, jump to an error-handling section.
`GOTO %1`	Jump to the label that corresponds to the first replaceable parameter. If the user uses a replaceable parameter that does not have a corresponding label, the batch file will abort on this line with a Missing Label error message.

`:NOTHING`
`ECHO This Batch File Requires`
`ECHO A Parameter. The Valid`
`ECHO Ways To Start It Are:`
`ECHO CAPITAL2 daily`
`ECHO CAPITAL2 monthly`
`ECHO CAPITAL2 annual`
`GOTO END`
`:END_NOTHING`
	Section that tells the user the batch file was run improperly and tells him how to run it properly.

`:DAILY`
`DAILY`
`GOTO END`
`:END_DAILY`
	Daily section.

Batch File Line	Explanation
:MONTHLY MONTHLY GOTO END :END_MONTHLY	Monthly section.
:ANNUAL ANNUAL GOTO END :END_ANNUAL	Annual section.

19-5 CAPITAL3.BAT creates an environmental variable to avoid the problems with capitalization.

Batch File Line	Explanation
@ECHO OFF	Turn command-echoing off.
REM NAME: CAPITAL3.BAT REM PURPOSE: Use Environmental REM Variables To Deal With REM Capitalization Problem REM VERSION: 1.00 REM DATE: May 10, 1991	Documentation remarks.
IF (%1)==(/?) GOTO HELP IF (%1)==(?) GOTO HELP	If the user starts the batch file with a request for help, jump to a section to display that help.
SET DAILY= SET MONTHLY= SET ANNUAL=	Reset the environmental variables used in this batch file.
SET %1=YES	Store YES to the environmental variable corresponding to the first replaceable parameter.
IF %DAILY%==YES GOTO DAILY IF %MONTHLY%==YES GOTO MONTHLY IF %ANNUAL%==YES GOTO ANNUAL	Test on the three environmental variables to decide which section to jump to.
GOTO ERROR	If the batch file reaches this point the user entered an invalid replaceable parameter, so jump to an error-handling section.
:ERROR ECHO This Batch File Requires ECHO A Parameter. The Valid ECHO Ways To Start It Are: ECHO CAPITAL3 daily ECHO CAPITAL3 monthly ECHO CAPITAL3 annual GOTO END :END_ERROR	Section that tells the user the batch file was run improperly and tells him how to run it properly.

Batch File Line	Explanation

`:DAILY`
`DAILY`
`GOTO END`
`:END_DAILY`
	Daily section.

`:MONTHLY`
`MONTHLY`
`GOTO END`
`:END_MONTHLY`
	Monthly section.

`:ANNUAL`
`ANNUAL`
`GOTO END`
`:END_ANNUAL`
	Annual section.

`:HELP`
`ECHO This Demonstration Batch File`
`ECHO Illustrates Dealing With Case`
`ECHO Problems In A Batch File`
`GOTO END`
`:END_HELP`
	Section that displays help when the user starts the batch file with a /? or a ? as the first replaceable parameter.

`:END`	Label marking the end of the batch file.

19-6 CAPITAL4.BAT's use of the path to convert the replaceable parameter avoids the problems with the GOTO %1 and environmental variable methods, but requires a large environment.

Batch File Line	Explanation
`@ECHO OFF`	Turn command-echoing off.

`REM NAME:      CAPITAL4.BAT`
`REM PURPOSE: Use Path To Deal With`
`REM          Capitalization Problem`
`REM VERSION: 1.00`
`REM DATE:     May 10, 1991`
	Documentation remarks.

`IF (%1)==(/?) GOTO HELP` `IF (%1)==(?)  GOTO HELP`	If the user starts the batch file with a request for help, jump to a section to display that help.
`SET OLDPATH=%PATH%`	Store the current path under the name OLDPATH.
`PATH;`	Reset the path to nul. This avoids problems when the user doesn't enter a replaceable parameter. Tests for this condition would also avoid the problem.

Batch File Line	Explanation
`PATH=%1`	Set the path equal to the first replaceable parameter. DOS converts the path to uppercase, so this will convert the first replaceable parameter to uppercase. Note that SET PATH=%1 won't work because not all versions of DOS convert the path to uppercase using this method.
`SET VARIABLE=%PATH%`	Store the uppercase replaceable parameter under another variable name.
`PATH=%OLDPATH%`	Restore the path.
`SET OLDPATH=`	Reset the temporary variable to empty.

`IF (%VARIABLE%)==(DAILY)`
`    GOTO DAILY`
`IF (%VARIABLE%)==(MONTHLY)`
`    GOTO MONTHLY`
`IF (%VARIABLE%)==(ANNUAL)`
`    GOTO ANNUAL`
	Jump to the appropriate section, depending on the replaceable parameter the user enters.

`GOTO ERROR`	If the batch file reaches this point the user entered an invalid replaceable parameter, so jump to an error-handling section.

`:ERROR`
`ECHO This Batch File Requires`
`ECHO A Parameter. The Valid`
`ECHO Ways To Start It Are:`
`ECHO CAPITAL4 daily`
`ECHO CAPITAL4 monthly`
`ECHO CAPITAL4 annual`
`GOTO END`
`:END_ERROR`
	Section that tells the user that the batch file was run improperly and tells him how to run it properly.

`:DAILY`
`ECHO DAILY`
`GOTO END`
`:END_DAILY`
	Daily section. In a working batch file, the ECHO DAILY command would be the actual command the batch file was to perform.

`:MONTHLY`
`ECHO MONTHLY`
`GOTO END`
`:END_MONTHLY`
	Monthly section. In a working batch file, the ECHO MONTHLY command would be the actual command the batch file was to perform.

Batch File Line	Explanation
:ANNUAL ECHO ANNUAL GOTO END :END_ANNUAL	Annual section. In a working batch file, the ECHO ANNUAL command would be the actual command the batch file was to perform.
:HELP ECHO This Demonstration Batch File ECHO Illustrates Dealing With Case ECHO Problems In A Batch File GOTO END :END_HELP	Section that displays help when the user starts the batch file with a /? or a ? as the first replaceable parameter.
:END	Label marking the end of the batch file.

19-7 CAPITAL5.BAT works very much like CAPITAL4.BAT except it stores the path to disk rather than in the environment.

Batch File Line	Explanation
@ECHO OFF	Turn command-echoing off.
REM NAME: CAPITAL5.BAT REM PURPOSE: Use Path To Deal With REM Capitalization Problem REM But Store Path On Disk REM VERSION: 1.00 REM DATE: December 21, 1991	Documentation remarks.
IF (%1)==(/?) GOTO HELP IF (%1)==(?) GOTO HELP	If the user starts the batch file with a request for help, jump to a section to display that help.
PATH>JUNK.BAT	Pipe the path to a temporary batch file. If your path is \DOS, then the batch file contains PATH=\DOS, which, when run, resets the path so no additional adjustments are needed.
PATH;	Reset the path to nul. This avoids problems when the user doesn't enter a replaceable parameter. Tests for this condition would also avoid the problem.

Batch File Line	Explanation
`PATH=%1`	Set the path equal to the first replaceable parameter. Because DOS converts the path to uppercase, this will convert the first replaceable parameter to uppercase. Note that SET PATH = %1 won't work because not all versions of DOS convert the path to uppercase using this method.
`SET VARIABLE=%PATH%`	Store the uppercase replaceable parameter under another variable name.
`CALL JUNK.BAT`	Run the temporary batch file to reset the path.
`DEL JUNK.BAT`	Delete the temporary batch file.

`IF (%VARIABLE%)==(DAILY)   GOTO DAILY`
`IF (%VARIABLE%)==(MONTHLY) GOTO MONTHLY`
`IF (%VARIABLE%)==(ANNUAL)  GOTO ANNUAL`
	Jump to the appropriate section, depending on the replaceable parameter the user enters.

`GOTO ERROR`	If the batch file reaches this point the user entered an invalid replaceable parameter, so jump to an error-handling section.

`:ERROR`
`ECHO This Batch File Requires`
`ECHO A Parameter. The Valid`
`ECHO Ways To Start It Are:`
`ECHO CAPITAL5 daily`
`ECHO CAPITAL5 monthly`
`ECHO CAPITAL5 annual`
`GOTO END`
`:END_ERROR`
	Section that tells the user the batch file was run improperly and tells him how to run it properly.

`:DAILY`
`ECHO DAILY`
`GOTO END`
`:END_DAILY`
	Daily section. In a working batch file, the ECHO DAILY command would be the actual commands the batch file was to perform.

Batch File Line	Explanation
| ```
:MONTHLY
ECHO MONTHLY
GOTO END
:END_MONTHLY
``` | Monthly section. In a working batch file, the ECHO MONTHLY command would be the actual command the batch file was to perform. |
| ```
:ANNUAL
ECHO ANNUAL
GOTO END
:END_ANNUAL
``` | Annual section. In a working batch file, the ECHO ANNUAL command would be the actual command the batch file was to perform. |
| ```
:HELP
ECHO This Demonstration Batch File
ECHO Illustrates Dealing With Case
ECHO Problems In A Batch File
GOTO END
:END_HELP
``` | Section that displays help when the user starts the batch file with a /? or a ? as the first replaceable parameter. |
| ```
:END
``` | Label marking the end of the batch file. |

19-8 TESTGOTO.BAT checks to see if the label entered on the command line exists before issuing a GOTO %1 command.

Batch File Line	Explanation
| ```
@ECHO OFF
``` | Turn command-echoing off. |
| ```
REM NAME:    TESTGOTO.BAT
REM PURPOSE: Show Testing For Labels
REM VERSION: 2.00
REM DATE:    December 21, 1991
``` | Documentation remarks. |
| ```
IF (%1)==(/?) GOTO HELP
IF (%1)==(?)  GOTO HELP
``` | If the user starts the batch file with a request for help, jump to a section to display that help. |
| ```
IF (%1)==() ECHO No Label To Test Entered
IF (%1)==() GOTO END
``` | If the user didn't enter a replaceable parameter to be used with the GOTO command, display an error message and exit the batch file. |

Batch File Line	Explanation
`TYPE TESTGOTO.BAT|FIND ":%1" /I > TESTED`	Type the batch file and pipe the results to the find filter. Once in the find filter, search for the first replaceable parameter with a colon added to the front. (Notice the /I to cause FIND to ignore the case.) Pipe the results to a file called TESTED.
`COPY TESTED C:\`	Copy the file called TESTED to the root directory of the C drive. If TESTED contains text (meaning FIND found the label) this copy will work. If TESTED is a zero-length file (meaning FIND didn't find the label) the copy won't work.
`DEL TESTED`	Delete the file.
`COPY C:\TESTED`	Try to copy the file back from the root directory of the C drive. If the file copied ok, this will work. If the file was a zero-length file it wasn't copied to C:\, so this won't work.
`IF EXIST C:\TESTED DEL C:\TESTED`	If C:\TESTED exists it's no longer needed, so delete it.
`IF EXIST TESTED ECHO LABEL FOUND` `IF EXIST TESTED GOTO %1`	If TESTED made it back to the current directory then the label existed, so display that information and jump to the appropriate label.
`IF NOT EXIST TESTED ECHO Label Not Found` `IF NOT EXIST TESTED GOTO END`	If TESTED didn't make it back to the current directory then the label didn't exist, so display an error message and exit the batch file.

`:ONE`
`ECHO One Entered`
`GOTO END`
`:END_ONE`
	Label that handles a replaceable parameter of ONE.

Batch File Line	Explanation

`:TWO`
`ECHO Two Entered`
`GOTO END`
`:END_TWO`
	Label that handles a replaceable parameter of TWO.

`:THREE`
`ECHO Three Entered`
`GOTO END`
`:END_THREE`
	Label that handles a replaceable parameter of THREE.

`:HELP`
`ECHO This Demonstration Batch File`
`ECHO Illustrates Verifying A Label Exists`
`ECHO Before Using The GOTO %1 Command`
`GOTO END`
`:END_HELP`
	Section that displays help when the user starts the batch file with a /? or a ? as the first replaceable parameter.

`:END`	Label marking the end of the batch file.
`IF EXIST TESTED DEL TESTED`	If the TESTED file exists, delete it because it's no longer needed.

19-9 NEST1.BAT tests for a Y or N answer to four IF tests.

Batch File Line	Explanation
`@ECHO OFF`	Turn command-echoing off.

`REM NAME:    NEST1.BAT`
`REM PURPOSE: Test For Y/N Input`
`REM VERSION: 1.00`
`REM DATE:    May 10, 1991`
	Documentation remarks.

`IF (%1)==(/?) GOTO HELP` `IF (%1)==(?)  GOTO HELP`	If the user starts the batch file with a request for help, jump to a section to display that help.
`IF (%1)==()   GOTO NONE`	If no replaceable parameter was entered, go to a special section.

`IF %1==Y GOTO OK`
`IF %1==y GOTO OK`
`IF %1==N GOTO OK`
`IF %1==n GOTO OK`
	If the user entered an upper- or lowercase n or y, jump to a section for an appropriate input.

`GOTO ERROR`	A nonacceptable input was used, so jump to a special error-handling section.

`:OK`
`ECHO CORRECT VALUE ENTERED`
`GOTO END`
`:END_OK`
	A correct command was entered, so normally there would be commands here to execute.

Batch File Line	Explanation

`:NONE`
`ECHO NO VALUE ENTERED`
`GOTO END`
`:END_NONE`
	No replaceable parameter was entered, so tell the user that and exit the batch file.

`:ERROR`
`ECHO INVALID VALUE ENTERED`
`GOTO END`
`:END_ERROR`
	An invalid replaceable parameter was entered, so tell the user that and exit the batch file.

`:HELP`
`ECHO This Demonstration Batch`
`ECHO File Illustrates Line-By-`
`ECHO Line IF Tests`
`GOTO END`
`:END_HELP`
	Section that displays help when the user starts the batch file with a /? or a ? as the first replaceable parameter.

`:END`	Label marking the end of the batch file.

19-10 NEST2.BAT simplifies string comparisons by means of multiple IF statements on one line.

Batch File Line	Explanation
`@ECHO OFF`	Turn command-echoing off.

`REM NAME:      NEST2.BAT`
`REM PURPOSE: Test For Y/N Input`
`REM          Using Consolidated`
`REM          IF Test`
	Documentation remarks.

`IF (%1)==(/?) GOTO HELP` `IF (%1)==(?)  GOTO HELP`	If the user starts the batch file with a request for help, jump to a section to display that help.
`IF (%1)==() GOTO NONE`	If no replaceable parameter was entered, jump to a special section to handle that error.

`IF NOT %1==Y IF NOT %1==y`
`   IF NOT %1==N IF NOT %1==n`
`   GOTO ERROR`
	If none of the four acceptable responses were entered, jump to an error-handling section.

`GOTO OK`	An acceptable response was entered, so go to the appropriate section.

`:OK`
`ECHO Correct Value Entered`
`GOTO END`
`:END_OK`
	A correct command was entered, so normally there would be commands here to execute.

`:NONE`
`ECHO No Value Entered`
`GOTO END`
`:END_NONE`
	No replaceable parameter was entered, so tell the user that and exit the batch file.

`:ERROR`
`ECHO Invalid Value Entered`
`GOTO END`
`:END_ERROR`
	An invalid replaceable parameter was entered, so tell the user that and exit the batch file.

Batch File Line	Explanation

`:HELP`
`ECHO This Demonstration Batch`
`ECHO File Illustrates Nested`
`ECHO IF Tests`
`GOTO END`
`:END_HELP`
	Section that displays help when the user starts the batch file with a /? or a ? as the first replaceable parameter.

`:END`	Label marking the end of the batch file.

19-11 TEXTFND4.BAT is a brute-force method of adding quotes for the Norton Text Search program.

Batch File Line	Explanation
`@ECHO OFF`	Turn command-echoing off.

`REM NAME:      TEXTFND4.BAT`
`REM PURPOSE: Brute-Force Approach`
`REM          To Building`
`REM          Environment Variable`
`REM VERSION: 1.45`
`REM DATE:    June 1, 1991`
	Documentation remarks.

`IF (%1)==(/?) GOTO HELP` `IF (%1)==(?)  GOTO HELP`	If the user starts the batch file with a request for help, jump to a section to display that help.
`IF (%1)==()   GOTO ERROR1`	If no replaceable parameters were entered, jump to an error-handling section.
`IF (%2)==()   GOTO ERROR2`	The program requires a minimum of two parameters, so if the second wasn't entered jump to an error-handling section.
`IF (%3)==() TS %1 %2` `IF (%3)==() GOTO END`	If no third parameter was entered, run the program with parameters and exit the batch file.
`IF (%4)==() TS %1 "%2 %3"` `IF (%4)==() GOTO END`	If no fourth parameter was entered, run the program with three parameters and exit the batch file.
`IF (%5)==() TS %1 "%2 %3 %4"` `IF (%5)==() GOTO END`	If no fifth parameter was entered, run the program with four parameters and exit the batch file.
`IF (%6)==() TS %1 "%2 %3 %4 %5"` `IF (%6)==() GOTO END`	If no sixth parameter was entered, run the program with five parameters and exit the batch file.

Batch File Line	Explanation
```IF (%7)==() TS %1 "%2 %3 %4 %5 %6"``` ```IF (%7)==() GOTO END```	If no seventh parameter was entered, run the program with six parameters and exit the batch file.
```IF (%8)==() TS %1 "%2 %3 %4 %5 %6 %7"``` ```IF (%8)==() GOTO END```	If no eighth parameter was entered, run the program with seven parameters and exit the batch file.
```IF (%9)==() TS %1 "%2 %3 %4 %5 %6 %7 %8"``` ```IF (%9)==() GOTO END```	If no ninth parameter was entered, run the program with eight parameters and exit the batch file.
```TS %1 "%2 %3 %4 %5 %6 %7 %8 %9"``` ```GOTO END```	If the batch file reaches this point then at least nine replaceable parameters were entered, so use all nine. Note that any replaceable parameters after %9 are lost. After running the program, exit the batch file.

```:ERROR1```
 ```ECHO No Files to Search Specified```
 ```GOTO END```
 ```:END_ERROR1```
	Error-handling section for no replaceable parameters.

```:ERROR2```
 ```ECHO No Text to Search For```
 ```GOTO END```
 ```:END_ERROR2```
	Error-handling section for only one replaceable parameter.

```:HELP```
 ```ECHO This Batch File Prepares```
 ```ECHO Inputs For The Norton```
 ```ECHO Utilities Text Search```
 ```ECHO Program```
 ```GOTO END```
 ```:END_HELP```
	Section that displays help when the user starts the batch file with a /? or a ? as the first replaceable parameter.

```:END```	Label marking the end of the batch file.

19-12 TEXTFND5.BAT is a finesse method of adding quotes for the Norton Text Search program by constructing a custom environmental variable.

Batch File Line	Explanation
```@ECHO OFF```	Turn command-echoing off.

```REM NAME: TEXTFND5.BAT```
 ```REM PURPOSE: Construct Environmental```
 ```REM   Containing Text To```
 ```REM   Search For```
 ```REM VERSION: 1.31```
 ```REM DATE: June 1, 1991```
	Documentation remarks.

Batch File Line	Explanation
`IF (%1)==(/?) GOTO HELP` `IF (%1)==(?)  GOTO HELP`	If the user starts the batch file with a request for help, jump to a section to display that help.
`IF (%1)==()   GOTO NOFILE`	If the user didn't enter files to search, jump to an error-handling routine.
`SET FILE=%1`	Store the files to search in the environment.
`SHIFT`	Move all the replaceable parameters down one level.
`IF (%1)==() GOTO NOTEXT`	If the user didn't enter any text to search for, jump to an error-handling routine.
`SET TEXT="%1`	Store the beginning quote and the text in the environment.
`SHIFT`	Move the replaceable parameters down one level.
`IF (%1)==() GOTO STOP`	If only one word was entered to search for, jump to the section named STOP to continue processing.
`:TOP`	Label marking the top of a loop.
`SET TEXT=%TEXT% %1`	Add a space and the next word to the environmental variable storing the text to search for. You must add the space because DOS strips out the spaces when it separates multiple words into individual replaceable parameters.
`SHIFT`	Move the replaceable parameters down one level.
`IF (%1)==() GOTO STOP`	Once the replaceable parameter are exhausted, jump to the next portion of the batch file to continue processing.
`GOTO TOP` `:END_TOP`	Continue the loop.
`:STOP`	Label marking the next section of the batch file.
`SET TEXT=%TEXT%"`	Add the closing quote to the environmental variable storing the text.

Batch File Line	Explanation
GOTO START : END_STOP	Jump to the section of the batch file that handles the actual searching.
: NOFILE	Label marking the error-handling section for when the user doesn't enter files to search.
ECHO No files to search entered	Tell the user what happened.
GOTO END : END_NOFILE	Exit the batch file.
: NOTEXT	Label marking the error-handling section for when the user doesn't enter text to search for.
ECHO No text to search for entered	Tell the user what happened.
GOTO END : END_NOTEXT	Exit the batch file.
: START	Label marking the section of the batch file that performs the actual searching.
TS %FILE% %TEXT% GOTO END : END_START	Run the Norton Utilities Text Search program and pass it the two values stored in the environment.
: HELP ECHO This Batch File Prepares ECHO Input For The Norton ECHO Utilities Text Search ECHO Program GOTO END : END_HELP	Section that displays help when the user starts the batch file with a /? or a ? as the first replaceable parameter.
: END	Label marking the end of the batch file.

19-13 SAVESPACE.BAT illustrates how to save disk space using environmental variables.

Batch File Line	Explanation
@ECHO OFF	Turn command-echoing off.
REM NAME: SAVESPACE.BAT REM PURPOSE: Replace Commands REM With Variables REM VERSION: 1.00 REM DATE: May 1, 1991	Documentation remarks.
IF (%1)==(/?) GOTO HELP IF (%1)==(?) GOTO HELP	If the user starts the batch file with a request for help, jump to a section to display that help.

Batch File Line	Explanation

`SET E=IF ERRORLEVEL`
`SET N=IF NOT ERRORLEVEL`
`SET O=ECHO`
	Set three environmental variables that will be used to shorten the batch file lines.

`%E% 255        %O% 255`	When DOS expands the environmental variables, this line becomes: IF ERRORLEVEL 255 ECHO 225.
`%E% 254 %N% 255 %O% 254`	When DOS expands the environmental variables, this line becomes: IF ERRORLEVEL 254 IF NOT ERRORLEVEL 255 ECHO 254.
`%E% 253 %N% 254 %O% 253`	When DOS expands the environmental variables, this line becomes: IF ERRORLEVEL 253 IF NOT ERRORLEVEL 254 ECHO 253.
The batch file continues in a similar fashion for 253-2	
`%E%   1 %N%   2 %O%   1`	When DOS expands the environmental variables, this line becomes: IF ERRORLEVEL 1 IF NOT ERRORLEVEL 2 ECHO 1.
`%E%   0 %N%   1 %O%   0`	When DOS expands the environmental variables, this line becomes: IF ERRORLEVEL 0 IF NOT ERRORLEVEL 1 ECHO 0.
`GOTO END`	Exit the batch file.

`:HELP`
`ECHO This Batch File Displays`
`ECHO The Errorlevel While`
`ECHO Demonstrating Using`
`ECHO Replaceable Parameters As`
`ECHO Commands In A Batch File`
`GOTO END`
`:END_HELP`
	Section that displays help when the user starts the batch file with a /? or a ? as the first replaceable parameter.

`:END`	Label marking the end of the batch file.

19-14 When one program or part of a program calls another program, the part being called is called a *subroutine*.

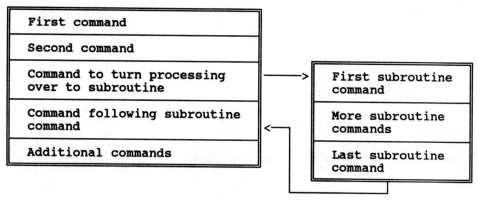

20

Batch file documentation

01.BAT
Chapter 11

Syntax: 01

01.BAT is a demonstration file that runs a make-believe application called BigApp, which requires a lot of memory. If 01.BAT finds that the machine wasn't booted using the configuration files stored under CONFIG.001 and AUTOEXEC.001, it will copy those on top of CONFIG.SYS and AUTOEXEC.BAT, respectively, reboot, and then start BigApp.

In order for the process to work, the AUTOEXEC.BAT file must run STARTAPP .BAT to check to see if a file called START.001 exists and, if it does, run 01.BAT. While you might find it useful to write similar batch files, 01.BAT performs no useful function beyond demonstrating how to deal with an inappropriate environment with a batch file. Note that 01.BAT uses Batcmd to reboot the computer, so Batcmd must be in the current subdirectory or path. *See also* 02.BAT and STARTAPP.BAT.

02.BAT
Chapter 11

Syntax: 02

02.BAT is a demonstration file that runs a make-believe application called TinyApp, which doesn't requires a lot of memory. If 02.BAT finds that the machine wasn't booted using the configuration files stored under CONFIG.002 and AUTOEXEC.002, it will copy those on top of CONFIG.SYS and AUTOEXEC.BAT, respectively, reboot, and then start BigApp.

In order for the process to work, the AUTOEXEC.BAT file must run STARTAPP .BAT to check to see if a file called START.002 exists and, if it does, run 02.BAT. 02.BAT performs no useful function beyond demonstrating how to deal with an inappropriate environment with a batch file. Note that 02.BAT uses Batcmd to reboot the computer, so

Batcmd must be in the current subdirectory or the path. *See also* 01.BAT and STARTAPP .BAT.

1-LOG.BAT
Chapter 2

Syntax: 1-LOG

1-LOG.BAT will pipe the date and time to the file C: \ LOG \ LOTUSLOG.TXT each time it's run, run Lotus, and then pipe the date and time Lotus was terminated to the same file. You might need to modify the name of the subdirectory or the 123 command that starts Lotus in order to use 1-LOG.BAT on your system.

ANSIDEMO.BAT
Chapter 18

Syntax: ANSIDEMO

ANSIDEMO.BAT is a demonstration batch file, and performs no useful function beyond demonstrating how to include ANSI escape sequences in a batch file. To run ANSIDEMO .BAT, you must load ANSI.SYS in your CONFIG.SYS file.

ANSIHIDE.BAT
Chapter 2

Syntax: ANSIHIDE

ANSIHIDE.BAT is a demonstration that shows how ANSI escape sequences can change the foreground and background colors to black, effectively hiding messages that are displayed through DOS. ANSIHIDE.BAT performs no useful function beyond demonstrating how to hide DOS messages in a batch file.

AUTOASK.BAT
Chapter 11

Syntax: AUTOASK

AUTOASK.BAT is an AUTOEXEC.BAT "fragment" that's designed for you to modify and include in your own AUTOEXEC.BAT—it isn't intended to be run from the command line. AUTOASK.BAT asks the user's permission before loading each of three memory-resident programs, and performs no useful function beyond demonstrating how to conditionally load memory resident software in the AUTOEXEC.BAT file.

AUTOBOOT.BAT
Chapter 11

Syntax: AUTOBOOT 001/002/003

AUTOBOOT.BAT allows the user to select from one of three sets of configuration files. AUTOBOOT.BAT then copies the appropriate set of files on top of the existing AUTOEXEC.BAT and CONFIG.SYS files, and reboots the computer. You'll have to supply your own versions of CONFIG.001, CONFIG.002, CONFIG.003, AUTOEXEC.001, AUTOEXEC.002 and AUTOEXEC.003, corresponding to the configurations you want to boot with. AUTOBOOT.BAT uses Batcmd to reboot the computer, so it must be in the current sub-directory or path.

BIGMENU.BAT
Chapter 4

Syntax: BIGMENU 1/2/3/4/5/6

BIGMENU.BAT saves disk space by consolidating six batch files into one massive batch file. Select the batch file to run by entering a 1−6 on the command line. BIGMENU.BAT contains demonstration batch files. You'll first need to modify it and replace its six batch files with batch files you use. There's no reason to limit BIGMENU.BAT to six batch files, so if you modify BIGMENU.BAT you might want to consolidate even more batch files into BIGMENU.BAT.

BLANK.BAT
Chapter 18

Syntax: BLANK

BLANK.BAT changes the foreground and background colors to black, effectively blanking the screen. Only programs that display their text through DOS will be blanked. If you want to run BLANK.BAT, you must load ANSI.SYS in your CONFIG.SYS file. *See also* UNBLANK.BAT.

CAPITAL1.BAT
Chapter 19

Syntax: CAPITAL1 daily/monthly/annual

CAPITAL1.BAT is a demonstration batch file that shows how to use multiple IF tests to partially deal with the problem of users using different capitalizations for text entered on the command line. While you might find it useful to include similar code in other batch files, CAPITAL1.BAT performs no useful function beyond demonstrating one approach to dealing with capitalization in a batch file. *See also* CAPITAL2.BAT, CAPITAL3.BAT, CAPITAL4.BAT, CAPITAL5.BAT, and PHONE.BAT.

CAPITAL2.BAT
Chapter 19

Syntax: CAPITAL2 daily/monthly/annual

CAPITAL2.BAT is a demonstration batch file that shows how to use the GOTO command to partially deal with the problem of entering different capitalizations for text on the command line. CAPITAL2.BAT performs no useful function beyond demonstrating one approach to dealing with capitalization in a batch file. See also CAPITAL1.BAT, CAPITAL3.BAT, CAPITAL4.BAT, CAPITAL5.BAT, and PHONE.BAT.

CAPITAL3.BAT
Chapter 19

Syntax: CAPITAL3 daily/monthly/annual

CAPITAL3.BAT is a demonstration batch file that shows how you can use environmental variables to partially deal with the problem of entering different capitalizations for text on the command line. CAPITAL3.BAT performs no useful function beyond demonstrating one approach to dealing with capitalization in a batch file. *See also* CAPITAL1.BAT, CAPITAL2.BAT, CAPITAL4.BAT, CAPITAL5.BAT, and PHONE.BAT.

CAPITAL4.BAT
Chapter 19

Syntax: CAPITAL4 daily/monthly/annual

CAPITAL4.BAT is a demonstration batch file that shows how to use the path to partially deal with the problem of entering different capitalizations for text on the command line. CAPITAL4.BAT performs no useful function beyond demonstrating one approach to dealing with capitalization in a batch file. See also CAPITAL1.BAT, CAPITAL2.BAT, CAPITAL3.BAT, CAPITAL5.BAT, and PHONE.BAT.

CAPITAL5.BAT
Chapter 19

Syntax: CAPITAL5 daily/monthly/annual

CAPITAL5.BAT is a demonstration batch file that shows how to use the path to partially deal with the problem of entering different capitalizations for text on the command line.

CAPITAL4.BAT used the environment to store the actual path and the path variable was used to convert the replaceable parameter to all uppercase, but CAPITAL5.BAT stores the path to disk. This reduces the environmental space required by the batch file. CAPITAL5.BAT performs no useful function beyond demonstrating one approach to dealing with capitalization in a batch file. See also CAPITAL1.BAT, CAPITAL2.BAT, CAPITAL3.BAT, CAPITAL4.BAT, and PHONE.BAT.

CASE.BAT
Chapter 19

Syntax: CASE

CASE.BAT is a demonstration batch file that shows how to simulate a case programming format in a batch file, and performs no useful function beyond demonstrating how to program the case format in a batch file.

CATALOG.BAT
Chapter 10

Syntax: CATALOG drive

CATALOG.BAT creates a listing of every file on the specified drive. This catalog is stored under the name C:\CATALOG\CATALOG.TXT. If you have more than one floppy drive, you might want to modify CATALOG.BAT to a different floppy drive. See also REMOVE.BAT.

CHECKERR.BAT
Chapter 17

Syntax: CHECKERR

This batch file displays the current errorlevel. CHECKERR.BAT is a large batch file that takes the brute-force approach of simply testing for all 256 possible errorlevel values. See also SAVE-ERR.BAT, CHECKER2.BAT, and SAVESPAC.BAT.

CHECKER2.BAT
Chapter 17

Syntax: CHECKER2

Like CHECKERR.BAT, CHECKER2.BAT displays the current errorlevel value by simply testing for every possible errorlevel value. Its advantage over CHECKERR.BAT is that it combines IF tests to reduce the size of the batch file. See also SAVE-ERR.BAT, CHECKERR.BAT, and SAVESPAC.BAT.

CHKDSKCD
Chapter 8

Syntax: CHKDSKCD *subdirectory*

CHKDSKCD.BAT runs CHKDSK/V to display all the subdirectories on your current drive, pipes that information to FIND to search for the subdirectory or subdirectory fragment entered on the command line, and then changes to the first matching subdirectory it finds. CHKDSKCD.BAT creates and deletes a temporary batch file called C: \ BAT \ JUNK.BAT. It also requires DIRECTOR.BAT to be in the path. CHKDSKCD.BAT works only on the current drive.

CL.BAT
Chapter 6

Syntax: CL # [*command__line*]

CL.BAT constructs and stores up to four command lines. If you specify a number with the command, e.g., CL 1, then it runs the command line stored under that number. If the number is followed by a command line, then it stores that command to the command line number and also executes the command line. Because CL.BAT stores its four command lines in the environment, you must have enough free environmental space to store all four command lines.

CL2.BAT
Chapter 6

Syntax: CL2 # [*command*]

CL2.BAT constructs and stores up to nine command lines. If it's started with just a number, e.g., CL2 1, then it runs the command line stored under that number. If the number is followed by a command, then it stores the command that follows to the command line number and then executes it. CL2.BAT stores its command lines in batch files named 1.BAT − 9.BAT in the C: \ CL2 subdirectory.

CNTBOOTS.BAT
Chapter 7

Syntax: CNTBOOTS

CNTBOOTS.BAT was designed to be called from the AUTOEXEC.BAT file rather than run from the command line. As written, CNTBOOTS.BAT will back up the entire C drive to the A drive using the DOS backup program and perform a disk test once every fiftieth booting, and perform an incremental backup every tenth booting. CNTBOOTS.BAT is a demonstration program designed to show you how to have a batch file run commands occasionally, and performs no useful function beyond this. *See also* OCCASION.BAT.

CNTFILES
Chapter 10

Syntax: CNTFILES [*drive*]

CNTFILES.BAT displays and counts all the files on the specified drive that have been changed since the last time they were backed up. If no drive is specified, the current drive is used. CNTFILES.BAT always displays all the files on the drive needing backup, even if it's run from a subdirectory other than the root directory.

CONFIG.BAT
Chapter 11

Syntax: CONFIG

CONFIG.BAT overwrites the current CONFIG.SYS file with a custom version by asking you a series of questions. It then reboots so the new CONFIG.SYS file can take effect. Warning: Before running CONFIG.BAT, you need to extensively modify the batch file. Failure to do this could result in the computer failing to boot properly. See the text for details.

CTTYKEY.BAT
Chapter 11

Syntax: CTTYKEY

CTTYKEY.BAT is a batch file that demonstrates how a batch file can accept keystrokes from the keyboard with a CTTY NUL command in effect, but performs no useful function beyond this.

CURRENT.BAT
Chapter 12

Syntax: CURRENT date is *day date*

AUTOEXEC.BAT echoes the date to a batch file and then runs that batch file. (Don't run it from the command line.) The batch file created by piping the date will contain text like *Current date is Tue 12-24-1991*. When that batch file is executed, it will run CURRENT-.BAT and pass it the day of the week as %3. As configured, CURRENT.BAT will perform a full backup on Friday and an incremental backup on Wednesday. You can modify CUR-

RENT.BAT to run your own backup program, and modify the days to improve their backup strategy. *See also* CURRENT1.BAT.

CURRENT1.BAT
Chapter 12

Syntax: CURRENT date is *day date*

CURRENT1.BAT is a modification of CURRENT.BAT, and will perform a backup only the first time the computer is booted on the specified days. CURRENT1.BAT must be renamed to CURRENT.BAT before it will work.

This version of CURRENT.BAT is designed to echo the date to a batch file and then run that batch file. The batch file created by piping the date will contain text like *Current date is Tue 12-24-1991*. When that batch file is executed, it will run CURRENT.BAT and pass it the day of the week as %3. As configured, CURRENT1.BAT will perform a full backup on Friday and an incremental backup on Wednesday, but only the first time the computer is booted on those days. Modify CURRENT1.BAT to run your own backup program and modify the days to improve their backup strategy. *See also* CURRENT.BAT.

DEL.BAT
Chapter 14

Syntax: DEL *files*

DEL.BAT replaces the internal DEL command when DOS has been modified to rename the DEL command to XXX.

DIGIT-1.BAT
Chapter 17

Syntax: DIGIT-1

DIGIT-1.BAT displays the hundreds value of the errorlevel. It was designed to be called by DIGIT-3.BAT rather than run directly from the command line, but it will work both ways.

DIGIT-2.BAT
Chapter 17

Syntax: DIGIT-2

DIGIT-2.BAT displays the tens value of the errorlevel. It was designed to be called by DIGIT-3.BAT rather than run directly from the command line. It will run directly from the command line, but only if DIGIT-1.BAT is run first; otherwise, its results are unpredictable.

DIGIT-3.BAT
Chapter 17

Syntax: DIGIT-3

DIGIT-3.BAT displays the current errorlevel value. It calls DIGIT-1.BAT to find the hundreds value and DIGIT-2.BAT to find the tens value. Then DIGIT-3.BAT finds the ones value. *See also* SAVE-ERR.BAT.

DIRECTOR.BAT
Chapter 8

DIRECTOR.BAT is called by CHKDSKCD.BAT to finish changing to a specified subdirectory. DIRECTOR.BAT isn't designed to run by itself from the command line. *See also* CHKDSK.BAT.

EDIT1.BAT
Chapter 13

Syntax: EDIT1 # *path*

EDIT1.BAT is designed to be called by EDITPATH.BAT and won't operate properly if called from the command line. EDIT1.BAT keeps the first number of elements of the path specified in the command and discards the rest. For example, if # is 2 and the path is C: \ ;C: \ DOS;C: \ WORD;C: \ BAT, then the path after EDIT1.BAT runs will be C: \ ;C: \ DOS. *See also* EDITPATH.BAT, EDITPAT2.BAT, and EDIT2.BAT.

EDIT2.BAT
Chapter 13

Syntax: EDIT2 *path*

EDIT2.BAT is designed to be called by EDITPAT2.BAT and won't operate properly if called from the command line. EDIT2.BAT asks you about each subdirectory in the path and retains only those you decide to keep. EDIT2.BAT uses Batcmd to ask questions and perform other tasks, so it must either be in the current subdirectory or the path. *See also* EDITPATH.BAT, EDITPAT2.BAT, and EDIT1.BAT.

EDITPAT2.BAT
Chapter 13

Syntax: EDITPAT2

EDITPAT2.BAT calls EDIT2.BAT and passes it the current path as a series of replaceable

parameters. This is required because a batch file is the only way to pass the path to EDIT2
.BAT in a form where its subdirectories can be used separately. *See also* EDITPATH.BAT,
EDIT1.BAT, and EDIT2.BAT.

EDITPATH.BAT
Chapter 13

Syntax: EDITPATH #

EDITPATH.BAT is the first step in editing your path. Start EDITPATH.BAT with the
number of subdirectories you want to keep specified on the command line. The number
must be 1−8. See also EDIT1.BAT, EDITPAT2.BAT, and EDIT2.BAT.

ENV_SIZE.BAT
Chapter 19

Syntax: ENV_SIZE

ENV_SIZE.BAT verifies that the environment contains 50 bytes of free space, but performs no useful function beyond demonstrating this function.

FASTFIND.BAT
Chapter 8

Syntax: FASTFIND *file*

FASTFIND.BAT will display all the files on disk matching the file specified on the command line. Wildcards are allowed. FASTFIND.BAT uses the DOS Attrib command, so it
must be in the current subdirectory or path. In addition, to work across all subdirectories,
you must be using DOS 3.3 or later.

GET-TIME.BAT
Chapter 12

Syntax: GET-TIME

GET-TIME.BAT displays the date and time on the screen. GET-TIME.BAT uses Batcmd,
so it must be in the current subdirectory or path. You might want to modify GET-TIME
.BAT to store the date and time in the environment rather than just displaying them to the
screen.

GETVOL.BAT
Chapter 12

Syntax: GETVOL

GETVOL.BAT is the first step in storing the volume label to an environmental variable. It pipes the volume to a file called STOREVOL.BAT and then executes that file. *See also* STOREVOL.BAT, VOLUME.BAT and VOLUME1.BAT.

HELP.BAT
Chapter 3

Syntax: HELP

HELP.BAT displays a brief description of available batch files. Note: The version of HELP.BAT on the enclosed disk describes only three of the batch files on disk. You must modify HELP.BAT to display help messages for your batch files before it will be useful.

HELP1.BAT
Chapter 3

Syntax: HELP1 *category*

HELP1.BAT displays a brief description of available batch files for the specified category. Note: The version of HELP1.BAT on the enclosed disk describes only several of the batch files on the disk in four categories. You must modify HELP1.BAT to display help messages for your own batch files, and use your own categories before it will be useful.

HELPBAT.BAT
Chapter 3

Syntax: HELPBAT

HELPBAT.BAT displays a brief description of each batch file in the C: \ BAT subdirectory. In order for HELPBAT.BAT to work, each batch file must be in the C: \ BAT subdirectory and have a remark line explaining the purpose of the batch file containing the word *PURPOSE* followed by a colon.

HELPBAT2.BAT
Chapter 3

Syntax: HELPBAT2 *topic*

HELPBAT2.BAT displays a brief description of each batch file in the C: \ BAT subdirectory that contains a phrase that exactly matches the *topic* entered on the command line. In order for HELPBAT2.BAT to work, each batch file must be in the C: \ BAT subdirectory and have a remark line explaining the purpose of the batch file containing the word *PURPOSE* followed by a colon. Note that HELPBAT2.BAT searches for only the specified topic on the PURPOSE: line. One drawback to HELPBAT2.BAT is that, while it shows the PURPOSE: line for batch files matching the search topic, it also displays the name of all the batch files.

HELPBAT3.BAT
Chapter 3

Syntax: HELPBAT3 *topic*

HELPBAT3.BAT displays a brief description of each batch file in the C: \ BAT subdirectory that contains a phrase that exactly matches the *topic* entered on the command line. In order for HELPBAT3.BAT to work, each batch file must be in the C: \ BAT subdirectory and have a remark line explaining the purpose of the batch file containing the word *PURPOSE* followed by a colon. Note that HELPBAT3.BAT searches for only the specified topic on the PURPOSE: line. Unlike HELPBAT2.BAT, HELPBAT3.BAT shows the name of the batch file only when the PURPOSE: line matches the search topic.

KEYASSGN.BAT
Chapter 15

Syntax: KEYASSGN

KEYASSGN.BAT creates a number of new DOS commands using the DOS 5.0 DOSKEY program. It requires that DOSKEY be loaded with a /BUFSIZE = 2000 or larger setting. Some of the commands also require that KEYERASE.BAT and MOVEIT.BAT be in the path.

KEYERASE.BAT
Chapter 15

Some of the DOSKEY macros created by KEYASSGN.BAT run KEYERASE.BAT, so it must be in the path. KEYERASE.BAT displays all the files to be deleted and will optionally prompt you before deleting each one. While designed to be run by DOSKEY, KEYERASE.BAT can be run from the command line with the command:

KEYERASE *file1 file2 file3*

As many files as will fit on the command line can be listed for deletion. Wildcards are supported.

LOCK.BAT
Chapter 2

Syntax: LOCK

LOCK.BAT locks the console and requires the user to enter a password before the computer can be used. Pressing Ctrl—Break will lock the computer and require it to be rebooted. LOCK.BAT gives the user three chances to enter the password. If the correct password (205 as written) isn't entered in three tries, LOCK.BAT will lock the computer so it must be rebooted.

LOGBOOT.BAT
Chapter 2

Syntax: LOGBOOT

LOGBOOT.BAT will pipe the date and time to a file called BOOTLOG.TXT each time it's run. While you might find it useful to include similar code in your AUTOEXEC.BAT or other batch files, LOGBOOT.BAT performs no useful function beyond demonstrating how to log usage in a batch file.

LOTUS.BAT
Chapter 7

Syntax: LOTUS

LOTUS.BAT first changes the prompt to a reminder that Lotus is running and then loads Lotus. After exiting Lotus, it changes the prompt back to pg. That way, if you're shelled out of Lotus using the /S command, you'll know that Lotus is still loaded in memory and will see how to return to Lotus. You'll need to modify LOTUS.BAT to use the subdirectory you use for Lotus. In addition, if you use a prompt other than pg, you'll need to modify LOTUS.BAT to reset the prompt to the one you use when Lotus terminates. *See also* LOTUS1.BAT.

LOTUS1.BAT
Chapter 7

Syntax: LOTUS1

LOTUS1.BAT is a modification of LOTUS.BAT that contains an EXIT command at the top. If you're shelled out of any program and try to load Lotus using this batch file, EXIT will return you to the original application instead.

If LOTUS1.BAT is run without another program in memory and therefore makes it past the EXIT command, it will change the prompt to a reminder that Lotus is running and then load Lotus. After exiting Lotus, it changes the prompt back to pg. That way, if you're shelled out of Lotus using the /S command, you'll know that Lotus is still loaded in memory and will see how to return to it. Modify LOTUS1.BAT to use your Lotus subdirectory and, if you use a prompt other than pg, to reset the prompt to the one you use when Lotus terminates. *See also* LOTUS.BAT.

MACRO.BAT
Chapter 6

Syntax: MACRO # [*command*]

MACRO.BAT constructs and stores up to four macros. If it's started with just a number, e.g., MACRO 1, then it runs the macro stored under that number. If the number is followed by a command, then it stores the command that follows to that macro number. Because MACRO.BAT stores its four macros in the environment, you must have enough free environmental space to store all four macros.

MACRO2.BAT
Chapter 6

Syntax: MACRO2 #[*command*]

MACRO2.BAT constructs and stores up to ten macros. If it's started with just a number, e.g., MACRO2 2, then it runs the macro stored under that number. If the number is followed by a command, then it stores the command that follows to that macro number. MACRO2.BAT stores its macros in batch files named 0.BAT−9.BAT in the C:\ MACRO2 subdirectory.

MATH.BAT
Chapter 5

Syntax: MATH A/S

MATH.BAT adds or subtracts one to or from the existing environmental variable MATH. An A on the command line tells it to add, while an S tells it to subtract. Before it will run, it requires the environmental variables ONE, TEN, and HUNDRED. These three variables are to contain the ones, tens, and hundreds digits of the number MATH.BAT is to add one to. While it checks to see if they exist, it doesn't check to see if they contain a single-digit number.

MATH1.BAT
Chapter 5

Syntax: MATH1 A/S

MATH1.BAT adds or subtracts one to or from the existing environmental variable MATH. An A on the command line tells it to add, while an S tells it to subtract. Unlike MATH.BAT, MATH1.BAT doesn't require the environmental variables ONE, TEN, and HUNDRED to be configured before using it.

MATH2.BAT
Chapter 5

Syntax: MATH2 A/S

MATH2.BAT adds or subtracts one to or from the existing environmental variable MATH. An A on the command line tells it to add, while an S tells it to subtract. MATH2.BAT uses the batch utility Batcmd, so it must be in the current subdirectory or the path for MATH2.BAT to work.

MOVEIT.BAT
Chapter 15

Some of the DOSKEY macros created by MOVEIT.BAT run MOVEIT.BAT, so it must be in the path. MOVEIT.BAT copies the files specified to the subdirectory specified and then deletes the original copy of the files. MOVEIT.BAT performs extensive error-checking prior to deleting the files. While designed to be run by DOSKEY, MOVEIT.BAT can also be run from the command line with the command:

    MOVEIT source_files target_subdirectory

Wildcards are supported, but, if any files exist in the target subdirectory that match the source file specification, MOVEIT.BAT will abort without performing the operation.

MULTI.BAT
Chapter 6

Syntax: MULTI command1 ^ command2 ^ . . .

MULTI.BAT allows you to enter multiple commands on the command line, separated by a caret and spaces, and it will run them one at a time. The commands can't contain DOS piping. MULTI.BAT stores each command in the environment so there must be enough free environmental space to store the longest command.

MULTI1.BAT
Chapter 6

Syntax: MULTI1

MULTI1.BAT allows you to enter multiple commands by creating a temporary batch file, halting execution while you enter commands into this temporary batch file, and then executing the temporary batch file. When it finishes, it deletes TEMP.BAT, the temporary batch file.

MULTI2.BAT
Chapter 6

Syntax: MULTI2

MULTI2.BAT allows you to enter up to five long commands, and then it executes those five commands. It does this by prompting you for each of the five commands using Batcmd and storing each command in an environmental. Due to a Batcmd limitation, commands are restricted to 65 characters. Once all five commands are entered, you have the option of changing them or running them. Because MULTI2.BAT uses the batch utility Batcmd, it must be in the current subdirectory or your path. Because MULTI2.BAT stores all five commands in the environment, you must have enough free environmental space to store all five commands.

MULTI3.BAT
Chapter 6

Syntax: MULTI3

MULTI3.BAT is a stripped-down version of MULTI2.BAT that doesn't give you the option of entering or editing commands. Prior to starting MULTI3.BAT, you must enter the five commands you want to execute in the environment under the names CMD1–CMD5. All five commands must be stored in the environment for MULTI3.BAT, so you must have enough free environmental space to store them.

MULTI4.BAT
Chapter 6

Syntax: MULTI4

MULTI4.BAT allows you to enter up to five long commands, and then it executes those five commands. It does this by prompting you for each of the five commands using Batcmd and storing each command in a batch file in the root directory of the C drive. It uses the names JUNK1.BAT through JUNK5.BAT. To prevent command echoing when these batch files are executed, it appends an @ to the front of each command. Due to a

Batcmd limitation, commands are restricted to 65 characters. Once all five commands are entered, you have the option of changing them or running them. Because MULTI4.BAT uses the batch utility Batcmd, it must be in the current subdirectory or your path.

NEST1.BAT
Chapter 19

Syntax: NEST1 y/n

NEST1.BAT is a demonstration batch file that simply reports if a Y or N keystroke was entered on the command line, but performs no useful function beyond demonstrating how to test a replaceable parameter in a batch file. *See also* NEST2.BAT.

NEST2.BAT
Chapter 19

Syntax: NEST2 y/n

NEST2.BAT is a demonstration batch file that simply reports if a Y or N keystroke was entered on the command line, but performs no useful function beyond demonstrating how to perform nested IF tests in a batch file. *See also* NEST1.BAT.

NEXTFILE.BAT
Chapter 5

Syntax: NEXTFILE

NEXTFILE.BAT starts with the filename JUNK.000 and increases the extension by one until it finds a filename that doesn't exist. It requires MATH.BAT to be in the current subdirectory or path to work. This is a demonstration batch file; it performs no useful function beyond demonstrating how to find a unique filename.

NICEPROM.BAT
Chapter 18

Syntax: NICEPROM

NICEPROM.BAT sets an attractive and useful prompt. It displays the date, time, and current subdirectory at the top of the screen along with the drive and subdirectory in the usual prompt position. It also sets the screen colors to bright white on blue. If you want to run NICEPROM.BAT, your CONFIG.SYS file must load ANSI.SYS.

NOT-DEL.BAT
Chapter 2

Syntax: NOT-DEL

NOT-DEL.BAT tries to delete a file that doesn't exist (C: \ QQQ) in order to demonstrate the power of the CTTY command. This batch file performs no useful function beyond demonstrating how to use the CTTY command in a batch file.

NUMBER.BAT
Chapter 5

Syntax: NUMBER

NUMBER.BAT takes a three-digit number stored in the environment under the name ANSWER and stores the hundreds digit under the environmental variable HUNDRED, the tens digit under the environmental variable TEN, and the ones digit under the environmental variable ONE. While NUMBER.BAT checks to see that the environmental variable ANSWER exists, it's unable to actually verify that it contains a three-digit number or even a number.

NUMBER1.BAT
Chapter 5

Syntax: NUMBER1

NUMBER1.BAT takes a three-digit number stored in the environment under the name ANSWER and stores the hundreds digit under the environmental variable HUNDRED, the tens digit under the environmental variable TEN, and the ones digit under the environmental variable ONE. While NUMBER1.BAT checks to see that environmental variable ANSWER exists, it's unable to actually verify that it contains a three-digit number or even a number. NUMBER1.BAT requires NUMBER2.BAT through NUMBER6.BAT be in the current subdirectory or in the path.

NUMBER2 – 6.BAT
Chapter 5

The batch files NUMBER2.BAT through NUMBER6.BAT are called by NUMBER1 .BAT. They shouldn't be run from the command line.

NUMBER9.BAT
Chapter 5

Syntax: NUMBER9

NUMBER9.BAT takes a three-digit number stored in the environment under the name

ANSWER and stores the hundreds digit under the environmental variable HUNDRED, the tens digit under the environmental variable TEN, and the ones digit under the environmental variable ONE. While NUMBER9.BAT checks to see that environmental variable ANSWER exists, it's unable to actually verify that it contains a three-digit number or even a number.

NUMBER9.BAT is functionally equivalent to NUMBER1.BAT. However, NUMBER9.BAT has built-in subroutines so it repeatedly calls itself, while NUMBER1.BAT has to repeatedly call the separate files NUMBER2.BAT – NUMBER6.BAT that contain its subroutines.

OCCASION.BAT
Chapter 7

Syntax: OCCASION

OCCASION.BAT was designed to be called from the AUTOEXEC.BAT file rather than run from the command line. As written, OCCASION.BAT will back up the entire C drive to the A drive using the DOS backup program once every tenth time it is run. OCCASION.BAT is a demonstration program designed to illustrate how commands can be run occasionally by a batch file, but performs no useful function beyond this. *See also* CNT-BOOTS.BAT.

PASSWRD2.BAT
Chapter 2

Syntax: PASSWRD2

PASSWRD2.BAT demonstrates how to require a password in a batch file, but performs no useful function beyond that. PASSWRD2.BAT uses Batcmd to get keystrokes from the user, so Batcmd must be in the current subdirectory or path for PASSWRD2.BAT to work.

PATH1.BAT
Chapter 13

Syntax: PATH1 *new_path*

PATH1.BAT stores the current path under the environmental variable OLDPATH, and then replaces the existing path with the new path entered on the command line. *See also* PATH2.BAT and PATH3.BAT.

PATH2.BAT
Chapter 13

Syntax: PATH2

PATH2.BAT restores the original path that was stored to the environmental variable OLDPATH by PATH1.BAT or PATH3.BAT. *See also* PATH1.BAT and PATH3.BAT.

PATH3.BAT
Chapter 13

Syntax: PATH3 *subdirectory*

PATH3.BAT stores the current path under the environmental variable OLDPATH, and then adds the subdirectory specified on the command line onto the end of the path. *See also* PATH1.BAT and PATH3.BAT.

PATH4.BAT
Chapter 13

Syntax: PATH4 1/2/3

PATH4.BAT demonstrates how to switch between alternative paths in a batch file, but performs no useful function beyond this.

PHONE.BAT
Chapter 19

Syntax: PHONE *name*

PHONE.BAT dials any Hayes-compatible modem for the number associated with the name entered on the command line. Currently, PHONE.BAT is configured with a few demonstration phone numbers. You'll need to modify PHONE.BAT before using it so it contains the names and phone numbers you'll be calling. PHONE.BAT is designed to work with a modem connected to COM1. If your modem is connected to COM2, you'll also need to modify the COM port used by PHONE.BAT. *See also* CAPITAL1.BAT, CAPITAL2.BAT, CAPITAL3.BAT, CAPITAL4.BAT, and CAPITAL5.BAT.

PREPARE.BAT
Chapter 2

Syntax: PREPARE

PREPARE.BAT resets the archive bit on all the *.BAK, *.TMP, JUNK*.*. and similar files so they won't be backed up in an incremental backup. PREPARE.BAT uses the Fileattr program from the Norton Utilities, so it must be in the current subdirectory or the path. You'll want to modify PREPARE.BAT before using it to reset the archive bits on the types of temporary files you have on your system. In addition, if you don't have Norton Utilities, you'll want to modify PREPARE.BAT to use the DOS Attrib program in place of Fileattr.

QCD.BAT
Chapter 8

Syntax: QCD *drive sub1 sub2 sub3*

QCD.BAT allows you to quickly change drives and subdirectories without having to enter the colon after the drive letter or the backslash between subdirectories. If the first replaceable parameter is A−D, it is treated as a drive letter; otherwise, it's treated as a subdirectory. QCD.BAT first changes drives, if necessary, and then constructs an environmental variable containing each subdirectory separated by a backslash. Once the environmental variable is constructed, QCD.BAT changes to that subdirectory. If you want to use QCD .BAT and have drives other than A−D, you'll need to modify QCD.BAT to either recognize the additional drives or not recognize the drives you don't have.

RCD.BAT
Chapter 8

Syntax: RCD *nickname*

RCD.BAT allows you to quickly change to any subdirectory by specifying a nickname for that subdirectory rather than the full path. For example, as written, the command RCD DOS changes to the C:\DOS subdirectory. RCD.BAT is configured with a few sample subdirectories. You'll need to modify RCD.BAT to contain the subdirectories and nicknames applicable to your system.

RECONFIG.BAT
Chapter 11

Syntax: RECONFIG

RECONFIG.BAT lets you select between one of eight sets of AUTOEXEC.BAT and CONFIG.SYS configuration files. It then copies the selected set to the root directory and reboots the computer. RECONFIG.BAT uses the C:\RECONFIG subdirectory and requires the eight sets of configuration files to be stored in this subdirectory under the names AUTOEXEC.1 to AUTOEXEC.8, and CONFIG.1 to CONFIG.8. You're given the opportunity to abort the process before any files are overwritten.

REMOVE.BAT
Chapter 10

Syntax: REMOVE *name*

REMOVE.BAT removes all the lines from the floppy disk catalog stored in C:\CATA-

LOG\CATALOG.TXT that contain the name entered on the command line. *See also* CATALOG.BAT.

RETURN.BAT
Chapter 8

Syntax: RETURN

RETURN.BAT constructs a custom batch file called RETURNTO.BAT in the C:\BAT subdirectory that will return you to the subdirectory you were in when you issued the RETURN command. RETURN.BAT requires a file called C:\BAT\RETURN that consists of a CD followed by a space and an end-of-file (eof) marker. Instructions for creating this file are contained in chapter 8.

RETURN2.BAT
Chapter 8

Syntax: RETURN2

Before this batch file will work, you must create an environmental variable called HOME that contains your home subdirectory, e.g., SET HOME = C:\WRITING\PENDING\ BOOK8. Once that environmental variable is created, RETURN2.BAT will change to that subdirectory when executed. *See also* RETURN3.BAT.

RETURN3.BAT
Chapter 8

Syntax: RETURN3 [*subdirectory*]

When RETURN3.BAT is run with a subdirectory also entered on the command line, e.g., RETURN3 C:\DOS, it will change to that subdirectory and store the subdirectory in the environment under the name HOME. When RETURN3.BAT is run without a subdirectory on the command line, it will change to the subdirectory stored in the environment.

RMD.BAT
Chapter 8

Syntax: RMD *subdirectory*

RMD.BAT first creates a subdirectory and then changes to that subdirectory. It's equivalent to an MD *subdirectory* command followed by a CD *subdirectory* command.

SAVE-ERR.BAT
Chapter 17

Syntax: SAVE-ERR

SAVE-ERR.BAT displays the current errorlevel value and saves it to the environmental variable ERROR. SAVE-ERR.BAT uses a FOR loop to keep the batch file small and quick. *See also* CHECKERR.BAT, CHECKER2.BAT, and SAVESPAC.BAT.

SAVESPAC.BAT
Chapter 19

Syntax: SAVESPAC

SAVESPAC.BAT displays the current errorlevel by testing for each possible errorlevel value. It also demonstrates how to shorten batch files by replacing long commands with environmental variables. *See also* CHECKERR.BAT, CHECKER2.BAT, and SAVE-ERR.BAT.

SENDANS2.BAT
Chapter 18

Syntax: SENDANS2 *ANSI_commands*

SENDANS2.BAT is a batch file that will send up to fifty ANSI escape sequences from the command without the Escape that usually precedes each command. You must load ANSI .SYS in your CONFIG.SYS file in order to use this batch file. *See also* SENDANSI.BAT.

SENDANSI.BAT
Chapter 18

Syntax: SENDANSI *ANSI_command*

SENDANSI.BAT is a batch file that will send a single ANSI escape sequence from the command line without the Escape that precedes the command. You must load ANSI.SYS in your CONFIG.SYS file in order to use this batch file. *See also* SENDANS2.BAT.

SERIAL.BAT
Chapter 12

Syntax: SERIAL

SERIAL.BAT stores a copy of the volume serial number in the environment under the name *SERIAL*. It creates a temporary batch file called JUNK.BAT in the current subdirectory and calls another batch file called VOLUME.BAT to actually place the serial number in the environment.

SETPATH.BAT
Chapter 13

Syntax: SETPATH

Prompts you for the elements to include in your path, one subdirectory at a time. After you've entered all the subdirectories, it gives you the option of making the path you just entered the current path. It also gives you the option of creating a batch file containing this path so you can easily reuse it.

SHOWLOOP.BAT
Chapter 5

Syntax: SHOWLOOP

SHOWLOOP.BAT goes through a simple loop 30 times. It requires MATH.BAT to be in the current subdirectory or path to work. This is a demonstration batch file; it performs no useful function beyond demonstrating how to loop in a batch file.

SMALLBAT.BAT
Chapter 4

Syntax: SMALLBAT *name*

SMALLBAT.BAT saves disk space by compressing all your batch files into one massive file using LHA. You run SMALLBAT by entering its name and the name of a batch file to run on the command line. For example, SMALLBAT CL2 would run CL2.BAT. SMALLBAT.BAT will uncompress the requested batch file and all associated batch files using LHA, run that batch file, and, when it terminates, deletes all the batch files. (Uncompressing doesn't affect the original copy inside the compressed file, so deleting the uncompressed copy won't delete the original copy of the batch file.)

Currently, SMALLBAT.BAT is designed to work with twelve of the sample batch files in the book. You'll need to modify the batch file to work with your own batch files before using it.

SMALLBAT.BAT uses LHA, a copyrighted but free utility program. LHA is included on the book's distribution disk so you can uncompress the batch files that come with the book. This allows you to use SMALLBAT.BAT as written, modify SMALLBAT .BAT to run your own files, and compress your batch files inside the SMALLBAT.LZH file used by SMALLBAT.BAT.

SMARTCHK.BAT
Chapter 10

Syntax: SMARTCHK [drive]

This batch file runs CHKDSK on the specified drive (or default if not specified) and reports the results. It also sets the errorlevel to one for noncontiguous files, two for lost clusters, and three for cross-linked files.

SP.BAT
Chapter 13

Syntax: SP

This batch file lists the subdirectories in your path, one per line, with a number to the left of the subdirectory indicating that subdirectory's position in your path.

STARTAPP.BAT
Chapter 11

Syntax: STARTAPP

STARTAPP.BAT is a demonstration batch file designed to run from the AUTOEXEC.BAT file rather than from the command line. Use it to see if an application is pending to run when the computer is rebooted. STARTAPP.BAT performs no useful function beyond demonstrating how to use a batch file to deal with an inappropriate environment. *See also* 01.BAT and 02.BAT.

STARTDAT.BAT
Chapter 7

Syntax: STARTDAT David/Ronny

STARTDAT.BAT is a demonstration program that activates one of two setups, depending on which user name is entered on the command line. STARTDAT.BAT performs no useful function beyond demonstrating how to reconfigure some application programs with a batch file. *See also* STARTWOR.BAT.

STARTWOR.BAT
Chapter 7

Syntax: STARTWOR David/Ronny

STARTWOR.BAT is a demonstration program that activates one of two setups of Microsoft Word, depending on which user name is entered on the command line, but performs no useful function beyond this. *See also* STARTDAT.BAT.

STORE.BAT
Chapter 5

Syntax: STORE S/R

STORE.BAT will write the contents of the ONE, TEN, and HUNDRED environmental variables to a file on the disk using the S option, or recall them from the disk file using the R option. The disk file it uses is C:\STORE-IT.BAT. If this file already exists, STORE .BAT will overwrite it.

STOREVOL.BAT
Chapter 12

Syntax: STOREVOL

STOREVOL.BAT is designed to be created and executed by GETVOL.BAT and should not be run from the command line. For a typical disk, STOREVOL.BAT will contain text like VOLUME in drive C is C DRIVE. When this is executed, it runs VOLUME.BAT and control doesn't pass back to STOREVOL.BAT. *See also* GETVOL.BAT, VOLUME.BAT, and VOLUME1.BAT.

TECH-AID.BAT
Chapter 12

Syntax: TECH-AID

TECH-AID.BAT creates a file in the root directory of the C drive called TECH-AID.TXT, which contains a detailed listing of the status of the computer. This file is useful for describing the status of your computer when calling for technical support. TECH-AID.BAT requires DOS 5.0 in order to work properly.

TESTCOM5.BAT
Chapter 9

Syntax: TESTCOM5

TESTCOM5.BAT tests COMMAND.COM against a known good copy to see if COMMAND.COM has been infected. TESTCOM5.BAT requires a known clean copy of COMMAND.COM stored as C:\MISC\TEST.TXT. In addition, TESTCOM5.BAT uses the DOS FC program, so it must be in the current subdirectory or in the path. TESTCOM5.BAT assumes that you have COMMAND.COM located in the C:\SYSLIB subdirectory. If you have COMMAND.COM located in the root directory or another sub-directory, you'll need to modify TESTCOM5.BAT before using it. As written, TEST-COM5.BAT requires DOS 5.0 to work, but you can easily modify it to work with any other DOS release.

TESTCOMM.BAT
Chapter 9

Syntax: TESTCOMM

TESTCOMM.BAT tests COMMAND.COM against a known good copy to see if COM-MAND.COM has been infected. TESTCOMM.BAT requires a clean copy of COM-MAND.COM stored as C:\MISC\TEST.TXT. In addition, TESTCOMM.BAT uses the DOS FC program, so FC must be in the current subdirectory or in the path. TEST-COMM.BAT assumes you have COMMAND.COM located in the C:\SYSLIB subdirec-tory. If COMMAND.COM is located in the root directory or another subdirectory, you'll need to modify TESTCOMM.BAT before using it.

TESTENVI.BAT
Chapter 19

Syntax: TESTENVI

TESTENVI.BAT is a batch file you can use to test the environment after using one of the techniques in the book to expand the environment. TESTENVI.BAT creates nineteen long environmental variables $(1-19)$ and then displays the environment, so you can see if all nineteen were successfully created.

TESTGOTO.BAT
Chapter 19

Syntax: TESTGOTO *label*

TESTGOTO.BAT issues a GOTO %1 command. Most batch files that use this command issue it blindly, assuming the user enters the replaceable parameter properly. TESTGO-TO.BAT doesn't; it tests the batch file first to make sure the requested label exists. TESTGOTO.BAT performs no useful function beyond this.

TEXTFND4.BAT
Chapter 19

Syntax: TEXTFND4 *text*

TEXTFND4.BAT is a brute-force approach for constructing an environmental variable containing all the replaceable parameters entered on the command line, with the variables %2 and higher separated with a single space and surrounded by quotation marks. TEXT-FND4.BAT uses multiple IF tests and has a different command line for each outcome. *See also* TEXTFND5.BAT.

TEXTFND5.BAT
Chapter 19

Syntax: TEXTFND5 *text*

TEXTFND5.BAT is a brute-force approach to constructing an environmental variable containing all the replaceable parameters entered on the command line, with the variables %2 and higher separated with a single space and surrounded by quotation marks. TEXT-FND5.BAT develops an environmental variable logically and is therefore a better method than the brute-force approach of TEXTFND4.BAT. *See also* TEXTFND4.BAT.

TP.BAT
Chapter 13

Syntax: TP

This batch file tests each subdirectory in your path to make sure that each one is valid, and reports any subdirectories in your path that don't exist. The technique used in TP.BAT can't be used to test for root directories, like C: \ , so it automatically passes C: \ and D: \ if they appear in your path. Users with additional drives where the root directories of those drives appear in their path don't need to modify TP.BAT.

UNBLANK.BAT
Chapter 18

Syntax: UNBLANK

UNBLANK.BAT sets the foreground color to bright white and the background color to blue, undoing the screen blanking of BLANK.BAT. Note that this color assignment is permanent and won't change with a CLS command. If you want to use UNBLANK.BAT, you must load ANSI.SYS in your CONFIG.SYS file. *See also* BLANK.BAT.

USEOVER.BAT
Chapter 6

Syntax: USEOVER [*command*]

If you run USEOVER.BAT followed by an optional command, it first stores that command in the environment and then executes it. If you run USEOVER.BAT without the optional command, it executes the last command stored in the environment. Because USEOVER .BAT stores the command in the environment, you must have enough free environmental space to store the command.

VERSION.BAT
Chapter 7

Syntax: VERSION

Beginning with DOS 3.3, you can immediately turn command-echoing off by preceding the command with an @. In addition, one batch file can call another and regain control when it terminates using the CALL command. VERSION.BAT allows people writing batch files running under both pre- and post-3.3 DOS systems to issue consistent commands.

VERSION.BAT configures three environmental variables. @ is set to nul for pre-3.3 DOS and to @ for post-3.3 DOS systems so commands can be preceded with a %@%. Echoing will be immediately turned off in post-DOS 3.3 systems, and pre-3.3 DOS systems will run normally with echoing on.

The environmental variable CALL is set to COMMAND/C on pre-3.3 DOS systems and CALL on post-3.3 DOS systems, so the command to call a batch file will work under either set of DOS. Finally, the environmental variable VERSION is set to either 2.0 or 3.3, giving batch files that will work only under post-3.3 DOS a method of testing for the version.

VOLUME.BAT
Chapter 12

Syntax: VOLUME in drive C is *volume*

VOLUME.BAT is designed to be run by STOREVOL.BAT or SERIAL.BAT, and not executed from the command line. When STOREVOL.BAT runs VOLUME.BAT, it passes VOLUME.BAT information on the command line. If the volume label contains no spaces, then it's passed to VOLUME.BAT as %5. If the volume label contains spaces, VOLUME .BAT won't work properly. For that, you need to use VOLUME1.BAT. *See also* GET-VOL.BAT, STOREVOL.BAT, and VOLUME1.BAT. When SERIAL.BAT passes the serial number to VOLUME.BAT, it's passed as %4. Serial numbers don't contain spaces.

VOLUME1.BAT
Chapter 12

Syntax: VOLUME in drive C is *volume*

VOLUME1.BAT is a replacement for VOLUME.BAT that will work when the volume label contains spaces. In order to work, VOLUME1.BAT must be renamed VOLUME .BAT.

VOLUME1.BAT is designed to be run by STOREVOL.BAT and not executed from the command line. When STOREVOL.BAT runs VOLUME1.BAT, it passes VOLUME1 .BAT information on the command line. If the volume label contains no spaces, then it's passed to VOLUME1.BAT as %5, %6, and so on. Because a volume label is limited to eleven characters, it contains a maximum of six single-character components separated by five single spaces. VOLUME1.BAT handles even this extreme case properly. *See also* GETVOL.BAT, STOREVOL.BAT, and VOLUME.BAT.

21

Batch file utilities

BatScreen

BatScreen was written by Doug Amaral of Hyperkinetix, the maker of Builder, especially for this book. The BatScreen screen compiler combines the ease of creating an ASCII file with much of the power of writing a program.

BatScreen takes an ASCII text file and converts it to a small .COM file. When you enter the name of the .COM file, the text will flash up on the screen almost instantly. To run BatScreen from DOS, simply enter BS at the command line.

When you run BatScreen, it first presents a screen showing all the nonblinking color choices with a box around the currently selected color combination. Use the cursor to move the box to the color combination you want. If you want the text to blink, press PgDn and select from the blinking text in the same fashion.

Next, BatScreen prompts you for the name of an ASCII file. To completely fill the screen, the ASCII file should contain 80 columns and 24 rows. If the file is larger, BatScreen will ignore the excess. If you enter the name incorrectly, BatScreen won't spot it until it tries to create the .COM file. Finally, BatScreen asks you if you want to clear the screen when the program displays. Answer Yes and the .COM file will clear the entire screen, set it to the colors you selected, and display the contents of the ASCII file. Answer No and the .COM file will clear off only enough lines to display the message. The original ASCII file isn't modified and doesn't need to be present for the .COM file to operate, so you can modify and recompile it if you ever need to change the screen.

BatScreen makes excellent menus. You can also use BatScreen to reset the cursor, change the screen colors, and generate colorful, attention-grabbing messages for your batch files. After trying BatScreen, I'm sure you'll agree that Doug has produced an excellent batch file tool. In fact, I use it almost exclusively for my batch file screens.

Batcmd

Like BatScreen, version 1.0 of Batcmd was written by Doug Amaral of Hyperkinetix for this book. I added a couple of commands and made some minor modifications to produce version 1.1, which is included in this book. Batcmd (short for *batch commands*) is a program designed to be run from inside a batch file. The general format of the command is

BATCMD *keyword* [*prompt*]

where *keyword* is a two letter command abbreviation that tells Batcmd what to do, and *prompt* is an optional message to the user to tell him what information to enter. The prompt can contain multiple words and shouldn't be enclosed in quotation marks.

Most of the Batcmd keywords cause Batcmd to either get information from the user or from the computer. In most cases, that information is passed back to the batch file through the errorlevel. The following is a description of the Batcmd commands, or keywords:

AD (add one to the math environmental variable)

This command adds one to the contents of the MATH environmental variable. If MATH doesn't exist, Batcmd will display an error message and do nothing. If MATH exists but contains something other than a number, its contents are treated as though they were a zero. As a result, its value is replaced with a one (zero plus one).

BE (beep the speaker)

This command beeps the speaker. If the command is entered as BATCMD BE, then it beeps the speaker once. If it's entered as BATCMD BE *n*, then it will beep the speaker *n* number of times. Once started, this beeping can't be aborted, so Batcmd limits *n* to 99. If you have a specific need to beep the speaker more than 99 times, you can repeatedly run BATCMD BE *n* or include it in a FOR loop.

BS (blank the screen)

This command clears the screen, the same way as the DOS CLS command. However, if you enter colors after the command, it will clear the screen to those colors. The command format is BATCMD BS *foreground background*. Table 21-1 shows the numbers that can be used with the BS command. You can use all sixteen numbers for the foreground color, but only 0−7 for the background color.

CC (check conventional memory)

This command checks to see how much conventional memory is available and returns the number of 32K blocks in the errorlevel. An errorlevel value of 10, therefore, indicates that 320K is free. Use this command to make sure enough memory is available; a program being run by a batch file is particularly sensitive to available memory. Keep in mind that available memory is reduced by the memory used by Batcmd before this measurement is made.

CE (check environmental memory)

This command checks to see how much environmental space is free and returns the number of bytes in the errorlevel. Because the errorlevel is limited to an integer between 0 and

Table 21-1 Colors you can use with the Batcmd BS command.

Number	Color	Number	Color
0	Black	8	Gray
1	Blue	9	Bright blue
2	Green	10	Bright green
3	Cyan	11	Bright cyan
4	Red	12	Bright red
5	Magenta	13	Bright magenta
6	Brown	14	Yellow
7	White	15	Bright white

255, this command will return 255 for any environment where the free environmental space exceeds 255 bytes. This is a good way for batch files that depend on the environment to check before running to make sure space is available.

CH (Check number of hard drives)

This command checks to see how many hard drives are installed. It sets the errorlevel equal to the number of hard drives. This command checks the number of physical hard drives, not the number of partitions. Thus, a 100Mg drive that's partitioned into three 32Mg partitions and a fourth 4Mg partition will still count as one physical drive to Batcmd. It doesn't include any CD ROM drives or other nonstandard drives in the calculation.

CL (Check LIM memory)

This command checks to see how much LIM memory is free and returns with an errorlevel equal to the number of 32K blocks of expanded memory.

CM (check the mouse)

This command sets the errorlevel to one if it finds a mouse, zero otherwise.

CS (check space)

This command checks to see how much free space is available on a drive and returns the number of 32K blocks of free space in the errorlevel. When free space exceeds $255 \times 32K$ or 8,160K, it returns 255. If the command is entered as BATCMD CS, it uses the default drive. If the command is entered as BATCMD CS *drive*, then it checks the amount of free space on the specified drive.

EX (Exit)

This command is entered as BATCMD EX *n*, where *n* is a number 0−255. Batcmd sets the errorlevel to the number specified and exits. If no number is specified, Batcmd sets the errorlevel to zero. If a fractional number is specified, Batcmd uses only the integer portion of the number. So BATCMD EX 33.3 would result in an errorlevel value of 33. If a number over 255 is specified, 256 will be repeatedly subtracted from the specified number until the resulting number is between 0 and 255, the only valid values for the errorlevel. If a number under zero is specified, 256 will be repeatedly added to the specified number until the resulting number is 0−255.

GE (get to environment)

This command accepts a multicharacter response and stores it in the master copy of the environment under the variable BATCMD. This command will display a prompt if one is entered on the command line after the GE. This command limits user inputs to 65 characters and will stop accepting keystrokes when that limit is reached. If there's inadequate free environmental space to store the response in the environment, the response will be lost and nothing will be stored in the environment.

GF (get from list)

This command accepts a keystroke only if it's on the list of acceptable keystrokes. The format of the command is BATCMD GF *list prompt*, where *list* is a listing of all valid keystrokes without spaces between them and *prompt* is the message to display. The list of keystrokes is case-sensitive so, in order to accept only A−C in either case, the command would have to be entered as BATCMD GF AaBbCc *prompt*. If you enter an invalid keystroke, Batcmd will beep and continue waiting for a valid keystroke. Once you enter a valid keystroke, Batcmd will set the errorlevel to that keystroke's position in the list. So, for the above example, if you entered a B the errorlevel would be set to three because a capital B is the third character in the list.

GK (get key)

This command accepts any keystroke and exits with the errorlevel set to the ASCII value of that keystroke. This command can display an optional prompt if it's included after the GK command.

GL (get letter)

This command accepts any letter and exits with the errorlevel set to one for an A, two for a B, and so on. If any other keystroke is entered, Batcmd will beep and continue waiting for a letter. This command can display an optional prompt if it's included after the command.

GN (get number)

This command accepts any single-digit number and exits with the errorlevel set to that number. If any other keystroke is entered, Batcmd will beep and continue waiting for a number. This command can display an optional prompt if it's included after the command.

GU (get uppercase letter)

This command accepts only uppercase letters. If you enter a lowercase letter or any non-letter keystroke, Batcmd will beep and continue waiting for an uppercase letter. This command can display an optional prompt if it's included after the command.

PC (position cursor)

This command positions the cursor at the specified coordinates on the screen. The format of the command is BATCMD PC *row column*, where *row* is the row number to move the cursor to $(1-24)$ and *column* is the column number to move the cursor to $(1-80)$. If a noninteger row or column number is used, the fractional portion of the number will be ignored. If a zero, negative number, or number outside the acceptable boundaries is used, Batcmd will abort with an error message and set the errorlevel to one.

RB (reboot the computer)

This command performs a warm reboot of the computer.

SD (store day)

This command stores the day of the month in the errorlevel. If the date is March 21, Batcmd SD would set the errorlevel to 21.

SH (store hour)

This command stores the hour of the day, in twenty-four hour format, in the errorlevel. If the time is 6:30 p.m., Batcmd SH would set the errorlevel to 18.

SL (skip line)

This command causes a batch file to skip a single line on the screen, just like echoing an Alt−255.

SM (store minute)

This command stores the minute of the hour in the errorlevel. If the time is 6:30 p.m., Batcmd SM would set the errorlevel to 30.

SO (store month)

This command stores the month of the year in the errorlevel. If the date is March 21, Batcmd SO would set the errorlevel to three.

SS (store second)

This command stores the second in errorlevel. Of course, this information changes rapidly, but the errorlevel is updated only each time the command is run. If the time is 6:30 and 15 seconds, Batcmd SS would set the errorlevel to 15.

SU (Subtract one from the math environmental variable)

This command subtracts one from the contents of the MATH environmental variable. If MATH doesn't exist, Batcmd will display an error message and do nothing. If MATH exists but contains something other than a number, its contents will be treated as though they were a zero.

SY (store year)

This command stores the last two digits of the year in the errorlevel, so 1992 is stored as 92 and 2000 is stored as zero.

YN (yes or no)

This command accepts only an N or Y keystroke in either upper- or lowercase. For an N, Batcmd YN would set the errorlevel to zero; for a Y, it would set it to one.

Table 21-2 shows a brief summary of the Batcmd keywords and their function.

Table 21-2   The Batcmd keywords.

Command abbreviation	Command name	Function
AD	Add	Adds one to the number stored in the MATH environmental variable.
BE	Beep	Beeps the speaker.
BS	BlankScreen	Clears the screen, optionally using the colors specified after the BS command.
CC	CheckConventional	Returns the amount of free conventional memory in 32K blocks.
CE	CheckEnvironment	Returns with an errorlevel equal to the amount of free environmental space up to 255 bytes, setting it to 255 for that amount and over.
CH	CheckHard	Returns with an errorlevel 0 if no hard disk is installed; otherwise sets the errorlevel equal to the number of logical hard disk drives installed.
CL	CheckLim	Returns with an errorlevel equal to the number of 32K blocks of expanded memory.
CM	CheckMouse	Returns with an errorlevel of 1 if there's a mouse, 0 otherwise.
CS	CheckSpace	Returns with an errorlevel equal to the number of 32K blocks free on the specified drive. If no drive specified, it uses the default.

Table 21-2   Continued.

Command abbreviation	Command name	Function
EX	Exit	Sets the errorlevel to the number specified after the EX and exit.
GE	GetEnvironment	Displays an optional prompt, accepts a multi-character input from the user, and stores it in the environment under the name BATCMD .
GF	GetFromList	Displays an optional prompt, accepts an input only if it's contained in the list following the prompt, and exits with an errorlevel equal to one for the first item in list, two for the second, and so on.
GK	GetKey	Displays an optional prompt, accepts any keystroke, and exits with the ASCII value of that keystroke.
GL	GetLetter	Displays an optional prompt, accepts a letter, and exits with an errorlevel of 1 for A, 2 for B, and so on. If the user presses any other keystroke, it beeps and continues waiting for a number.
GN	GetNumber	Displays an optional prompt, accepts a single-digit number, and exits with an errorlevel equal to that number. If the user presses any other keystroke, it beeps and continues waiting for a number.
GU	GetUpper	Displays an optional prompt, accepts an uppercase letter, and exits with an errorlevel equal to the ASCII value of the letter. If the user presses a lowercase letter or any nonletter keystroke, it beeps and continues waiting for an uppercase letter.
PC	PositionCursor	Positions the cursor on the row and column specified after the PC.
RB	Reboot	Reboots the computer.
SD	StoreDay	Returns with an errorlevel equal to the day of the month.
SH	ShowHour	Returns with an errorlevel equal to the hour of the day, in 24-hour format.
SL	SkipLine	Skips one blank line on the screen.
SM	StoreMinute	Returns with an errorlevel equal to the minute.
SO	StoreMonth	Returns with an errorlevel equal to the month.

Table 21-2 Continued.

Command abbreviation	Command name	Function
SS	StoreSecond	Returns with an errorlevel equal to the second.
SU	Subtract	Subtracts one from the number stored in the MATH environmental variable.
SY	StoreYear	Returns with an errorlevel equal to the last two digits of the year. If possible, have it work properly for 2000 and beyond.

LHA version 2.13

LHA is a file compression program written by Haruyasu Yoshizaki. It's a copyrighted program, but Haruyasu Yoshizaki doesn't charge for its use. A copy of LHA is included on the disk.

LHA reads a series of files, compresses them, and stores them in a common file. Once the files are compressed and consolidated, you can use LHA to remove and uncompress any of the files from the common file. This doesn't change the storage file. The general form of an LHA command is:

LHA [*command*][*options*] *storage_file files_to_include*

The commands that can be used on the command line are as follows:

A (Add)

This command compresses the files and adds them to the archive file. If the file doesn't exist, it will be created. If it does exist, files will be appended into it. If the archive file contains a file and a file with the same name is added to it, LHA will overwrite the one already contained in the archive file. For example, the command:

LHA A BAT *.BAT

would compress all the batch files in the current subdirectory and store them in a file called BAT.LZH. If BAT.LZH already contains files newer than those in the current subdirectory, the ones in BAT.LZH would be replaced.

D (delete)

This deletes a file stored in the archive file. For example, the command:

LHA D BAT EXAMPLE?.BAT

would delete all the EXAMPLE?.BAT files in BAT.LZH.

E (extract)

This extracts files from an archive file. If no name is included on the command line, all the files will be extracted; otherwise, just those files matching the file specification. Files aren't extracted if they will overwrite a newer file with the same name. For example, the command:

    LHA E BAT CAPITAL?.BAT

would extract all the CAPITAL?.BAT files stored in BAT.LZH as long as a newer version of one of those files doesn't already exist in the current subdirectory.

F (freshen)

This works identically to the update command (U) except that files are stored in the archive file only if they already exist in the file, and if the version to be added is newer than the one already in the archive file. For example, the command:

    LHA F BAT C: \ BAT \ TEXT*.BAT

would replace all the TEXT*.BAT files in BAT.LZH with any newer versions that exist in the C: \ BAT subdirectory.

L (List)

This lists the files stored in an archive file by name only. Using a /x switch will add the path stored in the archive to that file, if any.

M (move)

This works identically to the update command (U) except that, once files are stored in the archive file, the original version of the file is deleted. For example, the command:

    LHA U TXT *.TXT

will compress all the text files in the current subdirectory and store them in a file called TXT.LZH. If TXT.LZH already contains files newer than those in the current subdirectory, the ones in TXT.LZH won't be replaced. In addition, all the text files in the current subdirectory will be deleted.

P (Print)

This extracts the file and prints it to the screen. The output can also be piped to a printer. For example, the command

    LHA P FANCY *.DOC > LPT2

would extract all the *.DOC files from the FANCY.LZH archive file and print them to the printer attached to LPT2.

S (self-extract)

This turns an .LZH file into a self-extracting program. For example, the command

    LHA S BATCH

would take BATCH.LZH and turn it into BATCH.EXE. When the user runs BATCH .EXE, all the files stored in BATCH.LZH—and therefore BATCH.EXE—would be extracted without the user having LHA or knowing how to use it.

T (test)

This tests the integrity of the archive file using a cyclical redundancy check.

U (update)

This works identically to the add command (A) except when a file to be added is already stored in the archive file. In that case, the file is stored to the archive file only if it's newer than the one already stored in the file. For example, the command

    LHA U TXT *.TXT

would compress all the text files in the current subdirectory and store them in a file called TXT.LZH. If TXT.LZH already contains files newer than those in the current subdirectory, the ones in TXT.LZH wouldn't be replaced.

X (extract)

This is identical to the Extract command except that files stored in the archive file are extracted with their full path. For example, if the file EXE.LZH contains all the .EXE files from the C:\DOS subdirectory and they've been archived with their full path, the command

    LHA E EXE *.EXE

would extract those files to the current subdirectory, no matter what its name is. On the other hand, the command:

    LHA X EXE *.EXE

would extract the files to the C:\DOS subdirectory, no matter what the current subdirectory is.

LHA also has a number of switches to alter its operation. These are explained in full in the documentation file that accompanies the program on the disk.

Summary

- BatScreen (BS.EXE) will take an ASCII file and turn it into a small .COM file that quickly displays the contents of that ASCII file on the screen. When creating the .COM file, you have full control over its colors.

- Batcmd is a batch file utility that gives you a number of useful options when writing batch files. Many of the batch files in this book use Batcmd, so if you want to experiment you can copy BATCMD.EXE to a subdirectory in your path.
- LHA is a compression program that I used to archive the batch files that come with this book. It offers a wealth of features to reduce the amount of space files required on a hard disk.

Appendix A
DOS command summary

Command	Syntax and description	Version of DOS added	Internal or external
APPEND	Establishes a "path" for files other than .COM, .EXE, and .BAT. Useful with older programs that don't support subdirectories.	3.3	External
ANSI.SYS	DEVICE=ANSI.SYS (in CONFIG.SYS file) A program to extend control over the screen.	2.0	External
ASSIGN	ASSIGN B=A Reassigns drive letters so one drive appears to be another drive. Useful with inflexible programs that expect data to be on a specific drive.	2.0	External
ATTRIB	ATTRIB [+R][-R][+A][-A] *file* Changes the read-only and archive flags of files. Enhanced in DOS 3.3 to process subdirectories as well as files.	3.0	External
BACKUP	BACKUP C:*path**files* A: [/S][/M][/A][/D] Makes a copy of files from a hard disk to floppy disks. The files must be restored to be useful. DOS 3.0 adds the ability to automatically format disks while performing a backup, and the ability to back up files modified after a certain date. Backups created prior to DOS 3.0 aren't compatible with later RESTORE programs. Backups created prior to DOS 3.2 aren't compatible with later RESTORE programs. Beginning with DOS 3.3, BACKUP will format disks if the /F option is included. Also, only two files are created on each disk, CONTROL.# and BACKUP.#, where # is the disk number. Using this method, BACKUP is about one-third faster than prior versions. DOS 3.3 also adds a /T option to back up files modified after a specified date, and a /L option to create a log file to store the names of the backed-up files. Performance is also greatly improved. Beginning with DOS 4.0, BACKUP will format disks that need it automatically without using a command-line switch.	2.0	External

Command	Syntax and description	Version of DOS added	Internal or external
BASIC	BASIC Programming language built into ROM memory on IBM computers. Other brands don't generally support a ROM-based BASIC program. Enhanced in DOS 3.3 to be more compatible with BASICA.	1.0	Internal
BASICA	BASICA *filename* A programming language, more advanced than BASIC. Many clones will name this program BASICA or GWBASIC. DOS 1.05 removed major bugs.	1.0	External
BREAK	BREAK [=ON] [=OFF] Controls how often DOS checks for a Ctrl-Break from the keyboard. Can be used either as a DOS command or in the CONFIG.SYS file.	2.0	Internal
BUFFERS	BUFFERS=# Included in the CONFIG.SYS file. Enhanced in DOS 3.3 so the default is tied to the machine's configuration. Enhanced in DOS 4.0 so it can read additional sectors and use expanded memory.	2.0	Internal
CALL	CALL *batch file* Runs a second batch file from within a first batch file. When the second batch file finishes, control is automatically passed back to the first batch file. Because this doesn't load a second copy of COMMAND.COM, any changes the second batch file makes to the environment are passed back to the first batch file (and DOS) when the second batch file terminates.	3.3	Internal
CD or CHDIR	CD *directory* Change subdirectories.	2.0	Internal
CHCP	CHCP *n* Displays or changes the active code page, where *n* is the code page specification.	3.3	Internal
CHKDSK	CHKDSK [/F] [/V] A program that checks subdirectories and files against their file allocation table entries. DOS 2.0 makes the corrective action (/F) optional.	1.0	External
CLS	CLS Clears the screen.	2.0	Internal
COMMAND	COMMAND *path* [E:xx] /C *string* Loads a second command processor. Beginning with DOS 3.0, it optionally expands the environment. (This isn't documented until DOS 3.1.) You add it to the CONFIG.SYS file. In DOS 3.3, the Fail option was added to critical error messages to allow easier stopping of certain processes.	1.0	External

Command	Syntax and description	Version of DOS added	Internal or external
COMP	COMP *file set 1 file set 2* Compares the contents of two sets of files to see if they're the same. Beginning with DOS 2.0, it adds the use of wildcards.	1.0	External
COMSPEC	COMSPEC= Included in CONFIG.SYS file. Defines an alternate path to COMMAND.COM.	2.0	Internal
COPY	COPY *drive*:*path**file drive*:*path**file* [/A][/B][/V] Copies files from one location to another. DOS 2.0 adds binary (/b) copying and verification (/v) while copying.	1.0	Internal
COUNTRY	COUNTRY=# Included in CONFIG.SYS file. It was added as an internal command in DOS 3.0 and changed to an external command in DOS 3.3.	3.0/3.3	Internal/ External
CTTY	CTTY *device* Allows you to use a remote terminal in place of a console.	2.0	Internal
DATE	DATE Sets the system date. It was an external command prior to DOS 1.1. Beginning with DOS 3.3, it also sets the time in the CMOS clock.	1.0	Internal
DEBUG	DEBUG *file* Examines and modifies files, memory, and disk contents.	1.0	External
DEL	DEL *files* /P Removes files from a disk. /P (prompt before erasing each file) was added in DOS 4.0.	1.1	Internal
DEVICE	DEVICE=*driver* Attaches a device driver to DOS. Included in CONFIG.SYS.	2.0	Internal
DEVICEHIGH	DEVICEHIGH *driver* Loads device drivers into high memory. Requires a 80386SX, 80386, or 80486 computer and EMM386 loaded first.	5.0	Internal
DIR	DIR [*path*] *files* [/P][/W] [/O*option*] Lists files on a disk or in a subdirectory. DOS 2.0 adds a volume label and time to the directory display. Note that DIR handles wildcards differently from other programs. Specifically, DIR * will display the same files as will DIR *.* while other programs require the full file specification. This can cause some confusion when a batch file uses the DIR command to display files and then the DEL command to delete them. DOS 5.0 adds the option to sort the display with /O. Sorting methods are name, extension, date, and size. The normal sort is smallest to largest, but you can reverse it by preceding the switch with a negative sign.	1.0	Internal

Command	Syntax and description	Version of DOS added	Internal or external
DISKCOMP	DISKCOMP *drive drive* [/1][/8] Compares two floppy disks to see if they are the same.	1.0	External
DISKCOPY	DISKCOPY *drive drive* [/1] Makes an exact copy of one disk on a second disk.	1.0	External
DISPLAY.SYS	DEVICE=DISPLAY.SYS Device driver for displaying the character sets from other countries on the screen.	3.3	External
DO	FOR %J IN (*.*) DO *command* Part of the FOR command.	2.0	Internal
DOS	DOS=[HIGH/LOW] [UMB/NOUMB] DOS=HIGH loads most of DOS into high memory. The UMB option keeps certain links open, allowing memory-resident software to be loaded into free high memory. This requires a 80286 or higher processor.	5.0	Internal
DOSKEY	DOSKEY /reinstall /bufsize= /dmacs /dhist macro= [insert/overstrike] Loads a small (4K) program to recall prior commands and allow command alaising. Options include: o Loading more than one copy o Changing the buffer size o Listing the macros o Listing the available commands o Defining a macro o Altering the default insert/overstrike mode for editing	5.0	Internal
DOSSHELL	DOSSHELL [G[:*resolution*[#]] /T[:*resolution*[#]]] /B A DOS shell that allows users to run programs from a menu and rapidly switch between programs without exiting any of the programs (task switching.) It doesn't support multitasking.	4.0	External
DRIVER.SYS	DEVICE=DRIVER.SYS /D[/C][/F:*f*][/H:*hh*][/N][/S:*ss*][/T:*tt*] Gives new names to logical devices.	3.2	External
DRIVPRAM	DRIVPRAM /d:*number* /c /f:*factor* /h:*heads* /i /n /s:*sectors* /t:*tracks* Modifies the parameters used for an existing drive.	3.2	Internal
ECHO	ECHO ON/OFF or ECHO *message* Turns echo on and off, or displays a message on the screen.	2.0	Internal
EDIT	EDIT *filename* Runs the excellent ASCII editor included with DOS 5.0. This editor is very much like the editor built into QuickBasic.	5.0	External

Command	Syntax and description	Version of DOS added	Internal or external
EDLIN	EDLIN *file* Simple ASCII file editor. Major improvements were introduced with DOS 2.0.	1.0	External
EMM386	EMM386 [on/off/auto] [w=on/off] This is the DOS 5.0 memory manager for 80386SX, 80386, and 80486 computers. It simulates expanded memory using extended memory, and it allows you to load device drivers and memory-resident software into high memory. It also enables and disables support for the Weitek coprocessor.	5.0	External
ERASE	ERASE *files* /P Remove files from a disk. /P (prompt before erasing each file) was added in DOS 4.0.	1.0	Internal
ERRORLEVEL	IF ERRORLEVEL # DO *command* Batch file command for reading ERRORLEVEL as set by other programs.	2.0	Internal
EXE2BIN	EXE2BIN *files files* Convert .EXE files to binary format. (Not all files can be converted.)	1.1	External
EXIST	IF EXIST *.* *command* Batch file command for testing if a file is present. Part of the IF statement.	2.0	Internal
EXIT	EXIT Removes the most recently loaded COMMAND.COM from memory. Has no impact if only one copy is in memory.	2.0	Internal
EXPAND	EXPAND [*path*]*source* [*path*]*target* DOS 5.0 files are shipped compressed, and need to be decompressed by the installation program. If necessary, the EXPAND program can manually decompress individual files or groups of files.	5.0	External
FASTOPEN	FASTOPEN *drive:*=*xx,yy* The FASTOPEN command remembers where files are located on a disk once you use them. That makes repeated access to files much faster. The *drive* is the drive to use FASTOPEN on, and it should be a hard disk. The *xx* is the number of files and subdirectories to retain in memory. The range is 10-999 and the default is 34. The *yy* is the number of continuous space buffers for the files identified. You can omit this if you specify a drive letter but no value for xx; otherwise, its default is 34. FASTOPEN can use a /X switch to perform its functions in expanded memory beginning with DOS 4.0. FASTOPEN doesn't adjust the location it has for files if you run a disk optimizer. Therefore, you must reboot after optimizing or DOS won't be able to find your files when aided by FASTOPEN.	3.3	External

Command	Syntax and description	Version of DOS added	Internal or external
FC	FC *file1 file2* [/A/B/C/L/LB#/N/T/W/#] Compares two files and reports any differences. Also sets the DOS errorlevel to one if the files are different.	2.0	External (MS-DOS only)
FCBS	FCBS=# Controls the maximum number of file control blocks that can be simultaneously open. Included in the CONFIG.SYS file.	3.0	Internal
FDISK	FDISK Initializes and partitions a hard disk; required before you format the disk. Beginning in DOS 3.3, it supports multiple DOS partitions.	2.0	External
FILES	FILES=# Controls how many files the entire system can have open at once. Included in the CONFIG.SYS file.	2.0	Internal
FIND	FIND [/V][/C][/N] *"string"* A filter for locating lines that contain a specific set of ASCII characters. Must be an exact match, including case. Generally used with DOS piping commands.	2.0	External
FOR	FOR %%j IN (SET) DO *command* Loops through items in (SET) and performs the command once per item. Generally used in batch file although it can also be used from the command line. When used from the command line, only one percent sign is used.	2.0	Internal
FORMAT	FORMAT *drive* [/S][/1][/8][/V][/N][/4] A program to prepare a hard or floppy disk for use. On a floppy disk, FORMAT performs a low-level formatting, a partitioning, and a high-level format. On a hard disk, FORMAT performs only the high-level formatting. FDISK performs the partitioning. DOS contains no low-level formatting. Must be included with the drive or performed at the factory. DOS 2.0 adds a volume label (/v). DOS 3.2 adds protection to keep you from accidentally formatting a hard disk. You must include the drive letter to format the default drive. In addition, you must enter the volume label to format a hard disk.	1.0	External
GOTO	GOTO *label* Batch file looping command.	2.0	Internal
GOTO	GOTO *label* Batch file looping command.	2.0	Internal
GRAFTABL	GRAFTABL Memory-resident program to load high-order characters into memory for graphics mode.	3.0	Internal

Command	Syntax and description	Version of DOS added	Internal or external
GRAPHICS	GRAPHICS Memory-resident program to allow screenn printing of graphic screens. Beginning with DOS 3.3, it's compatible with thermal and LCD printers.	2.0	External
HELP	HELP *command* Displays the help screen for a particular DOS command. It displays the same information as starting the command with the /? switch. Entering HELP without a command after it will display a list of DOS commands.	5.0	External
IF	IF [NOT] *condition command* Batch command to conditionally execute commands.	2.0	Internal
IN	FOR %J IN (*.*) DO *command* Part of the FOR command.	2.0	Internal
INSTALL	INSTALL=*drive:\path\file* Runs a memory-resident program while processing the CONFIG.SYS file. Only a few memory-resident programs, like SHARE, can be run this way.	4.0	Internal
JOIN	JOIN *path* [/D] A command to treat all the files in one drive or subdirectory as though they were in another drive or subdirectory.	3.1	External
KEYB??	KEYB[FR][GR][IT][SP][UK] A memory-resident program to change the keyboard translation and date and time formats for other countries.	3.0	External
LABEL	LABEL *drive label* Enters or changes a volume label.	3.0	External
LASTDRIVE	LASTDRIVE= This is a CONFIG.SYS command to specify the last drive. This command might be unnecessary in DOS 3.1 and higher. In these versions, the default last drive is E. When you specify a LASTDRIVE, you add 2K of overhead to DOS.	3.0	Internal
LINK	LINK Runs the LINK program. Generally used only by programmers.	1.0	External
LOADHIGH	LOADHIGH *drive:\path\file* Loads a memory-resident program into high memory. This requires a 80386SX or higher processor.	5.0	Internal
MD or MKDIR	MD [*drive*] *name* Creates a subdirectory.	2.0	Internal
MEM	MEM [/program] [/debug] Displays the amount of memory a system has quickly, without having to run the slower CHKDSK. It can also display the programs and internal drivers loaded into memory.	4.0	External

Command	Syntax and description	Version of DOS added	Internal or external
MIRROR	MIRROR [drives:] [/t drives[-entries]] [/1] [/u] Records information on disks that UNDELETE and REBUILD use to recover deleted files or formatted disks.	5.0	External
MODE	MODE [LPT1=COM] A program that controls the screen, printer, speed, display, and other important functions. Exact usage will depend on the brand of computer and the version of DOS in use. Major improvements made in DOS 1.1. DOS 3.3 adds support for COM3 and COM4 and transfer rates up to 19.2 kbps.	1.0	External
MORE	DIR	MORE Program to scroll data to the screen one screenful at a time.	2.0	External
NOT	IF NOT Batch file command for reversing a DOS decision. If the IF test is true, then the IF NOT test is false.	2.0	Internal
NLSFUNC	NLSFUNC *filename* Used in either the CONFIG.SYS file or from the command line to support country-specific information and code-page switching.	3.3	External
PATH	PATH=C:\;B:\;A:\;*path* Controls what drives and subdirectories DOS searches for programs and batch files.	2.0	Internal
PAUSE	PAUSE Batch file command to suspend execution until a key is pressed.	1.0	Internal

PRINT	PRINT *drive:\path\file* [/D:*device*] [/B:*buffer size*]
	    [/U:*busyticks*] [/M:*maximum ticks*]
	    [/S:*time slice*] [/Q:*queue size*] [/T] [/C] [/P]
	Memory-resident program to print ASCII files in the background while the computer is doing something else. DOS 3.0 changes the way PRINT gets CPU time for printing.
		2.0	External

PRINTER.SYS	DEVICE=PRINTER.SYS Device driver for changing the printer character set to that for another country.	3.3	External
PROMPT	PROMPT=*new prompt* Command to change the DOS prompt.	2.0	Internal
QBASIC	QBASIC *file* [/b] [/nohi] [/b] [/*editor*] [/g] [/mbf] Loads interpretive Quickbasic.	5.0	External
RD or RMDIR	RD *drive:\subdirectory* Command to remove an empty subdirectory.	2.0	Internal
RECOVER	RECOVER *drive:\path\files* Command to rescue files from a disk with bad sectors. Warning: This command has the potential to do a lot of damage and should be used only by experienced users and only after making a complete backup.	2.0	External

Command	Syntax and description	Version of DOS added	Internal or external
REM	REM *text* Batch file command to enter remarks in a batch file. Nothing after REM is executed.	1.0	Internal
REN or RENAME	REN *old new* Command to change the name of files.	1.1	Internal
REPLACE	REPLACE *drive:\path\files drive:\path\files* [/A][/D][/P] [/R][/S][/W] Selectively replaces files on a target drive or subdirectory with files of the same name from a different drive or subdirectory.	3.2	External
RESTORE	RESTORE *drive:\path\files* [/S][/P] Replaces files on a hard disk with those created on floppy disks during a backup. Major enhancements were made with DOS 3.0. Backups created prior to DOS 3.0 aren't compatible with later RESTORE programs. Backups created prior to DOS 3.2 aren't compatible with later RESTORE programs. Version 3.3 of DOS adds many new features. The /B:*date*, /A:*date*, /E:*time*, and /L:*time* switches restore files modified before or after a specified date and time, /M restores files modified or deleted since the last backup, and /N restores the files that have been deleted since the last backup.	2.0	External
SELECT	SELECT [A:/B:] *drive:\path* AAA BB A program to pick alternate keyboard and time formats for different countries.	3.0	External
SET	SET *name=string* A command to enter or delete variables from DOS environment.	2.0	Internal
SETVER	SETVER *drive:\path\file version number* Causes DOS to "lie" about its version number to the specified program. That way, programs that require a specific DOS version can run under DOS 5.0. This command requires a DEVICE=*drive:\path*\SETVER.EXE statement in the CONFIG.SYS file.	5.0	External
SHARE	SHARE *drive:\path\files* [/L:*locks*] A memory-resident program that controls file sharing on a network.	3.0	External
SHELL	SHELL= CONFIG.SYS command to replace COMMAND.COM with an alternate command processor, or to expand the DOS environment.	2.0	Internal
SHIFT	SHIFT A batch file command to make additional replaceable parameters available to DOS.	2.0	Internal

Command	Syntax and description	Version of DOS added	Internal or external
SORT	SORT [/R][/+n] A program that rearranges text into ASCII order. Generally used with DOS piping commands.	2.0	External
STACKS	STACKS=x,y Included in CONFIG.SYS to change the number of stack frames used to process hardware interrupts and their size. Enhanced in DOS 3.3 so the default is tied to the machine's configuration.	3.2	Internal
SUBST	SUBST drive:\path drive [/D] A command to treat a subdirectory as a drive.	3.1	Internal
SYS	SYS drive Moves the hidden system files to a drive.	1.0	Internal
TIME	TIME Sets DOS time. It's external prior to DOS 1.1. Beginning with DOS 3.3 it also sets the CMOS clock.	1.0	Internal
TREE	TREE drive [/F] Displays the tree structure of a drive.	2.0	External
TRUENAME	TRUENAME file Displays the true name of a file. For example, if you enter the command ASSIGN A=B, then the response to the command TRUENAME B:file, where file is actually on the A drive, will be A:file. The command is not documented.	4.00	Internal
TYPE	TYPE drive:\path\file Displays an ASCII file to the screen.	1.0	Internal
UNDELETE	UNDELETE file list [/dt] [/dos] [/all] Unerases the specified files.	5.0	External
UNFORMAT	UNFORMAT [drive] [/j] [l] [/test] [/p] Unformats a hard disk.	5.0	External
VDISK.SYS	DEVICE=drive:\path\VDISK.SYS size sector size directory entries DOS command to create an electronic drive. The DOS 2.0 manual contains source code.	3.0	External
VER	VER Displays the DOS version number.	2.0	Internal
VERIFY	VERIFY [ON][OFF] Controls whether DOS checks data after it writes to disk.	2.0	Internal
VOL	VOL drive Displays the volume label.	2.0	Internal
XCOPY	XCOPY drive:\path\files drive:\path\files [/A][/E][/M] [/P][/S][/V][/W] Advanced copy command. Unlike COPY, XCOPY sets the DOS errorlevel when it terminates.	3.2	External

Batch file information
for popular software

Program	Vendor	Default subdirectory	Startup command	Special interest items for batch files
@Liberty	SoftLogic Solutions	\LIBERTY	Prepare	Doesn't use command-line switches.
Alpha Four	Alpha Software	\ALPHA	A4	
Back-It 4	Gazelle Systems	\BACKIT4	BK4	Back-It 4 can run presets from the command line if you include the preset name with the program at startup.
Better Working One Person Office	Spinnaker Software	\ONE	ONE	
BitFax/SR	BIT Software	\BITFAX	COMSHELL	
Brooklyn Bridge Filer	Fifth Generation Systems	\BRIDGE	F	The Brooklyn Bridge Filer uses a number of command-line switches to control its operation. You can see these by entering F? on the command line.
ClassFILE	SoftLogic Solutions	\CLFILE	CF	Doesn't use command-line switches.
Cubit	SoftLogic Solutions	\CUBIT \CU or \MM	Cubit	Doesn't use command-line switches.
DataEase 4.2	DataEase International	\DEASE	DEASE	Enter the name of a database to load after the DEASE command to load it automatically.
dBXL 1.3R	WordTech Systems	\XL13R	DBXL	You can include the name of a program to execute immediately on the command line.
DESQview 386	Quaterdeck	\DV	\DV	The command DV runs a batch file called DV.BAT, so you must use the CALL command if you're going to call DESQview from within other batch files.
Disk Optimizer	SoftLogic Solutions	\DISKOPT	OPTIMIZE	Doesn't use command-line switches.
DoubleDOS	SoftLogic Solutions	\DD	DOUBLEDO	Doesn't use command-line switches.

Program	Vendor	Default subdirectory	Startup command	Special interest items for batch files
DR DOS 5.0	Digital Research	\DRDOS	NA	All DR DOS 5.0 commands can run from batch files, just like MS-DOS.
DrawPerfect 1.1	WordPerfect Corporation	\DR11	DR	Enter a filename to edit after the DR to automatically load the file.
EzTape for DOS	Irwin Magnetic Systems	\EZTAPE	EZTAPE	EzTape can back up and restore disk information, and manage the tape under batch control. The numerous batch-file options are well documented in the manual.
FATCAT	SoftLogic Solutions	\FATCAT	FATCAT	Doesn't use command-line switches.
File Director	Fifth Generation Systems	\FD	FD	File Director uses a number of command-line switches to control its operation. You can see these by entering FD? on the command line.
FoxBASE+ /LAN 2.10	Fox Software	User Selected	MFOXPLUS	-NOTIBM switch for use with machines not fully IBM-compatible.
FoxBASE+ 2.10	Fox Software	User Selected	FOXPLUS	-NOTIBM switch for use with machines not fully IBM-compatible.
FoxPro /LAN 1.02	Fox Software	User Selected	FOXPROLN	Same as FoxPro 1.02
FoxPro 1.02	Fox Software	User Selected	FOXPRO	-C *file* to specify a configuration file -E to prevent using expanded memory -K to prevent using F11 or F12 -T to suppress sign-on screen It can also automatically run a program if you specify the program name on the command line.
FoxPro 2.0	Fox Software	\FOXPRO2	FOXPRO	Same as FoxPro 1.02
FoxPro/LAN 2.0	Fox Software	\FOXPRO2	FOXPROL	Same as FoxPro 1.02
GeoWorks Ensemble 1.0	GeoWorks	\GEOWORKS	GEOS	If you want to be able to launch non-GeoWorks Ensemble applications from the GeoManager window just like you launch native applications, put the batch file into the \GEOWORKS\WORLD subdirectory. It will then show up alongside your other program icons.
GeoWorks Ensemble 1.2	GeoWorks	\GEOWORKS	GEOS	See note for version 1.0. In addition, beginning with 1.2, the program starts with a batch file rather than an .EXE program. If you launch GeoWorks Ensemble from a menu with a batch file, you need to start it with a CALL GEOS command so the batch file can regain control when GeoWorks Ensemble terminates.
Grammatik IV for DOS	Reference Software	\GMK	GMK	With Grammatik IV for DOS, you can specify the name of the input and output files on the command line, along with switches that control its operation.

Program	Vendor	Default subdirectory	Startup command	Special interest items for batch files
Logical Connection Junior	Fifth Generation Systems	\LCJ	LCJMODE	Logical Connection Junior uses command-line switches to control many of the program settings. You can see these by entering LCJMODE SYNTAX at the command line.
Logical Connector Plus	Fifth Generation Systems	\LCPLUS	LCP	Logical Connector Plus uses several command-line switches to control its operation. To see this, enter LCPSETUP ? at the command line.
1-2-3 Release 2.3	Lotus Development Corporation	\123R23	123	1-2-3 doesn't allow you to enter a filename on the command line to load it automatically.
1-2-3 Release 3.1	Lotus Development Corporation	\123R31	123	1-2-3 doesn't allow you to enter a filename on the command line to load it automatically.
Magic Mirror	SoftLogic Solutions	\MM	MM	Doesn't use command-line switches.
MathCAD	Mathsoft	\MCAD	MCAD	MathCAD can load a file automatically if you include its name on the command line.

MathCAD has a number of switches to specify the graphics mode. See the manual for details. |
Microsoft Word 5.5	Microsoft Corporation	\WORD55	WORD	Enter a filename after the WORD command to load that file, or enter a /L to load the last file that was edited.
Norton Antivirus	Symantec	\NAV	NAV	
Norton Backup 1.0	Symantec	\NBACKUP	NBACKUP	To run an existing setup file, include its name after the NBACKUP command. Norton Backup includes a number of command-line switches that can be used in a batch file; see the manual for details.
Norton Backup 1.2	Symantec	\NBACKUP	NBACKUP	See notes on version 1.0.
Norton Editor	Symantec	User Selected	NE	The Norton Editor uses the environmental variable NE to determine the location of its configuration file. If you need to run the Norton Editor under different configurations, you can start each of those configurations with a batch file--but first have the batch file change the contents of the environmental variable to point to a different location for the configuration file.

Program	Vendor	Default subdirectory	Startup command	Special interest items for batch files
Norton Utilities	Symantec	\NORTON	NORTON	During installation, the Norton Utilities looks for an older version of the Norton Utilities and, if it finds one, will default to that subdirectory rather than the \NORTON subdirectory. Entering NORTON runs an integrated menu, and you can run the individual programs either from the command line or in a batch file. Beginning with version 6.0, the Norton Utilities include NDOS, a replacement for COMMAND.COM. This program offers its own batch language, which is far superior to the DOS batch language. See the manual for details.
Open Link Extender (OLE')	SoftLogic	\SC	OLE	Doesn't use command-line switches.
OPTune	Gazelle Systems	\OPTUNE	OPTUNE	The vendor distributes a sample batch file with the program that shows how to use Q-DOS 3 errorlevels.
Paradox 3.5	Borland	\PDOX35	PARADOX	If Paradox is in the path and a working subdirectory has been set using Paradox's configuration program, Paradox will switch to the working subdirectory when you start and switch back when done.
Paradox 3.0	Borland	\PARADOX3	PARADOX3	See Paradox 3.5.
Paradox 2.0	Borland	\PARADOX2	PARADOX2	See Paradox 3.5.
PC Paintbrush IV	ZSoft Corporation	\PBRUSH	PAINT	The program that loads PC Paintbrush IV is a batch file. If you plan on starting the program with another batch file, you must start it using the CALL PAINT command rather than the PAINT command. Otherwise, you menu won't regain control.
PC Paintbrush IV Plus	ZSoft Corporation	\PBRUSH	PAINT	The program that loads PC Paintbrush IV Plus is a batch file. If you plan on starting the program with another batch file, you must start it using the CALL PAINT command rather than the PAINT command. Otherwise, you menu won't regain control.
PFS: First Publisher	SPC Software Publishing	\PUB	FP	Have the batch file change to the \PUB subdirectory before starting PFS: First Publisher, or the program will have problems locating its data file.
Power Cache Plus	Intelligent Devices	\PCP	PCPFAST	

Program	Vendor	Default subdirectory	Startup command	Special interest items for batch files
Q&A	Symantec	\QA	QA	Enter the name of a database file after QA to load that database automatically. Before you install Q&A, the installation program scans the hard disk. If it finds an older version of Q&A, it will default to that subdirectory rather than \QA.
QEdit	SemWare	User Selected	Q QTSR	Q loads the stand-alone version, while QTSR loads the memory-resident version. There are switches that can be included in a batch file to jump to a specific line of the file, load and run a macro file, and load a file for editing.
Reflex	Borland	\REFLEX	REFLEX	Reflex uses a number of command-line switches to control its operation. If you use the same switches each time you start Reflex, you can avoid entering them each time by storing those switches in an environmental variable called REFLEX.
PC-Kwik Power Disk	Multisoft Corporation	\PCKWIK	PCKPDISK	All options that fine-tune the performance of PC-Kwik Power Disk are executable from the command line and covered in the manual.
PC-Kwik Power Pak	Multisoft Corporation	\PCKWIK	SUPERPCK PCKSCRN PCKKEK PCKSPL POWERON POWEROFF	PC-Kwik Power Pak includes five separate modules. Four are executable with their own command-line entry, and the fifth (PCKRAMD.SYS) loads in the CONFIG.SYS file. POWERON.BAT and POWEROFF.BAT are batch files included with the package to turn all the modules on and off.
Q-DOS 3	Gazelle Systems	\QDOS	QD3	
Quattro Pro 1.0 Quattro Pro 2.0 Quattro Pro 3.0	Borland	\QPRO	Q	Unlike Lotus 1-2-3, Quattro Pro can load a worksheet automatically if you include its name on the command line. You can also include the name of a macro to run automatically. The program uses several switches to control how it loads. These are covered in the manual.
Quicken 3	Intuit	\QUICKEN3	Q	Enter the name of the account in order to start Quicken with that account loaded.
Quicken 4	Intuit	\QUICKEN4	Q	See Quicken 3 If upgrading from Quicken 3, the installation program uses the \QUICKEN3 subdirectory rather than the \QUICKEN4 subdirectory.
Quicksilver 1.3R	WordTech Systems	\QS13R	DB3C	Quicksilver uses a number of command-line options. They're well documented in the manual.

Program	Vendor	Default subdirectory	Startup command	Special interest items for batch files
Sidekick 2.0	Borland	\SK2	SK2	Sidekick 2.0 should always be loaded from its own subdirectory. To accomplish this, have your AUTOEXEC.BAT change to the \SK2 subdirectory prior to loading Sidekick.
Software Carousel	SoftLogic Solutions	\SC	CAROUSEL	Doesn't use command-line switches.
Super PC-Kwik	Multisoft Corporation	\PCKWIK	SUPERPIC	All options that fine-tune the performance of Super PC-Kwik are executable from the command line and covered in the manual.
Windows 3.0	Microsoft	\WIN	WIN	If a program is in your path or in the \WIN subdirectory, you can automatically start it by including it on the command line. In addition, you can generally have that program load a file automatically by including the name of the file after the program name.
Word 5.5	Microsoft Corporation	\WORD55	WORD	Enter a filename after the WORD command to load that file, or enter a /L to load the last file that was edited.
WordPerfect 5.1	WordPerfect Corporation	\WP51	WP	Include the filename after the WP command to automatically load that file.
ZyIndex	ZyLAB Corporation	\ZY	ZYC (Cleanup) ZYI (Index) ZYL (List) ZYS (Search)	Each of the commands to operate ZyIndex is itself a batch file. As a result, you must be careful when calling these programs from other batch files in a menu system. Unless you use the call command, control won't return to the original batch file. The best way to write custom batch files for ZyIndex is to study the batch files ZyIndex uses to start itself and carefully modify copies of those batch files.

Index

01.BAT, 181
  documentation, 343
  source code, 190-192
02.BAT, 181
  documentation, 343-344
  source code, 192-193
1-LOG.BAT, 13
  documentation, 344
  source code, 14-16
@ symbol, 131
@ECHO OFF, 4, 12

A

Add (A) command, 380
Add (AD) command, 374
Amaral, Doug, xiii, 373
ANSI.BAT, 288
ANSI.SYS, 12, 386
  tutorial, 288-291
  working with, 287-302
ANSIDEMO.BAT, 287
  documentation, 344
  source code, 296-298
ANSIHIDE.BAT, 12, 291
  documentation, 344
  source code, 25-27
APPEND command, 386
archive flag, 239
ASSIGN command, 386
Atlanta Computer Currents, xix
ATTRIB command, 159, 167, 386
AUTOASK.BAT, 182, 184
  documentation, 344
  source code, 194-195
AUTOBOOT.BAT, 180, 184
  documentation, 345
  source code, 185-186
AUTOEXEC.BAT, 11, 127, 130, 179,
    184, 266, 320
  customizing, 179-183
  protecting, 238-239
  renaming, 239-240

B

BACKUP command, 169, 386
  errorlevel values, 275
backups, 129-131, 199-200
  automatic, 200
  counting files, 169
Bascom, Chris, xiii
BASIC, 386
BASICA, 386
batch files
  accessing global information,
    199-215
  advanced techniques for creating,
    305-341
  anatomy, 3
  combining, 42
  components of, 4-7
  DOS-based virus protection,
    159-166
  DOS configuring, 177-258
  DOS environment, 259-302
  DOS errorlevel, 273-286
  DOS versions, 131-132
  help, 29-40
  hiding what it does, 9-26
  indenting sections of, 6
  making DOS run smoothly, 127-144
  mathematical functions, 55-89
  message length, 7
  messages within, 10, 12
  miscellaneous, 167-176
  modifying DOS 5.0 with DOSKEY,
    247-258
  modifying DOS without version
    5.0, 237-245
  requiring less memory, 41-53
  section markers, 6
  software information, 397-407
  source code (*see* source code)
  stopping, 168
  structure, 1-28
  using keyboard macros, 97

using reserve names, 318-319
using SET variables, 265
using subroutines, 315-318
utilities (*see* utility programs)
working with DOS, 91-176
working with DOS ANSI.SYS,
    287-302
working with DOS subdirectories,
    145-158
working with PATH, 217-235
writing using spreadsheet program,
    306, 319
Batcmd, xiii, xviii, 60, 373-378
  commands, 374-378
  keywords, 378-380
  using, 201
BatScreen, xiii, xviii, 373
Beep (BE) command, 374
BIGMENU.BAT, 42
  documentation, 345
  source code, 44-46
BLANK.BAT, 289
  documentation, 345
  source code, 299
BlankScreen (BS) command, 374
boot disk, creating, 305, 307-308
BREAK, 183, 386
BUFFERS, 183, 238, 387

C

CALL command, 131-132, 316, 321,
    387
CAPITAL1.BAT, 308
  documentation, 345-346
  source code, 323-324
CAPITAL2.BAT
  documentation, 346
  source code, 325-326
CAPITAL3.BAT, 309
  documentation, 346
  source code, 327-328

CAPITAL4.BAT, 310
  documentation, 346
  source code, 328-330
CAPITAL5.BAT
  documentation, 346-347
  source code, 330-332
capitalization, 5, 305, 308-310
  case construction, 305-307
  environmental variables, 309
  GOTO %1, 308-309
  PATH command, 309-310
CASE.BAT, 307
  documentation, 347
  source code, 321-323
CATALOG.BAT, 167
  documentation, 347
  source code, 169-170
CD, 387
CHCP, 387
CHDIR, 387
CheckConventional (CC) command,
  374
CheckEnvironment (CE) command,
  374-375
CHECKER2.BAT, 274, 279, 315
  documentation, 347
  source code, 281
CHECKERR.BAT, 274, 279, 313
  documentation, 347
  source code, 280
CheckHard (CH) command, 375
CheckLim (CL) command, 375
CheckMouse (CM) command, 375
CheckSpace (CS) command, 375
CHKDSK, 312, 387
  making smarter, 168-169
CHKDSKCD.BAT, 147-148
  documentation, 348
  source code, 152-153
CL.BAT, 97-99
  documentation, 348
  source code, 120-122
CL2.BAT, 98, 99
  documentation, 348
  source code, 122-125
CLS command, 287, 387
clusters, 41, 44
CNTBOOTS.BAT, 130-131
  documentation, 348-349
  source code, 140-142
CNTFILES.BAT, 169
  source code, 174-176
COMMAND, 387
command aliasing, 96
command lines
  enhancing, 93-125
  entering multiple commands, 94
  recalling using DOSKEY, 252
  storing in a batch file, 98-99
  storing in the environment, 97-98
COMMAND.COM, 59-60, 97, 128,

162, 261-262, 266, 310, 316, 321
  hiding for virus-protection reasons,
    160-161
  testing critical files, 161
commands
  changing names, 240
  replacing with environmental
    variables, 306, 315
  reusing, 95-96
COMP command, 161, 387
computer, logging usage of, 9-10
Computer Monthly, xix
Computer Shopper, xix
COMSPEC, 387
CONFIG.BAT, 184
  documentation, 349
  source code, 195-197
CONFIG.SYS, 97, 179
  modifying, 183-184
  multiple files, 183
  protecting, 238-239
  renaming, 239-240
COPY command, 316-317, 387
COUNTRY command, 387
CTTY command, 9-10, 13, 388
CTTY CON command, 9
CTTY NUL command, 9-13
CTTYKEY.BAT, 10
  documentation, 349
  source code, 18
CURRENT.BAT, 200, 202
  documentation, 349-350
  source code, 202-203
CURRENT1.BAT, 200
  documentation, 350
  source code, 204-206

D

data compression, 42-44
DATE, 388
date and time, 199-200
DEBUG command, 388
DEBUG.COM, 266
DEL command, 240, 247, 388
DEL.BAT, 240
  documentation, 350
  source code, 243-245
Delete (D) command, 380
DEVICE, 388
device drivers, adding, 238
DEVICEHIGH, 388
DIGIT-1.BAT, 274, 279
  documentation, 350
  source code, 282
DIGIT-2.BAT, 274-275, 279
  documentation, 351
  source code, 282-283
DIGIT-3.BAT, 274-275, 279
  documentation, 351
  source code, 283-284
DIR, 388

DIRECTOR.BAT, 147-148
  documentation, 351
  source code, 153-154
disclaimer, xx
disk operating system (*see* DOS; DR
  DOS; MS-DOS)
DISKCOMP command, 388
  errorlevel values, 276
DISKCOPY command, 388
  errorlevel values, 276
DISPLAY.SYS, 388
DO command, 388
documentation, 3, 303-371
  self, 4
DOS, 388
  accessing global information,
    199-215
  changing, 239-240
  command summary, 385-395
  custom configurations, 179-197
  enhancing command lines, 93-125
  environment, 261-271
  errorlevel, 273-286
  issuing multiple commands, 93-94
  keyboard macros, 96-97
  making run smoothly, 127-144
  modifying without version 5.0,
    237-245
  reusing commands, 95-96
  running different versions, 131-132
  running inflexible programs, 129
  storing command lines in a batch
    file, 98-99
  storing command lines in the
    environment, 97-98
  upgrading, 41-42
  virus protection programs, 159-166
  warning statement, 237
  working with ANSI.SYS, 287-302
  working with subdirectories,
    145-158
  working with your path, 217-235
DOS 5.0, 93-94, 161-162, 237
  DOSKEY, 97, 237, 389
  FC program, 161, 390
  modifying with DOSKEY, 247-258
DOSKEY, 97, 237, 389
  basics, 248
  buffer size, 250
  changing command names, 249
  changing functions, 249
  functions, 248-249
  increasing memory, 249-250
  modifying DOS 5.0 using, 247-258
  recalling command lines, 252
  shortening commands, 248-249
  symbols, 248
DOSSHELL, 128-129, 389
DR DOS, 182-184
DRIVER.SYS, 389
DRIVPRAM command, 389

DUMMY.BAT, 314

E

ECHO command, 7, 10, 389
EDIT, 389
EDIT1.BAT, 219
  documentation, 351
  source code, 232-233
EDIT2.BAT, 219
  documentation, 351
  source code, 233-235
EDITPAT2.BAT, 219, 220
  documentation, 351-352
EDITPATH.BAT, 219, 220
  documentation, 352
  source code, 231
EDLIN, 389
EMM386, 389
environment, 261-271
  definition, 261-262
  increasing size, 265-267
  testing, 267
ENV_SIZE.BAT
  documentation, 352
  source code, 270-271
ERASE command, 318, 389
errorlevel, 273-286
  programs using, 275-279
  shorter tests, 274-275
ERRORLEVEL command, 389
escape sequences, 288
EXE2BIN, 390
EXIST command, 390
Exit (EX) command, 376
EXIT command, 128, 316, 390
EXPAND, 390
Extract (E) command, 381
Extract (X) command, 382

F

FASTFIND.BAT, 148
  documentation, 352
  source code, 157-158
FASTOPEN command, 390
FCBS, 390
FDISK, 390
file allocation table (FAT), 11, 320
FILES, 183, 238, 390
  zero-length, 320
FIND command, 167-168, 312, 391
flags, 239
floppy disks, cataloging, 167-168
Flores, Steven, 145
FOR command, 305, 391
  adding wildcard support, 311
  nested statements, 310-311
  running commands with FOR loop,
    311-312
  tricks, 310-312
FORMAT command, 391
  errorlevel values, 276

FORMAT.BAT, 319
Freshen (F) command, 381
FROM-SUB.BAT, 317
FROM.BAT, 317

G

GET-TIME.BAT, 201
  documentation, 352
  source code, 210-212
GetEnvironment (GE) command, 376
GetFrontList (GF) command, 376
GetKey (GK) command, 376
GetLetter (GL) command, 376
GetNumber (GN) command, 376
GetUpper (GU) command, 377
GETVOL.BAT, 200, 202
  documentation, 353
  source code, 206
GOTO, 168, 305, 320, 391
GOTO END, 306, 313-314, 321
GOTO TOP, 5
GRAFTABL command, 391
  errorlevel values, 277
GRAPHICS, 391

H

hardware, xviii
help, 29-40
  customized, 29-30
  specific, 30-31
HELP command, 391
HELP.BAT, 29, 31
  documentation, 353
  source code, 32
HELP1.BAT, 29, 31
  documentation, 353
  source code, 33-34
HELPBAT.BAT, 30, 31
  documentation, 353
  source code, 34-35
HELPBAT2.BAT, 31-32
  documentation, 353-354
  source code, 36-37
HELPBAT3.BAT, 31-32
  documentation, 354
  source code, 37-40
hidden flag, 239
Hyperkinetix, xiii, 373

I

IF statement, 306, 391
  combining, 274
  nesting, 313
IN command, 391
indenting, sections of batch file, 6-7
INFO.EXE, 319
INSTALL, 392

J

JOIN, 392

K

KEYASSGN.BAT
  documentation, 354
KEYASSIGN.BAT, 250
  commands created by, 250-251
  source code, 252-254
KEYB command, 392
  errorlevel values, 277
keyboard
  extended keystrokes, 292-295
  keys, xviii-xix
  reconfiguring using ANSI.SYS,
    291-295
KEYDEL.BAT, 247
KEYERASE.BAT, 250
  documentation, 354
  source code, 254-256

L

LABEL, 392
label testing, 305-306, 312-313
LASTDRIVE, 392
LHA, xviii, 42-44, 380-383
  commands, 380-382
LINK, 392
List (L) command, 381
LOADHIGH, 392
LOCK.BAT, 11
  documentation, 355
  source code, 21-23
LOGBOOT.BAT, 10, 13
  documentation, 355
  source code, 14
logging computer usage, 9-10
looping, 57-58
LOTUS.BAT, 128-129
  documentation, 355
  source code, 133
LOTUS1.BAT, 128-129
  documentation, 355-356
  source code, 134-135

M

MACRO.BAT, 96-99
  documentation, 356
  source code, 114-116
MACRO2.BAT, 97-99
  documentation, 356
  source code, 116-119
macros, 96-97, 252
  in a batch file, 97
MATH.BAT, 56-58, 60
  documentation, 356
  source code, 61-69
MATH1.BAT, 58, 60
  documentation, 357
  source code, 73-76
MATH2.BAT, 60-61
  documentation, 357
  source code, 88-89

mathematical functions, 55-89
    adding, 55-56
    basic math batch file, 56-60
    looping, 57-58
    rules, 55-56
    subtracting, 56
MD, 392
MEM, 392
memory
    data compression, 42-44
    expanded, 179
    extended, 179
    increasing amount available by
        upgrading DOS, 41-42
    RAM, 264
    saving, 127
    using less, 41-53
    using less by combining batch files,
        42
memory-resident programs, 238
    conditionally loading, 182
    unloading, 127-128
MENU.BAT, 42
message length, 7
messages, 10, 12
metacharacters, 290
MIRROR, 392
MKDIR, 392
MODE, 392
MORE, 392
Move (M) command, 381
MOVEIT.BAT, 250
    documentation, 357
    source code, 256-258
MS-DOS, 182-184
MULTI.BAT, 93-94, 99
    documentation, 357
    source code, 99-101
MULTI1.BAT, 94-95, 99
    source code, 101-102
MULTI2.BAT, 95, 99
    documentation, 358
    source code, 102-107
MULTI3.BAT, 95, 99
    documentation, 358
    source code, 108
MULTI4.BAT, 95, 99
    documentation, 358-359
    source code, 108-113

N

NEST1.BAT, 313
    documentation, 359
    source code, 334-335
NEST2.BAT
    documentation, 359
    source code, 335-336
NEXTFILE.BAT, 57, 60
    documentation, 359
    source code, 70-72
NICEPROM.BAT, 290

documentation, 359
source code, 301-302
NICEPROMPT.BAT, source code,
    300-301
NLSFUNC, 393
NOT, 393
NOT-DEL.BAT, 9
    documentation, 360
    source code, 13
NUMBER.BAT, 58-60
    documentation, 360
    source code, 76-78
NUMBER1.BAT, 59-61, 318
    documentation, 360
    source code, 78-79
NUMBER2.BAT, 59-61, 318
    documentation, 360
    source code, 79-80
NUMBER3.BAT, 59-61, 318
    source code, 80-81
NUMBER4.BAT, 59-61, 318
    source code, 81-82
NUMBER5.BAT, 59-61, 318
    source code, 82
NUMBER6.BAT, 60-61, 318
    source code, 83
NUMBER9.BAT, 60-61, 318
    documentation, 360-361
    source code, 83-87

O

OCCASION.BAT, 130
    documentation, 361
    source code, 138-140

P

password protection, 11
PASSWRD2.BAT, 11, 13
    documentation, 361
    source code, 18-21
PATH command, 217-235, 264-265,
    309-310, 393
    adding subdirectories, 218
    deleting subdirectories, 218-219
    editing, 219
PATH1.BAT, 218, 220
    documentation, 361
    source code, 227
PATH2.BAT, 218, 220
    documentation, 361
    source code, 228
PATH3.BAT, 218, 220
    documentation, 362
    source code, 228-229
PATH4.BAT, 218, 220
    documentation, 362
    source code, 229-230
PAUSE command, 393
PC/Computing, xix
PHONE.BAT, 305, 309

documentation, 362
source code, 326-327
PositionCursor (PC) command, 377
PREPARE.BAT, 10
    documentation, 362
    source code, 16-17
Print (P) command, 381
PRINT command, 393
PRINTER.SYS, 393
PROMPT command, 263, 393
    metacharacters, 290

Q

QBASIC, 393
QCD.BAT, 147-148
    documentation, 363
    source code, 154-156
quotation marks, 306, 314-315

R

RAM, 264
RCD.BAT, 146
    documentation, 363
    source code, 151-152
RD, 393
read only flag, 239
Reboot (RB) command, 377
RECONFIG.BAT, 181, 184
    documentation, 363
    source code, 186-190
RECOVER command, 393
REM, 393
REM DATE, 4-5
REM NAME, 4
REM PURPOSE, 4
REM VERSION, 4
REMOVE.BAT, 167
    documentation, 363-364
    source code, 170-172
REN, 393
RENAME command, 319, 393
REPLACE command, 393
    errorlevel values, 277
reserve names, 306
    using, 318-319
RESTORE command, 394
    errorlevel values, 278
RETURN.BAT, 146, 148
    documentation, 364
    source code, 148-149
RETURN2.BAT, 146, 148
    documentation, 364
    source code, 149-150
RETURN3.BAT, 146, 148
    documentation, 364
    source code, 150-151
Richardson, Ronny, xix
RMD.BAT, 148
    documentation, 364
    source code, 156-157
RMDIR, 393

S

SAVE-ERR.BAT, 279
  documentation, 365
  source code, 284-286
SAVESPACE.BAT, 315
  documentation, 365
  source code, 339-340
screen, changing color using
    ANSI.SYS, 287-291
sections
  indenting, 6-7
  markers, 6
SELECT, 394
Self-Extract (S) command, 382
SENDANS2.BAT, 292
  documentation, 365
SENDANSI.BAT, 288, 292
  documentation, 365
  source code, 298
serial number, 201
SERIAL.BAT, 201-202
  documentation, 365-366
  source code, 209-210
SET command, 217, 262-263, 310,
    394
  using variables in batch files, 265
SET COMSPEC, 263-264
SET PATH command, 264-265
SET PROMPT command, 263
SETPATH.BAT, 217, 220
  source code, 221-224
SETVER command, 394
  errorlevel values, 278
SHARE, 394
SHELL command, 267, 394
SHIFT command, 315, 394
ShowHour (SH) command, 377
SHOWLOOP.BAT, 58, 60
  documentation, 366
  source code, 72-73
SkipLine (SL) command, 377
SMALLBAT.BAT, xviii, 42-44
  documentation, 366
  source code, 47-53
SMALLBAT.LZH, 42-43
SMARTCHK.BAT, 168-169
  documentation, 367
  source code, 172-174
software
  batch file information, 397-407
  Compute, 160
  file compression program, 42-44
  LHA, xviii, 42-44
  Norton Utilities, 237
  Norton Utilities NCD, 145-147
  PrintCache, 182
  QC shareware program, 145
  Sidekick, 160, 182
  Superkey, 182
  technical support, 202

utility programs (see utility
    programs)
SORT, 394
source code
  01.BAT, 190-192
  02.BAT, 192-193
  1-LOG.BAT, 14-16
  ANSIDEMO.BAT, 296-298
  ANSIHIDE.BAT, 25-27
  AUTOASK.BAT, 194-195
  AUTOBOOT.BAT, 185-186
  BIGMENU.BAT, 44-46
  BLANK.BAT, 299
  CAPITAL1.BAT, 323-324
  CAPITAL2.BAT, 325-326
  CAPITAL3.BAT, 327-328
  CAPITAL4.BAT, 328-330
  CAPITAL5.BAT, 330-332
  CASE.BAT, 321-323
  CATALOG.BAT, 169-170
  CHECKER2.BAT, 281
  CHECKERR.BAT, 280
  CHKDSKCD.BAT, 152-153
  CL.BAT, 120-122
  CL2.BAT, 122-125
  CNTBOOTS.BAT, 140-142
  CNTFILES.BAT, 174-176
  CONFIG.BAT, 195-197
  CTTYKEY.BAT, 18
  CURRENT.BAT, 202-203
  CURRENT1.BAT, 204-206
  DEL.BAT, 243-245
  DIGIT-1.BAT, 282
  DIGIT-2.BAT, 282-283
  DIGIT-3.BAT, 283-284
  DIRECTOR.BAT, 153-154
  EDIT1.BAT, 232-233
  EDIT2.BAT, 233-235
  EDITPATH.BAT, 231
  ENV_SIZE.BAT, 270-271
  FASTFIND.BAT, 157-158
  GET-TIME.BAT, 210-212
  GETVOL.BAT, 206
  HELP.BAT, 32
  HELP1.BAT, 33-34
  HELPBAT.BAT, 34-35
  HELPBAT2.BAT, 36-37
  HELPBAT3.BAT, 37-40
  KEYASSIGN.BAT, 252-254
  KEYERASE.BAT, 254-256
  LOCK.BAT, 21-23
  LOGBOOT.BAT, 14
  LOTUS.BAT, 133
  LOTUS1.BAT, 134-135
  MACRO.BAT, 114-116
  MACRO2.BAT, 116-119
  MATH.BAT, 61-69
  MATH1.BAT, 73-76
  MATH2.BAT, 88-89
  MOVEIT.BAT, 256-258
  MULTI.BAT, 99-101

  MULTI1.BAT, 101-102
  MULTI2.BAT, 102-107
  MULTI3.BAT, 108
  MULTI4.BAT, 108-113
  NEST1.BAT, 334-335
  NEST2.BAT, 335-336
  NEXTFILE.BAT, 70-72
  NICEPROM.BAT, 301-302
  NICEPROMPT.BAT, 300-301
  NOT-DEL.BAT, 13
  NUMBER.BAT, 76-78
  NUMBER1.BAT, 78-79
  NUMBER2.BAT, 79-80
  NUMBER3.BAT, 80-81
  NUMBER4.BAT, 81-82
  NUMBER5.BAT, 82
  NUMBER6.BAT, 83
  NUMBER9.BAT, 83-87
  OCCASION.BAT, 138-140
  PASSWRD2.BAT, 18-21
  PATH1.BAT, 227
  PATH2.BAT, 228
  PATH3.BAT, 228-229
  PATH4.BAT, 229-230
  PHONE.BAT, 326-327
  PREPARE.BAT, 16-17
  QCD.BAT, 154-156
  RCD.BAT, 151-152
  RECONFIG.BAT, 186-190
  REMOVE.BAT, 170-172
  RETURN.BAT, 148-149
  RETURN2.BAT, 149-150
  RETURN3.BAT, 150-151
  RMD.BAT, 156-157
  SAVE-ERR.BAT, 284-286
  SAVESPACE.BAT, 339-340
  SENDANSI.BAT, 298
  SERIAL.BAT, 209-210
  SETPATH.BAT, 221-224
  SHOWLOOP.BAT, 72-73
  SMALLBAT.BAT, 47-53
  SMARTCHK.BAT, 172-174
  SP.BAT, 220-221
  STARTAPP.BAT, 193-194
  STARTDATA.BAT, 135-136
  STARTWORD.BAT, 136-138
  STOREVOL.BAT, 207
  TECH-AID.BAT, 212-215
  TESTCOM5.BAT, 163-166
  TESTCOMM.BAT, 162-163
  ESTENV1.BAT, 268-269
  TESTGOTO.BAT, 332-334
  TEXTFND4.BAT, 336-337
  TEXTFND5.BAT, 337-339
  TP.BAT, 224-226
  UNBLANK.BAT, 299-300
  USEOVER.BAT, 113-114
  VERSION.BAT, 143-144
  VOLUME.BAT, 207-208
  VOLUME1.BAT, 208-209
SP.BAT, 217, 220

SP.BAT *cont.*
  documentation, 367
  source code, 220-221
spacing, 5-6
STACKS, 394
STARTAPP.BAT, 182, 184
  documentation, 367
  source code, 193-194
STARTDATA.BAT, 129
  documentation, 367
  source code, 135-136
STARTWORD.BAT, 129
  documentation, 367-368
  source code, 136-138
STORE.BAT, 57
  documentation, 368
StoreDay (SD) command, 377
StoreMinute (SM) command, 377
StoreMonth (SO) command, 377
StoreSecond (SS) command, 377
STOREVOL.BAT, 200
  documentation, 368
  source code, 207
StoreYear (SY) command, 378
subdirectories
  batch file for each, 145
  batch file for returning home,
    145-146
  changing, 145
  locating files quickly, 148
  making/changing into new, 148
  using no backslashes to change, 147
  using only partial filename to
    change, 147
  using PATH command to add, 218
  using PATH command to delete,
    218-219
  working with, 145-158
subroutines, 306, 315-318
  DOS 3.3 and later, 316
  inside calling batch file, 317-318
  reasons for using, 316-317
  tricking early DOS to run, 316
SUBST command, 265, 394
Subtract (SU) command, 378
switches, 266

Symantec, 146
SYS, 395
system flag, 239

T

TECH-AID.BAT, 202
  documentation, 368
  source code, 212-215
technical support, 202
TEMP.BAT, 59, 289
terminate and stay resident (TSR), 12,
  262
Test (T) command, 382
TESTCOM5.BAT, 161, 162
  documentation, 368-369
  source code, 163-166
TESTCOMM.BAT, 161
  documentation, 369
  source code, 162-163
TESTENV1.BAT, 267
  documentation, 369
  source code, 268-269
TESTGOTO.BAT
  documentation, 369
  source code, 332-334
TEXTFND4.BAT, 314, 315
  documentation, 369-370
  source code, 336-337
TEXTFND5.BAT, 315
  documentation, 370
  source code, 337-339
TIME, 395
time and date, 199-200
TP.BAT, 218, 220
  documentation, 370
  source code, 224-226
TREE, 395
TRUENAME, 395
TS.EXE, 314
TYPE command, 30, 289, 312, 395

U

UNBLANK.BAT, 289
  documentation, 370
  source code, 299-300
UNDELETE command, 395

UNFORMAT command, 395
Update (U) command, 382
USEOVER.BAT, 96, 99
  documentation, 370-371
  source code, 113-114
utility programs, 60, 373-383
  Batcmd (*see* Batcmd)
  BatScreen (*see* BatScreen)

V

variables
  environmental, 305, 309, 310
  replacing commands with
    environmental, 306, 315
VDISK.SYS, 395
VER, 395
VERIFY, 395
VERSION.BAT, 131-132
  documentation, 371
  source code, 143-144
virus-protection
  DOS-based, 159-166
  writing programs, 159-160
VOL command, 201, 395
volume label, 200-201
VOLUME.BAT, 200
  documentation, 371
  source code, 207-208
VOLUME1.BAT, 201
  documentation, 371-372
  source code, 208-209

W

wildcards, 311
Windows, 128

X

XCOPY command, 317, 395
  errorlevel values, 279

Y

YN command, 378
Yoshizaki, Haruyasu, 42, 380

Z

zero-length files, 320

Other Bestsellers of Related Interest

BATCH FILES TO GO: A Programmer's Library
Ronny Richardson
Ronny Richardson, respected research analyst and programmer, has assembled this collection of ready-to-use batch files featuring over 80 exclusive keystrike-saving programs. These fully developed programs—all available on disk for instant access—can be used as they are, or altered to handle virtually any file management task. 352 pages, 100 illustrations, includes 5.25″ disk.

Book No. 4165 $34.95 paperback only

EASY PC MAINTENANCE AND REPAIR
Phil Laplante
Keep your PC running flawlessly—and save hundreds of dollars in professional service fees! This money-saving guide will show you how. It provides all the step-by-step instructions and troubleshooting guidance you need to maintain your IBM PC-XT, 286, 386, or 486 compatible computer. If you have a screwdriver, a pair of pliers, and a basic understanding of how PCs function, you're ready to go to work. 152 pages, 68 illustrations.

Book No. 4143 $14.95 paperback, $22.95 hardcover

NORTON UTILITIES® 6.0: An Illustrated Tutorial
Richard Evans
Richard Evans shows you how to painlessly perform the most dazzling Norton functions using the all-new features of Norton Utilities 6.0. He also reviews the best form previous releases, providing clear, easy-to-follow instructions and screen illustrations reflecting Norton's new developments. You'll also learn about NDOS, a new configuration and shell program that replaces COMMAND.COM.464 pages, 277 illustrations.

Book No. 4132 $19.95 paperback, $29.95 hardcover

ADVANCED BATCH FILE PROGRAMMING
—3rd Edition
Dan Gookin
Now updated to cover DOS 5.0, this book includes enhanced coverage of batch file commands, material on several new code compilers, and an expanded reference section. In addition, you'll get a number of sample programs, complete with line-by-line explanations—all of which are included on disk. 528 pages, 125 illustrations, includes 5.25″ disk.

Book No. 3986 $29.95 paperback only

BUILD YOUR OWN 386/386SX COMPATIBLE AND SAVE A BUNDLE—2nd Edition
Aubrey Pilgrim
Assemble an 80386 microcomputer at home using mail-order parts that cost a lost less today than they did several years ago. Absolutely no special technical know-how is required—only a pair of pliers, a couple of screwdrivers, and this detailed, easy-to-follow guide. 248 pages, 79 illustrations.

Book No. 4089 $18.95 paperback, $29.95 hardcover

MAINTAIN AND REPAIR YOUR COMPUTER PRINTER AND SAVE A BUNDLE
Stephen J. Bigelow
A few basic tools are all you need to fix many of the most common printer problems quickly and easily. You may even be able to avoid printer hangups altogether by following a regular routine of cleaning, lubrication, and adjustment. Why pay a repairman a bundle when you don't need to? With *Maintain and Repair Your Computer Printer and Save a Bundle*, repair bills will be a thing of the past! 240 pages, 160 illustrations.

Book No. 3922 $16.95 paperback, $26.95 hardcover

BASICs FOR DOS
Gary Cornell, Ph.D.
Use *BASICs for DOS* as your hands-on tutorial for this popular language. It's the most comprehensive guide available on using GW-BASIC, BASICA, and especially the new Microsoft QBasic being shipped with DOS 5.0. Whether you've just decided to break away from pre-packaged programs or are already a veteran at testing and debugging, you'll appreciate the programming skills that Gary Cornell describes. 448 pages, 68 illustrations.

Book No. 3769 $21.95 paperback, $31.95 hardcover

THE ENTREPRENEURIAL PC
Bernard J. David
Put that expensive home PC to work for you. You will learn about the profit-making potential of computers in typing, word processing, desktop publishing, database programming, hardware installation, electronic mail, and much more. David uses detailed, real-life examples to describe some of the more popular avenues of entrepreneurship for the home PC owner. 336 pages, 50 illustrations.

Book No. 3823 $19.95 paperback, $29.95 hardcover

WINDOWS® SHAREWARE UTILITIES
PC-SIG, Inc.

From personal information manages and telephone dialers to challenging games of skill and patience, *Windows® 3 Shareware Utilities* gives you a close-up look at the newest and most innovative shareware utilities that have been created for Windows. Plus, a FREE 5.25" disk includes trial versions of the programs reviewed in the book. Both novice and experienced Windows users will find this book extremely useful. 216 pages, 130 illustrations, includes 5.25" disk.

Book No. 3917   **$29.95 paperback only**

THE HAPPY MAC® : Using Utility Programs
Richard Evans

Keep your Macintosh in a mellow state of RAM with Richard Evans' advice on more than a dozen utility programs. He explains how to use these Mac utilities to manage disks and files, recover lost data, protect against viruses, and streamline everyday computer tasks. Evans covers the new Norton Backup and Disk Doctor programs, as well as general troubleshooting guidance that can take the headaches out of the daily operation of high-capacity Macintosh systems. 224 pages, 128 illustrations.

Book No. 3863   **$17.95 paperback only**

NETWARE® : The Macintosh® Connection
Marty Jost

Novell's Marty Jost discusses all the theoretical, technical, and practical issues involved in linking the Macintosh to Mac-only and Mac-PC networks. He provides a step-by-step skills development program and concentrates on critical issues in the Macintosh area, including the latest versions—2.15 and 385—of Mac under NetWare. In addition, you'll find a comprehensive glossary of networking terms for AppleTalk and NetWare networks. 248 pages, 226 illustrations.

Book No. 3756   **$22.95 paperback only**

THE INFORMATION BROKER'S HANDBOOK
Sue Rugge and Alfred Glossbrenner

Start and run a profitable information brokerage. You'll examine all of the search and retrieval options today's successful information brokers use, everything from conventional library research to online databases, special interest groups, CD-ROMs, and bulletin board systems. No successful information broker should be without this valuable reference tool for his or her office. 408 pages, 100 illustrations, includes 5.25" disk.

Book No. 4104   **$29.95 paperback, $39.95 hardcover**

ONLINE INFORMATION HUNTING
Nahum Goldmann

Cut down dramatically on your time and money spent online, and increase your online productivity with this helpful book. It will give you systematic instruction on developing cost-effective research techniques for large-scale information networks. You'll also get detailed coverage of the latest online services, new hardware and software, and recent advances that have affected online research. 256 pages, 125 illustrations.

Book No. 3943   **$19.95 paperback, $29.95 hardcover**

VISUAL BASIC: Easy Windows™ Programming
Namir C. Shammas

Enter the exciting new world of visual object-oriented programming for the Windows environment. *Visual Basic* is chock-full of screen dumps, program listings, and illustrations to give you a clear picture of how your code should come together. You'll find yourself referring to its tables, listings, and quick-reference section long after you master Visual Basic. As a bonus, the book is packaged with a 3.5-inch disk filled with all the working Visual Basic application programs discussed in the test. 480 pages, 249 illustrations, includes 3.5" disk.

Book No. 4086   **$29.95 paperback only**

USING ONLINE SCIENTIFIC & ENGINEERING DATABASES
Harley Bjelland

With this authoritative guide, you'll discover how to conduct successful online searches that take advantage of databases dedicated to computers, physics, electronics, mathematics, and other disciplines. Emphasizing efficiency, jargon-free language, and simple procedures, Bjelland shows you how to use modern online services to locate information with minimal time, effort, and expense. 232 pages, 31 illustrations.

Book No. 3967   **$26.95 paperback only**

WRITING AND MARKETING SHAREWARE: Revised and Expanded—2nd Edition
Steve Hudgik

Profit from the lucrative shareware market with the expert tips and techniques found in this guide. If you have new software ideas, but are not sure they'll be competitive in today's dynamic PC market, this reference will show you how to evaluate and sell them through shareware distribution. Plus, you get a 5.25" disk—featuring a shareware mailing list management program and a database with over 200 shareware distributors—through a special coupon offer. 336 pages, 41 illustrations.

Book No. 3961   **$18.95 paperback only**

Look for These and Other TAB Books at Your Local Bookstore

To Order Call Toll Free 1-800-822-8158
(in PA, AK, and Canada call 717-794-2191)

or write to TAB Books, Blue Ridge Summit, PA 17294-0840.

Title	Product No.	Quantity	Price

☐ Check or money order made payable to TAB Books

Charge my ☐ VISA   ☐ MasterCard   ☐ American Express

Acct. No. _____ Exp. _____

Signature: _____

Name: _____

Address: _____

City: _____

State: _____ Zip: _____

Subtotal $ _____

Postage and Handling
($3.00 in U.S., $5.00 outside U.S.) $ _____

Add applicable state and local
sales tax $ _____

TOTAL $ _____

TAB Books catalog free with purchase; otherwise send $1.00 in check or money order and receive $1.00 credit on your next purchase.

Orders outside U.S. must pay with international money in U.S. dollars

TAB Guarantee: If for any reason you are not satisfied with the book(s) you order, simply return it (them) within 15 days and receive a full refund.   **BC**

The enclosed disk contains the programs BatScreen, Batcmd, and LHA, each of which resides in its own subdirectory. The disk also contains a fourth subdirectory, BATCH, which contains all the batch files listed in the book. For additional information, put the disk in your floppy drive and, at the floppy-drive prompt, type README and hit Enter.